History Education and Conflict Transformation

Charis Psaltis · Mario Carretero
Sabina Čehajić-Clancy
Editors

History Education and Conflict Transformation

Social Psychological Theories,
History Teaching and Reconciliation

Editors
Charis Psaltis
Department of Psychology
University of Cyprus
Nicosia, Cyprus

Sabina Čehajić-Clancy
School of Science and Technology
University Sarajevo
Sarajevo, Bosnia and Herzegovina

Mario Carretero
Autonoma University of Madrid
Madrid, Spain

ISBN 978-3-319-54680-3   ISBN 978-3-319-54681-0 (eBook)
DOI 10.1007/978-3-319-54681-0

Library of Congress Control Number: 2017937491

© The Editor(s) (if applicable) and The Author(s) 2017. This book is an open access publication.
Open Access This book is licensed under the terms of the Creative Commons Attribution 4.0 International License (http://creativecommons.org/licenses/by/4.0/), which permits use, sharing, adaptation, distribution and reproduction in any medium or format, as long as you give appropriate credit to the original author(s) and the source, provide a link to the Creative Commons license and indicate if changes were made.
The images or other third party material in this book are included in the book's Creative Commons license, unless indicated otherwise in a credit line to the material. If material is not included in the book's Creative Commons license and your intended use is not permitted by statutory regulation or exceeds the permitted use, you will need to obtain permission directly from the copyright holder.
The use of general descriptive names, registered names, trademarks, service marks, etc. in this publication does not imply, even in the absence of a specific statement, that such names are exempt from the relevant protective laws and regulations and therefore free for general use.
The publisher, the authors and the editors are safe to assume that the advice and information in this book are believed to be true and accurate at the date of publication. Neither the publisher nor the authors or the editors give a warranty, express or implied, with respect to the material contained herein or for any errors or omissions that may have been made. The publisher remains neutral with regard to jurisdictional claims in published maps and institutional affiliations.

Printed on acid-free paper

This Palgrave Macmillan imprint is published by Springer Nature
The registered company is Springer International Publishing AG
The registered company address is: Gewerbestrasse 11, 6330 Cham, Switzerland

Preface and Acknowledgements

Social representations of history are fundamental in forming social identities and are consequently critical for understanding intergroup relations. Social psychological approaches are vital for understanding how history education can contribute to conflict transformation and reconciliation processes. In this volume, we discuss the effects, models and implications of history teaching in relation to conflict transformation with an emphasis on how social psychological theories can enrich our understanding of history teaching in relation to conflict transformation and reconciliation processes.

This book is based on the contributions made by members of COST Action IS 1205, "Social psychological dynamics of historical representations in the enlarged European Union" coming from various countries who specialize in the study of post-conflict societies. In addition to COST IS 1205 members, renowned academics were also invited to offer an international perspective on the role of history teaching in conflict transformation including contributors from North and South America.

The contributors comprise a mix of well-established, mid-career and young researchers and academics who study various actors and factors involved in history education ranging from policy making, school curricula, textbooks, civil society organizations, teachers and teaching practices themselves. Many of the contributors are particularly interested in the role of social representations of the past and of history, and of the role of group-based emotions in intergroup conflicts and reconciliation processes. The contributors are also in the in processes of prejudice reduction, intergroup contact, apologies, guilt, shame, regret, forgiveness, moral exemplars and conflict transformation. They all draw on various social psychological theories that attempt to understand processes of conflict transformation and reconciliation in the context of post-colonialism, post-cold-war transition, post-conflict societies, genocide and the holocaust drawing valuable links between social psychological theories and various aspects of history education.

A distinct characteristic of this volume is that it stresses the importance of an approach to history teaching that is transformative at all levels of analysis (intrapersonal, interpersonal, intergroup/positional and social representational/ideological). The list of contributors comprises social, developmental, cognitive and educational psychologists, historians and educators referring to various social psychological theories and models to better understand the way that history teaching could be enriched from an interdisciplinary perspective. Such an interdisciplinary perspective is described as *transformative history teaching*, in another outcome of the COST IS1205 network of researchers which is the publication of the "Recommendations for the History Teaching of Intergroup Conflicts" (Psaltis et al. 2017). Transformative history teaching attempts a critical understanding of the conflictual past through the cultivation of historical thinking, empathy, an overcoming of ethnocentric narratives and the promotion of multiperspectivity.

The first part of this volume discusses the state of the art from an international perspective on developments relating to (a) history textbook writing in post-conflict societies (b) work from international, regional and local civil society organizations on history teaching and reconciliation with the purpose of identifying the various strategies, theories and models that inspired these initiatives and the extent to which they draw on social psychological theory explicitly or implicitly in conflict transformation processes, and (c) lay representations of people in relation to master narratives in post-conflict societies in South Eastern Europe (Croatia, Serbia) and the Eastern Mediterranean (Cyprus) that give ample evidence of the pernicious effects of adherence to master narratives at the representational level as a block to conflict transformation, reconciliation and political compromise.

The second part of the volume deals with the question of perpetrator–victim dynamic and the specific tensions arising from the asymmetrical configurations of these different contexts (colonialism and holocaust) when it comes to the question of how to best deal with the legacies of the past, ingroup past wrongdoings, master narratives and counter-narratives as well as the phenomenon of genocide and the holocaust in a way that can be informed by social psychological theory. This part makes clear that well-established approaches in history teaching, in this context, can be problematic not only because they fail to achieve their proclaimed reconciliation or moral aims but because they often run the danger of reproducing problematic aspects of history teaching that fail to promote the historical thinking skills of the students.

The third part focuses on history textbooks and teachers as the main mediators of classroom teaching practice in post-transition and post-conflict settings that pose unique challenges due to the fact of reversals in asymmetric configurations of status and power. In such contexts, one interesting question is how history teachers from both the new and old minorities adjust to the rapture of a transition into a new constitution of a newly established nation state. The chapters of this section make clear the important role of the quality of deliberations and communication around textbook writing and actual teaching practice.

Finally, in the fourth part of the volume the focus moves to pedagogy and a comparison of various possible approaches that could be taken in post-conflict settings at the level of both formal and non-formal education through the work of civil society organizations. The context of Israel, Northern Ireland and Cyprus is very relevant to explore such questions because they all have by now gathered a lot of experience on the topic of this volume either through research on history teaching or through reflection on the work of civil society organizations in this field.

The concluding chapter written by M. Carretero, a co-editor of the volume, draws on his experience on history teaching in relation to patriotism, nationalism, social identity processes and reconciliation in various parts of the world. It tries to be a reflective commentary establishing a meaningful relation between present trends in history education and how to rethink them in relation to the teaching of historical contents in post-conflict societies. Therefore, this chapter tries to focus not only on what to teach but also on how to teach it and how this could contribute to conflict transformation. Also, this chapter intends to develop a meaningful relation between social psychology contributions and present ideas coming from history education, historiography and related fields.

We have enjoyed the process of preparing our edited volume and in particular the support of our colleagues and friends who have been helpful and challenging at the same time. Believing that our work will be useful for academics and practitioners living and working in (post-) conflict contexts has sustained us with positive energy throughout this process. We want to especially thank members of the COST Action IS 1205 (http://www.cost.eu/COST_Actions/isch/IS1205) coming from various European countries and beyond.

COST IS 1205 is supported by COST (European Cooperation in Science and Technology), which is a pan-European intergovernmental framework. Its mission is to enable breakthrough scientific and technological developments leading to new concepts and products and thereby contribute to strengthening Europe's research and innovation capacities. It allows researchers, engineers and scholars to jointly develop their own ideas and take new initiatives across all fields of science and technology, while promoting multi- and interdisciplinary approaches. COST aims at fostering a better integration of less research intensive countries to the knowledge hubs of the European Research Area. The COST Association, an International not-for-profit Association under Belgian Law, integrates all management, governing and administrative functions necessary for the operation of the framework. The COST Association has currently 36 Member Countries (www.cost.eu).

Without the intellectual and experiential contributions of researchers and academics from this COST Action and the generous funding from COST for the various working group meetings, this volume would not have been possible. We would like to extend special thanks to the chair of the COST Action IS 1205, Laurent Licata, who originally had the idea of such a volume in a meeting of COST IS 1205 working groups 2 and 4 in Cyprus.

We also would like to thank our publishers for their enthusiasm, encouragement and support and specifically Eleanor Christie, Laura Aldridge and Andrew James.

Charis Psaltis would like to thank all contributors for their valuable chapters and their enthusiasm for this project. He would also like to thank his co-editors; without them, this volume would not become a reality. Last but not least, he wishes to thank his wife Chara Makriyianni not only for her own pioneering work, in this field, in the civil society of Cyprus but also the valuable discussions along the process of writing up parts of this book. Last but not least, for her sacrifice of a lot of her valuable time taking care of Maximos when he could not be around due to the editing of the volume. Charis hopes that this volume will contribute to both the process of reconciliation in Cyprus and other parts of the world and the cultivation of critically minded citizens so that children of the world like Maximos live in a more peaceful and co-operative world compared to the one we currently experience.

Mario Carretero would like to thank all the members of the COST IS 1205 Project, and particularly Charis Psaltis who invited him to be co-editor of this volume, because their intellectual inputs were essential to achieve a better understanding of history education in post-conflicts societies. He would also like to thank Prof. Giovanna Leone and the CORIS Department of La Sapienza University (Rome) who supported his Fellowship as Visiting Scholar for one semester providing excellent academic conditions for his work on this book.

Sabina Čehajić-Clancy wishes to thank her colleagues and friends that have mentored and supported her throughout her career as a psychologist working in conflict environments, especially Rupert Brown, Emanuele Castano and Eran Halperin. She would also like to thank her parents and her husband for their unconditional support, love and faith. She dedicates this volume to Noah and Ardan, her two greatest achievements.

Nicosia, Cyprus   Charis Psaltis
Madrid, Spain   Mario Carretero
Sarajevo, Bosnia and Herzegovina   Sabina Čehajić-Clancy

REFERENCE

Psaltis, C., McCully, A., Agbaria, A., Makriyianni, C., Pingel, F., Karahasan, H., Carretero, M., Oguz, M., Choplarou, R., Philippou, S., Wagner, W. & Papadakis, Y. (2017). Recommendations for the History Teaching of Intergroup Conflicts. COST IS 1205 Working Group. Retrieved from http://docs.wixstatic.com/ugd/89ca3b_a592bbe79ece4d218cbf9858928b5d10.pdf.

Contents

Conflict Transformation and History Teaching:
Social Psychological Theory and Its Contributions 1
Charis Psaltis, Mario Carretero and Sabina Čehajić-Clancy

Part I Global and Regional Perspectives on Textbook Writing, Civil Society Organizations and Social Representations

History Textbook Writing in Post-conflict Societies: From
Battlefield to Site and Means of Conflict Transformation 37
Denise Bentrovato

Confronting History and Reconciliation: A Review of Civil
Society's Approaches to Transforming Conflict Narratives 77
Rezarta Bilali and Rima Mahmoud

Social Representations of the Past in Post-conflict Societies:
Adherence to Official Historical Narratives and Distrust
Through Heightened Threats 97
Charis Psaltis, Renata Franc, Anouk Smeekes, Maria Ioannou
and Iris Žeželj

xi

Part II Social Psychological Perspectives of Perpetrators and Victims

Power Struggles in the Remembering of Historical Intergroup Conflict: Hegemonic and Counter-Narratives About the Argentine "Conquest of the Desert" 125
Alicia Barreiro, Cecilia Wainryb and Mario Carretero

When History Teaching Turns into Parrhesia: The Case of Italian Colonial Crimes 147
Giovanna Leone

How to Teach about the Holocaust? Psychological Obstacles in Historical Education in Poland and Germany 169
Michal Bilewicz, Marta Witkowska, Silviana Stubig, Marta Beneda and Roland Imhoff

Part III Textbook and Teacher Perspectives in Post-transition and Post-conflict Societies

History Teaching as 'Propaganda'? Teachers' Communication Styles in Post-Transition Societies 201
Katrin Kello and Wolfgang Wagner

A Clash of Communication? Intervening in Textbook Writing and Curriculum Development in Bosnia and Herzegovina After the War of 1992–1995 231
Falk Pingel

Textbook Narratives and Patriotism in Belarus 257
Anna Zadora

Part IV Pedagogical Approaches to History Teaching and Reconciliation

The Official, The Empathetic and The Critical:
Three Approaches to History Teaching
and Reconciliation in Israel   277
Tsafrir Goldberg

History Teaching to Promote Positive Community
Relations in Northern Ireland: Tensions
Between Pedagogy, Social Psychological Theory
and Professional Practice in Two Recent Projects   301
Alan McCully and Jacqueline Reilly

Formal and Non-formal Reform Efforts of History
Teaching in Cyprus: Openings and Closures for Dangerous
Memories and Reconciliation Pedagogies   321
Michalinos Zembylas and Hakan Karahasan

The Teaching of Recent and Violent Conflicts
as Challenges for History Education   341
Mario Carretero

Index   379

About the Editors

Charis Psaltis is an Associate Professor of Social and Developmental Psychology at the University of Cyprus. His research interests fall in the areas of genetic social psychology, social interaction in learning and cognitive development, social representations of gender, intergroup contact and intergroup relations between Greek Cypriots and Turkish Cypriots, development of national identities and history teaching and collective memory. He published papers in *Journal of Personality and Social Psychology, European Journal of Social Psychology, British Journal of Developmental Psychology, Culture & Psychology and Human Development*. Since 2014, he is a member of the Editorial Board of the *British Journal of Developmental Psychology* and since 2015 Associate Editor of *European Journal of Psychology of Education*. In April 2014, his book co-authored with Anna Zapiti entitled *Interaction, Communication and Development: Psychological Development as a social process* was published by Routledge, and in 2015, his co-edited volume *Social Relations in Human and Societal Development* by Palgrave Macmillan.

Mario Carretero is a Professor of Cognitive Psychology at Autonoma University of Madrid, Spain, where he was Dean of the Faculty of Psychology, and Researcher at FLACSO, Argentina. He has carried out an extensive research on history education from both cognitive and sociocultural approaches. He has published in *Journal of the Learning*

Sciences and *Cognition and Instruction*. His last books are *History Education and the Construction of National Identities* (2012) (co-ed.) and *Constructing Patriotism* (funded by the Guggenheim Foundation) (2011). He has been Santander Visiting Scholar at the David Rockefeller Center for Latin American Studies of Harvard University (2009) and Bliss Carnochan Visiting Professor at the Humanities Center of Stanford University (2011). His present research interests have to do with an interdisciplinary attempt to study history education issues as it can be seen in *Palgrave Handbook of Research in Historical Culture and Education* (2017) (co-edited along with S. Berger and M. Grever).

Sabina Čehajić-Clancy works as an Associate Professor of Social and Political Psychology at the Sarajevo School of Science and Technology in Bosnia and Herzegovina. She works in the field of intergroup relations, more specifically on reconciliation in post-conflict societies. She has published numerous papers in peer-reviewed journals such as *Journal of Personality and Social Psychology, European Journal of Social Psychology, Political Psychology, Group Processes and Intergroup Relations and Psychological Inquiry*. Sabina has also over thirteen years of experience in working as an expert consultant for various international and local NGO's such as UNICEF, UNDP, Post-conflict Research Centre, Catholic Relief Service, Save the Children, and USAID designing and evaluating reconciliation-oriented interventions. Her work has received wide media coverage due to its unique methodological approaches used in (post-) conflict contexts. She is also a member of the Editorial Board for the Political Psychology Journal..

List of Figures

Social Representations of the Past in Post-conflict Societies: Adherence to Official Historical Narratives and Distrust Through Heightened Threats

Fig. 1　Effects of adherence to ingroup narratives on outgroup trust, mediated by perceived realistic, symbolic and group-esteem threat. *Note* Standardized coefficients presented and separated by a slash (Cyprus/Serbia/Croatia); the correlation between the two mediators was accounted for. † $p < 0.01$, * $p < 0.05$, ** $p < 0.01$, *** $p < 0.001$　　111

History Teaching as 'Propaganda'? Teachers' Communication Styles in Post-Transition Societies

Fig. 1　Contextual dimensions of the history teacher's action space　　204

Fig. 2　'Propagation' as spanning a continuum between 'propaganda' and 'dissemination'　　207

Fig. 3　Opposite styles of propaganda and dissemination cross-cut by two opposite approaches in history teaching　　208

The Official, The Empathetic and The Critical: Three Approaches to History Teaching and Reconciliation in Israel

Fig. 1　Path diagram for the effects of teaching approach on responsibility and interest in out-group perspective on acknowledgement of responsibility and out-group partner reaction　　291

LIST OF TABLES

Social Representations of the Past in Post-conflict Societies: Adherence to Official Historical Narratives and Distrust Through Heightened Threats

Table 1	Means, SDs and correlations between variables, Cyprus	109
Table 2	Means, SDs and correlations between variables, Serbia	109
Table 3	Means, SDs and correlations between variables, Croatia	110

How to Teach about the Holocaust? Psychological Obstacles in Historical Education in Poland and Germany

Table 1	Correlation between knowledge, understanding of history, attitudes and school education among Warsaw students. Pearson correlation coefficients (r)	178

The Official, The Empathetic and The Critical: Three Approaches to History Teaching and Reconciliation in Israel

Table 1	Means and standard deviations for defense of in-group narrative (DIN), interest in the other's perspective (IO) perceived in-group responsibility (IR), glorification (GLO) and attachment (ATT) by condition and national group	282
Table 2	Bivariate correlations between liberal political affiliation, initial interest in other and responsibility following learning	284
Table 3	Mean Jewish Arab difference scores for the dominance of discussion time and control of discussion by condition	288

Table 4	Mean percentage of agreement and opposition utterances by condition and frequency of agreement on solution for the refugee problem, by condition	288
Table 5	Descriptive statistics and bivariate correlations of IGR and proportion of agreement, rejection, opposition and compliance utterances (% of total utterances), by ethnic group	289

Conflict Transformation and History Teaching: Social Psychological Theory and Its Contributions

Charis Psaltis, Mario Carretero and Sabina Čehajić-Clancy

It is widely recognized that the number of international wars has declined continuously since the mid-1960s, whilst internal conflicts and civil wars became more numerous than those fought between nation states. Internal divisions of societies and separatism within a single political unit have also become a more frequent form of conflict. The nature of armed conflicts is also changing claiming the lives of more civilians compared to military personnel in relation to the past (Hobsbawm 2002). As Kelman (2004, 2008) convincingly argued, this changing nature of wars ignited the recent research interest in the notion of *reconciliation*. In such a context the primary challenge is for former enemies

---

C. Psaltis (✉)
Social and Developmental Psychology, University of Cyprus, Nicosia, Cyprus
e-mail: cpsaltis@ucy.ac.cy

M. Carretero
Cognitive Psychology, Autonoma University of Madrid, Madrid, Spain

S. Čehajić-Clancy
Social and Political Psychology, Sarajevo School of Science and Technology, University Sarajevo, Sarajevo, Bosnia and Herzegovina

© The Author(s) 2017
C. Psaltis et al. (eds.), *History Education and Conflict Transformation*,
DOI 10.1007/978-3-319-54681-0_1

to find the way to not only live together peacefully but even at times cooperate and share power.

Today, almost two decades in the twenty-first-century humanity is witnessing both a revival of nationalism, separatism, sectarianism, terrorism and radical fundamentalism and proxy wars resulting in a vast number of casualties, refugees and internally displaced people. Despite the changing nature of these conflicts, it is clear that representations of the past and history teaching are still weaponized for these collective struggles (Bentrovato et al. 2016; Carretero 2011). Given the circumstances, the time is ripe for the human kind to take stock of the knowledge gained from the study of peace and conflict in the social sciences and in particular of the way history teaching and representations of the past are used and abused in this context. In order to enable this process, we ought to systematically understand the process of conflict transformation, the influences exerted by the past and more specifically the contributions made by the field of social psychology.

Conflict Transformation, Conflict Resolution and Reconciliation: The Social Psychological Perspective

The recent turn in the study of peace and conflict towards "conflict transformation" rather than "conflict resolution", being the process of reaching a durable and mutually satisfactory solution between former enemies (Kelman 2008), is a desired development because such a shift contributes to a greater understanding of the conflict context whilst focusing on more productive aspects of the conflict. In comparison the conflict resolution approach can be regarded as more restrictive in scope (Galtung 2000; Lederach 1997). Conflict transformation puts emphasis not only on the end of direct violence but rather a constant orientation to positive peace and the end of structural (e.g. inequality, social exclusion and exploitation) and cultural forms of violence (e.g. perceived realistic and symbolic threats, prejudice, distrust). In other words, conflict transformation is concerned with transforming the systems, structures and relationships that give rise to violence and injustice.

All available theoretical models of conflict transformation that go beyond conflict management and conflict resolution (Galtung 2000;

Lederach 1997) emphasize the importance of understanding the processes that enable the transformation of conflict from its destructive and violent forms into a more productive form which is recognized as part of our everyday life to be resolved through dialogue, creative and peaceful means; conflict resolution and conflict transformation are not antithetical and the notion of transformation in the post-conflict period is often presented as a stepping stone to resolution, especially in the case of protracted conflicts (Constantinou 2015).

A notion that occupies a crucial role in both approaches is the notion of reconciliation as both a process and an outcome that not only diminishes the possibility for violent conflict in cases of structural inequalities and political instability but also facilitates peace settlements and supports their viability afterwards. Social psychological concepts and theories are recently making a unique contribution to our understanding of reconciliation. Kelman (2004, 2008) proposes a notion of reconciliation from a social psychological perspective beyond any religious connotations. In this context, reconciliation is of vital importance not only for reaching a peace settlement that will bring up a sense of justice and redress of inequality issues but also for its future viability through the cultivation of the element of trust (Marková and Gillespie 2012; Psaltis 2012a). Čehajić-Clancy et al. (2016) conceptualize intergroup reconciliation as an emotion-regulation process involving positive affective change towards the outgroup, and they offer a framework that integrates the emotion regulation and intergroup reconciliation literatures. In this account, the emotions of intergroup hatred and anger towards the outgroup need to be downregulated, whereas guilt for ingroup wrongdoings, hope and empathy need to be upregulated for deep psychological changes to be made possible. These psychological changes include alterations in beliefs, emotions, identity and behavioural intentions. Such an approach is premised on *Intergroup Emotions Theory* by Smith (1993) who argued that when group memberships are salient, people can feel emotions on account of their group's position or treatment, even if they have had little or no personal experience of the actual intergroup situations themselves. Behind Smith's (1993) theory is the by-now classic *Social Identity and Self-categorization theory* (Tajfel and Turner 1979) which informs a great number of research in the social psychology of intergroup relations.

Seeing reconciliation as simply an emotional regulation process was criticized for reducing reconciliation into a psychological and individualistic process not recognizing the need for structural and societal transformation (Vollhardt and Twali 2016; Shnabel and Ulrich 2016) which is part of what we described earlier as the broader process of conflict transformation. From a social representations perspective (Psaltis 2012a) reconciliation as a process and outcome entails the shift from an identity position in the representational field of mistrust, high prejudice, low quantity and quality contact, low perspective taking, low forgiveness and high threats (realistic and symbolic) into a position of high trust, low prejudice, high quantity and quality of contact, high perspective taking, high forgiveness and low threats (realistic and symbolic). Intergroup contact is also of crucial importance as the motor of change in microgenetic processes of representational change in social interaction (Psaltis 2015b) which is both constrained and enabled by the legal macro-structures and infrastructures of peace and their representations. In this process, the building of trust occupies a central position as it is an organizing principle of the representational field altogether being both a predictor and outcome of intergroup contact. Similar formulations were proposed by Nadler and Shnabel (2015) who also recognize the crucial position of trust in the reconciliation process which they define as both a process and outcome that concerns structural, relational and identity-related transformations.

An important idea behind theories that study *transformative* processes is that they understand social or national identity and representations as socially constructed and they are compatible with recent developments in social and developmental psychology (Duveen 2001, 2002, 2007; Psaltis et al. 2015) that aim at the study of human and societal change as the transformation of social relations. Such approaches have the potential to overcome the often narrow perspective of the classical *Social Identity Theory* (Tajfel 1978) which is mostly interested in categorization processes and offers limited insight into the role of social representations of the past in the formation of intergroup relations.

Still, most of the findings of intergroup relations research today is indeed trying to explain the creation of prejudice, negative stereotyping and the escalation of conflict by putting emphasis on the central role of categorization (Tajfel 1978) and social identification processes but often overlooking the content of these categorizations (Psaltis and Cakal 2016). Ingroup identification processes often lead to emotions on behalf of their group and/or group's actions. Events and situations that affect the group have an effect for the self as well. In (post-)conflict situations, such emotions stemming from group's actions or those oriented towards out groups such as intergroup anxiety directly impact intergroup interactions and contribute to further divisions and polarizations. Consequently, assumptions and implications as postulated by the *Theory of* Intergroup Emotions *(Smith 1993) and the model of intergroup anxiety in the Intergroup Threat Theory* (Stephan et al. 2009; Psaltis et al., Chap. 4) are highly relevant in understanding conflict transformation. In the present volume, we aim to shed light on how social representations of the past and history teaching in particular could be related to all these social psychological concepts.

To sum up, after political transition periods, successful conflict resolution or cessation of the conflict, war, colonialism and a genocide itself, societies are left with many questions such as disputes over the understanding of the past, issues of identification, responsibility, victimization and justice. These and similar issues ought to be addressed not only from a historical and legal or transitional justice perspective but also from a social psychological angle which concerns itself with issues of ameliorating intergroup relations. How do various actors involved in the process of history teaching (teachers, ministries of education, civil society organizations, historians) see these issues in relation to a social psychological understanding of reconciliation which implies both a process of positive changes in relations between adversaries and an outcome characterized by humanization, acceptance of both similarity and difference, outgroup malleability (Halperin et al. 2011), responsibility for ingroup past wrongdoing (Leach et al. 2013), intergroup contact, prejudice reduction and the cultivation of trust? These processes of humanization, empathy, intergroup contact and dialogue are just a few socio-psychological pillars which can help individuals and groups to become more inclusive, open-minded and accepting of the Other and as a consequence contribute to sustainable peace (Čehajić and Brown 2010). To what extend could they inform in any way the various approaches to history education currently in use in various post-conflict or post-transition settings?

REPRESENTATIONS OF THE PAST, HISTORY TEACHING APPROACHES AND RECONCILIATION

One aspect of the reconciliation process concerns primarily the existence of present co-operative relations between individuals and institutions through intergroup contact for a common goal (described as the instrumental route to reconciliation by Nadler and Shnabel 2015). Another part concerns the conflict resolution and peace settlement efforts that are usually future oriented (Tint 2010a, b) as they strive to build a common vision or design new institutional structures of power sharing (Loizides 2015) that will resolve structural inequalities. However, at the heart of the reconciliation effort the primary orientation concerns the past and its representations, or what is called by Nadler and Shnabel (2015) the socio-emotional route to reconciliation (apologies, forgiveness, guilt/shame). In this sense, the social representations of a group or a community about the past are directly related to processes of conflict transformation and reconciliation. For example in August 2016 on the 30th anniversary of the killing of "Yoyes[1]", and six years after the last ceasefire by ETA, public discussion in newspapers shows that in the Basque Country three positions around this killing were still evident: (a) the people who condemn this killing; (b) the people who still approve it; and (c) the people who think that it is not possible to make a moral judgement.

These representations of the past (Liu and Hilton 2005; Psaltis 2016) have also been discussed in the social sciences as *historical culture* (Carretero et al. 2017), which expresses another way of approaching and understanding the effective and affective relationship that different groups have with its past. In this vein, the notion of culture should be best understood as a system of social representations (Duveen 2007; Psaltis 2012b) thus avoiding any fossilized, reified or essentialist connotations that often go with the notion of "culture". Representations of the past describe a dynamic process of dialogue, through which interpretations of the past are disseminated, negotiated and debated between perspectives from academic history, school history and public history (monuments, commemorations, museums, films, historical novels, etc.) (Papadakis 2008; Carretero, Chap. 14).

In this vein, an important question is the following: "*What is the place of representations of the past and history teaching in reconciliation?*" It has rightly been argued (Cole 2007) that representations of the past and history teaching could be used to either facilitate conflict transformation processes or to block conflict transformation and even reinforce antagonism and conflict through the traditional romantic role of the promotion of blind and essentialist forms of patriotism (Carretero et al. 2012). In countries where the traumatic experiences of identity-based conflict are recent, there are questions about whether, how and at what age children should learn about parts of the nation's past relating to conflict (Cole 2007) which naturally influences the curriculum aims, content to be taught and textbooks or supplementary teaching material to be used in the classroom.

A recent review of how the history of the conflict is dealt in post-conflict societies (Paulson 2015) revealed that depending on the conflict setting one can identify various approaches to history education. For example, there are conflict settings where guidance on recent conflict is included in national curricula and where it is not thus letting teachers deal with these issues without any direction. Some post-conflict settings saw the establishment of moratoria, namely where they temporarily suspend history education or its recent history segment, including its textbooks (Bentrovato, Chap. 2; Bentrovato et al. 2016) like Afghanistan, BaH, Cambodia, Guatemala, Lebanon or Libya. It is worth noting that in most of these countries one can find a very weak tradition of history teaching methodology which makes history teaching an unlikely candidate to contribute to a transformative process. An interesting case is that of Northern Ireland. Here there is silence regarding the recent history of conflict as until recently they did not have compulsory national curriculum content about recent conflict. In Northern Ireland however, due to the long and quite strong tradition of "New History" (see Carretero, Chap. 14) students have the chance to cultivate their historical thinking skills through an evidence-based, analytic approach that emphasizes multiple perspectives. In particular, the cultivation of historical thinking mostly concerns the development of "historical literacy", gaining a deep understanding of historical events and processes through active engagement with historical texts, establishing historical significance, identifying continuity and change, analysing cause and consequence, taking historical perspectives and understanding the ethical dimensions of historical interpretations (Seixas 2004).

However, according to Kitson (2007) and McCully and Barton (2010) this disciplinary approach is not enough to facilitate reconciliation (McCully 2012; McCully and Reilly, Chap. 12). Many times students assimilated the other community perspective to their own community narrative, and at others, they were completely dismissive of community histories not being able to reflect on the connections between the past and present in regard to their national identities in the context of the collective struggles of their communities and the identity politics around it.

As a remedy, they argue for the need for a more interdisciplinary approach to history teaching that benefits from the social psychological literature of the study of intergroup relations (McCully and Reilly, Chap. 12). From this perspective, what is needed is a curriculum that attends more directly to the student's active construction of historical meaning and supports them in constructing critical perspectives on the contemporary relevance of the past through the cultivation of emotional empathy for the outgroupers. It is also important to understand through *Social Identity Theory* (Tajfel 1978) how simplistic binary oppositions are created through categorizations and the consequences of that for the formation of homogenizing views of the ingroup and the outgroup. Students must be helped to understand why some people feel the need to use and abuse history. Recent social psychological work offers one possible answer to this question. Smeekes et al. (2017) show that in both Northern Ireland and Cyprus when individuals experience a perceived sense of realistic or symbolic or identity threats (Branscombe et al. 1999) it becomes more likely that they attempt to regain a sense of ingroup pride through recourse to a sense of collective continuity (Sani 2008; Smeekes 2015; Smeekes and Verkuyten 2015). Recent studies have pointed out that the continuity motive is an important part of various types of group identity (e.g. Easterbrook and Vignoles 2013) and plays an important role in intergroup relations (e.g. Smeekes and Verkuyten 2015). It has, for example, been shown that collective self-continuity forms an important basis for national identification, but at the same time drives ingroup defensive reactions in the context of group threat (Smeekes and Verkuyten 2015) by creating more negative attitudes towards immigrants.

In other words, representations of the past premised on notions of continuity relate to fears of a threatened political or financial status of the ingroup or an identity threat coming from the other group. This dynamic helps us understand the mechanisms behind the phenomenon of resistance (Duveen 2001) when microgenetic processes (Duveen and Lloyd 1990; Psaltis 2015b) of engagement with alternative perspectives and representations of the past are made possible but often undermined by the use of semantic barriers who defend the self from change (Gillespie 2008, 2015).

On the other hand, as it is shown by Psaltis et al. (Chap. 4) in the post-conflict context of Cyprus, Serbia and Croatia, the threats themselves are heightened by internalization and adherence of the official master narratives of conflict in all three contexts; through a heightened feeling of threat, distrust between ingroup and outgroup is also increased, thus becoming a major impediment to reconciliation. This kind of research leads to the conclusion that essentialist representations of the past and an ahistorical conception of essentialist and reified national identifications can entrap individuals and societies into a vicious circle of frozen or even escalated conflict (Makriyianni and Psaltis 2007).

In post-conflict settings where the state decides to indeed offer guidelines for the history of conflict in their curriculum and textbooks this is, in the majority of cases, done in a manner that blocks conflict transformation or event reinforces conflict by insisting, even after educational reforms taking place in the twenty-first century, on a culture of preservation of the memory of conflict and a simplistic master narrative of the conflict. This is the case, for example, in Israel (Bekerman and Zembylas 2011) and Cyprus for both the Greek Cypriot and the Turkish Cypriot community (Klerides and Philippou 2015; Makriyianni et al. 2011; Perikleous 2010; Psaltis 2015a, b; Zembylas and Karahasan, Chap. 13) with directions pointing to the need for a preservation of the memory of one-sided victimization and an ethnocentric orientation to history teaching. In the case of Cyprus, as in the case of Israel, this gap is successfully filled by the work of local NGOs who work either intercommunally like the *Association for Historical Dialogue and Research* (AHDR) *or monocommunally and in co-operation with international organizations like the Council of Europe promoting the idea of a transformative* form of history teaching that cultivates both the critical historical thinking skills of the students (Seixas 2004; Wineburg 2001; Carretero, Chap. 14) and reconciliation through a critical approach to ethnocentric master narratives. The pioneering approach of AHDR[2] has been one that deals with both non-controversial social history—like the supplementary teaching material produced by teachers from both communities and international experts, called *A look at our past* published in English, Greek and Turkish from a multi-perspective approach—and controversial issues like approaching the issue of the missing people (Chapman et al. 2011) by applying a multiperspectivity approach. AHDR is a pioneer of the interdisciplinary and transformative approach to history teaching as its work has been enriched by social psychological and developmental theory from its very first steps (Makriyianni and Psaltis 2007). It is noteworthy that in the last decades an international "eduscape" (Klerides and Zembylas 2017) is expanding where the disciplinary approach to history teaching is used as a way to achieve conflict transformation aims supported by various international organizations: Council of Europe, UNESCO and OECD (Bentrovato, Chap. 2). The contribution of various local and international NGOs like EUROCLIO has been instrumental in this effort (Bilali and Mahmut, Chap. 3; McCully and Reilly, Chap. 12).

However, not all efforts towards reconciliation have treated history teaching with respect for critical historical enquiry since some post-conflict societies following the early example of the Franco-German textbook decided simply to delete from textbooks offensive sentences or material (e.g. BaH) or harmonizing conflicting narratives through a process of political negotiation which was the result of a political compromise rather than that of critical enquiry. In some cases they even decided to promote a nation building approach, by writing up a single authoritative narrative; this is the case of Rwanda where the government enforced a new, hegemonic narrative of past events, applying a narrow understanding of what is to be taught. This narrative promotes the concept of "Rwandanness", emphasizing the nation's alleged primordial unity and dismissing ethnic identities as a historically unfounded colonial invention that was supposedly the primary cause of genocide in Rwanda (Bentrovato, Chap. 2). Despite the epistemological weaknesses of single-narrative approaches, there is an emerging realization that common history textbook commissions (Korostelina and Lässig 2013), provided they respect the principles of cultivating historical thinking skills, can indeed produce valuable textbooks or supplementary teaching material. Moreover, probably the most significant contribution of joint textbook commissions is the performative and transformative aspects of the co-operative writing up itself (Pingel, Chap. 9). This is only expected from the social psychological and well-established paradigm of prejudice reduction through intergroup contact (Allport 1954; Brown and Hewstone 2005; Tausch et al. 2010) given its potential to deconstruct negative stereotypes, facilitate perspective taking and forgiveness, reduce threat and intergroup anxiety, and more importantly build trust.

It could be claimed that depending on the implicit lay social psychological theories of change or practice, and conflict transformation processes held by both practitioners in civil society (Bilali and Mahmut, Chap. 3) variations in the strategies followed to tackle representations of the past can also be expected at the level of civil society initiatives.

The NGOs usually try to find ways to fill the gaps of silence, evasion and elision in official history textbooks and curricula. This is because civil society actors are less constrained by the pressures and political agendas that elites and governments face; for example, in Cyprus NGOs like the AHDR are not constrained by the inability of the internationally recognized ministry of education and culture of the Republic of Cyprus to officially co-operate with the corresponding ministry in the Turkish Cypriot community which is internationally recognized only by Turkey. NGOs like AHDR in Cyprus or *History that Connects* project which invites history educators from Bosnia, Croatia, and Serbia to co-operate are usually engaged in professional development and capacity building for teachers. This kind of teacher training focuses on innovative pedagogies and methods, oral histories, digital media, production of educational materials to supplement traditional textbooks that incorporate new pedagogies and more inclusive historical experiences across conflicting groups. They also often get involved in the creation of forums for dialogue like the building of educational centres[3], seminars or conferences to foster co-operation among teachers across division, conflict lines or borders.

What civil society organizations are aiming at is to transform the social representations at the grassroots level by deconstructing master narratives and overcoming ethnocentric representations of the past. Sometimes NGOs explicitly aim at raising awareness of the dynamics of intergroup conflict and the social psychological and other roots of conflicts. At other times according to Bilali and Mahmoud (Chap. 2) they engage in oral history projects so that they bring in the public eye personal histories of traumatization of victims of the conflict or the perspectives of members of marginalized or oppressed groups.

Most local and international NGOs prioritize teacher training because educators are the main mediators between historiographical traditions, school history in the classroom and public history. Depending on the specific country they could be trained as historians or not, be trained in history didactics or not. When such pre-service training is absent, they often function more as "lay historians" (Klein 2013) than academic historians. This could in fact be one of the greatest impediments for successful conflict transformation since their teaching will be constrained by social representations of the past that take the form of master narratives of the conflict (Carretero 2011; Bar-Tal and Salomon 2006; Páez and Liu 2011; Psaltis 2012a, 2016).

Unfortunately, actual teaching practice in many post-conflict societies ends up enhancing collective memory or collective remembering (Wagoner 2015) of victimization, and promoting exclusive and essentialist views of patriotism and national identities (Carretero 2011; Hein and Selden 2000) by teaching the past as an ontological and fixed "heritage" (Lowenthal 1996; Makriyianni and Psaltis 2007) which promotes notions of cultural continuity, nativist or autochthony beliefs of the kind "We were here first" (Martinovic and Verkuyten 2013) regret for a decadent present and nostalgia for a better past (Smeekes and Verkuyten 2015). This is done at the cost of challenging such simplistic representations of the past that Moscovici would call *Social Representations based on belief*[4] (Moscovici 1998/2000; Psaltis 2016). Such representations are often polemical and are enacted through forms of communication that Moscovici (1961/2008) described as propaganda (Kello and Wagner, Chap. 8) in his seminal work on social representations of psychoanalysis.

The "charters" (Liu and Hilton 2005) on which collective memory (Páez and Liu 2011) master narratives as social representations (Psaltis 2016) of the past are structured serve identity functions, on the basis of either glorification or victimization. Interestingly both notions strengthen an ethnocentric perception of the past that contributes to distancing from other groups and thus not only obstruct conflict transformation but also limit the cultivation of historical thinking as they distort students understanding of significance in favour of events and characters relating to what is perceived as the ingroup at any given time, they also distort understanding of continuity and change, through the use of simplistic circular and *Rise-and-fall* views of history or linear progression schemes (Páez et al. 2017). They also obstruct the understanding of causality through the romantic or great men perspective and the use of historical analogies and deterministic or attribution schemes that fail to capture contingence, randomness and multi-causality (Carretero, Chap. 14). An attribution style which is characteristic for its ingroup serving bias and its pernicious effects is what has been described by Thomas Pettigrew (1979) as the *ultimate attribution error* which is the tendency to internally attribute negative outgroup and positive ingroup behaviour and to externally attribute positive outgroup and negative ingroup behaviour. Similarly, such master narratives feed moral disengagement from past wrongdoings of the ingroup (Bandura 1999; Bilali 2013) by moral justification of the act, denial, displacement, or diffusion of responsibility, disregarding or minimizing the negative consequences of the violent acts, and attribution of blame to the victim or circumstances. Finally, this kind of representations of the past often actively promote a sense of *intergroup competitive victimhood* (Noor et al. 2012) which describes the efforts of members of groups involved in violent conflicts to establish that their group has suffered more than their adversarial group which is a mindset that obstructs reconciliation efforts and the support of peace processes.

TENSIONS AND DILEMMAS ARISING FROM ASYMMETRICAL POST-CONFLICT CONTEXTS FOR HISTORY TEACHING

Given that conflict transformation engages issues of structural inequality and justice it is also necessary to think about conflict settings where one could argue that competitive victimhood is less likely to be germane because there is clear division, or at least wider consensus, between either the roles of perpetrator and victim or a clear case of structural inequalities favouring one (e.g. a majority) over the other group (e.g. a minority). Such settings are discussed in the papers by Barreiro et al. (Chap. 5) in the case of the Mapuche minority group who struggle for recognition from the majority group in Argentina. It is also discussed by Leone (Chap. 6) in the case of colonial Italy (cf. Licata and Klein 2010 on the Belgium heritage of colonialism) facing the past wrongdoings of their ingroup in Ethiopia. Also, Bilewicz et al. (Chap. 7) discuss how to best deal with the Holocaust in the context of history teaching.

In such cases, whenever an asymmetrical dynamic of majority–minority or perpetrator–victim dynamic enters the scene interesting tensions become relevant on how to best deal with history and representations of the past. One kind of tension is when minority counter-narratives fall back to the use of simplistic narratives themselves, or enter into an identity politics of strategically using reified (Hammack 2010) or essentialist identities (Zeromskyte and Wagner 2016) to gain public awareness or "preserve" what they see as their identity (Barreiro et al., Chap. 5) which is also one of the strategies sometimes used by NGOs in some parts of the world. Such examples are instructive because they help us clarify the cases when the cultivation of historical thinking skills might not be served by what is perceived as working towards reconciliation (Bilali and Mahmut, Chap. 3).

In social psychological theory, recent debates reflect exactly these tensions when the prejudice reduction paradigm is pitted against the collective action model. Research interest in collective action was rekindled, albeit in its more radical and revolutionary form, after the so-called Arab spring revolutions with the proposal of new social psychological models of collective action (Van Zomeren et al. 2008) which tried to identify the conditions under which various groups embark on collective action, or even become radicalized engaging in violent forms of struggle. Social identity processes have been identified as a crucial ingredient in understanding such collective actions. Recent theories of collective action suggest that a feeling of relative deprivation, strong identification with the ingroup and group efficacy are key predictors of collective action on behalf of the ingroup (Van Zomeren et al. 2008). But here exactly lies some of the most recent tensions in the field of Social Psychology as it would appear that what is being proposed by collective action theorists is the contestable claim that groups who have an ethically legitimate struggle to wage, as that of ending structural violence could or should be agitating, activating or facilitating exactly the same social psychological mechanisms that the prejudice reduction and reconciliation literature, discussed earlier, has been criticizing for years or exposing as unproductive in processes of conflict transformation (see debate in Dixon et al. 2012).

Some of the collective action theorists even went as far as to argue that the promotion of strategies for emancipatory action to end structural inequalities against the oppressed minorities is incompatible with the promotion of co-operative relations between the groups and the well-established paradigm of prejudice reduction through intergroup contact (Brown and Hewstone 2005) because prejudice reduction interventions might be working towards regimenting a structural inequality in society by reconciling the weak group with an unfavourable for them *status quo* (Dixon et al. 2012). Indeed the same mediators of prejudice reduction and reconciliation through intergroup contact (threats, intergroup anxiety, stereotyping) (Stephan et al. 2009) could be used in the reverse direction in the collective action paradigm to enhance solidarity and cohesion within the dominated group, facilitating sacrifices (even giving one's life for the ingroup). In that sense the revolt model of social relations implied in the collective action paradigm (usually studied in the context of overthrowing totalitarian regimes or dictatorships as we have recently seen in the Arab spring revolts or in the eighties against authoritarian leaders in the Eastern Europe) appears at first glance to be a whole different context where non-normative, violent action and the escalation of conflict would even be seen as legitimate. However, this rationale despite its positive role in bringing to our attention the issue of structural inequality, moving away from individualist assumptions, is built on some problematic premises: first, it presupposes that the oppressed have a false consciousness and do not know what is best for them (Howarth et al. 2012). Secondly, the whole argument is built on a very weak ethical standpoint because the logical conclusion of it is that the oppressed in fact need to keep their simplistic conflict narratives intact and their low-level historical thinking or consciousness just to end up instruments of some enlightened elites that would guide them to go sacrifice themselves for the common good. What collective action theorists failed to discuss is also the applicability of such a model in Western democracies, post-conflict or divided societies and the similarities of forms of representation produced through collective action with historically well-rehearsed doctrines and ideologies like nationalism, racism, fundamentalism and extremism (see Obradovic and Howarth 2017; Psaltis et al. 2015). For example, in divided societies like Israel and Palestine, Northern Ireland, Serbia, Croatia or Cyprus (Psaltis et al., Chap. 4) "two can play that game" of collective action for the interest of the ingroup that will eventually lead to either stalemate or the escalation of conflict, without compromise or reconciliation (Psaltis 2012a). The critics of the "prejudice reduction" paradigm (Dixon et al. 2012) also failed to recognize the existence of joint ingroup–outgroup collective action for the benefits of both groups by segments of former enemy groups for which intergroup contact and co-operation is actually a necessary precondition for joint collective action. Finally, they did not recognize post-colonial writings that argue along the emancipation of both groups in the process of tackling structural inequalities (Howarth et al. 2012).

The negative consequences of strategic decisions to use essentialist representations of the past or reified identities for collective struggles in asymmetric contexts relating to nation building efforts of new states can be seen in differing degrees in the context of the Baltic states (Kello and Wagner, Chap. 8) and Belarus (Zadora, Chap. 10) where in a post-transition context just before and after the dissolution of the Soviet Union nationalism was on the rise. In Estonia, a more disciplinary approach to history teaching is becoming more widely accepted after joining the EU, whereas in Latvia a more clear involvement by politicians in history teaching in a similar context led to more references to patriotism as an aim of history teaching according to Kello and Wagner (Chap. 8). The situation is more problematic in Belarus where an authoritarian administration is clearly using history teaching for political purposes in a very centralized way. The result of such pressures for the actual teaching practice is that teachers trying to balance a romantic and enlightened way of history teaching end up making use of communicative styles that Moscovici described as "propagation", a communicative style which is a middle road between propaganda and diffusion (Moscovici 1961/2008). Indeed the denial of citizenship rights to a significant number of inhabitants of the Baltic states of Russian origin should not come as a surprise given the link between essentialist representations of the past, ethnic identity and exclusionary notions of citizenship (Kadianaki and Andreouli 2015; Kadianaki et al. 2016).

The fact that the collective action paradigm is premised on predetermined roles of oppressor and oppressed, majority–minority, perpetrator and victim can be also challenged in that groups historically can pass from both roles and thus it is rather unlikely that there will ever be a clear case of a group being constantly in the same position. This problem is very clear in Cyprus, for example, not only because at different times in history both groups were oppressed and oppressors, victims and perpetrators, minorities and majorities but also because Greek Cypriots can always claim that they are the victims of a huge country like Turkey and the Turkish Cypriots at the same time claim that they are the victims of the 80% of the population (Greek Cypriots) in Cyprus. So in fact there is an interaction of social representations of the Cyprus issue with representations of the past (the main tension being whether it is a problem of intercommunal conflict vs a problem of violation of international law by Turkey which invaded Cyprus) which is not very far from the spirit of competitive victimhood already discussed for its pernicious effects.

From the Disciplinary to the Interdisciplinary Approach in History Teaching: From Representations of the Past Based on Belief to Representations Based on Knowledge

History educators have been increasingly realizing the need to deepen their understanding of the role of history teaching in conflict transformation (see Carretero 2011; Perikleous and Shemilt 2011).

As it will become clear to the reader of this volume, such concerns are now global and historically have their roots in the genetic epistemology of Jean Piaget in the International Bureau of Education (IBE) (Pingel 2016) when he advocated international dialogue of educators in an effort to de-centre history teaching from the ethnocentric orientations in the period between World War I and World War II. In the same vein, the work of the Spanish historian Altamira (1891) earlier was also pioneering for policy on history teaching in the League of Nations. The early epistemological distinctions made by Jean Piaget (1932) between social relations of co-operation (based on mutual respect) and social relations of constraint (unilateral respect/inequality of status) are still as relevant as ever since they offer a robust and clear epistemological social constructivist standpoint (Psaltis et al. 2015) for the construction of historical knowledge and advancement of historical consciousness. Such a conciousness should aim to move away from social relations of constraint towards relations of co-operation as they are enacted in social interaction successfully resolving socio-cognitive conflicts of various perspectives and producing more advanced forms of knowledge (Makriyianni and Psaltis 2007).

In this vein, the discussion of stages of historical consciousness by Rüsen (2004) and the higher form of consciousness described as "genetic" relates to Piaget's higher forms of transformative knowledge and interacting that he described as genuine dialogue characteristic of a democratic mentality. The Moscovician *Genetic Model of Social Influence* (Moscovici 1976) recognizes the harsh reality of asymmetries and inequalities in the conflict-ridden worlds we live in, but it is largely based on convincing by peaceful means, dialogue and communication the population for the stance of the minority in a struggle for recognition and change of social representations. This model as well as the more recent approach of *genetic social psychology* (Duveen and Psaltis 2008; Psaltis et al. 2015) recognizes that ideal relations of mutual respect are rarely achieved in reality since social identities are shot through with inequalities of status. However, it recognizes that conflicting asymmetries could create the conditions for productive forms of dialogue that can lead to more advanced forms of thinking. This approach is aiming at the integration of the processes of microgenetic, ontogenetic and sociogenetic changes of social representations; here the forms of communication described Kello and Wagner (Chap. 8) drawing inspiration from the second part of Moscovici's *Psychoanalysis* and the recent work of Gerard Duveen (Moscovici et al. 2013) become directly relevant. The processes of socio-cognitive conflict (Doise et al. 1976) between representations of the past, resistance to change (Duveen 2001) through the use of symbolic resources (Zittoun et al. 2003) and symbolic barriers (Gillepie 2015) discussed in the papers by Barreiro et al. (Chap. 5) can form a vibrant research agenda for the future. The in-depth studies of social interaction by Tsafrir Goldberg (2013; Chap. 11) in relation to the dual-narrative/empathetic textbook approach and the critical/disciplinary approach in Israel suggest that microgenetic processes in the classroom are indeed influenced by a complex interplay between the voices and perspectives made available in textbooks and the asymmetrical status of the groups in conflict.

THE MAJOR CHALLENGE: FACILITATING CONFLICT TRANSFORMATION THROUGH INTERDISCIPLINARY RESEARCH AND DIALOGUE

What this volume makes clear is the need for various stakeholders in the process of conflict transformation (policy makers, teachers, civil society and the grassroots) to engage in a process of reconstruction of their representations of the past. This cannot be done by replacing a master narrative with another well-intentioned simplistic peace narrative or with the strategic use of essentialist and reified forms of identity and social representations of the past. What is needed is a history teaching that is epistemologically more advanced compared to collective memory or the teaching of history as heritage (Lowenthal 1996; Makriyianni and Psaltis 2007), not only because more de-centred and multi-perspective forms of knowledge as we know from the genetic epistemology of Jean Piaget are more advanced forms of knowing compared to monoperspective accounts (see Makriyianni and Psaltis 2007) but also because developing the historical literacy, and their epistemological stance of history (Nasie et al. 2014), allows them to take an informed, critical and reflective stance on diverse representations and interpretations of the past. The main message of this volume is that we need to move from the disciplinary to the interdisciplinary teaching of history. History teachers who have enriched their history teaching skills with knowledge of social psychological theories will be in a position to engage with historical texts, establish historical significance, identify continuity and change, analyse cause and consequence, take historical perspectives and understand the ethical dimensions of historical interpretations as described by Seixas (2004) in a more successful way as proposed by McCully and Reilly (Chap. 12). Such teaching will enlarge the notion of historical literacy into a study of historical culture (Grever and Stuurman 2007) and historical consciousness (Rüsen 2004) in the classroom so that students become reflective of the role of collective memory and history teaching in processes of conflict transformation and understand the ways in which various forms of historical consciousness relate the past, present and future (Van Alphen and Carretero 2015; Psaltis 2016). This can be done through a better grasp of the way attributions of past wrongdoings (Doosje and Branscombe 2003) relate to processes of moral disengagement, apology, guilt, shame or regret (Imhoff et al. 2012); how realistic and symbolic threats can become an obstacle for prejudice reduction, confidence building and reconciliation; and how intergroup contact can lead to reconciliation. This kind of history teaching is interdisciplinary in nature and can be called *transformative history teaching* to the extent that it facilitates both the cultivation of historical thinking and conflict transformation.

Part I: Global and Regional Perspectives on Textbook Writing, Civil Society Organizations and Social Representations

The first part of this volume discusses the state of the art from an international and regional perspective on developments at the level of policy making and history textbooks in particular, local and international civil society organizations working on reconciliation projects in post-conflict societies all the way down to the representation of the past of lay people.

In her chapter Bentrovato (Chap. 2) examines history textbook work as an intervention for the promotion of reconciliation in intergroup conflict settings. It maps current practices and emerging trends in this field and considers their value and limitations. The analysis, combining a narrative framework with the conflict transformation paradigm, questions the value of models involving narrative evasion or elision and of single-narrative approaches and advocates for multi-narrative and multi-perspective textbook designs. In proposing a model of collaborative textbook work based on the concept of dialogical narrative transformation, this analysis elucidates its potential value as a catalyst for positive intergroup engagement and dialogue and ultimately for the redefinition of relationships. It thus shows that history textbook writing, often a battleground of narratives and interests, may act as a site and means of conflict transformation.

Bilali and Mahmoud (Chap. 3) review the work of civil society organizations that focus on confronting history as an avenue to achieving intergroup reconciliation in the aftermath of conflict. The chapter sheds light on practitioners' lay theories and strategies to address history for conflict transformation and reconciliation and contrasts these approaches to the scholarship in this area. Bilali and Mahmoud review the impressive number of 127 civil society projects that focus on confronting history in forty-five countries. They draw parallels between practitioners' approaches and the research literature and theory on intergroup conflict and discuss scholarly evidence on the assumptions underlying praxis from a social psychological perspective.

In their contribution in Chap. 4, Charis Psaltis, Renata Franc, Anouk Smeekes, Maria Ioannou and Iris Žeželj explore the role of social representations of the past, known as master narratives, in three cases of post-conflict societies (Cyprus, Serbia, Croatia). Their findings point to a *past–present–future* connection in all contexts; adherence to official master narratives of conflict relates to threats to ingroup well-being, an exaggerated sense of difference as an identity threat and the attribution of negative intentions to the outgroup today. These various types of threats mediate the negative effects of adherence to master narratives on the building of distrust thus undermining reconciliation.

Part II: Social Psychological Perspectives of Perpetrators and Victims

The second part of the volume deals with the question of perpetrator–victim dynamic and the ways that master narratives could be resisted in two different contexts (colonialism and holocaust) that however both involve a more widely accepted asymmetric perpetrator–victim dynamic.

In their contribution (Chap. 5) Alicia Barreiro, Cecilia Wainryb and Mario Carretero discuss the "Conquest of the Desert", a military campaign carried out by the Argentine State at the end of the 19th century, which involved the massacre and enslavement of indigenous communities. They analyse the hegemonic narrative concerning this historical process as conveyed by a museum's exhibits along with the indigenous counter-narrative as registered and supported by the local Mapuche community. Their analysis shows that the hegemonic narrative tends to negate the conflict between the two groups by rendering the indigenous group invisible and representing their identity in an anachronistic fashion. The counter-narrative evidences a tension between indigenous people's need to assert their identification with their ancestors and secure recognition from the dominant group, whilst also allowing for change and transformation in their midst.

In Chap. 6 Giovanna Leone describes what happens when history teaching breaks down social denials of past ingroup wrongdoings. These denials often occur when former victims of past violence are weak or isolated. She argues that reactions to teaching dealing with sensitive historical issues have to be set apart from reactions to teaching dealing with historical facts denied in the general social discourse. The article proposes to consider the latter as a special instance of *parrhesia*. Foucault's theoretical stance is discussed, who expects that *parrhesia* may lead to positive effects for listeners able to accept a difficult truth. Then, a case study on reactions by Italians to evidence of socially denied Italian colonial crimes is presented.

Michal Bilewicz, Marta Witkowska, Silviana Stubig, Marta Beneda and Roland Imhoff (Chap. 7) relate their social psychological research to Holocaust education which is one of the most widely taught historical matters: it is present in school curricula as part of history classes, but also in human rights education, ethics, philosophy and general social studies. Yet, many studies point to the fact that Holocaust education is not effective in providing knowledge and raising an emotional approach to this genocide. This chapter reviews empirical research conducted in Germany and Poland showing the main shortcomings of current Holocaust education and interpreting them from a social psychological perspective. Alternatively, they propose three alternative approaches to Holocaust education based on their findings. They suggest (1) using regret- instead of guilt-inducing narratives about the past, based on empathic concern about the victim, (2) incorporating moral exemplars narratives and (3) basing the education on local identities rather than national ones.

PART III: TEXTBOOK AND TEACHER PERSPECTIVES IN POST-TRANSITION AND POST-CONFLICT SOCIETIES

The third part focuses on history textbook and teacher perspectives with a special emphasis on the main mediators of history teaching, that is history teachers.

In Chap. 8 Kello and Wagner analyse history teaching through the lens of a distinction of communication styles—dissemination, propagation and propaganda—as proposed by Social Representation Theory. They see a history classroom as a communicative space and history teaching as situated standpoints-in-action. These standpoints can occupy different places on a continuum between the two extremes—dissemination versus propaganda—that is between an academic instruction style, neutrally presenting different perspectives about the past, versus straightforward ideological teaching. The authors analyse interviews with Estonian and Latvian history teachers and show how communication styles are defined both by the teacher's perceived action space, delimited by social, political, educational and academic demands and contexts, and by understandings of the past and history.

Falk Pingel (Chap. 9) focuses on history textbook revision and communicative processes around this practice at different levels. Various international organizations and local stakeholders in education participate in projects on the revision of history textbooks and curricula in conflict-ridden countries. Falk Pingel examines whether theories of social psychology help explain strategies of intervention. In Bosnia and Herzegovina, it was crucial to overcome ethnic, cultural and religious divides that split the Bosnian society and imprint the whole education system. Whereas at the beginning of the revision process Bosnian participants showed strong ingroup attitudes to protect their ethnic identity, continuous joint work decreased the impact of political difference and increased a common understanding of acting as education experts. Communication no longer went along the model of political negotiation and legitimation but followed the paradigm of an intersubjective, truth-finding process.

In her contribution Anna Zadora (Chap. 10) analyses textbook narratives in the specific context of Belarus—a post-totalitarian and authoritarian state. School history teaching has often been a powerful instrument for patriotism and identity building in Belarus. Political authorities tend to control the school history textbook writing and the transmission of sentiment of loyalty to the motherland. History teaching is often used for identity building processes, because history is relating to continuity and stability as fundamental notions for identity building. The article will provide a chronological analysis of the evolution of history textbooks writing in Belarus and the transmission of patriotism discourse trough the history textbooks and the prism of the construction of the dividing line between "us": patriots, belonging to the nation and the "other": "the strangers".

Part IV: Pedagogical Approaches to History Teaching and Reconciliation

In the fourth and final part of the volume, the focus moves to various pedagogical practices of history teaching in relation to reconciliation and a comparison of various possible approaches practically taken in formal and non-formal education. Such approaches intend to deal with issues of conflict transformation and reconciliation through history teaching in the post-conflict societies of Israel, Northern Ireland and Cyprus, where an interdisciplinary understanding of history teaching can be found either in civil society organisations or the formal educational system in various degrees.

Tsafrir Goldberg in Chap. 11 describes an intervention where Jewish and Arab Israeli adolescents were randomly allocated to learn the history of the Jewish-Arab conflict in one of three competing history teaching approaches—a single official narrative, an empathetic dual-narrative and a multiple-perspective critical enquiry. Later, Jewish and Arab participants were matched by teaching approach into small groups to discuss the roots and solution to the conflict. Analysis of learners' writing and discussion shows one-sided history teaching reduces openness to outgroup perspective, egalitarian intergroup interaction and reconciliatory decisions. Openness to outgroup perspective and acknowledgement of responsibility predicted reconciliatory interaction and discussion outcome in line with the *needs-based reconciliation model.*

In Chap. 12, McCully and Reilly discuss the role of history teaching in promoting positive community relations in Northern Ireland with specific reference to two publicly funded projects. The Northern Ireland context for history teaching is outlined, followed by an overview of relevant social psychological theory, concepts and research. Educational responses to the conflict and post-conflict situations are explored including development of the history curriculum. The extent to which history teachers might employ ideas from social psychology to contribute to improved relationships between young people is examined. They conclude that history teachers may privilege disciplinary outcomes and curriculum over other project aims; therefore, outcomes in relation to promoting community relations may be less consistent than discipline-related outcomes without additional input from social psychologists.

Michalinos Zembylas and Hakan Karahasan in Chap. 13 explore the potential of history teaching in formal and non-formal education spaces to facilitate conflict transformation processes, focusing on the role of dangerous memories and reconciliation pedagogies. The chapter is divided into four parts. First, there is a theoretical discussion on memory, history and identity in relation to dangerous memories and conflict transformation. Second, a brief review of recent formal reform efforts on history teaching is provided in the Greek Cypriot and Turkish Cypriot educational systems. Third, the work of NGOs working with both Greek Cypriot and Turkish Cypriot teachers shows some openings for reconciliation pedagogies and dangerous memories. The chapter ends with a broader discussion of the role that could be played by reconciliation pedagogies to promote dangerous memories through both formal and non-formal education efforts.

The concluding chapter written by M. Carretero, a co-editor of the volume, draws on his experience on history teaching in relation to patriotism, nationalism, social identity processes and reconciliation in various parts of the world. It tries to be a reflective commentary establishing a meaningful relation between present trends in history education and how to rethink them in relation to the teaching of historical contents in post-conflict societies. Therefore this chapter tries to focus not only on what to teach but also on how to teach it and how this could contribute to conflict transformation. Also, this chapter intends to develop a meaningful relation between social psychology contributions and present ideas coming from history education, historiography and related fields.

Notes

1. Yoyes was an ETA terrorist that decided to abandon the terrorist actions and was later killed by her former terrorist colleagues. Story retrieved from El Pais newspaper (http://politica.elpais.com/politica/2016/09/21/actualidad/1474483613_429957.html).
2. In recognition of its pioneering work at the level of civil society organizations, AHDR has recently been awarded with the Max van der Stoel Award of OSCE in 2016 (http://www.osce.org/hcnm/256056).
3. In Cyprus, the major project of the AHDR was the establishment of the Home for Co-operation (http://www.home4cooperation.info/). A renovated derelict building in the Nicosia UN patrolled Buffer Zone to be used as an educational centre and meeting place for AHDR and other intercommunal NGOs working for reconciliation and co-operation between the two communities in Cyprus.
4. Moscovici's (1998/2000, p. 136) distinction is between (a) social representations "whose kernel consists of beliefs which are generally more homogenous, affective, impermeable to experience or contradiction, and leave little scope for individual variations" and (b) social representations founded on knowledge "which are more fluid, pragmatic, amenable to the proof of success or failure, and leave a certain latitude to language, experience, and even to the critical faculties of individuals"; this distinction clearly relates back to his social influence model of minority influence and through that to Piaget's (1932/1997) social psychological model of relations of constraint vs relations of co-operation.

References

Allport, G. (1954). *The nature of prejudice*. Cambridge, MA: Addison-Wesley.
Altamira, R. (1891). *La enseñanza de la Historia* (History education). Madrid: V. Suárez.
Bandura, A. (1999). Moral disengagement in the perpetration of inhumanities. *Personality and Social Psychology Review, 3*, 193–209.
Bar-Tal, D., & Salomon, G. (2006). Israeli-Jewish narratives of the Israeli-Palestinian conflict: Evolvement, contents, functions and consequences. In R. I. Rotberg (Ed.), *Israeli and Palestinian narratives of conflict: History's Double Helix*. Bloomington: Indiana University Press.
Bekerman, Z., & Zembylas, M. (2011). The emotional complexities of teaching conflictual historical narratives: The case of integrated Palestinian-Jewish schools in Israel. *Teachers College Record, 113*(5), 1004–1030.

Bentrovato, D., Korostelina, K. V., & Schulze, M. (Eds.). (2016). *History can bite: History education in divided and postwar societies*. Göttingen: V&R Unipress.

Bilali, R. (2013). National Narrative and Social Psychological Influences in Turks' Denial of the Mass Killings of Armenians as Genocide. *Journal of Social Issues, 69,* 16–33.

Branscombe, N. R., Ellemers, N., Spears, R., & Doosje, B. (1999). The context and content of social identity threat. In N. Ellemers, R. Spears, & B. Doosje (Eds.), *Social identity: Context, commitment, content* (pp. 35–58). Oxford, United Kingdom: Basil Blackwell.

Brown, R., & Hewstone, H. (2005). An integrative theory of intergroup contact. In M. Zanna (Ed.), *Advances in experimental social psychology* (Vol. 37, pp. 255–343). San Diego, CA: Academic Press.

Carretero, M. (2011). *Constructing patriotism. Teaching history and memories in global worlds*. Charlotte: Information Age Publishing.

Carretero, M., Asensio, M., & Rodriguez-Moneo, M. (Eds.). (2012). *History education and the construction of national identities*. Charlotte: Information Age Publishing.

Carretero, M., Berger, S., & Grever, M. (2017). Introduction: Historical cultures and education in transition. In: Carretero, M., Berger, S., & Grever, M. (Eds.). (2017). *Palgrave handbook of research in historical culture and education* (pp. 1–35). Basingstoke: Palgrave.

Čehajić, S., & Brown, R. (2010). Silencing the past: Effect of intergroup contact on acknowledgment of ingroup atrocities. *Social Psychological and Personality Science, 1*(2), 190–196.

Čehajić-Clancy, S., Goldenberg, A., Gross, J., & Halperin, E. (2016). Social-Psychological interventions for intergroup reconciliation: An emotion regulation perspective. *Psychological Inquiry, 27*(2), 73–88.

Chapman, A., Perikleous, L., Yakinthou, C., & Zincir Celal, R. (2011). *Thinking historically about missing persons: A guide for teachers*. Nicosia: AHDR.

Cole, E. (Ed.). (2007). *Teaching the violent past: History education and reconciliation*. Lanham, MD: Rowman and Littlefield.

Constantinou, C. M. (2015). Conflict transformation and homodiplomacy. In C. Psaltis, A. Gillespie, & A. N. P. Perret-Clermont (Eds.), *Social relations in human and societal development* (pp. 114–133). London, United Kingdom: Palgrave Macmillan.

Dixon, J., Levine, M., Reicher, S., & Durrheim, K. (2012). Beyond prejudice: Are negative evaluations the problem and is getting us to like one another more the solution? *Behavioural and Brain Sciences, 35*(6), 411–466.

Doosje, B., & Branscombe, N. R. (2003). Attributions for the negative historical actions of a group. *European Journal of Social Psychology, 33,* 235–248.

Doise, W., Mugny, G., & Perret-Clermont, A. N. (1976). Social interaction and cognitive development: Further evidence. *European Journal of Social Psychology, 6*, 245–247.
Duveen, G. (2001). Representations, identity, resistance. In K. Deaux & G. Philogene (Eds.), *Representations of the social* (pp. 257–284). Oxford: Blackwell.
Duveen, G. (2002). Construction, belief, doubt. *Psychologie et Societé, 3*, 139–155.
Duveen, G. (2007). Culture and social sepresentations. In J. Valsiner & A. Rosa (Eds.), *The Cambridge handbook of sociocultural psychology*. Cambridge: CUP.
Duveen, G., & Lloyd, B. (1990). Introduction. In G. Duveen & B. Lloyd (Eds.), *Social representations and the development of knowledge* (pp. 1–10). Cambridge: Cambridge University Press.
Duveen, G., & Psaltis, C. (2008). The constructive role of asymmetries in social interaction. In U. Mueller, J. Carpendale, N. Budwig & B. Sokol (Eds.), *Social life and social knowledge: Toward a process account of development* (pp. 183–204). Mahwah, NJ: Lawrence Erlbaum.
Easterbrook, M., & Vignoles, V. (2013). What does it mean to belong? Interpersonal bonds and intragroup similarities as predictors of felt belonging in different types of groups. *European Journal of Social Psychology, 43*(6), 455–462.
Galtung, J. (2000). *Conflict transformation by peaceful means: The Transcend method*. United Nations.
Gillespie, A. (2008). Social representations, alternative representations and semantic barriers. *Journal for the Theory of Social Behaviour, 38*, 375–391.
Gillespie, A. (2015). Non-transformative social interaction. In C. Psaltis, A. Gillespie & A. N. P Perret-Clermont (Eds.), *Social relations in human and societal revelopment* (pp. 97–113). London: Palgrave Macmillan.
Goldberg, T. (2013). "It's in my veins": Identity and disciplinary practice in students' discussions of a historical issue. *Theory & Research in Social Education, 41*(1), 33–64.
Grever, M., & Stuurman, S. (Eds.). (2007). *Beyond the canon: History for the twenty-first century*. Basingstoke: Palgrave Macmillan.
Halperin, E., Russell, A. G., Trzesniewski, K. H., Gross, J. J., & Dweck, C. S. (2011). Promoting the Middle East peace process by changing beliefs about group malleability. *Science, 333*, 1767–1769.
Hammack, P. (2010). Identity as burden or benefit? Youth, historical narrative, and the legacy of political conflict. *Human Development, 53*, 173–201.
Hein, L., & Selden, M. (Eds.). (2000). *Censoring history: Citizenship and memory in Japan, Germany, and the United States*. New York: M.E. Sharpe.

Hobsbawm, E. (2002, February 23). War and peace: Newspaper article published in *The Guardian*. Retrieved September 21, 2016 from https://www.theguardian.com/education/2002/feb/23/artsandhumanities.highereducation.

Howarth, C., Wagner, W., Kessi, S., & Sen, R. (2012). The politics of moving beyond prejudice. *Behavioural and Brain Sciences, 35*(6), 437–438.

Imhoff, R., Bilewicz, M., & Erb, H. P. (2012). Collective guilt versus collective regret. Different emotional reactions to ingroup atrocities. *European Journal for Social Psychology, 42*, 729–742.

Kadianaki, I., & Andreouli, E. (2015), Essentialism in social representations of citizenship: An analysis of Greeks' and Migrants' discourse. *Political Psychology. Advance online publication*. doi: 10.1111/pops.12271.

Kadianaki, I., Andreouli, E., & Carretero, M. (2016). Using national history to construct the boundaries of citizenship: An analysis of Greek citizens' discourse about immigrants' rights. *Qualitative Psychology*. http://dx.doi.org/10.1037/qup0000087.

Kelman, H. C. (2004). Reconciliation as identity change: A social psychological perspective. In Y. Bart-Siman-Tov (Ed.), *From conflict resolution to reconciliation* (pp. 111–124). Oxford: Oxford University Press.

Kelman, H. C. (2008). Reconciliation from a social-psychological perspective. In A. Nadler, T. Malloy & J. D. Fisher (Eds.), *Social psychology of intergroup reconciliation* (pp. 15–32). Oxford: Oxford University Press.

Kitson, A. (2007). History teaching and reconciliation in Northern Ireland. In E. A. Cole (Ed.), *Teaching the violent past: History education and reconciliation* (pp. 123–155). Lanham, MD: Rowman & Littlefield.

Klein, O. (2013). The lay historian: How ordinary people think about history. In R. Cabecinhas & L. Abadia (Eds.), *Narratives and social memory: Theoretical and methodological approaches* (pp. 25–45). Braga, Portugal: University of Minho.

Klerides, E., & Philippou, S. (2015). Cyprus: Exploring educational reform 2004–2014. In T. Corner (Ed.), *Education in the European Union: Post-2003 member states* (pp. 51–73). London: Bloomsbury.

Klerides, E., & Zembylas, M. (2017). Ideology as immunology: History teaching in two ethnic borders of Europe. *Compare: A Journal of Comparative and International Education, 47*(3), 416–433.

Korostelina, K., & Lässig, S. (Eds.). (2013). *History education and postconflict reconciliation: Reconsidering joint textbook projects*. Abingdon, UK: Routledge.

Leach, C., Zeineddine, F., & Čehajić-Clancy, S. (2013). Moral immemorial: The rarity of self-criticism for previous generations' genocide or mass violence. *Journal of Social Issues, 69*(1), 34–53.

Lederach, J. P. (1997). *Building peace: Sustainable reconciliation in divided societies*. Washington, D.C: United States Institute of Peace Press.

Licata, L., & Klein, O. (2010). Holocaust or benevolent paternalism? Intergenerational comparisons on collective memories and emotions about Belgium's colonial past. *International Journal of Conflict and Violence, 4*(1), 45–57.
Liu, J. H., & Hilton, D. J. (2005). How the past weighs on the present: Social representations of history and their role in identity politics. *British Journal of Social Psychology, 44,* 537–556.
Loizides, N. (2015). *Designing peace: Cyprus and institutional innovations in divided societies.* Pennsylvania: University of Pennsylvania Press.
Lowenthal, D. (1996). *The heritage crusade and the spoils of history.* Cambridge: CUP.
Makriyianni, C., & Psaltis, C. (2007). History teaching and reconciliation. *Cyprus Review, 19,* 43–69.
Makriyianni, C., Psaltis, C., & Latif, D. (2011). History teaching in cyprus. In E. Erdmann & W. Hasberg (Eds.), *Facing mapping, bridging diversity: Foundations of a European discourse on history education, part 1* (pp. 91–138). Germany: Wochen Schau Wissenschaft.
Marková, I., & Gillespie, A. (Eds.). (2012). *Trust and conflict: Representation, culture and dialogue.* London: Routledge.
Martinovic, B., & Verkuyten, M. (2013). 'We were here first, so we determine the rules of the game': Autochthony and prejudice towards out-groups. *European Journal of Social Psychology, 43,* 637–647.
McCully, A. (2012). History teaching, conflict and the legacy of the past. *Education, Citizenship and Social Justice, 7*(2), 145–159.
McCully, A., & Barton, K. C. (2010). "You can form your own point of view": Internally persuasive discourse in Northern Ireland students' encounters with history. *Teachers College Record, 112*(1), 142–181.
Moscovici, S. (1976). *Social influence and social change.* London: Academic Press.
Moscovici, S. (1998/2000). The history and actuality of social representations. In G. Duveen (Ed.), *Social representations: Explorations in social psychology.* (pp. 120–154). Cambridge: Polity Press.
Moscovici, S., Jovchelovitch, S., & Wagoner, B. (2013). (Eds.), *Development as a social process: Contributions of Gerard Duveen.* UK: Routledge.
Moscovici, S. (1961/2008). *Psychoanalysis: Its image and its public.* Cambridge: Polity Press.
Nadler, A., & Shnabel, N. (2015). Intergroup reconciliation: Instrumental and socio-emotional processes and the needs-based model. *European Review of Social Psychology, 26,* 93–125.
Nasie, M., Bar-Tal, D., Pliskin, R., Nahhas, E., & Haperin, E. (2014). Overcoming the barrier of narrative adherence in conflicts through awareness of the psychological bias of naive realism. *Personal and Social Psychology Bulletin, 40,* 1543–1557.

Noor, M., Shnabel, N., Halabi, S., & Nadler, A. (2012). When suffering begets suffering: The psychology of competitive victimhood between adversarial groups in violent conflicts. *Personality and Social Psychology Review, 16*(4), 351–374.

Obradovic, S., & Howarth, C. (2017). Everyday Reconciliation. In C. Howarth & E. Andreouli (Eds.), *The social psychology of everyday politics*. UK: Routledge.

Papadakis, Y. (2008). Narrative, memory and history in divided Cyprus: A comparison of school books on the history of cyprus. *History & Museum, 20*, 128–148.

Páez, D., & Liu, J. H. (2011). Collective memory of conflicts. In D. Bar-Tal (Ed.), *Intergroup conflicts and their resolution: A social psychological perspective* (pp. 105–124). New York, NY: Psychology Press.

Páez, D., Bobowic, M., & Liu, J. H. (2017). Social representations of the past and competences in history education. In M. Carretero, S. Berger & M. Grever (Eds.), *Handbook of research in historical culture and history education* (pp. 491–510). Palgrave Macmillan.

Paulson, J. (2015). "Whether and how?" History education about recent and ongoing conflict: A review of research. *Journal on Education in Emergencies, 1*(1), 14–47.

Perikleous, L. (2010). At a crossroad between memory and thinking: The case of primary history education in the Greek cypriot educational system, education 3–13: *International Journal of Primary, Elementary and Early Years Education, 38*(3), 315–328.

Perikleous, L., & Shemilt, D. (Eds.). (2011). *The future of the past: Why history education matters*. Nicosia: AHDR.

Pettigrew, T. F. (1979). The ultimate attribution error: Extending Allport's cognitive analysis of prejudice. *Personality and Social Psychology Bulletin, 5*, 461–476.

Psaltis, C. (2012a). Intergroup trust and contact in transition: A social representations perspective on the Cyprus conflict. In I. Markova & A. Gillespie (Eds.), *Trust and conflict: Representations, culture and dialogue* (pp. 83–104), London: Routledge.

Psaltis, C. (2012b). Culture and social representations: A continuing dialogue in search for heterogeneity in social developmental psychology. *Culture & Psychology, 18*(3), 375–390.

Psaltis, C. (2015a). Genetic social psychology: From microgenesis to ontogenesis and sociogenesis…and back. In C. Psaltis, A. Gillespie & A. N. P Perret-Clermont (Eds.), *Social relations in human and societal development*, UK: Palgrave, Macmillan.

Psaltis, C. (2015b). Communication and the microgenetic construction of knowledge. In G. Sammut, E. Andreouli, G. Gaskell & J. Valsiner (Eds.), *Handbook of social representations* (pp. 113–127). Cambridge: CUP.

Psaltis, C. (2016). Collective memory, social representations of intercommunal relations and conflict transformation in divided Cyprus. *Peace and Conflict: Journal of Peace Psychology, 22*(1), 19–27.
Psaltis, C., & Cakal, H. (2016). Social identity in divided Cyprus. In S. McKeown, R. Haji & N. Ferguson (Eds.), *Understanding peace and conflict through social identity theory: Contemporary and world-wide perspectives* (Springer Peace Psychology Book Series) (pp. 229–244). UK: Springer.
Psaltis, C., Gillespie, A., & Perret-Clermont, A. N. P. (Eds.). (2015). *Human relations in human and societal development*. UK: Palgrave-Macmillan.
Piaget, J. (1932/1997). *The moral judgment of the child*. New York: Free Press Paperbacks.
Pingel, F. (2016). Textbook revision programme: History, concepts, and assumptions. In A. Kulnazarova & C. Ydesen (Eds.), *UNESCO without borders. Educational campaigns for international understanding* (pp. 13–31). New York: Routledge.
Rüsen, J. (2004). Historical consciousness: Narrative structure, moral function, and ontogenetic development. In P. Seixas (Ed.), *Theorizing historical consciousness* (pp. 63–85). Toronto: University of Toronto Press.
Sani, F. (2008). *Self continuity: Individual and collective perspectives*. New York: Psychology Press.
Seixas, P. (Ed.). (2004). *Theorizing historical consciousness*. Toronto: University of Toronto Press.
Shnabel, N., & Ullrich, J. (2016). Putting emotion regulation in context: The (Missing) role of power relations. Intergroup Trust, and Groups' Need for Positive Identities in Reconciliation Processes. *Psychological Inquiry, 27*(2), 124–132.
Smeekes, A. (2015). National nostalgia: A group-based emotion that benefits the in-group but hampers intergroup relations. *International Journal of Intercultural Relations, 49*, 54–67.
Smeekes, A., & Verkuyten, M. (2015). The presence of the past: Identity continuity and group dynamics. *European Review of Social Psychology, 26*(1), 162–202.
Smeekes, A., McKeown, S., & Psaltis, C. (2017). Endorsing narratives under threat: Maintaining perceived collective continuity through the protective power of ingroup narratives in Northern Ireland and Cyprus. *Journal of Social and Political Psychology*.
Smith, E. R. (1993). Social identity and social emotions: Toward new conceptualizations of prejudice. In D. M. Mackie & D. L. Hamilton (Eds.), *Affect, cognition, and stereotyping: Interactive processes in group perception* (pp. 297–315). San Diego, CA: Academic Press.
Stephan, W. G., Ybarra, O., & Rios Morrison, K. (2009). Intergroup threat theory (pp. 43–59). In T. Nelson (Ed.), *Handbook of prejudice*. Mahwah, NJ: Lawrence Erlbaum Associates.

Tajfel, H. (Ed.). (1978). *Differentiation between social groups: Studies in the social psychology of intergroup relations*. London: Academic Press.

Tajfel, H., & Turner, J. C. (1979). An integrative theory of intergroup conflict. In W. G. Austin & S. Worchel (Eds.), *The social psychology of intergroup relations* (pp. 7–24). Monterey, CA: Brooks-Cole.

Tausch, N., Hewstone, M., Kenworthy, J., Psaltis, C., Schmid, K., Popan, J., et al. (2010). Secondary Transfer Effects of Intergroup Contact: Alternative Accounts and Underlying Processes. *Journal of Personality & Social Psychology*, 99, 282–302.

Tint, B. (2010a). History, memory, and intractable conflict. *Conflict Resolution Quarterly*, 27, 239–256.

Tint, B. (2010b). History, memory, and conflict resolution: Research and application. *Conflict Resolution Quarterly*, 27, 369–399.

Vollhardt, J. R., & Twali, M. S. (2016). Emotion-based reconciliation requires attention to power differences, critical consciousness, and structural change. *Psychological Inquiry*, 27, 136–143.

Wagoner, B. (2015). Collective remembering as a process of social representations. In G. Sammut, E. Andreouli, G. Gaskell, & J. Valsiner (Eds.), *Cambridge handbook of social representations* (pp. 143–162). Cambridge: Cambridge University Press.

Wineburg, S. (2001). *Historical thinking and other unnatural acts*. Philadelphia: Temple University Press.

Van Zomeren, M., Postmes, T., & Spears, R. (2008). Toward an integrative social identity model of collective action: A quantitative research synthesis of three socio-psychological perspectives. *Psychological Bulletin*, 134, 504–535.

Van Alphen, F., & Carretero, M. (2015). The construction of the relation between national past and present in the appropriation of historical master narratives. *Integrative Psychological and Behavioral Science.*, 49(3), 512–530.

Zittoun, T., Duveen, G., Gillespie, A., Ivinson, G., & Psaltis, C. (2003). The use of symbolic resources in developmental transitions. *Culture & Psychology*, 9, 415–448.

Zeromskyte, R., & Wagner, W. (2016). When a majority becomes a minority: Essentialist intergroup stereotyping in an inverted power differential. *Culture & Psychology.* 23, 1, 88–107.

Authors' Biography

Charis Psaltis is an Associate Professor of Social and Developmental Psychology at the University of Cyprus. His research interests fall in the areas of genetic social psychology, social interaction in learning and cognitive development, social representations of gender, intergroup contact and intergroup relations between Greek Cypriots and Turkish Cypriots, development of national identities and history teaching and collective memory. He published papers in *Journal of Personality and Social Psychology, European Journal of Social Psychology, British Journal of Developmental Psychology, Culture & Psychology and Human Development*. Since 2014, he is a member of the Editorial Board of the *British Journal of Developmental Psychology* and since 2015 Associate Editor of *European Journal of Psychology of Education*. In April 2014, his book co-authored with Anna Zapiti entitled *Interaction, Communication and Development: Psychological Development as a social process* was published by Routledge, and in 2015, his co-edited volume *Social Relations in Human and Societal Development* by Palgrave Macmillan.

Mario Carretero is a Professor of Cognitive Psychology at Autonoma University of Madrid, Spain, where he was Dean of the Faculty of Psychology, and Researcher at FLACSO, Argentina. He has carried out an extensive research on history education from both cognitive and sociocultural approaches. He has published in *Journal of the Learning Sciences* and *Cognition and Instruction*. His last books are *History Education and the Construction of National Identities* (2012) (co-ed.) and *Constructing Patriotism* (funded by the Guggenheim Foundation) (2011). He has been Santander Visiting Scholar at the David Rockefeller Center for Latin American Studies of Harvard University (2009) and Bliss Carnochan Visiting Professor at the Humanities Center of Stanford University (2011). His present research interests have to do with an interdisciplinary attempt to study history education issues as it can be seen in *Palgrave Handbook of Research in Historical Culture and Education* (2017) (co-edited along with S. Berger and M. Grever).

Sabina Čehajić-Clancy works as an Associate Professor of Social and Political Psychology at the Sarajevo School of Science and Technology in Bosnia and Herzegovina. She works in the field of intergroup relations, more specifically on reconciliation in post-conflict societies. She has published numerous papers in peer-reviewed journals such as *Journal of Personality and Social Psychology, European Journal of Social Psychology, Political Psychology, Group Processes and Intergroup Relations and Psychological Inquiry*. Sabina has also over thirteen years of experience in working as an expert consultant for various international and local NGOs such as UNICEF, UNDP, Post-conflict Research Centre, Catholic Relief Service, Save the Children and USAID designing and evaluating reconciliation-oriented interventions. Her work has received wide media coverage due to its unique methodological approaches used in (post-)conflict contexts. She is also a member of the Editorial Board for the Political Psychology Journal.

Open Access This chapter is licensed under the terms of the Creative Commons Attribution 4.0 International License (http://creativecommons.org/licenses/by/4.0/), which permits use, sharing, adaptation, distribution and reproduction in any medium or format, as long as you give appropriate credit to the original author(s) and the source, provide a link to the Creative Commons license and indicate if changes were made.

The images or other third party material in this chapter are included in the chapter's Creative Commons license, unless indicated otherwise in a credit line to the material. If material is not included in the chapter's Creative Commons license and your intended use is not permitted by statutory regulation or exceeds the permitted use, you will need to obtain permission directly from the copyright holder.

PART I

Global and Regional Perspectives on Textbook Writing, Civil Society Organizations and Social Representations

History Textbook Writing in Post-Conflict Societies: From Battlefield to Site and Means of Conflict Transformation

Denise Bentrovato

Societies emerging from violent conflict face daunting challenges. One of the many challenges they face relates to the question of how to deal with the divisive past in ways that promote peace and reconciliation. The profusion of transitional justice (TJ) practices and of related scholarship since the 1990s evidences the systematic attention recently given to this question in post-conflict societies (Buckley-Zistel et al. 2014; Clark and Palmer 2012). TJ measures, such as truth commissions, tribunals, official apologies, reparation programmes and institutional reforms, have increasingly become key elements in the stock of interventions designed to help societies come to terms with their past in order to break cycles of violence and prevent its recurrence. The expansion of the field of TJ has been accompanied by an increasing appreciation of the role of education in the non-repetition of violence (Leach and Dunne 2007; Smith 2010). A growing

---

The author is grateful to Luigi Cajani, Alan McCully and Falk Pingel for their valuable comments on this paper.

D. Bentrovato (✉)
University of Pretoria, Pretoria, South Africa
e-mail: denise.bentrovato@up.ac.za

© The Author(s) 2017
C. Psaltis et al. (eds.), *History Education and Conflict Transformation*,
DOI 10.1007/978-3-319-54681-0_2

body of research has consequently emerged that examines the distinct role of history education in conflict and peace, inspiring lively debates on how to teach history after conflict (Bentrovato et al. 2016; Cole 2007; Paulson 2015). Embedded in these debates, this chapter focuses on one particular aspect of post-conflict history education, namely school textbooks—a central element in history teaching practices across the globe, though only one among various sources within the "complex medial space" (Lässig 2013: 4) that may shape historical consciousness (Rüsen 2004; Seixas 2004). More specifically, it examines the revision and development of history textbooks as one aspect, often marginalised in scholarly research, in the plethora of interventions designed to promote reconciliation in societies transitioning from violent conflict to peace and democracy.

Drawing from a wide range of case-studies from around the world as its empirical base, this chapter reviews past and present work around history textbook writing in divided and post-conflict societies in order to reflect upon the conciliatory value and limitations of current practices in this field. Its aim is to shed light on key approaches, challenges and opportunities related to textbook work in the context and aftermath of conflict and mass violence, and also on actors and conditions that have had an influence on related processes and outcomes. The chapter starts from the premise of the complex role of history textbooks in conflict and peace before examining recent experiences in textbook writing and takes stock of some of the different models and underlying assumptions that have marked this field. A narrative framework is adopted to structure the analysis of the processes and outcomes characterising these endeavours. Within this framework, the chapter first examines the promises and pitfalls of a variety of prominent short-term and longer-term approaches to post-conflict textbook work, thereby focusing on the narrative strategies employed to deal with contentious and potentially divisive histories in the wake of intergroup conflict. Moving beyond a focus on the concrete outcomes of textbook projects, it then relies on the "conflict transformation" paradigm to highlight the less tangible conciliatory value inherent in the performative dimension of these projects. It thereby draws attention to the transformative potential of communicative processes involved in collaborative textbook work that is geared towards the production of inclusive, multiperspective educational resources.

The chapter argues that, while history textbook revision poses daunting challenges for societies emerging from recent violent conflict, often serving as a battlefield for opposing narratives and interests, such processes also offer largely unexploited opportunities as potential sites and means of conflict transformation. Specifically, it suggests that the added value of post-conflict textbook work lies in its potential to provide a context for positive intergroup engagement and dialogue which could facilitate reconciliation, and the intrinsic "redefinition of relationships" (Lederach 2001: 847), through encouraging a process of "narrative transformation." Ultimately, this study aims to contribute to further mapping and conceptualising an eclectic and still undertheorised field that has been largely driven by practice as well as to distil lessons for the purpose of enhancing the role of such initiatives in processes of peacebuilding and reconciliation.

The Janus-Face of History Textbooks in Conflict and Peace

History textbooks are not of little significance. Their conspicuous role in society has been underscored by extensive textbook research describing them as powerful "cultural artefacts" that have traditionally served as conveyors of official knowledge (Apple 1993; Apple and Christian-Smith 1991; Foster and Crawford 2006; Marsden 2001; Nicholls 2006). Across the globe, they have functioned as central instruments of nation-building and citizenship formation and as important sites for the construction and transmission of collective identities and memories and of particular concepts of nationhood (Carretero 2011; Williams 2014). As such, history textbooks have been commonly politicised, becoming a significant pawn and a key stake in struggles and conflicts over identity and power. Critical textbook studies have shown that, as a result and a reflection of these struggles, their content, far from being neutral, has reproduced and legitimised the beliefs, values and norms of dominant groups in society (e.g. Apple and Christian-Smith 1991).

Growing research into the politics of history textbooks has indicated the conflict potential of these powerful media. Time and again, their role in promoting attachment to a particular "imagined community" (Anderson 1991) has been fulfilled through glorification of some and marginalisation and vilification of others. In the aftermath of violent conflict, history textbooks are frequently found to have played a particularly deleterious role in society by conveying and cementing prejudice, stereotypes and enemy images through their dissemination of largely mythical narratives that depict in- and outgroup identities as primordial, monolithic and antagonistic. They have construed and legitimised images of age-old intergroup enmity and of ingroup natural superiority, collective victimhood, heroism, and historical entitlement to territory, power and resources, while presenting negative portrayals of the "other" (Bentrovato et al. 2016; Dimou 2009; EUROMID 2006; Richter 2008; Vickers and Jones 2005). In so doing, history textbooks have reinforced antagonistic perceptions and inequalities which, in the conflict transformation literature, have been identified as characterising protracted identity-based conflict in deeply divided societies (Bar-Tal 2000; Kriesberg 2004; Lederach 1997; Oberschall 2007).

Conversely, as observed by various authors, history textbooks can also "help transform society by challenging the deep-rooted prejudices and inequalities at the heart of the conflict" (Leach and Dunne 2007: 11). With history textbooks having regularly been seen as a factor contributing to conflict, post-war interventions have often included the establishment of bodies with a mandate to re-examine textbooks in order to screen and purge them of objectionable content and to (re)write more appropriate materials or produce guidelines for this purpose. These activities have been considered an important confidence-building and peacebuilding strategy able to contribute to the deconstruction of negative perceptions and the promotion of dialogue, mutual understanding and social cohesion. Today these activities can count on a longstanding "conciliatory tradition" of textbook work (Foster 2011), which, developed in Europe especially after World War II, has inspired both scholarship and practice around the world (Pingel 2008, 2010; Stöber 2013). Historically promoted to advance interstate peace and international understanding, traditional goals of conciliatory textbook work have consisted in convening historians and teachers from across the divide with a view to "disarming" and "decontaminating" textbooks and to producing new resources "so that they (a) are underpinned by common historical understandings of the past and (b) are more sensitive to the histories of other nations" (Foster 2011: 7).

Since then, textbook activities have slowly found a place in peace agreements and TJ processes in contexts of intrastate conflicts and their resolution. The 1989 Taif peace agreement, for instance, which ended civil war in Lebanon after fifteen years of sectarian strife, explicitly, though largely unsuccessfully (Daher 2012; Kriener 2012), urged the revision of curricula "in a manner that strengthens national belonging, fusion, spiritual and cultural openness, and that unifies textbooks on the subjects of history and national education" (art. III.F.5). The peacebuilding role of history education and textbooks is also both implicitly and explicitly recognised in key TJ documents issued by the United Nations, which hint at the need to expediently revise and update textbooks to accurately deal with a violent past. Particularly, the UN *Impunity* and *Reparation Principles* respectively highlight the importance of educative measures to facilitate "A people's knowledge of the history of its oppression" in fulfilment of a state's "duty to preserve memory" and counter impunity (United Nations Commission on Human Rights 2005), and, on that premise, further call for the "[i]nclusion of an accurate account of the violations [...] in educational material at all levels" as a symbolic reparation measure for victims of historical wrongs (United Nations General Assembly 2006, in De Baets 2015: 18).

Fulfilling these demands and expectations is not an easy task, but rather one that is itself ridden with conflict. History textbook revision is an inherently contested and selective process conducted and influenced "by real people with real interests" (Apple 1993: 46). It entails negotiations and deliberations, which may provoke tensions that are part and parcel of struggles for recognition and legitimacy. In societies emerging from violent intergroup conflict, history textbook revision faces particular challenges. Here, the contentions surrounding the selection of textbook content are compounded by a meta-conflict that is typically manifest in the existence of viscerally held, one-sided and mutually contested narratives of victimisation. Competing group narratives may diverge regarding the causes of conflict, the number and identity of the victims, actors' roles and responsibilities, and the motivations, legitimacy and implications of their actions. They also commonly differ as to the terminology they use to define violent events, each presenting different connotations and meanings. Definitions of one and the same event have ranged from "liberation" to "aggression", "invasion" or "occupation", and from "incident" or "crisis" to "civil war", "killings", "massacre" or "genocide". Daniel Bar-Tal poignantly summarises this predicament by suggesting that "Over the years, groups involved in conflict selectively form collective memories about the conflict. On the one hand, they focus mainly on the other side's responsibility for the outbreak and continuation of the conflict and its misdeeds, violence and atrocities; on the other hand, they concentrate on their own self-justification, self-righteousness, glorification, and victimization" (Bar-Tal 2003: 78; see also Cairns and Roe 2003). In such contexts, the fundamental lack of consensus on the shared but divisive past is often recognised as an obstacle to reconciliation. Yet, at the same time, efforts aimed at confronting and teaching the violent past and its various controversies are commonly feared as possibly destabilising for the fragile peace that tends to characterise post-conflict societies.

As will be outlined in the next sections, post-conflict societies have taken various routes in responding to the demands and challenges related to teaching younger generations about histories of violent intergroup conflict through textbooks. The variety of approaches and strategies adopted in this field includes shorter-term stopgap measures often promoting narrative silence, evasion or elision, notably through the establishment of moratoria and the banning or the emergency revision of existing textbooks. It also includes longer-term textbook development work, espousing different concepts and methods, including single-narrative or multinarrative and multiperspective approaches. As a result of these various strategies, in different contexts violent histories will be shown to have been alternatively sidestepped, repressed, sanitised, mystified or meaningfully dealt with in post-conflict school textbooks, possibly affecting intergroup reconciliation.

SHORT- AND MEDIUM-TERM TEXTBOOK REVISION: NARRATIVE SILENCE, EVASION AND ELISION

History Textbooks and Post-war Moratoria

Post-conflict societies face two immediate concerns when it comes to history textbooks: one is to review and revise existent materials to eliminate biased and conflict-ridden content; the other is to update their content drawing on recent historical research and to include discussions on the more recent past. This represents a difficult and time-consuming endeavour, especially so in cases where both curricula and textbooks may not have been revised for decades. Confronted with these tasks, numerous countries around the world have opted, at least temporarily, for an amnesiac or evasive approach to history education, particularly in relation to the most contested and painful recent past. As Alan McCully (2012) observes, after conflict, "Dealing with the recent past is especially problematic because the situation is still heavily disputed, raw, and characterized by personal trauma, anger, and grief" (p. 154).

Against this backdrop, a common strategy in the immediate aftermath of violent conflict has been the establishment of moratoria, namely "the temporary suspension of history education or its recent history segment, including its textbooks" (De Baets 2015: 6). This measure was officially implemented, for instance, in Afghanistan (Sarwari 2012), Bosnia and Herzegovina (Ahonen 2013), Cambodia (Dy 2008, 2013), Croatia (Koren and Baranović 2009), Guatemala (Bellino 2014), Lebanon (van Ommering 2015), Libya (Duncan 2011), Rwanda (Bentrovato 2015) and South Africa (Weldon 2010)—their time span varying from a few years to several decades. While countries such as Cambodia, Croatia, Rwanda and South Africa have gradually moved away from narrative silence and have variously dealt with their past in schools, recent conflict remains largely unaddressed in compulsory history education in all the other cases mentioned, despite ongoing efforts to revise curricula and textbooks. In yet other contexts, including numerous countries in sub-Saharan Africa such as Burundi and Sierra Leone, silence surrounding the violent past, while not officially sanctioned by a formal moratorium, has been virtually maintained in the classrooms due to the continuing lack of updated official history curricula and textbooks. Here, the turbulent post-colonial past is either omitted outright or, at best, is reduced to lists of names and dates as a way to avoid controversy (Bentrovato 2017).

The choice of a "rhetoric of silence" (Ondek and Laurence 1993) underlying official post-conflict textbook work has been determined by a number of considerations, most of which are underpinned by a belief, or a political pretext, relating to the benefit of the passage of time (see also De Baets 2015). At least four main arguments have been regularly raised by stakeholders around the world to legitimise this option. First, this approach has been rationalised as a necessity for national healing and reconciliation by supposedly allowing time for society to come to terms with the past. Evasive strategies towards history textbooks have been dictated by concerns that, in the immediate aftermath of violent conflict, when wounds are still fresh and memories and legacies of violence pervasive, confronting the painful past may be too sensitive and may provoke controversy and commotion that could hamper intergroup reconciliation. Such concerns underlying the choice to temporarily edit out historical conflict seem justified by research showing that revisiting traumatic events can be shattering for those who lived through the violence, be they survivors, perpetrators or bystanders (e.g. Hamber 2009), as well as their offspring (Danieli 1998). Consequently, a belief has been expressed in the desirability of allowing sufficient temporal distance in order for later generations, less constrained by a too recent perspective which may lock societies into Manichean discourses, to take on the task of addressing the violent past in a more objective and less emotional manner. A second argument, equally related to fears connected to the risk of jeopardising peace, concerns political constraints to the possibility of objectively and safely confronting the past when actors who were involved in the conflict still hold powerful positions. The weight of this particular consideration is largely contingent on the ways in which conflict ends, be it by unilateral military victory or negotiated agreement, and on the subsequent power constellations. A third argument for a temporarily evasive approach underscores the need to allow sufficient time for scientific and legal investigation and documentation to uncover "the truth" and to reach consensus about the past. This argument typically highlights the role of TJ mechanisms as well as historians in providing society with answers to open historical questions and controversies before new textbooks can be developed. A fourth reason concerns more pragmatic issues. In the short term, post-war countries commonly face so many different challenges, including insecurity, poverty and institutional weakness, that history textbook revision may not be considered as a priority or even a possibility. Within the education sector alone, post-conflict countries may face the challenge of having to rehabilitate a derelict system following the destruction of educational facilities and the loss or displacement of educational personnel and academics, a group often deliberately targeted during armed conflict (GCPEA 2014; UNESCO 2011; World Bank 2005). Undoubtedly, behind such arguments are often vested interests of political actors concerned with delaying all confrontation with the past in order to secure power and legitimacy.

While they may be dictated by more or less legitimate concerns, evasive approaches to post-conflict history textbook revision are not uncontroversial or unproblematic. For those who consider themselves as victims of historical wrongs, textbook silence on their past experience of suffering may be resented as renewed injustice and may thus provide political entrepreneurs with a chance to manipulate grievances for their vested interests, thus perpetuating conflict. This cautionary note echoes the warnings widely articulated in the peace-and-conflict literature against the dangers to peace posed by a politics of oblivion, facilitating collective amnesia, denial and impunity, and scholars' virtual consensus on the importance of recognition and redress of historical injustice for intergroup reconciliation (e.g. Bar-Tal and Bennink 2004; Minow 1998). In Bosnia, for instance, the moratorium that was placed by the government on teaching the recent war was vehemently protested by opponents of this policy "as 'an attack on the truth'" and "as a call for 'lies and silence'", hindering rather than promoting reconciliation (De Baets 2015: 12). Evasive strategies that leave the past unsettled, especially if for a longer period of time, need to be further applied with due caution as they may leave a vacuum providing fertile ground for entrenched polarisation. This vacuum may allow the unchallenged thriving of sectarian and partisan conflict narratives in society while forestalling opportunities for younger generations to critically examine and make sense of the past and its pervasive legacy. In the face of curricular and textbook silence, these narratives have indeed been found to be commonly embraced by young people, thus favouring societal rifts (Barton and McCully 2005; Van Ommering 2015). Against this backdrop, one may argue that evasive strategies are likely to be beneficial as long as they are pursued temporarily and the ensuing vacuum effectively serves the purpose of revising textbooks based on unobstructed academic research and unrestricted public debate. As warned by De Baets (2015), suspicion should be raised by prolonged evasive strategies, which might be "censorship-induced" and aimed at promoting "'repressed memory', 'selective amnesia' and 'historical taboo'" (p. 24), which are unlikely to be conducive to reconciliation.

"Emergency Textbooks" and the Removal of Objectionable Content

Besides the establishment of moratoria and the temporary suspension of history textbooks, another short-term form of post-conflict activities consists in the instant elision of biased and objectionable content from existing textbooks. This measure has been widely recommended by the international community as a minimum standard of textbook quality to be upheld after violent conflict. The Guidance Notes on Teaching and Learning developed by the Inter-Agency Network for Education in Emergencies (2010), for instance, highlight the "immediate need" to expunge "conflict-inciting materials and ideologically-loaded content" from textbooks (p. 2).

This measure was famously applied in the immediate post-WWII era by the Allied Powers, who, upon their victory, either banned or purged of militaristic and ultra-nationalist content textbooks that had been used in countries belonging to the Axis Powers, notably Germany, Italy and Japan (UNESCO 1949). Similar strategies have been adopted more recently in the wake of civil wars, in some cases showing a level of interventionism reminiscent of the post-WWII experience. Such interventionist models of emergency textbook revision, initiated and controlled by international actors, have been applied in Bosnia, Afghanistan and Iraq. In Bosnia, the moratorium on the teaching of the recent war, which had been negotiated through the Office of the High Representative as the body overseeing the implementation of the civilian aspects of the 1995 Dayton peace agreement, was accompanied by the screening and removal of "offensive or misleading" content from the largely ethno-nationalist textbooks that have characterised this country's segregated education system catering in parallel for Bosnian Serbs, Bosnian Croats and Bosniaks. This measure was leveraged by the Council of Europe, making it a requirement for the country's aspired membership in this body. Under the supervision of an international monitoring team, textbook passages that had been identified as being problematic by a commission equally representing the country's "constituent peoples" were either blacked out or annotated as being "currently under review". Such measures have not been without controversies, having provoked public outcry as well as arousing pupils' heightened curiosity towards the censored content (Pingel 2009; Torsti 2007).

In Afghanistan and Iraq, two countries that underwent US-led foreign military intervention, similar emergency strategies were driven and controlled by the US and the US Agency for International Development (USAID) as the sponsoring organisation. In Afghanistan, emergency textbook revisions, which were launched after the toppling of Taliban rule in 2001, were partly sponsored by the US Commander's Emergency Response Programme and were aimed at erasing propagandistic and militant textbook content, including Jihadist teachings, which USAID had previously supported in the context of the Cold War (Burde 2014). Similarly, the violent overthrow of Saddam Hussein in Iraq in 2003 was immediately followed by rapidly implemented textbook revisions that were conducted by UNESCO and UNICEF on behalf of the Coalition Provisional Authority (CPA). The emergency revisions entailed the "de-Baathification" of textbooks, namely the erasure of Baath party ideology, as well as the elimination of signs of sectarianism and xenophobia (Al-Tikriti 2010; Rohde 2013a). Pointing to the influence of foreign actors on textbook revision, guidelines developed for this purpose in Iraq stipulated, among other things, the removal from textbooks of "any religious references in order to comply with the American constitution" as well as the erasure of "statements which promoted fighting, for example, against the USA or against Israel" (cited in Al-Tikriti 2010: 356).

International experiences in such contexts have illuminated a critical "tension between *intervention and empowerment*" (Lässig 2013: 10), with analyses indicating common failures to substantially engage local stakeholders and to ensure their ownership of processes and outcomes. This reported failure calls for caution if one considers that lack of ownership and empowerment is widely held to critically undermine the effectiveness and sustainability of any initiative, especially so if its aim is to positively affect local dynamics of peace and reconciliation (e.g. Lee and Özerdem 2015). This failure clearly emerges from a draft report on internationally driven textbook revision activities in Iraq issued by UNESCO—presently the leading international agency in this field in the country. The document points to tensions and serious "communication gap[s]" having emerged both between UNESCO and USAID officials, and, more crucially, between international actors and local partners. According to the report, the textbook revision guidelines "were not discussed properly among Iraqi and other education specialists", further remarking that "one should make sure that Iraqi educators are comfortable with the revision parameters" (cited in Al-Tikriti 2010: 356).

*Longer-Term Models of Post-conflict Textbook Work:
Single- and Multinarrative Approaches*

In transitional societies, longer-term and more substantial post-conflict history textbook work is often principally left to a later date, at times coinciding with the end of the transition and the expected coming of a democratically elected government.[1] In the post-transition phase, calls have been made to undertake a democratic process of post-conflict history textbook writing, which may include the development of materials jointly authored by representatives from across historical conflict lines. Such activities can count on a longstanding international tradition of conciliatory textbook work, originally undertaken between former enemies across state borders (Pingel 2008, 2010) and now increasingly "diffused" to also cater for the needs of societies emerging from intrastate conflict. Jointly developed resources that have been the result of long-term post-conflict textbook work are wide-ranging. They comprise recommendations or guidelines for textbook authors and editors; supplementary alternative materials or teaching units on specific historical topics in the form of teacher guides, source books or pupil's workbooks; and common textbooks aligned to curricular content. These collaborative projects, examples of which can be found across the globe, have been either government-sponsored or privately sponsored, or again they have been the fruit of state/non-state partnerships (Korostelina and Lässig 2013).

Many of the joint textbook development activities undertaken to date have resorted to relational approaches to history, their aim being to transcend narrow (ethno)national(ist) perspectives which tend to perpetuate conflict. Among the relational approaches adopted in these projects are comparative history, history of cultural transfers, transnational history, and *histoire croisée* or entangled history (Paulmann 1998; Werner and Zimmermann 2004)—all of which may or may not include explicit discussions on recent histories of violence. Paradigmatic examples of joint conciliatory textbook work include the experiences of the Franco-German and the German-Polish Textbook Commissions, two quasi-official bodies whose work culminated in the drafting of joint recommendations and the production of politically endorsed curricular resources based on a reciprocal critical review of textbooks in the respective countries (Defrance and Pfeil 2013; Lässig and Strobel 2013). Their notable work continues to inspire other societies around the world, most notably in East Asia, a region where history "textbook wars" have regularly made headlines, straining diplomatic relations (Mueller-Sainy 2011; Yang and Sin 2013). Whereas the conflict-ridden past and its related historical controversies have been intently addressed both in the Franco-German and the German-Polish cases, in other instances, such as in the Balkans, several non-governmental textbook projects have opted for a more evasive approach. While addressing intergroup relations from a historical perspective, they have focused, for instance, on a less contentious distant past or on selected themes in social and cultural history as strategies to promote rapprochement through the exploration of commonalities and instances of peaceful coexistence and cooperation (e.g. EUROCLIO 2008).

These projects today also differ as to whether they openly show and discuss, or rather "hide", controversy when addressing and narrating the contentious past. On this basis, two main alternative narrative approaches have been adopted in collaborative textbook projects: a traditional single-narrative approach, presenting a mutually accepted "consensual", "bridging" or "compromise narrative" that synthetises common understandings of a shared or connected history; and a pluralistic multinarrative and multiperspective approach, which refrains from supplying an authoritative narrative, instead presenting contrasting narratives for critical enquiry. As outlined below, these different approaches to textbook revision and development reflect divergent perceptions of the nature, function and value of history education in society and, more specifically, of the ways history textbooks can foster peace.

The Elusive Value of the Single-Narrative Approach: Consensus or Hegemonic History?

The single-narrative approach to history textbook work entails collaboratively constructing, through negotiation and compromise, a mutually agreed-upon narrative, which harmonises the perspectives of conflicting parties. Originally prevalent in international textbook projects, this consensus-based model has entailed joint efforts to negotiate a common narrative, whereby special care is given to both eliminating enemy images, bias and stereotypes, and emphasising historical elements possibly conducive to reconciliation, such as positive interactions in history (Pingel 2008). In countries emerging from civil strife and marked by profound societal and historical rifts, the conventional single-narrative approach has often been favoured as a strategy to foster unity and social cohesion in response to an acutely felt need to mend the torn social fabric. This concern is demonstrated in recent research indicating the prominence of traditional, national(istic) single narratives in textbooks developed in post-conflict countries (Lerch 2016) despite global trends towards denationalisation (Hansen 2012). In such contexts, governments typically see the added value of teaching the nation a "usable" (Wertsch 2002: 70) and "monumental" national past (Nietzsche 1997: 69) through textbooks disseminating an authoritative and uniform "closed national 'historical' narrative" (Nakou and Barca 2010: 8). This approach not only contravenes current historiographical and didactic trends; it also appears problematic, as a conciliatory strategy, if one considers that the public dominance of particular narratives in society has frequently been the object of grievances that have adversely factored into the conflict itself.

In divided societies emerging from violent conflict, the appeal to "consensus history", consisting in blending different views in a single narrative, risks degenerating into "hegemonic history" as a result of political hijacking. A new state-sanctioned and uncontested master-narrative or "official truth" may emerge, which is top-down, normative, expediently narrow and selective, homogenising and excluding or dismissive of alternative memories and narratives, and at odds with the historical record. In this narrative, difference and diversity are often glossed over or depicted as a menace to a precious unity to be safeguarded. While presented as embodying a nation's shared historical memory, single narratives are likely to reproduce existing power relations by endorsing the beliefs, values, norms and identity of dominant groups, thus possibly feeding new or renewed inequalities and societal rifts. In this sense, as Friedrich Nietzsche (1997) once warned us, "Sufficient danger remains should (specific narratives) grow too mighty and overpower the other modes regarding the past" (p. 75).

The experience in reforming history education in Rwanda represents a telling example of the pitfalls of the single-narrative approach to history textbook revision in contested post-conflict societies. In the early 1990s, the country experienced civil war and state-orchestrated genocide during which hundreds of thousands, primarily of the Tutsi minority, were killed by their Hutu neighbours. The violence ended with the military victory and political takeover by a Tutsi-dominated rebel movement. As part of a broader agenda of "national unity and reconciliation" and related memory politics, during the emergency moratorium phase launched in 1995, the post-genocide government worked towards revising purportedly divisive history curricula and textbooks. Recent research shows that, through revised history textbooks, the government has been enforcing a new, hegemonic narrative of past events, endorsing a narrow understanding of "legitimate knowledge" (Anyon 1978). This narrative promotes the concept of "Rwandanness", emphasising the nation's alleged primordial unity and dismissing ethnic identities as a historically unfounded colonial invention that was supposedly the primary cause of genocide in Rwanda. This official truth has been widely criticised by observers for forcibly repressing salient identities as well as related discussions on ongoing divisions in the present, while both underscoring Tutsi historical victimisation and silencing "Hutu memories" of suffering. This particular approach to history textbook revision, and to history politics in general, appears to rest on a quest for political legitimation and social control, effectively ensured in Rwanda through laws against "divisionism" and "genocide ideology", which have apparently coerced many into self-censorship while alienating a large part of the population (Bentrovato 2015; King 2014). Against this backdrop, developing and implementing alternative materials has proven largely unsuccessful. The constraints posed by strictly state-controlled contexts are illustrated by the experience of the US-based NGO Facing History and Ourselves in helping develop a collaborative history resource book for Rwandan secondary schools based on participatory methods. Eventually, the initiative was severely undermined by the withdrawal of local stakeholders' committed participation in the project due to widespread concerns connected to a political leadership that had grown increasingly intolerant of historical accounts diverging from the state-sanctioned "truth" (Freedman et al. 2008).

Post-Saddam Iraq is another case in point, which highlights the shortcomings of single-narrative textbooks that espouse a dominant or hegemonic rhetoric of illusive national unity when communal divisions and grievances remain unaddressed under increasingly authoritarian regimes. Textbooks produced in Iraq after the emergency phase and under the current Shi'i-dominant government have been disseminating a similarly homogenising nationalist single narrative, which clashes with realities on the ground. Through outright evasions that exceed the expediently selective approach adopted in Rwanda to study the country's history of violence, revised Iraqi textbooks elude references to sectarian fault lines by neglecting Shi'i and Sunni history altogether in order to preserve "the image of a unified Arab nation" (Rohde 2013a: 724). They further omit such divisive issues as the 2003 US-led military overthrow of the Sunni-dominated regime of Saddam Hussein and its aftermath, and the Kurdish question. This generally "unifying" narrative notwithstanding, observers have indicated the risks related to a creeping Shi'i bias in textbooks which could possibly estrange and disaffect non-Shi'i groups (*Ibid.*: 725).

The Promises of a Multinarrative and Multiperspective Approach: Narrative Plurality and Diversity

Reflecting new trends in historiography and history didactics, the main alternative to the single-narrative approach to post-conflict textbook revision is the enquiry-based multinarrative and multiperspective approach, a model widely advocated since the 1990s as the "most effective way for history teaching to contribute to postconflict understanding" (McCully 2012: 146). Contrary to teaching a definite narrative, this approach, being grounded in the discipline of history, is centred on an interpretive and evidence-based process of historical enquiry, which regards all narratives as "provisional and open to question" (McCully 2012: 148; see also Seixas 2000; Stradling 2003). One common format for this particular model consists in source-based material presenting multiple narratives and perspectives for evaluation. An example of this approach is the "Joint History Project" supplementary teaching material for Southeast Europe (CDRSEE 2005). The material consists of four source-based workbooks that were jointly produced by a regional team of authors on the history of the Balkans. While the material excludes discussions on the particularly sensitive recent history, it occasionally addresses controversial topics by juxtaposing divergent historical interpretations in line with a multiperspective methodology (see also Fajfer 2013; Milosheva and Krushe 2010).

A different and uniquely creative example of the multinarrative and multiperspective approach is the "dual-narrative" methodology. This model finds its most renowned application in the non-governmental Israeli–Palestinian joint history textbook project "Learning Each Other's Historical Narrative". Launched in the midst of conflict, this binational resource, which, however, has not been officially approved for classroom use, juxtaposes two competing nationalist narratives of the conflict-ridden history of Israeli–Palestinian bilateral relations. These opposing narratives consist of accounts which authors from both sides mutually recognised as legitimate and which were cleansed of excessively offensive or emotive language upon the authors' dialogue and exchanges that marked the development stage of the material. The joint resource presents these narratives side by side on two columns of each page, separating them through a blank space designed to encourage pupils to develop their own understanding of the contested past. The intention underlying the project was for students to "become equipped to acknowledge, understand, and respect (without having to accept) the narrative of the other" (Adwan et al. 2012: x). This was seen as an "essential intermediate phase" in a context where "there is not enough common ground for Israelis and Palestinians to create a single historical narrative" (Bar-On and Adwan 2006: 310; see also Rohde 2012, 2013b). A similar multinarrative history textbook project was launched in India and Pakistan in 2013. Drawing on regular school history textbooks used in the two countries, this material puts their "different (often opposite) historical narratives side by side", covering key events in the tense history of Hindu–Muslim relations in this region (Daftuar 2013).

Arguably, by exposing pupils to narrative plurality and diversity regarding the past, this approach is deemed to be more democratic and to create opportunities for dialogue and rapprochement by encouraging pupils to question, critique and revisit exclusive and apparently irreconcilable group narratives and preconceived truths. The actual effects and impact of the internationally acclaimed multinarrative and multiperspective methodology on intergroup relations, however, remain empirically understudied, thus precluding definite conclusions as to its value and limitations. The implementation of this methodology faces a number of concerns, which relate to the complexities and challenges of teaching contested and conflictual narratives being laid bare in ethnographic studies in schools in several divided societies (e.g. Bekerman and Zembylas 2012). For example, while being presumably better suited for contested societies, the multinarrative and multiperspective approach has raised the concern that the permanent questioning it encourages may produce undesired uncertainty in fragile contexts and may thus be potentially more destabilising than supplying the nation with a definite and positive or progressive linear narrative of the shared past. It also raises the concern that, unless both teachers and pupils are effectively equipped with the tools and dispositions of the historical profession, this approach, by exposing differences and controversies, may further entrench polarisation rather than help communities transcend sectarian group narratives and encourage rapprochement. In relation to the Israeli–Palestinian project, in particular, critics have raised questions about the conciliatory value of a dual-narrative approach, which both confirms and "cements the bipolar structure of the conflict itself" by failing to take into account the diversity inherent within each society and related narratives (Rohde 2013a: 189).

Beyond Content: The Transformative "Performative Dimension" of Post-conflict Textbook Work

Research in post-conflict textbook writing, particularly regarding joint projects, suggests that, while such initiatives have been inevitably daunting and, in fact, often unsuccessful in effectively translating their outcomes into classroom practice, the processes involved have proved valuable in themselves. One of the most crucial, though less tangible, achievements identified in various case-studies from around the world is the attitudinal change induced by collaborative initiatives bringing together representatives from opposing conflict sides to produce textbooks or related guidelines (see case-studies in Korostelina and Lässig 2013). These observations serve as a fundamental starting point for reconsidering the conciliatory potential of post-conflict textbook revision from a processual perspective that may help further conceptualise the nexus between history textbooks and intergroup reconciliation. Upon this premise, this section moves beyond a discussion of history textbook designs and strategies that are the outcome of related activities in order to also include a reflection on the often overlooked yet significant "performative dimension" (Lässig 2013: 8) of post-conflict textbook work. Drawing on discourses on conflict and peacebuilding, this section argues the utility of a narrative-based approach to conflict transformation for a better understanding and assessment of the value of textbook projects. It uses this approach as a framework to conceptualise what can be termed a "transformative model of post-conflict textbook work". The contention underlying this model is that the conciliatory potential of textbook activities lies partly in the capacity of the processes of collaborative textbook development to encourage a process of "narrative transformation" of the competing accounts that typically accompany conflict—a process whose transformative dynamics and effects may further trickle down during the implementation phase in the classroom.

Theoretically grounded in social constructionism (Berger and Luckmann 1966), the framework from which the proposed model borrows places the reframing of conflict narratives and related "mythico-histories" (Malkki 1995) at the centre of conflict transformation processes geared towards instigating changes in intergroup perceptions and attitudes that are considered key to reconciliation (Austin et al. 2011; Kelman 2004; Kriesberg 2007; Lederach 1997). It regards narrative re-examination and reconfiguration as a critical step towards "un-sticking" conflict-relationships between opposing "mnemonic communities" that are often trapped within competing victimisation-based "schematic narrative templates" (Wertsch 1998: 60) through which they make sense of "reality". As Sara Cobb (2003) suggests, "Unless these stories are transformed or evolved, they retain their coherence, collecting 'data' that confirm the myths as events unfold". She further argues that "If there is to be an end to the cycle of violence, if there is to be an opening for building new relationships, [...] these myths must lose their totalitarian grip; they must be opened to new information, new plots, new character roles, and new themes" (p. 295; see also Cobb 2013; Mack 1990).

This section argues that textbook revision and development processes are well positioned to undermine the coherence of competing conflict narratives warned against by Cobb. Specifically, textbook work appears to hold great potential for creating a "dialogical space" (Hermann 2004) in which to engage participants from former conflict sides in reassessing and redefining their narratives, and their underlying antagonistic perceptions and belief systems. This can be achieved through textbook work that involves and that facilitates sustained cooperative interaction and critical and "constructive confrontation with the painful past" (Nadler and Shnabel 2008: 44)—two processes otherwise respectively described in the conflict transformation literature as "instrumental" and "socioemotional" forms of "social learning" conducive to intergroup reconciliation (Aiken 2013; Nadler et al. 2008; Nadler and Shnabel 2008). By engaging former enemies in such processes of "social learning", textbook work may act as a catalyst for "narrative transformation" directed towards increased "narrative complexity" (Cobb 2003). It can, in other words, contribute towards broadening the narrow and uniform stock of stories that often define intergroup relations and towards crafting more complex and nuanced narratives on the basis of dialogical interaction and critical enquiry. The processes involved in this transformative model of textbook work may ultimately allow a transition from competing narratives that one-sidedly emphasise incompatible historical claims towards more inclusive and pluralistic narratives, which are at once shared and heteroglossic and which accept, expose and discuss multiple understandings of the divisive past on scientific bases while also being appreciative of the often overlooked positive interactions and transfers that marked histories of intergroup relations.

Based on worldwide experiences in post-conflict societies, a number of key procedural principles and prerequisites can be highlighted as being fundamental for this transformative process to occur within the proposed model of textbook work. The first regards the importance of adopting an inclusive, symmetrical, and democratic collaborative approach to textbook revision and development, which ensures a sense of empowerment and ownership for the various parties and sides involved. A review of case-studies on textbook projects indicates the importance of respecting a concern for inclusiveness and equality both in the configuration of participant groups and in the perspectives and stories discussed and eventually presented in the newly designed textbooks. This approach may both initiate and signal a crucial shift from a common practice whereby "legitimate knowledge" is determined by dominant groups towards more democratic practices, whereby history is co-authored by representatives of different groups, resulting in diverse voices in society being equally represented and heard in the textbooks. Failing to do so risks undermining the legitimacy and public perception of the impartiality of these projects and, more broadly, it risks perpetuating marginalisation and ultimately conflict. Past experience with unofficial textbook consultations in Northeast Asia, for instance, warns against the pitfalls of textbook activities that are based on asymmetrical communication. The one-sidedness that characterised these pioneering activities in the region, and which was manifest in their exclusive critique towards Japan as the only historical wrongdoer, undermined the initiative. It caused it to be perceived "as an appendage to the political debate" geared towards apology "rather than a driving force that could lend a new direction to the public discourse" (Pingel 2008: 196). This served as a clear lesson for later joint projects in Northeast Asia, which were markedly more considerate of the impediments to rapprochement posed by asymmetrical dialogue in textbook work (Han et al. 2012).

The proposed transformative model of post-conflict textbook work further presupposes a shift from a common practice of hiding conflict, controversies and diversity—be it behind utter silence or behind politically correct consensus—to acknowledging and openly confronting differences. Critical foundations for a meaningful and constructive dialogue on the shared but divisive past include the participants' basic acknowledgement of the both inevitable and legitimate existence of multiple and divergent perspectives and narratives on history. This acknowledgement entails the acceptance of the importance attached by each group to its ability to tell particular stories in which its identity is grounded. The model also necessitates the participants' willingness to respectfully engage with "conflicting views that fall within the range of reasonable disagreement", and this "without either endorsing them as clearly correct or rejecting them as clearly incorrect" (Gutmann and Thompson 2000: 22, 41).

The process of respectfully engaging with each other's narratives, including each other's painful experiences and sensitivities, further presupposes the participants' questioning of assumptions and preconceptions that may inhibit rational and constructive intergroup dialogue on the shared history. Inhibitors include assumptions of negative intentionality of "the other" (Cobb 1994) and assumptions of moral superiority and legitimate entitlement of the ingroup. The former are associated with practices of demonisation and dehumanisation of the perceived enemy typically accompanying violent conflict. Martha Nussbaum (1992) critically observes that, in conflict situations, "awareness of the enemy's similar humanity is easily lost from view" (p. 282), keeping groups trapped into dichotomous victim/perpetrator discourses that perpetuate cycles of violence and prevent rapprochement. The latter imply engaging in critical self-reflexivity, involving both awareness of ingroup suffering and an honest appraisal of the nature of ingroup actions and their supposed morality. This critical inward- and outward-looking process should be part of larger deconstructionist endeavours consisting in confronting and debunking respective myths, which, by their very nature, tend to hinder "narrative transformation" as mechanisms that "see[k] to establish the sole way of ordering the world and defining world-views" (Schöpflin 1997: 19).

These transformative processes are undoubtedly challenging to bring about, and can only be the result of long-term efforts. They may necessitate extensive and ongoing groundwork towards building mutual recognition and mutual trust, especially in the initial phase of the project, when opposing sides may hold rigid defensive and offensive positions. One should indeed foresee and intently address the challenges posed to these processes by the legacy of conflict and by related psychological barriers, with memories of violence and associated emotions often crippling intergroup receptive and empathic abilities that are fundamental to these projects. In the light of the inherent complexity and sensitivity of these endeavours, it may be beneficial, as has often been the case, for the dialogic processes that are at the core of such undertakings to be facilitated by a neutral third party in order to ensure "controlled communication" (Ellis 2006: 143) as part of an effort at "narrative mediation" (Winslade and Monk 2000). It may be equally beneficial for these processes to be grounded in exchanges of personal experiences and thus to aim at fostering basic personal relationships before moving to professional discussions.

Being geared towards mutual recognition of the experiences and painful legacy of each conflict side, the proposed approach to post-conflict textbook work ultimately holds significant potential towards contributing to an enhanced sense of justice that is widely considered key to reconciliation (Gibson 2004; Kriesberg 2004; Lederach 1997; Minow 1998). Particularly, it may contribute to victims' restored sense of dignity, which may have been undermined by denial or silence of experienced harm. Arguably, however, the most immediate value of this transformative model of post-conflict textbook work lies in its potential to build and empower a cooperative community of practice by acting as a forum for constructive intergroup engagement and collaboration directed towards a shared goal and vision. Experiences across the world, for instance in the Balkans, the Middle East and Northeast Asia, have illustrated the power of dialogical and cooperative textbook activities in prompting the participants' transformative shift from acting as representatives of a particular group to recasting themselves as "experts who acted independently from a political agenda" (Pingel 2008: 193). Joint ventures of this kind can act as evidence of the possibility of rapprochement and cooperation and can thus build trust in a shared peaceful and democratic future where differences can be accepted and embraced rather than suppressed and silenced. Ideally, these same processes and experiences, if echoed in the classroom, can lend such projects a multiplier or ripple effect. In the long term, they may impact younger generations' knowledge and attitudes and may, through young people, stimulate transformation within families and communities, eventually laying the foundation for a new social contract that is grounded on respect for pluralism, democracy and human rights.

Actors and Interactions in Post-conflict Textbook Work

In keeping with a processual perspective on post-conflict textbook work, an important factor to be considered when analysing and assessing these activities relates to the interplay between grassroots, national and international actors, and to the nature and level of interaction and intersection between top-down and bottom-up processes and initiatives. Post-conflict textbook work ought to be understood as a multi-actor and multilevel process, involving a variety of stakeholders, including state actors and agencies, international organisations, NGOs and academic institutions. It is equally understood as an interdisciplinary field which, as declared by UNESCO (1949), "must involve the closest cooperation of scholars, educators, and psychologists, who understand the implications of materials presented to pupils" (p. 60). As Stuart Foster (2011) observes, it is also "a transnational field, resulting from co-operation, competition and transfers" (p. 33).

When it comes to textbook activities, governments and their agencies, notably national ministries of education, are undoubtedly key actors, whose political endorsement has proven essential for these initiatives' legitimacy and practical implementation. Research on official textbook commissions in post-WWII Europe has indicated that their viability and perceived success largely stemmed from their institutional backing by the respective governments. Conversely, abundant research points to lack of political support and commitment as a recurring disabling factor. Numerous cases have been reported of innovative materials having been banned, boycotted or withdrawn by governments upon damning reaction by powerful spoiler-groups, who time and again have slandered and even threatened their authors for supposedly betraying the ingroup. This has been the unfortunate fate of many initiatives by civil society groups, which, in post-conflict contexts, have often taken the lead in conciliatory textbook work, but whose power has been regularly undermined by highly centralised education systems. With many (post-conflict) countries being characterised by strictly state-controlled textbook screening and authorisation processes, any failure to secure official approval almost inevitably implies the books' absence from the classrooms. That being said, state involvement is also potentially problematic as it may translate into political compromise and lead to these activities being less likely to critically address highly controversial issues.

With these projects having to rely on substantial funding, worldwide experience has shown international actors as being highly instrumental in supporting both official and unofficial textbook work in post-conflict societies. Some of them, notably the Council of Europe and UNESCO, have a proven record of active and influential involvement in this field. Historically, these organisations have been the drivers of conciliatory textbook work, sponsoring history textbook dialogue and cooperation, and the production of recommendations and guidelines for textbook authors (e.g. CoE 2001, 2009; Minkina-Milko 2012; Pingel 2010; Stobart 1999). Throughout the decades, an expanding network of international actors have provided funding and expertise and have played a consultative, coordinating, supervising and/or mediating role—visibly resulting in the diffusion of certain dominant concepts and models, such as multiculturalism and multiperspectivity. They have been involved in the design, development, production and distribution of new teaching materials as well as in local stakeholders' professional training in related activities. Their level of influence in setting agenda, goals and outcomes has thereby varied and has been the greatest in contexts characterised by institutional weakness and aid dependency. As hinted at earlier in relation to highly interventionist emergency textbook activities, ensuring local ownership of related processes and outcomes remains a challenge in which failure has risked undermining the legitimacy and credibility of these projects, feeding popular perceptions of outside imposition of foreign models.

Contextual Constraints and Possibilities of Conciliatory Textbook Work

Evidently, post-conflict textbook work is a hard task which, more often than not, has faced formidable challenges and constraints, especially of a political nature. As worldwide experiences indicate, at all levels from conception to implementation, perseverance and risk-taking have marked these initiatives. The inclusive, balanced and complex narratives and texts that are the ideal product of conciliatory textbook work typically represent counter-discourses and are therefore commonly resisted. Time and again, they have been the object of fierce public debates, political dispute and protest, which have regularly proven fatal to these projects.

As a general rule, the most successful initiatives, notably those officially approved, could only be realised after years, if not decades, of dialogue, debate and negotiation. For instance, it took the German-Polish textbook commission over a decade to negotiate and gain formal acceptance of its bilateral recommendations. Similarly, the joint guidelines for textbook authors that were developed by an expert commission in Bosnia in line with a multinarrative and multiperspective model underwent protracted negotiations before being officially endorsed (Pingel 2008: 193, this volume). Several other conciliatory initiatives have been short-lived or never reached fruition, often as a result of vehement criticism from powerful conservative groups. In Croatia, for example, a temporary textbook supplement produced in 2005, which acknowledged Croat crimes perpetrated against Serbs during the conflict in the early 1990s, was swiftly withdrawn following public protests on account of its supposedly "'sacrificing' the sufferings of Croats in the war for the sake of reconciliation" (De Baets 2015: 11). The initiative, however, prepared the groundwork for later textbook work, which resulted in new textbooks adopting a comparatively balanced approach to the conflict-ridden past (Koren and Baranovic 2009). In some contexts, compromise, possibly induced by a desire to accommodate political and/or societal sensitivities, led to evasion and/or political correctness coming at the expense of historical accuracy in new textbooks dealing with the divisive past. In

Cambodia, for example, the first state-approved history textbook covering Khmer Rouge history, which was produced by a local NGO (Dy 2007) and was recently endorsed by the ministry of education to teach younger generations about the genocide that marked Cambodia in the 1970s, circumvents several sensitive questions of responsibility in a context where a number of former members of the Khmer Rouge presently occupy prominent positions in government (De Baets 2015: 14). In Guatemala, accuracy is similarly compromised in new social studies textbooks in a context where silence on the recent violent past is, however, maintained in official curricula. Adopting a predominant human rights perspective, current textbooks present a superficial narrative of the conflict which evades discussions on historical agency as they point the finger at the abstract concept of "culture of violence" as the cause of the country's decades-long civil war (Bellino 2014; Oglesby 2007).

Conciliatory textbook work that did succeed in coming to fruition has frequently faced further serious challenges related to the implementation of its products and their translation into classroom practice. This is again particularly true for unofficial supplementary material, whose use, being left to teachers' discretion, has proven to be limited across the board. Described by Simone Lässig (2013) as "probably the most important translators (or obstructers) of reform ideas" (p. 14), teachers, upon whom the multiplier effect of conciliatory textbook work in the classroom largely depends, have been found to resist and subvert innovative textbook content. Especially in "hot spots", as found in, for instance, Northern Ireland (Kitson 2007) and Israel (Gordon 2005), educators have often pre-emptively avoided or abandoned material addressing sensitive and controversial historical issues related to intergroup conflict. They have done so out of fear of opening fresh wounds in the classroom, of receiving angry reactions by pupils or their parents and, ultimately, for safety reasons (Bentrovato 2016). A shift away from adverse or safe pedagogical practices necessarily requires specific teacher training. It requires training encompassing not only attention to new content knowledge and teaching methods, but also to offering opportunities for history educators to deal with their own painful experiences and memories of conflict, to question their own preconceptions and bias, and to learn how to responsibly and constructively deal with conflict and discomfort that may arise in the classroom upon discussing controversial perspectives prompted by textbook use. From a more practical perspective, the meaningful use of multiperspective materials by teachers may be constrained by curriculum content overload and knowledge-based examination, and by limited access to these materials in typically resource-poor post-conflict settings.

Naturally, possibilities and constraints of post-conflict history textbook work are determined by the specific context and circumstances, which inevitably influence the processes, outcome and impact of such initiatives. A variety of enabling or disabling contextual conditions may affect textbook work and its conciliatory potential. These include, *inter alia*: the nature of the conflict, including its more or less extensive scope and length and related levels of collective trauma, as well as its temporal proximity; its stage and outcome, namely whether the conflict has been settled, notably through one-sided military victory or through negotiated agreement resulting from military stalemate and combat fatigue, or, again, whether the conflict is still openly or latently ongoing; the TJ path chosen to deal with the past, be it one focused on amnesia, truth-telling and/or criminal accountability; the larger political system, including the level of symmetry in power relations between (former) parties to the conflict; and the degree of foreign involvement in the conflict settlement and its aftermath as well as the strength of civil society. Whereas the distinct effects of different scenarios yet remain to be systematically investigated, what is evident is the defining role of the general political climate in which these projects are embedded, the latter having proven to be closely tied to political contingencies.

Worldwide experience in history textbook revision points to a number of contextual conditions in which these activities are more likely to have a conciliatory and transformative effect on intergroup relations. Existing case-studies suggest the favourability of a political environment marked by relative stability and by a broader policy of rapprochement. A good example of such a case is the German-Polish textbook project, which was enabled by the specific historical-political context of detente inaugurated by Willy Brandt's German *Ostpolitik* (Lässig and Strobel 2013). Conversely, ongoing (or renewed) violence and injustice and the absence of a larger conciliatory context may cause similar endeavours to become hostage to political caprice and may additionally lessen the population's receptiveness to the initiatives. The PRIME project in Israel/Palestine illustrates well the high probability of unresolved tensions and renewed violence causing collaborative textbook projects to reach a deadlock and to be viewed with suspicion and be rejected both by politicians and by teachers, pupils and society at large across the divide (Eid 2010; Rohde

2013a). The case of post-genocide Rwanda further demonstrates that peace and stability are not sufficient elements for a favourable context for conciliatory textbook work. A democratic political environment, where textbook work can rely on open and unrestricted public and scholarly debate, is equally crucial for new educational materials not to convey a highly problematic "hegemonic history". Furthermore, experiences around the world, for instance in the self-proclaimed Turkish Republic of Northern Cyprus, point to the constraints exercised on conciliatory textbook work by the political contingency of regime change, notably the coming to power of conservative parties. In the case of Northern Cyprus, political change marked a return to ethno-nationalist history textbooks after a short-lived introduction of more conciliatory materials that had been promoting a sense of common identity (Evripidou 2010). Another significant factor affecting these initiatives relates to the nature of broader educational policies and structures in which they are embedded, specifically the extent to which these policies are conducive to intergroup integration or segregation. In Bosnia, Cyprus, Israel/Palestine and Lebanon, for instance, where formal history curriculum and textbook revision has been (tentatively) undertaken in the wake of peace processes, such educational policies and structures appear to have severely undermined efforts to harmonise history teaching and reconcile conflicting narratives through textbooks. Here, sectarianism continues to be pervasive within the context of highly segregated education systems, pointing to the obstinacy of competing group narratives in such contexts (Nasser and Nasser 2008; Torsti 2009; Van Ommering 2015; Zembylas 2013).

If it is true that the existence of supportive institutional structures, and particularly of institutional rapprochement, is likely to provide a favourable context for conciliatory textbook revision, formal TJ processes may lend unique opportunities for this purpose. As highlighted by emerging research advocating for crafting stronger connections between the fields of education and TJ (Cole 2007; Ramírez-Barat and Duthie 2015), there is considerable value in seeing post-conflict textbook revision anchored in a TJ framework, particularly so within the context of the work of official truth (and reconciliation) commissions (TRCs). As part of their mandate, truth commissions are expected to produce a public record of historical injustice and abuse, including their causes, scope, dynamics and consequences, through investigation that typically relies on statement-taking from victims, perpetrators and witnesses (Hayner 2002).

Their prominent work in dealing with the recent violent past is still limitedly exploited as an opportunity to support history education reform and textbook revision. Their work may provide an institutional framework for the re-examination of textbooks as part of an investigation into the role of the education sector in contributing to conflict while also dispensing source material for new textbooks deriving from their broader investigative work on the conflict as outlined in their final reports. This, however, should be considered with the understanding that the record produced by such entities is neither complete nor definitive, but rather is a selective representation of the violent past (Hayner 2002; Imbleau 2004). Hitherto, only timid and largely unsuccessful attempts have been made to integrate TRC findings into mainly supplementary educational materials, most notably in Guatemala, Peru and Sierra Leone. In Guatemala and Peru, these attempts were called to a halt by the government (Paulson 2010, 2015), while in Sierra Leone, TRC-related school materials appear to have fallen into oblivion mainly as a result of lack of government follow-up towards including these resources into what largely remains an outdated and evasive official curriculum (Bentrovato 2017).

Conclusion

This chapter is based on the premise that history textbooks are significant means that can either support or hinder reconciliation in the context of intergroup conflict. On that basis, it analysed history textbook revision and development as one component of broader peacebuilding and reconciliation efforts in societies emerging from violent conflict. The chapter surveyed some of the key approaches to post-conflict textbook work and their related narrative strategies as they have been employed in countries across the globe. In reviewing current practices and emerging trends in this field, it pointed to a number of pitfalls and opportunities having marked these endeavours. In relation to the narrative strategies adopted in textbook activities in both the shorter and longer term, this chapter questioned the rationale and the possible implications of different responses to the common challenge of dealing with societal conflict, diversity and controversy in history textbooks. In particular, it questioned the value of post-conflict models of textbook work that espouse either narrative evasion or elision, or single-narrative approaches. Its review of worldwide experiences suggests that these strategies, while ostensibly conciliatory in divided societies, are unlikely to be conducive to improved intergroup relations as they both preclude a chance for younger generations to make sense of a complex and contentious violent past and to transcend competing group narratives that hinder historical understanding. They may in fact counter intergroup reconciliation efforts, reinforcing sectarian divisions by leaving young people at the mercy of narrow and partisan family and community narratives that may openly or covertly circulate in society. While it acknowledges existing concerns related to the possible destabilising effects of less evasive and more complex narratives, this chapter argues for the comparative value of alternative multinarrative and multiperspective textbook designs. It thereby agrees with other scholars' contentions regarding the particular value of teaching contested history "as a 'mosaic of intercommunicating stories and memories', which transcend communalist and nationalist boundaries while acknowledging their existence" (Rohde 2013a: 189–190, citing Naveh 2006). That being said, this chapter is cautious not to overestimate the overall significance of textbooks within educational settings. It acknowledges textbooks as being only one among the multiple resources directing an effective enquiry-based and multiperspective approach to history education. Concomitantly, it recognises the critical role of teachers, who, even in the most unfavourable circumstances, could turn a biased textbook into a great resource for a transformative lesson.[2]

Having taken stock of some of the popular approaches and designs characterising current practices in post-conflict history textbook work, this chapter highlighted the less tangible value potentially inherent in collaborative processes of textbook revision and development, arguing for the benefit for this intrinsic potential to be capitalised upon and to be explicitly considered in the conception, implementation and evaluation of such initiatives. On that premise, it proposed a transformative model of post-conflict history textbook work, presenting this as a potential catalyst for instrumental and socioemotional reconciliation entailing the participants' challenging and transforming antagonistic narratives and underlying belief systems through sustained dialogical and cooperative interaction and constructive confrontation with the past. Built around the concept of dialogical "narrative transformation", the suggested model of post-conflict textbook work is proposed as having the potential to foster intergroup reconciliation by creating opportunities towards promoting former enemies' (re)humanisation, reciprocal empathy and acknowledgement of respective past suffering and common ground, and their envisioning of a shared future. In recognition of the complexity and contingency of these undertakings, the chapter further draws attention to the actors and contextual factors and conditions that may either hinder or enable history textbook revision playing a conciliatory role in divided societies. This potential is thereby held to be especially dependent upon these activities taking place within a favourable political and social environment and upon their being anchored in a broader institutional framework of rapprochement as an integral part of holistic efforts aimed at addressing the violent past and its legacies.

While this chapter seeks to make a contribution to further mapping and conceptualising the field of post-conflict history textbook revision and development, it also calls for a continued need for in-depth analysis and sophisticated frameworks of evaluation to examine and capitalise upon the conciliatory and transformative potential of such projects. Particularly, more empirical research is needed to assess the processes and dynamics involved, the societal reception of the material by its targeted audiences, and the effects and impact of textbook activities on intergroup relations in their different forms and in different contexts. These undoubtedly are fundamental, yet complex, emerging questions, the answers to which will help us chart the way forward.

Notes

1. Notable exceptions to this particular trend are cases in post-revolutionary contexts, where far-reaching textbook changes may have been introduced in the immediate aftermath of political overhaul, provided sufficient resources are available to do so. The author is thankful for Falk Pingel's observation that in the cases of post-war Germany and Japan, for instance, the most innovative textbooks and curricula were produced immediately after WWII under American occupation, whereas more conservative textbooks appeared after the occupation.
2. The author is grateful to Alan McCully for stressing this important point.

References

Adwan, S., Bar-On, D., & Naveh, E. (Eds.). (2012). *Side by side: Parallel histories of Israel-Palestine*. New York: New Press.

Ahonen, S. (2013). Postconflict history education in Finland, South Africa and Bosnia-Herzegovina. *Nordidactica: Journal of Humanities and Social Science Education, 1,* 90–103.

Aiken, N. T. (2013). *Identity, reconciliation and transitional justice: Overcoming intractability in divided societies*. New York: Routledge.
Al-Tikriti, N. (2010). War, state collapse and the predicament of education in Iraq. In A. E. Mazawi & R. G. Sultana (Eds.), *Education and the Arab "world": Political projects, struggles, and geometries of power* (pp. 350–360). London: Routledge.
Anderson, B. (1991). *Imagined communities: Reflections on the origin and spread of nationalism* (Rev ed.). London: Verso.
Anyon, J. (1978). Elementary social studies textbooks and legitimate knowledge. *Theory and Research in Social Education, 6*, 40–55.
Apple, M. W. (1993). *Official knowledge: Democratic education in a conservative age*. London: Routledge.
Apple, M. W., & Christian-Smith, L. K. (Eds.). (1991). *The politics of the textbook*. New York: Routledge.
Austin, B., Fischer, M., & Giessmann, H. J. (Eds.). (2011). *Advancing conflict transformation. The Bergh of handbook II*. Opladen/Farmington Hills: Barbara Budrich Publishers.
Bar-On, D., & Adwan, S. (2006). The PRIME shared history project: Peace-building project under fire. In Y. Iram, H. Wahrman, & Z. Gross (Eds.), *Educating toward a culture of peace* (pp. 309–323). Charlotte, NC: Information Age Publishing.
Bar-Tal, D. (2000). From intractable conflict through conflict resolution to reconciliation: Psychological analysis. *Political Psychology, 21*(2), 351–365.
Bar-Tal, D. (2003). Collective memory of physical violence: Its contribution to the culture of violence. In E. Cairns & M. D. Roe (Eds.), *The role of memory in ethnic conflict* (pp. 77–93). Houndmills, UK: Palgrave Macmillan.
Bar-Tal, D., & Bennink, G. H. (2004). The nature of reconciliation as an outcome and as a process. In Y. Bar-Siman-Tov (Ed.), *From conflict resolution to reconciliation* (pp. 11–38). Oxford: Oxford University Press.
Barton, K. C., & McCully, A. W. (2005). History, identity and the school curriculum in Northern Ireland: An empirical study of secondary students' ideas and perspectives. *Journal of Curriculum Studies, 37*(1), 85–116.
Bekerman, Z., & Zembylas, M. (2012). *Teaching contested narratives: Identity, memory and reconciliation in peace education and beyond*. Cambridge: Cambridge University Press.
Bellino, M. J. (2014). Whose past, whose present? Historical memory among the "postwar" generation in Guatemala. In J. H. Williams (Ed.), *(Re) constructing memory: School textbooks and the imagination of the nation* (pp. 131–153). Rotterdam: Sense Publishers.
Bentrovato, D. (2015). *Narrating and teaching the nation: The politics of education in pre- and post-genocide Rwanda*. Göttingen: V&R Unipress.

Bentrovato, D. (2016). Whose past, what future? Teaching contested histories in contemporary Rwanda and Burundi. In D. Bentrovato, K. V. Korostelina, & M. Schulze (Eds.), *History can bite: History education in divided and postwar societies* (pp. 221–242). Göttingen: V&R Unipress.

Bentrovato, D. (2017). Beyond transitional justice: Evaluating school outreach programmes and educational materials in post-war Rwanda and Sierra Leone. In C. Ramírez-Barat & M. Schulze (Eds.), *Transitional Justice and Education: Engaging Children and Youth in Justice and Peacebuilding through Educational Media, Curricula and Outreach*. Göttingen: V&R Unipress.

Bentrovato, D., Korostelina, K. V., & Schulze, M. (Eds.). (2016). *History can bite: History education in divided and postwar societies*. Göttingen: V&R Unipress.

Buckley-Zistel, S., Koloma Beck, T., Braun, C., & Mieth, F. (Eds.). (2014). *Transitional justice theories*. Abington: Routledge.

Burde, D. (2014). *Schools for conflict or for peace in Afghanistan*. New York: Columbia University Press.

Berger, P., & Luckmann, T. (1966). *The social construction of reality: A treatise in the sociology of knowledge*. New York: Anchor Books.

Cairns, E., & Roe, M. D. (Eds.). (2003). *The role of memory in ethnic conflict*. New York: Palgrave.

Carretero, M. (2011). *Constructing patriotism: Teaching history and memories in global worlds*. Charlotte, NC: Information Age Publishing.

CDRSEE. (2005). *Teaching modern Southeast European history. Alternative educational materials* (Vol. 1–4). Thessaloniki: Center for Democracy and Reconciliation in Southeast Europe.

Clark, P., & Palmer, N. (2012). Challenging transitional justice. In N. Palmer, P. Clark, & D. Granville (Eds.), *Critical perspectives in transitional justice* (pp. 1–16). Antwerp: Intersentia.

Cobb, S. (1994). "Theories of responsibility": The social construction of intentions in mediation. *Discourse Processes, 18*(2), 165–186.

Cobb, S. (2003). Fostering coexistence in identity-based conflicts: Towards a narrative approach. In A. Chayes & M. Minow (Eds.), *Imagine coexistence* (pp. 294–310). San Francisco: Jossey Bass.

Cobb, S. (2013). *Speaking of violence: The politics and poetics of narrative in conflict resolution*. New York: Oxford University Press.

CoE (Council of Europe). (2001). *Recommendation Rec(2001)15 on history teaching in twenty-first-century Europe*. Retrieved July, 3, 2017, from https://rm.coe.int/16805e2c31.

CoE (Council of Europe). (2009). *Recommendation 1880 (2009)1 history teaching in conflict and post-conflict*. Retrieved July, 3, 2017, from http://assembly.coe.int/nw/xml/XRef/Xref-XML2HTML-en.asp?fileid=17765&lang=en.

Cole, E. A. (2007). Transitional justice and the reform of history education. *International Journal of Transitional Justice, 1*, 115–137.

Daftuar, S. (2013, September 16). One story, two sides. *The Hindu*. Retrieved July, 3, 2017, from http://www.thehindu.com/features/magazine/one-story-two-sides/article5124147.ece.

Daher, M. (2012). On the impossibility of teaching history in Lebanon: Notes on a textbook controversy. In S. Alayan, A. Rohde, & S. Dhouib (Eds.), *The politics of education reform in the Middle East. Self and other in textbooks and curricula* (pp. 97–111). New York: Berghahn Books.

Danieli, Y. (Ed.). (1998). *International handbook of multigenerational legacies of trauma*. New York: Plenum Press.

De Baets, A. (2015). Post-conflict history education moratoria: A balance. *World Studies in Education*, *16*(1), 5–30.

Defrance, C., & Pfeil, U. (2013). Symbol or reality? The background, implementation and development of the Franco-German history textbook. In K. Korostelina & S. Lässig (Eds.), *History education and postconflict reconciliation: Reconsidering joint textbook projects* (pp. 52–68). London: Routledge.

Dimou, A. (Ed.). (2009). *"Transition" and the politics of history education on Southeast Europe*. Göttingen: V&R Unipress.

Dy, K. (2007). *A history of democratic Kampuchea 1975–1979*. Phnom Penh: Documentation Center of Cambodia.

Dy, K. (2008). *Teaching genocide in Cambodia: Challenges, analysis, and recommendations*. Retrieved July, 3, 2017, from http://d.dccam.org/Projects/Genocide/Boly_Teaching_Genocide_in_Cambodia1.pdf.

Dy, K. (2013). Challenges of teaching genocide in Cambodian secondary school. *Policy and Practice: Pedagogy about Holocaust and Genocide Papers*. Paper 4. Retrieved July, 3, 2017, from http://commons.clarku.edu/pedagogy2013/4.

Duncan, D. (2011). Education in Libya after Gaddafi. Retrieved July, 3, 2017 from http://www.pri.org/stories/2011-11-11/education-libya-after-gaddafi.

Eid, N. (2010). The inner conflict: How Palestinian students in Israel react to the dual narrative approach concerning the events of 1948. *Journal of Educational Media, Memory, and Society*, *2*(1), 55–77.

Ellis, D. G. (2006). *Transforming conflict: Communication and ethnopolitical conflict*. Lanham, MD: Rowman & Littlefield.

Evripidou, S. (2010). Taking a step back in the history books in the North. *Cyprus Mail*, 5 March.

EUROCLIO. (2008). *Ordinary people in an extraordinary country. Everyday life in Bosnia and Herzegovina, Croatia and Serbia between East and West 1945–1990*. The Hague: EUROCLIO.

EUROMID (Resource Centre on Euro-Middle East Affairs). (2006). *The role of textbooks in the Middle East conflict*. Retrieved July, 3, 2017, from http://www.europarl.europa.eu/meetdocs/2004_2009/documents/fd/il20062006_05/il20062006_05en.pdf.

Fajfer, L. (2013). Reconnecting history: The joint history project in the Balkans. In K. Korostelina & S. Lässig (Eds.), *History education and postconflict reconciliation: Reconsidering joint textbook projects* (pp. 140–154). London: Routledge.

Foster, S. J. (2011). Traditions in international textbook research and revision. *Education Inquiry, 2*(1), 5–20.

Foster, S. J., & Crawford, K. A. (Eds.). (2006). *What shall we tell the children? International perspectives on school history textbooks.* Charlotte, NC: Information Age Publishing.

Freedman, S. W., Weinstein, H. M., Murphy, K., & Longman, T. (2008). Teaching history after identity-based conflicts: The Rwanda experience. *Comparative Education Review, 52*(4), 663–690.

GCPEA (Global Coalition to Protect Education from Attack). (2014). *Education under attack, 2014.* New York: GCPEA.

Gibson, J. L. (2004). *Overcoming apartheid: Can truth reconcile a divided nation?.* New York: Russel Sage Foundation.

Gordon, D. (2005). History textbooks, narratives, and democracy: A response to Majid Al-Haj. *Curriculum Inquiry, 35*(3), 367–376.

Gutmann, A., & Thompson, D. (2000). The moral foundations of truth commissions. In R. Rotberg & D. Thompson (Eds.), *Truth V. Justice: The morality of truth commission* (pp. 22–44). Princeton: Princeton University Press.

Hamber, B. (2009). *Transforming societies after political violence: Truth, reconciliation, and mental health.* New York: Springer.

Han, U., Kondo, T., Yang, B., & Pingel, F. (2012). *History education and reconciliation: Comparative perspectives on East Asia.* Frankfurt am Main: Peter Lang.

Hansen, J. M. (2012). De-nationalize history and what have we done? Ontology, essentialism, and the search for a cosmopolitan alternative. In M. Carretero, M. Asensio, & M. Rodriguez-Moneo (Eds.), *History education and the construction of national identities* (pp. 17–32). Charlotte, NC: Information Age Publishing.

Hayner, P. B. (2002). *Unspeakable truths: Facing the challenge of truth commissions.* New York: Routledge.

Hermann, T. (2004). Reconciliation: Reflections on the theoretical and practical utility of the term. In Y. Bar-Siman-Tov (Ed.), *From conflict resolution to reconciliation* (pp. 39–60). Oxford: Oxford University Press.

Imbleau, M. (2004). Initial truth establishment by transitional bodies and the fight against denial. In W. Schabas & S. Darcy (Eds.), *Truth commissions and courts: The tension between criminal justice and the search for the truth* (pp. 159–192). New York: Kluwer Academic.

INEE (Inter-Agency Network for Education in Emergencies). (2010). *Guidance notes on teaching and learning.* New York: INEE.

Kelman, H. C. (2004). Reconciliation as identity change: A social psychological perspective. In Y. Bar-Siman-Tov (Ed.), *From conflict resolution to reconciliation* (pp. 111–124). Oxford: Oxford University Press.

King, E. (2014). *From classrooms to conflict in Rwanda*. New York: Cambridge University Press.
Kitson, A. (2007). History teaching and reconciliation in Northern Ireland. In E. A. Cole (Ed.), *Teaching the violent past: History education and reconciliation* (pp. 123–155). Lanham, MD: Rowman & Littlefield.
Koren, S., & Baranović, B. (2009). What kind of history education do we have after eighteen years of democracy in Croatia? Transition, intervention and history education politics (1990–2008). In A. Dimou (Ed.), *"Transition" and the politics of history education in Southeastern Europe* (pp. 91–140). Göttingen: V&E Unipress.
Korostelina, K., & Lässig, S. (Eds.). (2013). *History education and postconflict reconciliation: Reconsidering joint textbook projects*. Abingdon, UK: Routledge.
Kriener, J. (2012). Different layers of identity in Lebanese textbooks. In S. Alayan, A. Rohde, & S. Dhouib (Eds.), *The politics of education reform in the Middle East: Self and other in textbooks and curricula* (pp. 131–153). New York: Berghahn Books.
Kriesberg, L. (2004). Comparing reconciliation actions within and between countries. In Y. Bar-Siman-Tov (Ed.), *From conflict resolution to reconciliation* (pp. 81–110). Oxford: Oxford University Press.
Kriesberg, L. (2007). Reconciliation: Aspects, growth, and sequences. *International Journal of Peace Studies, 12*, 1–21.
Lässig, S. (2013). Introduction: Post-conflict reconciliation and joint history textbook projects. In K. Korostelina & S. Lässig (Eds.), *History education and postconflict reconciliation: Reconsidering joint textbook projects* (pp. 1–18). Abingdon, UK: Routledge.
Lässig, S., & Strobel, T. (2013). Towards a joint German-Polish history textbook: Historical roots, structures and challenges. In K. Korostelina & S. Lässig (Eds.), *History education and postconflict reconciliation: Reconsidering joint textbook projects* (pp. 90–119). Abingdon, UK: Routledge.
Leach, F., & Dunne, M. (Eds.). (2007). *Education, conflict and reconciliation: International perspectives*. Bern: Peter Lang.
Lederach, J. P. (1997). *Building peace: Sustainable reconciliation in divided societies*. Washington, DC: United States Institute of Peace Press.
Lederach, J. P. (2001). Civil society and reconciliation. In C. A. Crocker, F. O. Hampson, & P. Aall (Eds.), *Turbulent peace: The challenges of managing international conflict* (pp. 841–854). Washington, DC: USIP.
Lee, S. Y., & Özerdem, A. (Eds.). (2015). *Local ownership in international peacebuilding: Key theoretical and practical issues*. Abingdon, UK: Routledge.
Lerch, J. (2016). Embracing diversity? Textbook narratives in countries with a legacy of internal armed conflict (1950 to 2011). In D. Bentrovato, K. V. Korostelina, & M. Schulze (Eds.), *History can bite: history education in divided and postwar societies*. Göttingen: V&R Unipress.

Mack, J. E. (1990). The psychodynamics of victimisation among national groups in conflict. In V. Volkan, D. A. Julius, & J. V. Montville (Eds.), *The psychodynamics of interpersonal relationships* (pp. 119–129). Lexington, MA: Lexington Books.

Malkki, L. H. (1995). *Purity and exile: Violence, memory, and national cosmology among Hutu refugees in Tanzania*. Chicago: University of Chicago Press.

Marsden, W. E. (2001). *The school textbook: Geography, history and social studies*. London: Routledge.

McCully, A. W. (2012). History teaching, conflict and the legacy of the past. *Education, Citizenship and Social Justice, 7*(2), 145–159.

Milosheva, M., & Krushe, D. (2010). *Out of the broken mirror: Learning for reconciliation through multi-perspective history teaching in Southeast Europe*. n.p.: USAID.

Minkina-Milko, T. (2012). Teaching and learning history for strengthening reconciliation and the peace-building process: Experience of the council of Europe. In M. Shuayb (Ed.), *Rethinking education for social cohesion: International case studies* (pp. 232–243). Basingstoke, UK: Palgrave Macmillan.

Minow, M. (1998). *Between vengeance and forgiveness: Facing history after genocide and mass violence*. Boston: Beacon Press.

Mueller-Sainy, G. (Ed.). (2011). *Designing history in East Asian textbooks: Identity politics and transnational aspirations*. New York: Routledge.

Nadler, A., Malloy, T., & Fisher, J. D. (2008). Intergroup reconciliation: Dimensions and themes. In A. Nadler, T. Malloy, & J. D. Fisher (Eds.), *The social psychology of intergroup reconciliation* (pp. 3–12). Oxford: Oxford University Press.

Nadler, A., & Shnabel, N. (2008). Instrumental and socioemotional paths to intergroup reconciliation and the needs-based model of socioemotional reconciliation. In A. Nadler, T. Malloy, & J. D. Fisher (Eds.), *The social psychology of intergroup reconciliation* (pp. 37–56). Oxford: Oxford University Press.

Nakou, I., & Barca, I. (Eds.) (2010). Contemporary public debates over history education. In *International review of history education series*. Charlotte, NC: Information Age Publishing.

Nasser, R., & Nasser, I. (2008). Textbooks as a vehicle for segregation and domination: State efforts to shape Palestinian Israelis' identities as citizens. *Journal of Curriculum Studies, 40*(5), 627–650.

Naveh, E. (2006). The dynamics of identity construction in Israel through education. In R. I. Rotberg (Ed.), *Israeli and Palestinian narratives of conflict: History's double helix* (pp. 244–270). Bloomington: Indiana University Press.

Nicholls, J. (2006). *School history textbooks across cultures: International debates and perspectives*. Oxford: Symposium Books.

Nietzsche, F. (1997). *Untimely meditations*. D. Breazeale (Ed.), trans. R. J. Hollingdale. Cambridge: Cambridge University Press.

Nussbaum, M. C. (1992). Tragedy and self-sufficiency. Plato and Aristotle on fear and pity. In A. O. Rorty (Ed.), *Essays on Aristotle's poetics* (pp. 261–290). Princeton: Princeton University Press.

Oberschall, A. (2007). *Conflict and peace building in divided societies. Responses to ethnic violence.* New York: Routledge.

Oglesby, E. (2007). Historical memory and the limits of peace education: Examining Guatemala's memory of silence and the politics of curriculum design. In E. A. Cole (Ed.), *Teaching the violent past: History education and reconciliation* (pp. 175–205). Lanham, MD: Rowman & Littlefield.

Ondek Laurence, P. (1993). *The reading of silence: Virginia Woolf in the English tradition.* Stanford: Stanford University Press.

Paulmann, J. (1998). Internationaler Vergleich und interkultureller Transfer. Zwei Forschungsansäntze zur eurpäischen Geschichtedes 18. bis 20 Jahrhunderts (International comparison and intercultural transfer. Two research approaches to European history of the 18th until the 20th centuries). *Historische Zeitschrift, 3,* 649–685.

Paulson, J. (2010). Truth commissions and national curricula: The case of recordandonos in Peru. In S. Parmar, M. J. Roseman, S. Siegrist, & T. Sowa (Eds.), *Children and transitional justice: Truth telling, accountability and reconciliation* (pp. 327–364). Cambridge, MA: Harvard University Press.

Paulson, J. (2015). "Whether and how?" History education about recent and ongoing conflict: A review of research. *Journal on Education in Emergencies, 1*(1), 14–47.

Pingel, F. (2008). Can truth be negotiated? History textbook revision as a means to reconciliation. *Annals of the American Academy of Political and Social Science, 617,* 181–198.

Pingel, F. (2009). From ownership to intervention—or vice versa? Textbook revision in Bosnia and Herzegovina. In A. Dimou (Ed.), *"Transition" and the politics of history education in Southeast Europe* (pp. 251–305). Göttingen: V&R Unipress.

Pingel, F. (2010). *UNESCO guidebook for textbook research and textbook revision* (2nd rev. ed.) Paris: UNESCO with support of Georg Eckert Institute for International Textbook Research.

Ramírez-Barat, C., & Duthie, R. (2015). *Education and transitional justice: Opportunities and challenges for peacebuilding.* New York: International Center for Transitional Justice.

Richter, S. (Ed.). (2008). *Contested views of a common past: Revisions of history in contemporary East Asia.* Frankfurt am Main/New York: Campus.

Rohde, A. (2012). Bridging conflicts through history education? A case study from Israel/Palestine. In S. Alayan, A. Rohde, & S. Dhouib (Eds.), *The politics of education reform in the Middle East: Self and other in textbooks and curricula* (pp. 237–260). New York: Berghahn Books.

Rohde, A. (2013a). Change and continuity in Arab Iraqi education: Sunni and Shi'i discourses in Iraqi textbooks before and after 2003. *Comparative Education Review*, 57(4), 711–734.

Rohde, A. (2013b). Learning each other's historical narrative: A road map to peace in Israel/Palestine? In K. V. Korostelina & S. Lässig (Eds.), *History education and postconflict reconciliation: Reconsidering joint textbook projects* (pp. 177–191). Abingdon, UK: Routledge.

Rüsen, J. (2004). Historical consciousness: Narrative structure, moral function, and ontogenetic development. In P. Seixas (Ed.), *Theorizing historical consciousness* (pp. 63–85). Toronto: University of Toronto Press.

Sarwary, B. (2012). Why Afghanistan's past is being "rewritten". *BBC News*. Retrieved July, 3, 2017, from http://www.bbc.com/news/world-asia-18579315.

Schöpflin, G. (1997). The functions of myth and a taxonomy of myths. In G. Hosking & G. Schöpflin (Eds.), *Myths and nationhood* (pp. 19–35). London: Hurst.

Seixas, P. (2000). Schweigen! Die Kinder! or does postmodern history have a place in the schools? In P. N. Stearns, S. Wineburg, & P. Seixas (Eds.), *Knowing, teaching and learning history: National and international perspectives* (pp. 19–37). New York: University Press.

Seixas, P. (Ed.). (2004). *Theorizing historical consciousness*. Toronto: University of Toronto Press.

Smith, A. (2010). *The influence of education on conflict and peace building, Background paper prepared for the education for all global monitoring report 2011 The Hidden Crisis: Armed conflict and education. Paris: UNESCO.* Education For All, Global Monitoring Report. Paris: UNESCO.

Stobart, M. (1999). Fifty years of European co-operation on history-textbooks: The role and contribution of the Council of Europe. *Internationale Schulbuchforschung*, 21, 147–161.

Stöber, G. (2013). From textbooks comparison to common textbooks? Changing patterns in international textbook revision. In K. Korostelina & S. Lässig (Eds.), *History education and postconflict reconciliation: Reconsidering joint textbook projects* (pp. 26–51). London: Routledge.

Stradling, R. (2003). *Multi-perspectivity in history teaching: A guide for teachers*. Strasbourg: Council of Europe.

Taif Agreement. (1989). Retrieved from http://peacemaker.un.org/lebanon-taifaccords89

Torsti, P. (2007). How to deal with a difficult past? History textbooks supporting enemy images in post-war Bosnia-Herzegovina. *Journal of Curriculum Studies*, 39(1), 77–96.

Torsti, P. (2009). Segregated education and texts: A challenge to peace in Bosnia and Herzegovina. *International Journal on World Peace*, 26(2), 65–82.

United Nations Commission on Human Rights. (2005). *Updated set of principles for the protection and promotion of human rights through action to combat impunity* (E/CN.4/2005/102/Add.1).
UNESCO. (1949). *A handbook for the improvement of textbooks and teaching materials as aids to international understanding.* Paris: UNESCO.
UNESCO. (2011). *The hidden crisis: Armed conflict and education—Education for all global monitoring report 2011.* Paris: UNESCO.
United Nations General Assembly. (2006). *The basic principles and guidelines on the right to a remedy and reparations for victims of gross violations of international human rights law and serious violations of international humanitarian law* (A/Res/60/147).
Van Ommering, E. (2015). Formal history education in Lebanon: Crossroads, past conflicts and prospects for peace. *International Journal of Educational Development, 41,* 200–207.
Vickers, E., & Jones, A. (Eds.). (2005). *History education and national identity in East Asia.* London: Routledge.
Weldon, G. (2010). *A comparative study of the construction of memory and identity in the curriculum in societies emerging from conflict: Rwanda and South Africa.* Saarbrücken: Lambert Academic Publishing.
Werner, M., & Zimmermann, B. (2004). Penser l'histoire croisée: entre empirie et réflecivité (Thinking about entangled history. Between empirical data and reflexivity). In M. Werner & B. Zimmermann (Eds.), *De la comparaison à l'histoire croisée* (pp. 15–52) (From comparison to entangled histories). Paris: Seuil.
Wertsch, J. V. (1998). *Mind as action.* New York: Oxford University Press.
Wertsch, J. V. (2002). *Voices of collective remembering.* Cambridge, UK: Cambridge University Press.
Williams, J. H. (Ed.). (2014). *(Re) constructing memory: School textbooks and the imagination of the nation.* Rotterdam: Sense Publishers.
Winslade, J., & Monk, G. (2000). *Narrative mediation. A new approach to conflict resolution.* San Francisco: Jossey-Bass.
World Bank. (2005). *Reshaping the future: Education and postconflict reconstruction.* Washington, DC.: World Bank.
Yang, D., & Sin, J.-B. (2013). Striving for common history textbooks in Northeast Asia (China, South Korea and Japan): Between ideal and reality. In K. Korostelina & S. Lässig (Eds.), *History education and postconflict reconciliation: Reconsidering joint textbook projects* (pp. 209–229). London: Routledge.
Zambylas, M. (2013). Integrated schooling in divided Cyprus: Impossible or indispensable? *Studies in Ethnicity and Nationalism, 13*(3), 442–454.

Author Biography

Denise Bentrovato is a Research Fellow in the Department of Humanities Education at the University of Pretoria and the co-founder and co-director of the African Association for History Education. Her research combines an interest in post-conflict memory politics, transitional justice and history education and primarily focuses on Africa, notably the Great Lakes Region, for which she is a special advisor at the Institute for Historical Justice and Reconciliation in the Netherlands. Throughout her career, she has worked both in academia and for international organisations and NGOs in Europe and Africa, including UNESCO. Dr. Bentrovato holds a Ph.D. in History and an M.A. in Conflict Resolution. Among her most recent publications are *Narrating and Teaching the Nation: The Politics of Education in Pre- and Post-Genocide Rwanda* (2015) and *History Can Bite: History Education in Divided and Postwar Societies* [with K. Korostelina and M. Schulze (eds.)] (2016).

Open Access This chapter is licensed under the terms of the Creative Commons Attribution 4.0 International License (http://creativecommons.org/licenses/by/4.0/), which permits use, sharing, adaptation, distribution and reproduction in any medium or format, as long as you give appropriate credit to the original author(s) and the source, provide a link to the Creative Commons license and indicate if changes were made.

The images or other third party material in this chapter are included in the chapter's Creative Commons license, unless indicated otherwise in a credit line to the material. If material is not included in the chapter's Creative Commons license and your intended use is not permitted by statutory regulation or exceeds the permitted use, you will need to obtain permission directly from the copyright holder.

Confronting History and Reconciliation: A Review of Civil Society's Approaches to Transforming Conflict Narratives

Rezarta Bilali and Rima Mahmoud

Historical narratives pose one of the most challenging obstacles to peaceful resolution of conflicts and reconciliation. Narratives of conflict typically emphasize the in-group's suffering (Nadler and Saguy 2004; Noor et al. 2008), morality, and the justness of the in-group's goals and actions while delegitimizing the opponent (Bar-Tal 2000). For instance, each group's account of the history of the conflict highlights different events and interprets the same events differently. Typically, each group in conflict blames the opponent for the violence (Staub and Bar-Tal 2003). Narratives of historical events are often manipulated by leaders and elites to justify aggressive action toward the out-group (Berlin 1979; Ramanathapillai 2006). In this manner, historical memory might provide lessons that are not conducive to peace building, and become a basis for the continuation of conflict. The two groups' conflicting views

---

R. Bilali (✉)
New York University, New York, NY, USA
e-mail: rb190@nyu.edu

R. Mahmoud
Boston University School of Law, Boston, MA, USA

© The Author(s) 2017
C. Psaltis et al. (eds.), *History Education and Conflict Transformation*,
DOI 10.1007/978-3-319-54681-0_3

of the past have negative consequences for coexistence and reconciliation and might provoke new hostilities and violence. Because of the role of history in fueling new conflicts and impeding reconciliation between groups, addressing the history of conflict is considered important for reconciliation (e.g., Bar-Tal 2000). Reconciliation requires a change in the orientation by groups toward the previous enemy, including acceptance of the other (Staub 2011). Such acceptance requires addressing and coming to terms with the conflictual and violent past, by mutually acknowledging past suffering. Around the world, numerous efforts are underway aiming to deal with the history of conflict in order to promote peace. Some of them, such as revisions of history education curricula in schools or establishment of historical and truth commissions, are government-driven programs. A large number of nongovernmental actors (civil society and international organizations) also design and implement programs that focus on addressing a violent conflict history and transforming conflict narratives to prevent violence and promote reconciliation. Following these practices, there is a growing scholarship on top-down approaches to transforming the narrative of conflict, such as on truth-and-reconciliation commissions (e.g., Hayner 2000) or on revising history education curricula in conflict and postconflict settings (for a review, see Paulson 2015). However, we know little about civil society's approaches to transforming conflict narratives.

There are multiple reasons for examining civil society's practices that target the transformation of conflict narratives. We know little about strategies and approaches that deal effectively with the history of conflict to foster positive intergroup relations. The little empirical evidence on top-down policies and programs reveals a mixed effect on target populations (e.g., Brouneus 2010; Kanyangara et al. 2007; Rime et al. 2011). One important constraint of top-down approaches is that they are often a result of negotiated political processes and might serve specific political agendas, which, in turn, limit the scope and the effectiveness of the implemented programs. By contrast, civil society actors are less constrained by the pressures and political agendas that elites and governments face; therefore, they are likely to use more diverse approaches and more creative strategies to confront the past. Practitioners, through their knowledge and expertise in working directly with communities, might gain important insights on how to effect change. Therefore, in this chapter we review projects developed by practitioners that focus on confronting the in-group's history around the world in order to gain insights about the principles used to achieve peace and reconciliation.

In the following discussion, we first present our review of civil society's practices that focus on confronting the in-group's history. Then, we report our analysis of the theories of practice underlying these projects. We also link practitioners' theories with research and theory in social psychology and discuss their potential and limits for effecting change. By linking practice with research and theory, we aim to increase communication between scholars and practitioners. Scholars can gain insights into the potential mechanisms of change that might work in the field and design studies to test them, whereas practitioners can assess their strategies and improve their programs based on empirical evidence.

Review Method

To identify projects and organizations working on confronting history, we used a variety of tools. First, we compiled a list of scholars and practitioners who work in related fields (historical memory, intergroup dialogue, transitional justice) and sent them an inquiry regarding our search criteria. Second, we posted an advertisement of our research on the *Peace and Collaborative Development Network* web page—an online network of professionals working in conflict settings. Lastly, we conducted a Google search of relevant organizations and projects by using a list of key words related to "confronting history" jointly with each country in the globe. The key words that we used included "writing history," "historical dialogue," "facing history," "history education," "reconciliation and memory," "antagonistic narratives," "storytelling," "remembering," "truth telling," "commemoration," and "conflicting narratives." We also used key words denoting different types of projects that might be implemented in this area, such as "history teaching," "mass media," "dialogue groups," "transitional justice," "photo exhibit," and "museum." We examined the information available on relevant projects and retained information only on projects that explicitly focused on confronting history to achieve peace and reconciliation.

We sought information about the goals and the scope of the project, the specific activities, and the target population of the intervention. We collected available project materials online or through e-mail inquiries in order to identify the assumptions underlying each project and their mechanisms of change. We also conducted 16 Skype interviews. After collecting the available information on each project (documents, transcripts of the interviews, etc.), we produced summaries of those materials. Then, we conducted thematic analyses on the summaries of the projects to extract the underlying assumptions and theories of change.

OVERVIEW OF CONFRONTING HISTORY PROJECTS

We reviewed 127 projects implemented by more than 60 organizations in 45 countries around the world. The projects included a wide range of activities, such as writing history books or textbooks; oral history projects; lectures, seminars, conferences, and workshops; dialogue between adversary groups; exhibits; Web site projects; training of teachers; tours and site/museum projects; public dialogue; and documentaries, children's books, and a variety of other media projects.

A large number of projects that we reviewed focused on teaching history in school settings. The aim of these projects was to provide an alternative more conducive to peace building and democratic values than traditional history education, which typically endorses a nationalistic approach focused on disseminating a linear narrative of the nation. The activities conducted in these projects can be grouped into three interconnected categories: (1) professional development and capacity building for teachers on innovative pedagogies and methods, such as oral histories and digital media; (2) production of educational materials to supplement traditional textbooks that incorporate new pedagogies and more inclusive historical experiences across conflicting groups and borders; and (3) creation of forums to foster cooperation among teachers across borders and conflict lines. Often, history teachers from antagonistic groups are brought together to design history-teaching tools and educational materials that are acceptable to all sides. For example, the *History that Connects* project invites history educators from Bosnia, Croatia, and Serbia to assist in developing a curriculum for teaching the history of the region and to set up workshops for training history educators. By bringing together teachers from different countries and groups, the project aims not only to provide professional training but also to stimulate cross-border cooperation and dialogue.

Another set of projects focuses on educating the public and raising awareness about the historical roots and factors that contribute to extremism, prejudice, and xenophobia. These projects engage the public in an examination of racism, prejudice, or anti-Semitism, by exposing historical materials such as witness accounts, oral histories, and testimonies. Some of these projects also educate and disseminate information about events in world history that are not specific to the targeted population, such as the Holocaust or other genocides.

Other projects include the establishment of physical and virtual museums and galleries or the creation of different art forms as a means of remembering the past. Some of these projects aim to teach the new generations about the devastating effects of conflict and remind them of the historical periods of peaceful coexistence among antagonistic groups. Museums, galleries, and other art expressions give victims time and space to be heard, serving a healing purpose. Intergroup dialogue among members of antagonistic groups with a focus on historical narratives is also common. Such dialogue aims to promote peace by fostering intergroup interactions that would not otherwise occur, in an environment designed to build trust and eradicate stereotypes. The *Peace Processes and Dialogue* project, for example, brings together young Georgians and Abkhaz who have never met before, to jointly analyze the roots of their conflict and better understand the other's concerns as a means to achieve peace.

PRACTITIONERS' THEORIES OF BRINGING PEACE THROUGH CONFRONTING HISTORY

All practice is based on beliefs about how the world works. These beliefs, here referred to as *theories of practice*, explain why and how practitioners expect their programs and activities to have the intended effect (Ross 2000). Theories of practice are often implicit, as civil society organizations do not always explicitly state the mechanisms through which their programs are assumed to impact the target population. Our goal in this research was to make these theories of practice explicit and link them to scientific research and theory. Making theories of practice explicit provides an opportunity to examine each belief closely, test its impact, and assess whether it has the intended effect. We identified the theories of practice by inferring them through analyses of the documents made available by the organizations. Our thematic analysis sheds light on several assumed psychological mechanisms (i.e., theories) regarding how addressing history should influence peace building and reconciliation. The following strategies are thought to effectively confront history to prevent future violence, counteract xenophobic myths, and foster reconciliation: (1) raising awareness and increasing understanding of history, (2) adopting historical thinking and multiperspectivity, (3) engaging plural perspectives and narratives, (4) creating shared historical narratives, and (5) healing and overcoming trauma. We discuss these mechanisms under the following subheadings, provide examples from practice to illustrate them, and draw links to relevant theory and research in social psychology.

Raising Awareness and Increasing Understanding of History

A large number of civil society projects aim to educate the public by raising awareness about the history of relations between antagonistic groups. The assumption underlying these projects is that if people understand the past, they will be able to prevent violence in the future and will work to build peaceful relations. It draws on the idea that ignorance, lack of understanding, and myths and propaganda are the causes of conflict and violence. The idea that ignorance and lack of understanding is the cause of conflict and prejudice has its roots in the Human Relations Movement of the twentieth century (e.g., Pettigrew and Tropp 2011). Combating misinformation about history should thus dispel myths about the past that perpetuate violence and community divisions. Increasing knowledge and understanding of history and its consequences is thought to prevent violent conflicts from happening again and, it is believed, will lead to intergroup tolerance.

Two approaches are used in civil society projects to promulgate knowledge about the past. In the first approach, the projects provide factual truths and disseminate knowledge about specific historic events or about the history of intergroup relations. Many projects that we reviewed do not simply disseminate knowledge about the past but also are involved in history making by gathering evidence to establish the truth and counter the distortions of facts and misinformation that often prevail in conflict and postconflict contexts. For instance, the Documenta project in Croatia and in other countries of the former Yugoslavia aims to establish the factual truths about the war through a systematic collection of materials related to war, human losses, and personal memories. In collaboration with human rights organizations, through oral histories, the project strives to establish the facts about the war and build memory based on facts rather than myths, so that the war does not become subject to political manipulation and serve to justify further violence. In another example in Poland, the *School of Dialogue* project aims to foster Poles' knowledge of the long-standing presence of Jews in Poland through commemoration of prewar Jewish history. It aims to teach tolerance and eradicate anti-Semitism by connecting knowledge regarding the history of discrimination of Jews in Poland to present-day issues.

In the second approach, rather than providing factual knowledge about the history of relations between the two relevant groups, some civil society projects raise awareness about the roots of conflict and the influences that lead to violence more generally. The assumption is that a general understanding of the influences that contribute to intergroup conflict will equip people with the tools and analytical frameworks to understand their own context (Staub 2011). That is, if people understand the universal roots of xenophobia, prejudice, and violence, then they will be able to prevent and resist such influences in their own society in the future. For instance, projects that focus on exposing the roots and the devastating consequences of the Holocaust and other genocides aim to bring change by increasing people's understanding of the causes of prejudice and violence. This approach might be effective, as it might be easier for people to engage with new ideas by examining a conflict in which they are not emotionally invested. Then, they can apply the lessons learned to their own conflict. In a unique use of this approach, the Dutch NGO *Radio La Benevolencija* produces soap operas to educate the populations in Rwanda, Burundi, and the Democratic Republic of the Congo about the roots and evolution of mass violence. Rather than making use of existing cases of genocide or violence to explain the roots of genocide, they disseminate fictional stories via media, which listeners can then apply to their own context. The underlying assumption of this approach is that knowledge about the universal factors that contribute to violence will empower people to take action to resist and counteract such influences in their society (e.g., Staub 2011).

In assessing whether and how increasing knowledge of history influences reconciliation, two pertinent questions should be considered. First, to what extent are beliefs about conflict history malleable? For example, does correcting specific misinformation result in changes in the narratives of the past? Second, does change in beliefs about historical events influence intergroup attitudes and behaviors? Historical narratives are coherent and persuasive. They build on cultural schemes and are often immune to criticism; therefore, they are hard to change. Because historical memory is central to the construction of group identities, information counteracting established historical memories and narratives can threaten people's sense of identity. Self and group images are self-perpetuating, driving schema-consistent interpretations of the past (Hirshberg 1993). Therefore, even in the face of contradictory information, the evidence is likely to be ignored, downplayed, or reinterpreted in ways that reaffirm preexisting beliefs. In the context of history education, Porat (2004) has shown that encounter with history textbooks does not change deeply held views about historical issues.

In the second approach, in which people learn about the influences that lead to violence through distant or fictional conflicts, people are less emotionally invested. Therefore, this approach has the potential to transform beliefs about group-based conflict and violence. However, whether a better understanding or more knowledge about conflicts in general contributes to more positive intergroup attitudes and behaviors is not clear. Research on other forms of interventions, such as intergroup contact, suggests that knowledge (about the other) per se might have only a minor influence in reducing prejudice (Pettigrew and Tropp 2008). Furthermore, it is unclear whether participants will draw lessons from the distant or fictional cases and see the parallels between those conflicts and the ones in which they are personally involved or emotionally invested. For instance, the media programs that use fictional conflict to raise awareness about the roots and evolution of violence in Rwanda, Burundi, and the Democratic Republic of the Congo have shown positive effects on intergroup attitudes but not on knowledge about the intergroup conflict (Bilali and Staub 2016; Paluck 2009).

Adopting Historical Thinking and Multiperspectivity

Some projects focus on fostering historical thinking (i.e., thinking as historians) as a way to deal with historical memory of conflict (Stradling 2003). Historical thinking is designed to teach students how to think critically about the past. Students learn to read primary and secondary sources and to construct narratives based on these sources. In historical thinking, multiperspectivity is especially emphasized as students learn how to analyze, interpret, and reconstruct historical events from a variety of perspectives. Students learn that history can be interpreted differently and subjectively by social groups, as each group can construct starkly different narratives by using and selecting different primary and secondary sources and evidence and highlighting different aspects of the evidence. Multiperspectivity allows students to take into account the perspectives of marginalized and silenced social categories, including ethnic and linguistic minorities, women, the poor, and ordinary people more generally (see Stradling 2003).

Civil society projects that encourage historical thinking and multiperspectivity in history teaching typically design and implement training programs for history teachers and prepare new educational materials and curricula to supplement traditional history textbooks. Such curricula include oral histories, primary and secondary sources of historical events, and the historical perspectives of different groups. As an example, the Association for Historical Dialogue and Research is an organization whose mission is to contribute to history education in Cyprus by focusing on enhancing the teaching of historical thinking. Specifically, the group aims to foster critical thinking skills with regard to understanding the past, respect for the people of the past, appreciation of the distance between the past and the present, and evaluation of competing narratives of the past (Psaltis et al. 2011). Students are taught to evaluate claims of different narratives and analyze how interpretations of evidence of historical events change over time and are dependent on historical actors.

There are two potential mechanisms through which historical thinking might influence intergroup outcomes positively: critical thinking and perspective taking. Historical thinking raises awareness about the limits of historical knowledge and evidence. Critical thinking pushes students to analyze, interpret, and think critically about historical events. Learning to think historically is likely to counteract traditional history education, which is often ethnocentric and presents only a dominant group's view of the past. Historical thinking breaks down historical myths, propaganda, and monolithic narratives of the past and also encourages perspective taking—the ability to view a situation from different angles. A large body of work in social psychology research has revealed the positive impact of perspective taking for intergroup relations. For instance, perspective taking is associated with less prejudice (Galinsky and Moskowitz 2000; Galinsky and Ku 2004), more positive evaluation of out-groups (Batson et al. 2002), and higher levels of intergroup forgiveness (Noor et al. 2008b). However, recent studies have also shown that the benefits of perspective taking might be limited in conflict contexts (e.g., Bruneau and Saxe 2012; Paluck 2010, but also see Bilali and Vollhardt

2013). Negative emotions toward the adversary might reduce willingness to engage with the adversary's perspective. Therefore, it is important to examine the conditions under which multiperspectivity is most influential in improving intergroup attitudes and when it might not be as effective. Barton and McCully (2012) argue that an analytic approach that encourages detachment might leave history solely to the domain of academic study and enterprise but does little to change deeply held narratives. Instead, stronger emotional and empathetic engagement with narratives might be necessary for deeper change.

ENGAGING PLURAL NARRATIVES OF HISTORY

We differentiate between interventions that focus on multiperspectivity as a set of tools and skills necessary to engage with different perspectives and interventions that focus on the content—that is, on creating educational materials that include multiple narratives and exposing people to these different versions of the same historical events. The assumption is that engaging with multiple narratives of the conflict's past will lead to reconciliation and positive relations between groups. In some instances, civil society projects expose group members to each group's dominant or master narrative of the conflict. For example, a textbook project undertaken by the Peace Research Institute in the Middle East (PRIME), led by Professors Dan Bar-On and Sami Adwan, created a joint history textbook titled *Learning Each Other's Historical Narrative: Palestinians and Israelis* that aimed to give teachers and pupils the opportunity to learn the other's perspective with regard to significant historical events in the Israeli–Palestinian conflict (see Adwan and Bar-On 2004). Each page of the booklet provides side-by-side Palestinian and Israeli narratives of a historical event. In the middle of the two narratives, it provides space for students to write their own comments on the two master narratives. Rather than revising the existing narratives of each side or creating a common narrative, the project aims to introduce pupils from both sides to the other group's narrative and engage them with both master narratives. Students are required not only to learn their perspective of the history but to engage with the other group's perspective as well. The idea is not to legitimize or accept the other's narrative but to recognize it (Adwan and Bar-On 2004).

Rather than focusing on each group's master narratives, other projects highlight a variety of narratives and experiences within each group.

This is achieved by providing access to oral histories and testimonies by ordinary people, thereby showing both commonalities and differences in experiences within and across groups in conflict. For instance, the Living Memorial Museum aims to demonstrate that there are different perspectives on the conflict in Northern Ireland—beyond the two master narratives—and that these perspectives can be preserved and shared in a respectful and tolerant way. The Apartheid Archives Project in South Africa examines the nature of ordinary South Africans' experiences of racism in the apartheid period and its continued effects in the present. Rather than highlighting grand narratives disseminated by elites, it focuses on gathering personal stories and individual narratives of ordinary South Africans who might have been silenced.

The plural narrative approach aims to promote an inclusive understanding of the past and foster respect for different experiences, which, in turn, would lead to tolerance toward others. However, it is important to empirically assess this claim: Does exposure to and engagement with different narratives of the past influence intergroup outcomes? In the Israeli–Palestinian context, Bar-On and Adwan (2006) report that exposure to dual narratives of the PRIME project led to resentment and anger among some students. Because students view their group's version of history as fact, some students had a hard time understanding why they were taught the enemy's propaganda. The characteristics and the phase of conflict might also influence how plural narratives are received. For instance, in the context of the PRIME project, acceptance and recognition of the other's narrative were particularly hard for Palestinian kids who lived under occupation (Bar-On and Adwan 2006). This finding is in line with recent research suggesting that engaging with an adversary's perspective might backfire under conditions of heightened conflict (e.g., Bilali and Vollhardt 2015; Paluck 2010).

In a study in Northern Ireland, Barton and McCully (2012) found that despite the presentation of multiple interpretations of historical events in school curricula, students' identification with their communities' historical perspective became stronger over time. Many students drew selectively from the curriculum to form reasoned arguments to support their community's perspectives (Barton and McCully 2012).

In a unique experimental study of the effects of different historical teaching approaches in Israel, Goldberg and Ron (2014) found that both dual-narrative and historical thinking (they call it a critical-disciplinary approach) approaches were effective in increasing students' agreement about the solutions to various conflict-driven problems. Dual narratives also increased interest in out-group perspectives, especially for members of the Arab minority (Goldberg and Ron 2014). Interestingly, a dual-narrative approach led to a reduction of perceived in-group responsibility among majority group members, Israeli Jews, whereas the critical-disciplinary approach led to an increase in perceived in-group responsibility among members of the Arab minority (Goldberg and Ron 2014).

These mixed findings call for further research and theorizing on the effects of exposure and engagement with multiple narratives in conflict settings. As we argued earlier, it is likely that exposure to plural narratives is more effective when people engage empathetically with different perspectives. However, engaging empathetically with the adversary's position might be difficult when out-group prejudices are high, when the conflict is intense, or when the out-group narrative denies one's experiences of conflict.

CREATING SHARED NARRATIVES OF THE PAST

A number of civil society projects focus on creating a common narrative from the divergent narratives and experiences of the past. The rationale underlying this practice is that if antagonistic and clashing narratives of the past contribute to fueling conflict between groups, then a common and shared understanding of the past should be a basis for overcoming differences. For instance, Kriesberg (2004) argues that for reconciliation to occur, conflicting groups should develop shared beliefs about what happened in the past. Similarly, Staub (2011) also claims that shared narratives of the past are important in developing a common orientation about the future. In order to build a shared peaceful future together, it is important to create a shared common narrative of the past. A common narrative of the past should serve to humanize the adversary, fight xenophobic myths, and promote reconciliation.

Civil society projects use different strategies to create shared narratives, such as through identifying the commonalities in the narratives of antagonist groups, highlighting the similar experiences across groups in conflict, emphasizing the shared struggles of the members of each group, or uncovering shared positive experiences (e.g., periods of peaceful coexistence) in the past. For instance, in the countries of the former Yugoslavia, the Institute for Historical Justice and Reconciliation (IHJR) brings together historians, researchers, policy makers, and civil society representatives to create and disseminate shared narratives of the past that highlight similarities in experiences across societies. However, in the context of the Armenian–Turkish dialogue, IHJR creates a shared narrative by uncovering the two groups' shared cultural heritage and by highlighting historical periods when the two antagonistic groups lived peacefully side by side. The goal is to show that conflict is not inevitable and that peaceful coexistence is realistic. By contrast, the Citizens Archive of Pakistan emphasizes the shared struggles of individual members of each group during conflict. Although different projects use different approaches to achieve commonality and shared narratives, they have the same underlying objective of reducing negative attitudes and creating space for a common shared vision for the future.

Because of the important role of narratives in identity construction, creating a common narrative might be an effective strategy to improve intergroup relations: A shared historical narrative can be the basis for establishing a common or superordinate in-group identity. A common in-group identity, in turn, should give rise to positive intergroup attitudes as former out-group members are considered in-group members at the superordinate level (Gaertner and Dovidio 2000). One important constraint is that a shared narrative might be hard to negotiate in conflict contexts in which groups hold opposing and competing narratives. However, building commonality based on similar experiences and struggles of individual group members across conflict lines might be easier to achieve. Yet a focus on commonality might be altogether problematic in contexts of asymmetric conflict, if commonality is used by the dominant group as a tool to silence or undermine the experiences of the minority group members. For instance, research (Bilali 2013; Bilali, Tropp, and Dasgupta 2012) in the context of the Armenian genocide shows that the Turkish narrative of that period highlights both groups' suffering and victimization. In this context, a narrative highlighting similarities might serve to equalize the victimization experiences of the two groups, undermine the victim group's experience, and absolve the in-group of its responsibility for the violence.

Healing and Overcoming Trauma

Violence and conflict have an immense impact on all segments of society: victims, survivors, and bystanders (Staub, Pearlman, and Bilali 2010). Traumas from past violence are thought to contribute to perpetuating cycles of violence. For instance, Staub et al. (2010) argue that past violence makes people feel vulnerable and see the world as dangerous, thereby making it more likely for people to engage in defensive violence. In consequence, healing from trauma is thought to facilitate reconciliation. Confronting, acknowledging, and sharing the traumatic experiences under empathetic and supportive conditions can contribute to recovery. Several civil society organizations that we have surveyed have an explicit goal of contributing to the healing process as a way of achieving peace and reconciliation. Most projects in this domain address the historical traumas by exploring and acknowledging the emotional and spiritual wounds due to conflict and seek to address and transform the negative emotions that remain from the past and that might impede reconciliation. For instance, the Remembering Quilt project in Northern Ireland provides therapeutic support for the bereaved and injured of the conflict within a safe environment. The community comes together for remembrance through a creative activity: They create quilt blocks memorializing an experience to share with others and build empathy surrounding it. The Healing the Wounds of History project in the USA uses drama and expressive arts to help participants from different conflicts to heal historical traumas by dealing with grief and transforming their emotions from the conflict.

The degree to which these activities contribute to recovery from trauma and whether healing at an individual level contributes to reconciliation at a societal level are important questions that, to our knowledge, have not yet been explored empirically. The idea that healing is important for reconciliation underlies much of the practice in postconflict contexts. For instance, various truth-and-reconciliation commissions were expected to contribute to healing. However, empirical evidence has questioned this assumption. For instance, in Rwanda, Brouneus (2010) found that witnesses participating in Gacaca tribunals, the Rwandan local truth-and-reconciliation tribunals, reported higher levels of depression and PTSD than those who did not witness the tribunals. Government-sanctioned truth commissions have several limitations and constraints and often do not create the safe environments for sharing traumatic experiences that are necessary for healing. Therefore, it is important to examine whether civil society projects that engage participants in creative activities in safe environments have a positive effect on healing from trauma and whether, in turn, these activities influence attitudes toward reconciliation.

CONCLUSION

History in conflict contexts is a double-edged sword. History is often instrumentalized to perpetuate conflict. Therefore, delving into the past can be dangerous, as it has the potential to fuel negative emotions and actions that might be destructive for intergroup relation. At the same time, ignoring the past is also dangerous, because the legacies of the past tend to linger in the present. Therefore, finding the truth and coming to grips with the past are considered necessary for reconciliation. For instance, the UN document (2004) on the Rule of Law and Transitional Justice in Conflict and Post-Conflict Societies proposes that finding the truth about the past may promote reconciliation. Despite the proliferation of the practice in this domain (i.e., programs and interventions that aim to address the past), we know little about the approaches used, their effectiveness, and the assumptions made about how confronting the past contributes to reconciliation. The review presented in this chapter sheds light on the strategies and assumptions underlying the practice of confronting history to achieve peace and reconciliation. We identified five theories of practice and drew links to theory and research in social psychology. Although we considered each mechanism separately, they are not exclusionary and do not contradict one another. Practitioners use an amalgam of tools and emphasize multiple strategies in order to maximize their impact for social change. Indeed, most of the projects and organizations that we have reviewed, including those that we have mentioned in this chapter, conduct activities that tap into multiple mechanisms simultaneously. For instance, the organization Facing History and Ourselves combines a series of tools to teach history by infusing history with teaching about stereotypes, biases, and democratic values. This method increases knowledge and understanding of past violence, counteracting misinformation, ignorance, stereotyping, and prejudice. At the same time, it adopts multiperspectivity as a pedagogical tool to encourage critical thinking and offers students a variety of voices, perspectives, and conflicting points of view. It also links the study of violence in the past with the study of human behavior and with knowledge about identity formation and understanding of attitudes and beliefs, democracy, race, and nationalism. Studies assessing the impact of Facing History and Ourselves classrooms have shown positive effects on moral development, intergroup attitudes, and critical thinking skills (e.g., Schultz et al. 2001). However, because multiple tools are used simultaneously, it is not possible to draw conclusions about which strategies, or which combination of strategies, are most or least effective, limiting our understanding of the processes of narrative transformation.

Overall, by linking practice with research and theory, scholars can gain insight into the potential mechanisms of change that might work in the real world, whereas practitioners can assess their theories and improve their programs based on evidence. The present review raised multiple questions and hypotheses that are important to examine empirically. Social psychology can be usefully employed toward this goal, as it is equipped to understand the interaction between social representations and people's attitudes and beliefs. Therefore, it can examine how different approaches affect change in beliefs and attitudes toward peace and reconciliation.

References

Adwan, S., & Bar-On, D. (2004). Shared history project: A PRIME example of peace building under fire. *International Journal of Politics, Culture, and Society, 17,* 513–522. doi:10.1023/B:IJPS.0000019616.78447.5e.

Bar-On, D., & Adwan, S. (2006). The PRIME shared history project. Peacebuilding project under fire. In Y. Iraam (Ed.). *Educating toward a culture of peace* (pp. 309–323). Information Age Publishing.

Bar-Tal, D. (2000). *Shared beliefs in a society: Social psychological analysis.* Thousands Oaks, CA: Sage Publications.

Barton, K. C., & McCully, A. (2012). Trying to "see things differently": Northern Ireland students' struggle to understand alternative historical perspectives. *Theory & Research in Social Education, 40,* 371–408.

Batson, C., Chang, J., Orr, R., & Rowland, J. (2002). Empathy, attitudes, and action: Can feeling for a member of a stigmatized group motivate one to help the group? *Personality and Social Psychology Bulletin, 28,* 1656–1666. doi:10.1177/014616702237647.

Berlin, I. (1979). Nationalism: Past neglect and present power. *Partisan Review, 46,* 344–361.

Bilali, R. (2013). National narrative and social psychological influences in Turks' denial of the mass killings of Armenians as genocide. *Journal of Social Issues, 69,* 16–33.

Bilali, R., & Staub, E. (2016). Interventions in real world settings. Using media to overcome prejudice and promote intergroup reconciliation in Central Africa. In C. Sibley, & F. Barlow (Eds.), *Cambridge handbook of the psychology of prejudice* (pp. 607–631). Cambridge University Press.

Bilali, R., & Vollhardt, J. R. (2013). Priming effects of a reconciliation radio drama on historical perspective-taking in the aftermath of mass violence in Rwanda. *Journal of Experimental Social Psychology,* 49, 144–151.

Bilali, R., & Vollhardt, J. R. (2015). Do mass media interventions effectively promote peace in contexts of ongoing violence? Evidence from Eastern Democratic Republic of Congo. *Peace & Conflict: Journal of Peace Psychology,* 21, 604–620.

Bilali, R., Tropp, L. R., & Dasgupta, N. (2012). Attributions of responsibility and perceived harm in the aftermath of mass violence. *Peace & Conflict: Journal of Peace Psychology,* 18, 21–39.

Brouneus, K. (2010). The trauma of truth telling: Effects of witnessing in the Rwandan Gacaca courts on psychological health. *Journal of Conflict Resolution,* 54, 408–437.

Bruneau, E. G., & Saxe, R. (2012). The power of being heard: The benefits of 'perspective-giving' in the context of intergroup conflict. *Journal of Experimental Social Psychology,* 48, 855–866. doi:10.1016/j.jesp.2012.02.017.

Gaertner, S., L., & Dovidio, J., F. (2000). *Reducing intergroup bias: The common ingroup identity model.* Philadelphia, PA: Psychology Press.

Galinsky, A. D., & Moskowitz, G. B. (2000). Perspective-taking: Decreasing stereotype expression, stereotype accessibility, and in-group favoritism. *Journal of Personality and Social Psychology,* 78, 708–724. doi:10.1037/0022-3514.78.4.708.

Galinsky, A. D., & Ku, G. (2004). The effects of perspective-taking on prejudice: The moderating role of self-evaluation. *Personality and Social Psychology Bulletin,* 30, 594–604. doi:10.1177/0146167203262802.

Goldberg, T., & Ron, Y. (2014). 'Look, Each Side Says Something Different': The impact of competing history teaching approaches on Jewish and Arab adolescents' discussions of the Jewish–Arab conflict. *Journal of Peace Education,* 11, 1–29. doi: 10.1080/17400201.2013.777897.

Hayner, P. (2000). Past truths, present dangers. The role of official truth seeking in conflict resolution and prevention. In P. C. Stern & D. Druckman (Eds.). *International conflict resolution after cold war* (pp. 338–387). Washington, D.C.: National Academies Press.

Hirshberg, M. (1993). The self-perpetuating national self-image: Cognitive biases in perceptions of international interventions. *Political Psychology,* 14, 77–93.

Kanyangara, P., Rime, B., Philippot, P., & Yzerbyt, V. (2007). Collective rituals, emotional climate, and intergroup perception: Participation in "Gacaca" tribunals and assimilation of the Rwandan genocide. *Journal of Social Issues,* 2, 387–403.

Kriesberg, L. (2004). Comparing reconciliation actions within and between countries. In Y. Bar-Siman-Tov (Ed.), *From conflict resolution to reconciliation* (pp. 81–110). New York: Oxford University Press.

Nadler, A., & Saguy, T. (2004). Reconciliation between nations: Overcoming emotional deterrents to ending conflicts between groups. In H. J. Langholtz & C. E. Westport (Eds.), *The psychology of diplomacy* (pp. 29–46). Westport, CT: Praeger Publishers/Greenwood Publishing Group.

Noor, M., Brown, R., & Prentice, G. (2008a). Precursors and mediators of intergroup reconciliation in Northern Ireland: a new model. *British Journal of Social Psychology, 47,* 481–495.

Noor, M., Brown, R., Gonzalez, R., Manzi, J., & Lewis, C. A. (2008b). On positive psychological outcomes: What helps groups with a history of conflict to forgive and reconcile with each other? *Personality and Social Psychology Bulletin, 34,* 819–832. doi:10.1177/0146167208315555.

Paluck, E. L. (2009). Reducing intergroup prejudice and conflict using the media: A field experiment in Rwanda. *Journal of Personality and Social Psychology, 96,* 574–587. doi:10.1037/a0011989.

Paluck, E. L. (2010). Is it better not to talk? Group polarization, extended contact, and perspective-taking in eastern Democratic Republic of Congo. *Personality and Social Psychology Bulletin, 36,* 1170–1185. doi:10.1177/0146167210379868.

Paulson, J. (2015). "Whether and how?" History education about recent and ongoing conflict. A review of research. *Journal on Education in Emergencies, 1,* 14–47.

Pettigrew, T. F., & Tropp, L. R. (2008). How does intergroup contact reduce prejudice? Meta-analytic tests of three mediators. *European Journal of Social Psychology, 38,* 922–934.

Pettigrew, T. F., & Tropp, L. (2011). *When groups meet: The dynamics of intergroup contact.* New York: Psychology Press.

Porat, D. A. (2004). It's not written here, but this is what happened: Students' cultural comprehension of textbook narratives on the Arab-Israeli conflict. *American Educational Research Journal, 41,* 963–996.

Psaltis, C., Lytras, E., & Costache, S. (2011). *History educators in the Greek Cypriot and Turkish Cypriot community of Cyprus: Perceptions, beliefs, and practices.* United Nations Development Programme—Action for Cooperation and Trust.

Ramanathapillai, R. (2006). The politicizing of trauma: A case study of Sri Lanka. *Peace and Conflict: Journal of Peace Psychology, 12,* 1–18.

Rime, B., Kanyangara, P., Yzerbyt, V., & Paez, D. (2011). The impact of Gacaca tribunals in Rwanda: Psychosocial effects of participation in a truth and reconciliation process after a genocide. *European Journal of Social Psychology, 41,* 695–705. doi:10.1002/ejsp.822.

Ross, M. H. (2000). Creating the conditions for peacemaking: Theories of practice in ethnic conflict resolution. *Ethnic and Racial Studies, 23,* 1002–1034.

Schultz, L. H., Barr, D. J., & Selman, R. L. (2001). The value of a developmental approach to evaluating character development programmes: An outcome study of facing history and ourselves. *Journal of Moral Education, 30,* 3–27.

Staub, E. (2011). *Overcoming evil: Genocide, violent conflict and terrorism.* New York: Oxford University Press.

Staub, E., & Bar-Tal, D. (2003). Genocide, mass killing and intractable conflict: Roots, evolution, prevention and reconciliation. In D. Sears, L. Huddy, & R. Jarvis (Eds.), *Handbook of political psychology.* New York: Oxford University Press.

Staub, E., Pearlman, L., & Bilali, R. (2010). Understanding the roots and impact of violence and psychological recovery as avenues to reconciliation after mass violence and intractable conflict. In G. Salomon, & E. Cairns (Eds.). *Handbook on peace education* (pp. 269–286). Psychology Press.

Stradling, R. (2003). *Multiperspectivity in history teaching: A guide for teachers.* Germany: Council of Europe.

United Nations. (2004). *The rule of law and transitional justice in conflict and post-conflict societies* (Report of the secretary general, S/2004/616). New York: United Nations.

Authors' Biography

Rezarta Bilali is Assistant Professor of Applied Psychology at New York University. She received her Ph.D. in Social Psychology with a concentration in peace and violence from the University of Massachusetts at Amherst. In one line of research, Dr. Bilali seeks to understand the psychological underpinnings of destructive conflict narratives, in order to shed light on strategies to reduce intergroup conflicts. In another line of research, she merges theory and practice by working with non-governmental organizations to develop and rigorously evaluate violence prevention and reconciliation media programmes in conflict-affected settings.

Rima Mahmoud is a second-year law student at Boston University School of Law. A Palestinian-American, she grew up in Jordan before immigrating to the USA during high school. She completed her bachelor's degree in Political Science and International Relations at the University of Massachusetts Boston, where she also earned her master's degree in Conflict Resolution, focusing her thesis on the Palestinian—Israeli conflict. Since then, she has served on the board of American Friends of Wahat Al-Salam/Neve Shalom. She also works at Ropes & Gray LLP as a Senior Intake & Compliance Specialist and serves as a Staff Member on the Student Board of Editors (2016–2017) of the *American Journal of Law & Medicine*.

Open Access This chapter is licensed under the terms of the Creative Commons Attribution 4.0 International License (http://creativecommons.org/licenses/by/4.0/), which permits use, sharing, adaptation, distribution and reproduction in any medium or format, as long as you give appropriate credit to the original author(s) and the source, provide a link to the Creative Commons license and indicate if changes were made.

The images or other third party material in this chapter are included in the chapter's Creative Commons license, unless indicated otherwise in a credit line to the material. If material is not included in the chapter's Creative Commons license and your intended use is not permitted by statutory regulation or exceeds the permitted use, you will need to obtain permission directly from the copyright holder.

Social Representations of the Past in Post-conflict Societies: Adherence to Official Historical Narratives and Distrust Through Heightened Threats

Charis Psaltis, Renata Franc, Anouk Smeekes, Maria Ioannou and Iris Žeželj

---

The authors would like to acknowledge the contribution of COST IS 1205 in making the meetings for conceptualizing the paper and the writing up possible.

C. Psaltis (✉)
Social and Developmental Psychology, The University of Cyprus, Nicosia, Cyprus
e-mail: cpsaltis@ucy.ac.cy

R. Franc
Ivo Pilar Institute of Social Sciences, Zagreb 10 000, Croatia

A. Smeekes
ERCOMER, Utrecht University, Utrecht, The Netherlands

M. Ioannou
University College Groningen, University of Groningen, Groningen, The Netherlands

I. Žeželj
Social Psychology, The University of Belgrade, Belgrade, Serbia

© The Author(s) 2017
C. Psaltis et al. (eds.), *History Education and Conflict Transformation*, DOI 10.1007/978-3-319-54681-0_4

Introduction

It is by now well recognized that one of the major obstacles in the cultivation of historical thinking (Seixas 2004) in the formal educational system of post-conflict societies is the collective memory and narratives of the conflict itself (Carretero 2011; Ferro 1984; Makriyianni and Psaltis 2007; McCully 2012; Carretero and Van Alpen 2014; Psaltis et al. 2017).[1] This is because many of the actors involved in the educational process, teachers, students, parents and policy makers often share social representations of the past, and the conflict in particular, that closely align with the official master narratives characteristic for their conflict ethos, monoperspectival, selective view of history and naïve epistemology (Bar-Tal and Salomon 2006; Psaltis 2016).

In this chapter, we argue based on empirical evidence from three post-conflict settings (Cyprus, Serbia and Croatia) that such representations of the past and their uncritical internalization that leads to adherence to master narratives of conflict construct a threatened self and generate distrust towards the outgroup. A threatened self and intergroup distrust are in our opinion obstacles to conflict transformation (Galtung 2000) and to a peaceful settlement of intergroup conflicts.

Representations Based on Belief vs Representations Based on Knowledge

The main tension in post-conflict societies around history teaching is well captured by the classic distinction by David Lowenthal (1985a, b) between *Heritage* vs *History* or by Wertsch (2007) as *collective memory* vs *history*, or Seixas (2004) as *collective memory* vs *disciplinary approach* to teaching history. This is not a claim of course that academic history is in any way objective and that collective memory is necessarily false. What we are claiming, however, is that there are two basic orientations that capture two distinct epistemological orientations. History teaching can be oriented towards the one or the other orientation depending on curriculum aims (Perikleous 2010), textbook content and structure and the ideological orientations and training of the educators (Psaltis et al. 2011; Makriyanni et al. 2011). The consequences of taking the one or the other orientation for the representations of the past formed in the classroom will be important, not only for communication in the classroom (Goldberg 2013, this volume; Goldberg et al. 2011), the cognitive and moral development of the students (Makriyianni and Psaltis 2007) and their historical consciousness (Rüsen 2004), but also for conflict transformation in the wider societal context. In the field of social psychology, Moscovici (1998) makes an important distinction between *social representations based on belief* and *social representations based on knowledge* (Psaltis 2016) which captures the epistemological intention that we are implying here. The distinction is premised on the idea that characteristics of beliefs are homogeneous, affective and impermeable to experience or contradiction that leave little scope for individual variation. They are thus similar to the "dogma" characteristics that Lowenthal attributes to approaching the past as an essentialist *heritage*. By contrast, social representations founded on knowledge are similar to Lowenthal's approach to the past as *history* since they are more fluid, pragmatic and amenable to the proof of success or failure and leave certain latitude to language, experience and even to the critical features of individuals.

The Social Psychological Contribution

The social developmental and social psychological literature stands in a privileged position to render intelligible the reasons behind the resiliency of representations of the past based on beliefs, but at the same time it can critically evaluate the consequences of this approach for intergroup relations in their local context. According to Hammack (2010), the tensions around "history wars" is one between theories that present development and the construction of identity in the youth as a *benefit* and theories that present the development and the construction of identity in the youth as a *burden*. Identity can be viewed as a burden to the extent that young people come to uncritically appropriate, reproduce and reify the narrative basis of conflict. The view of identity as a *burden* that characterizes the narrative identity development of youth is derived from a critical account of the hegemonic nature of identity as a *received* social taxonomy. Such internalization of a reified and polarized narrative of collective identity would curtail the agency the young people might otherwise possess to make meaning of the social world. In this approach, the nonsense of conflict gains meaning by situating oneself in a community whose collective trauma is anchored in a common narrative (Bekerman and Zembylas 2011) as well as a feeling of perceived collective victimization (Bar-Tal et al. 2009).

On the contrary, the set of theories that view identity as a *benefit* stress the liberating potential of identities in the context of a collective struggle for recognition of a weak and marginalized group that is forced to face a dominant, more powerful and suppressive group. This position is largely drawing on writings on national liberation, civil rights movement and collective action. From this position, "national liberation struggles have and continue to embrace the strategic use of reified identities to mobilize and motivate individuals for collective action against an oppressive configuration of intergroup relations" (Hammack 2010). The assumption here is that the internalization of national master narratives of collective victimization can become a valuable symbolic resource (Zittoun et al. 2003) for the construction of a patriotic, proud, self and a society that is homogeneous and socially cohesive. The use of a symbolic resource can both enable and constrain certain actions, and in the case of master narratives, it is worth exploring how their structure and content canalizes the past, present and future of the person.

According to Carretero et al. (2012), master narratives have six common features: (a) exclusion–inclusion as a logical operation contributing to establish the historical subject; (b) identification processes that function as both cognitive and affective anchors; (c) frequent presence of mythical and heroic characters and motives; (d) search for freedom or territory as a main and common narrative theme; (e) inclusion of a moral orientation; and (f) A romantic and essentialist concept of both the nation and the nationals. Van Alpen and Carretero (2015) showed that such master narratives create a very problematic interpretation of the relation between past and present which often takes three forms: (a) collapsing past and present; (b) the past is idealized in a way that the present is a decadent version of the past; and (c) relating the past to a teleological end. All three forms of thinking were found to hinder the historical thinking of 16-year-old high school students in Argentina.

The narratives of conflict also sustain a temporal sense of continuity (Smeekes et al. 2017), and this sense of continuity is closely related to self-identification processes. Groups generally tend to have an understanding of their ethnic and national identities as entities that possess a past, present and future (Sani et al. 2008). During the last few years, social psychological researchers started to examine the importance of a sense of continuity between the past, present and future for collective identities. A series of studies by Sani et al. (2008) revealed that the perception that one's group has temporal endurance over time (i.e.

perceived collective continuity) is associated with stronger attachment to one's ingroup and it bolsters social connectedness with the ingroup. Importantly, however, recent studies found that ingroup members tend to oppose social developments and outgroups that undermine group continuity (Jetten and Hutchison 2011; Jetten and Wohl 2012).

Moreover, an emerging body of research started to address the underlying psychological mechanisms that drive these relationships by examining the role of feelings of collective self-continuity (for an overview, see Smeekes and Verkuyten 2015). Self-continuity refers to having a sense of connection between one's past, present and future self. Following the social identity perspective (Turner and Reynolds 2001), people should be able to derive a sense of self-continuity from their memberships in social groups. Thus, collective self-continuity refers to the feeling that the part of the self that is derived from group membership has temporal endurance.

There are various groups that can provide people with a sense of self-continuity, but this is particularly likely for national groups. The reason is that nations are mainly defined and understood as communities that live together through time (e.g. Anderson 1983; Bhaba 1990), and are often perceived as having a shared culture and identity that is passed on from generation to generation (Bar-Tal and Teichman 2005). This identity, according to Anderson, is imagined, but people perceive it as real. From this point of view, continuity is also imagined but perceived as real. In intergroup conflicts, both groups may develop historical narratives that help them to maintain a sense of collective self-continuity. Previous studies indicate that individuals tend to identify with groups that they see as temporally enduring, because this satisfies their need for self-continuity (e.g. Smeekes and Verkuyten 2013, 2014a, b). This is particularly the case when these groups are seen to possess essentialist continuity, which refers to the perception that core features of the group's culture and identity are stable and continuous even for centuries.

Continuity is not the only way in which group members draw on time to understand their group identity. Lowenthal (1985a, b) proposes that the collective past is used to validate national identity in the present in two ways: by *preservation* and by *restoration*. Preservation connects to the concept of collective continuity as discussed within social psychological work (e.g. Sani et al. 2008) and refers to the notion that people find comfort in the belief that their social identities have temporal endurance and are therefore likely to believe that "we" are (and should be) the way we have always been. This means that most people want to preserve their collective ways of life, symbols and practices in order to maintain a sense of collective continuity. In times of social change and transition, groups may get the feeling that they are losing their connection to "who we were" in the past, and this is likely to result in attempts to restore a sense of collective continuity. Attempting to restore a national culture and identity that is perceived to be lost or undermined is another way in which the past validates the present. That is, people often refer back to the way things were done in the past, such as customs and traditions, in order to legitimize how things should be done in the present. Lowenthal (1985a, b) suggests that preservation and restoration often exist simultaneously. People are likely to preserve their group identity by affirming its continuity over time, and this is alternated with attempts to restore traditions and ways of life that are seen to be undermined by foreign flavours. One manifestation of this alternation between preservation and restoration is feelings of *national nostalgia*. National nostalgia is understood as a sentimental longing for the good old days of the country. It is a group-based emotion that can be experienced on the basis of one's social identity. Scholars have proposed that national nostalgia emerges in times of social change and transition, because it has a restorative function (Boym 2001; Lowenthal 1985a, b). The reason is that in longing for those good old days of the national past, group members become more aware of the importance of their original national culture and traditions as a basis for preserving their national identity. In other words, national nostalgia can help group members to restore a sense of collective continuity. At the same time, national nostalgia is often an expression of the mourning and regret over these changes that have taken place (Duyvendak 2011). A fond remembrance of the national past can serve as a painful reminder of the good things that are lost, and this is likely to result in attempts to restore "the way we were". Recent work has shown that national nostalgia is related to feelings of threat to the continuity of group identity (Smeekes and Verkuyten 2015) and results in negative attitudes towards immigrant outgroups (e.g. Smeekes et al. 2015).

The focus on group history observed in public discourses over intergroup conflict in various European countries explicitly frames the collective past as the rooted basis for group identity. However, within these discourses there are different representations of what this collective past looks like. This means that people are both capable of understanding their group identity as a temporal entity, and to attribute *content* to its temporality. This latter aspect is relevant for the study of intergroup relations, because depending on the particular historical narratives that are endorsed, people may position themselves favourably or unfavourably towards the presence of others. These historical narratives are socially shared as they are expressed in public and political discourses (Ashmore et al. 2004; Psaltis 2012, 2016). In these discourses, the collective past is often reconstructed and used flexibly to fit the interests of the present (Lowenthal 1985a, b). That is, strategic representations of group history are often employed in politics to justify present arrangements (Reicher and Hopkins 2001).

The historical perspective to group dynamics has been integrated to social psychological research. There is, for instance, a considerable body of research on how representations of historical wrongdoings of ingroups, such as slavery, colonialism and genocide, impact current intergroup relations via group-based emotions (Branscombe and Doosje 2004; Doosje et al. 1998). Group-based emotions refer to the emotions that people can feel on account of their ingroup's behaviour towards others, such as guilt or shame, even when not personally involved in this intergroup conflict. Most studies within this line of research have examined whether experiencing group-based emotions for historical wrongdoings impacts attitudes towards the harmed outgroup. Several studies show that feelings of group-based guilt for past ingroup atrocities are related to reparation and compensation intentions towards the harmed outgroup in the present (e.g. Brown and Cehajic 2008). A related body of research has examined how group members, despite not being directly harmed, regard themselves as victims of past group conflict (i.e. collective victimhood), and how this impacts intergroup relations (Bar-Tal et al. 2009). Furthermore, studies by Liu and colleagues (e.g. Liu and Hilton 2005; Liu and László 2007; Sibley et al. 2008) examined how representations of national history guide current sociopolitical attitudes, such as support for military action, and legitimation of social inequality (Sibley et al. 2008). Importantly, these social representations also hinder the development and attainment of some central historical thinking skills (Seixas 2004) like historical significance, change and continuity, cause and effect and historical empathy (Páez et al. 2017, pp. 491–510; Psaltis et al. 2017).

We argue that something that is missing from the above line of research is the study of historical narratives of intergroup conflict in relation to a basic ingredient of reconciliation which is trust given that trust is not only a prerequisite for reaching a political settlement, an organizing principle of identity positions in the representational field of conflict, but also an essential element of the viability of any peace settlement (Psaltis 2012a).

The Present Study

Our aim in this study was to further our understanding of the way adherence to master narratives of conflict relates to feelings of intergroup threat and distrust. We put into test the hypothesis that adherence to master narratives is associated with intergroup distrust and feelings of threat. We more specifically propose that the positive relationship between (greater) adherence to ingroup's master narratives and (greater) outgroup distrust is mediated by (increased) feelings of threat.

We test this hypothesis in three post-conflict contexts (Cyprus, Serbia and Croatia), all of which are characterized by violent conflicts between ethnic groups. As is explained next, the adversarial ethnic groups in each of these settings have developed their own accounts of the history of their conflict thus resulting in differing and opposing historical narratives. Despite this major similarity, Cyprus, Serbia and Croatia remain to be three qualitatively distinct contexts. Of interest to us was to assess whether the proposed course of relationships between adherence to the ingroup's master narrative and intergroup distrust via feelings of threat could be validated in all three contexts.

The studied "ingroup" in Cyprus was Greek Cypriots, in Serbia it was Serbs and in Croatia it was Croats. The respective outgroups were Turkish Cypriots in Cyprus, Kosovar Albanians in Serbia and Serbs in Croatia. A brief description of the three contexts follows.

Cyprus: The conflict in Cyprus originates in the 1950s when Cyprus was a British colony. Greek Cypriots (82% of the population) sought for political union with Greece, which elicited the reaction of the Turkish Cypriot minority (18%) who embarked on a struggle for the partition of Cyprus between Greece and Turkey. In 1960, Cyprus gained its independence and a power sharing partnership between Greek Cypriots and Turkish Cypriots was established along with the Republic of Cyprus. A coup against the Greek Cypriot president in 1974 engineered by the Greek military junta prompted a military intervention by Turkey that led to the division of the island into two ethnically homogeneous areas.

According to Papadakis (2008), the central nationalistic historical narrative in the Greek Cypriot community (henceforth GC) as represented in history textbooks is one that begins with the arrival of Greeks (14th century BC) in Cyprus that leads to its Hellenization. The moral centre is Greeks (of Cyprus), and the major enemy is Turks. The plot concerns a struggle for survival of the Cypriot Hellenism against foreign conquerors. The "tragic end" of this struggle is the "Barbaric Turkish Invasion" in 1974 and occupation of 37% of the island's territory since then.

The corresponding Turkish Cypriot (henceforth TC) narrative is one that begins with the arrival of Turks in Cyprus (in 1571 AD), the moral self is Turks (of Cyprus) and the major enemy are Rums (Greek Cypriots). The plot concerns a struggle for survival by the Turks of Cyprus against Greek Cypriot domination. The military intervention of 1974 marks a happy ending of their struggle for survival. For this reason, it is regarded as the "Happy peace operation" by Turkey in Cyprus which saved Turkish Cypriots from a pending union of Cyprus with Greece.

Serbia: Kosovo is a territory located between Albania, Montenegro, Macedonia and Serbia. The region is burdened by history of long-term ethnic tensions between Albanian and Serb population. Following the violent breakdown of former Yugoslavia during the 1990s, an armed conflict erupted in Kosovo in 1998. Between 1998 and 1999, more than 10,000 people were killed and about 3000 were abducted, whilst approximately 800,000 people fled to neighbouring countries (O'Neill 2002). The conflict ended by NATO intervention, after which a UN protectorate secured by international peacekeeping force was established. Kosovo unilaterally declared its independence in 2008, and its status is still disputed by Serbia. Kosovo and Serbian officials are currently engaged in EU-facilitated dialogue aimed at normalizing their relations.

Kosovar Albanians and Serbs have very different narratives explaining the origin and course of the conflict: Kosovar Albanians consider Kosovo's independence reflecting their large majority status, whilst Serbs view the territory as historically belonging to Serbia. Above a territorial claim, Kosovo is a vital national idea for each group (Bieber 2002).

Croatia: Within the context of collapse of communism in Eastern Europe, significant political and historical changes occurred in the Socialist Federal Republic of Yugoslavia. The political leaderships of Slovenia and Croatia (two out of six Yugoslav republics) elected on the first multi-party elections proposed a new confederal agreement (October 1990) to other Yugoslav republics, proposing each republic's right to free self-determination. After the Yugoslav state presidency rejected this proposal, in Croatia a referendum for independence was held in May 1991, whereas 93% of voters (with 83.6% turnout) voted for independence from Yugoslavia (Jović 2007). However, the ethnic Serbs in parts of Croatia with ethnic Serb majorities boycotted this referendum wanted Croatia to remain a part of Yugoslavia. Croatian independence from Yugoslavia was declared in June 1991, followed by international recognition in January 1992.

The tensions with Serbs minority who opposed Croatian independence escalated in August 1991, and grew into 1991–1995 war between Croatian forces and the Croatian Serbs rebel forces with the help of the JNA and Serbia (UN-ICTY). Around 54% of Croatian territory inhabited by 36% of the Croatian population was directly affected by war, and around 26% of Croatian territory was occupied for several years (Perković and Puljiz 2001). Direct demographic losses counted 22,192 people; out of them, 36.7% were members of Croatian military forces, 29.8% civilians, 5.5% missing Croatian forces and civilians and 28% missing and killed members of the army of the so-called Republic of Serbian Krajina and Serbian civilians from the same territory (Živić and Pokos 2004).

Dominant narratives about the war 1991–1995 between the two sides are still very different. According to dominant Croatian historical narrative, the 1991–1995 war in Croatia or Homeland war is legitimate international war by which Croatia established its independence and defended itself from Serbian and Slobodan Milošević's aggression and aspirations for so-called Great Serbia (Banjeglav 2013). Such narrative is promoted also by Declaration about Homeland war adopted by Croatian parliament in 2000 (Narodne novine 2000). On the other side, according to dominant Serbs narrative the 1991–1995 war is primarily internal conflict or civil war with emphasis on Serb's suffering (Mirkovic 2000, p. 364; Subotić 2013).

METHODS

Participants

Our sample consisted of a total of 478 university students, studying in the capital cities of the three countries under study: Cyprus, Nicosia ($N = 145$); Serbia, Belgrade ($N = 173$); and Croatia, Zagreb ($N = 160$).[1] The mean age of the total sample was 21.2 ($SD = 2.47$), and this was comparable across countries, Cyprus: $M = 21.2$ ($SD = 2.82$), Serbia: $M = 21.3$ ($SD = 2.32$) and Croatia: $M = 21.25$ ($SD = 2.34$). Of the participants who indicated their gender (9% was missing), the vast majority were females (82%), and males made up 18%. The gender distribution was similar across countries, Cyprus: 77% females, Serbia: 81% females and Croatia: 87% females.

Procedure

Participants were recruited from university classes using opportunity sampling. The participation was voluntary and anonymous. Upon agreeing to take part, participants were asked to fill in the questionnaire either electronically or via paper and pencil as truthfully as they could. The master questionnaire was developed in English, and it was translated into the mother tongue of the participants in each country by two independent native speakers. Local research coordinators compared the two versions against one another and corrected minor discrepancies. As this study was part of a larger cross-cultural survey, we are only reporting the variables relevant to the purposes of this paper.

Measures

Adherence to ingroup's historical narratives was measured by a three-item scale in Serbia and Croatia, and a two-item scale in Cyprus. The items comprising the scale were designed to convey the ingroup's mainstream narrative of the conflict (as it can be found in textbooks and mainstream media) which is typically placing the blame for the eruption or/and the continuation of the conflict on the outgroup(s). The items differed (in content) by country. Examples of items for each country are the following: Cyprus: (1) "In 1974 Turkey invaded Cyprus with the aim of partitioning the country" and (2) "The declaration of the 'Turkish

Republic of Northern Cyprus' prevents the solution of the Cyprus problem"; Serbia: (1) "the Kosovo conflict erupted primarily because Kosovo Albanians wished for Greater Albania" and (2) "Throughout their history, Serbs have been repeatedly forcefully displaced from Kosovo"; and Croatia: (1) "The war in Croatia was entirely a consequence of Serbian aggressive politics" and (2) "War in Croatia happened because the Serbs refused to accept the creation of Croatia as an independent state". Participants assessed their agreement with each statement on a 7-point Likert scale ranging from 1 = strongly disagree to 7 = strongly agree. Cronbach's *alpha* for this scale was 0.76 in Serbia and 0.80 in Croatia, whereas the correlation coefficient in Cyprus where this construct was measured by two items was 0.33, $p < 0.001$.

Realistic threat was measured by four items which participants had to assess by declaring their agreement or disagreement on a 7-point scale (e.g. in Cyprus: (1) The more power Turkish Cypriots gain in Cyprus, the more difficult it will become for Greek Cypriots; (2) I am afraid that allowing Turkish Cypriots to decide on political issues would mean that Greek Cypriots will have less to say in how this country is run). Cronbach's alpha for this scale was 0.86 (Cyprus: 0.88, Serbia: 0.86, Croatia: 0.77).

Symbolic threat was measured by a four-item scale. Participants had to declare their agreement or disagreement with each of the four statements on a 7-point scale (e.g. in Serbia: (1) Some of the customs and traditions of Albanians undermine the traditional way of life of Serbs; (2) Albanians are beginning to project their identity in a way that I find threatening). The Cronbach's alpha for this scale was 0.78 (Cyprus: 0.73, Serbia: 0.80, Croatia: 0.80).

Group-esteem threat was measured by four items (e.g. Croatia: (1) Serbs have little respect for Croatians; (2) Serbs think positively about Croatians (reverse-coded)). Cronbach's alpha was 0.86 (Cyprus, 0.92; Serbia: 0.85, Croatia: 0.82).

Outgroup trust was measured via three items to which participants had to respond on a 4-point scale. The three items were the following (e.g. Cyprus): (1) Do you think most Turkish Cypriots would try to take advantage of you if they got a chance, or would they try to be fair? (1, *definitely try to take advantage*; 4, *definitely try to be fair*), (2) Would you say that most Turkish Cypriots can be trusted or that you can't be too trusting of them? (1, *definitely can't be too trusting*; 4, *definitely can be trusted*) and (3) Would you say that most of the time Turkish Cypriots try to be helpful or that mainly they are interested only in themselves?

(1, *definitely interested only in themselves*; 4, *definitely try to be helpful*). Cronbach's alpha was 0.81 for the whole sample (Cyprus: 0.87; Serbia: 0.87; Croatia: 0.75).

RESULTS

Descriptive Statistics

Tables 1, 2 and 3 show the means (M) and standard deviations (SD) for all variables, as well as the correlations between variables, in all three contexts. As can be seen in these tables, the mean levels of adherence to ingroup narratives were above the mid-point level (4.0) in all countries suggesting a tendency to overall agree with the ingroup's narrative of the conflict. The means of realistic, symbolic and group-esteem threats were above mid-point (4.0) for Serbia, close to mid-point for Cyprus and slightly below mid-point for Croatia, thus showing that the nature of the

Table 1 Means, SDs and correlations between variables, Cyprus

	1	2	3	4	5	Mean (SD)
Adherence to ingroup's historical narrative	1	0.25**	0.39**	0.16*	−0.21*	4.69 (1.19)
Group-esteem threat		1	0.64**	0.71**	−0.73**	3.84 (1.26)
Realistic threat			1	0.77**	−0.60**	4.74 (1.26)
Symbolic threat				1	−0.66**	3.55 (1.18)
Trust towards outgroup					1	2.34 (0.67)

*$p < .05$
**$p < .01$

Table 2 Means, SDs and correlations between variables, Serbia

	1	2	3	4	5	Mean (SD)
Adherence to ingroup's historical narrative	1	0.54**	0.67**	0.59**	−0.33**	4.56 (1.24)
Group-esteem threat		1	0.67**	0.66**	−0.39**	4.59 (1.13)
Realistic threat			1	0.68**	−0.31**	5.09 (1.32)
Symbolic threat				1	−0.48**	4.28 (1.32)
Trust towards outgroup					1	2.73 (0.56)

*$p < .05$
**$p < .01$

Table 3 Means, SDs and correlations between variables, Croatia

	1	2	3	4	5	Mean (SD)
Adherence to ingroup's historical narrative	1	0.54**	0.67**	0.59**	−0.33**	5.33 (1.08)
Group-esteem threat		1	0.67**	0.66**	−0.39**	3.30 (1.12)
Realistic threat			1	0.68**	−0.31**	3.44 (1.32)
Symbolic threat				1	−0.48**	2.51 (1.32)
Trust towards outgroup					1	2.10 (1.50)

*$p < .05$
**$p < .01$

conflict, or the nature of intergroup relations rather, varies somewhat in the three countries. Finally, the levels of outgroup trust were moderate in the three countries (just above 2 at a 4-point scale).

The correlations between variables were in the expected direction across contexts, and they were all significant. Adherence to ingroup narratives was found to be positively correlated with all types of threat and negatively correlated with outgroup trust. Greater adherence to ingroup narratives was associated with feeling greater levels of realistic, symbolic and group-esteem threat and being less trusting of the outgroup. Furthermore, all types of threats were found to be negatively correlated with trust: experiencing more realistic, symbolic and group-esteem threat for the outgroup was associated with lower levels of trust towards the outgroup.

We proceeded to test the hypothesized relationships between adherence to ingroup narratives, threats and trust with a path model, using AMOS. We first tested the model with the whole sample and then on each context separately. In this model, adherence to ingroup narratives was inserted as the predicting variable, outgroup trust as the outcome variable and the three types of threats as mediators. The proposed relationships between these variables were that adherence to ingroup narratives would be negatively associated with outgroup trust and that this relationship would be mediated by the three types of threat.

The results of the proposed model on the whole sample mostly supported our hypothesized relationships between variables. Adherence to ingroup narratives was found to be associated with higher realistic threat, $\beta = 0.325$, $p < 0.001$, higher symbolic threat, $\beta = 0.167$, $p < 0.01$, and higher group-esteem threat, $\beta = 0.228$, $p < 0.001$. Higher symbolic and higher group-esteem threat were related to less outgroup trust ($\beta = -0.085$, $p < 0.01$, $\beta = -0.159$, $p < 0.001$, respectively), but there was no significant association between realistic threats and trust. In order to identify the mediators accounting for the indirect effects, we then applied a bootstrapping procedure using 95% confidence intervals based on 5,000 bootstrap resamples with the use of PROCESS (Preacher and Hayes 2008). In general, adherence to ingroup narratives had a negative total indirect effect on trust, TIE = –0.055 [–0.086, –0.026]. Two of the three specific indirect effects of adherence to ingroup narrative on trust were significant. The first involved the mediation of symbolic threat, IE = −0.014 [−0.034, −0.003], and the second involved the mediation of group-esteem threat, IE = −0.035 [−0.061, −0.017]. The indirect effect of realistic threat was not significant, IE = −.004 [−0.026, 0.015].

The results for the proposed model for each of the three countries are shown in Fig. 1. As can be seen, adherence to ingroup narratives was indeed found to strongly and significantly correlate with every type of threat in all contexts. The only exception to this was a solely marginal effect between adherence to ingroup narrative and symbolic threat in Cyprus. The relationships between threat and outgroup trust were less conclusive, however. In all three contexts, group-esteem threat was found to significantly correlate with outgroup trust in the expected

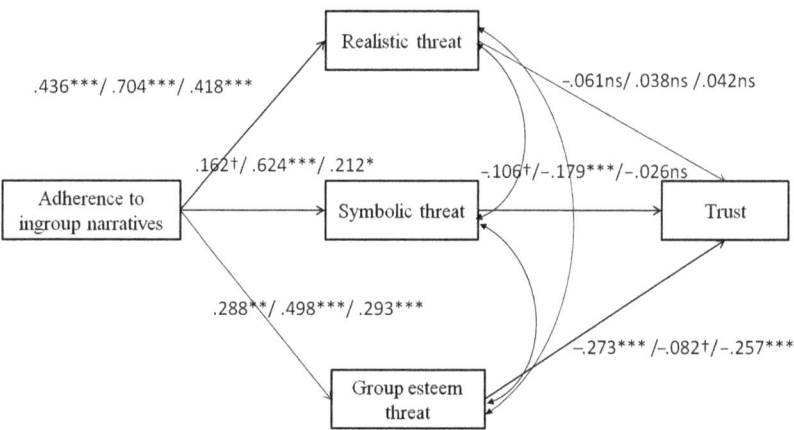

Fig. 1 Effects of adherence to ingroup narratives on outgroup trust, mediated by perceived realistic, symbolic and group-esteem threat. *Note* Standardized coefficients presented and separated by a slash (Cyprus/Serbia/Croatia); the correlation between the two mediators was accounted for. † $p < 0.01$, *$p < 0.05$, **$p < 0.01$, ***$p < 0.001$

direction: higher perceived group-esteem threat associated with lower trust. The effect was only marginal for Cyprus nevertheless. Realistic threat was not found to be significantly related to outgroup trust in any of the three countries. Symbolic threat was found to be associated with outgroup trust only for Serbia, and marginally for Cyprus.

In particular, for Serbia adherence to ingroup narratives had a negative total indirect effect on trust, TIE = -0.107 [-0.179, -0.041]. One of the three specific indirect effects of adherence to ingroup narrative on trust was significant. This involved the mediation of symbolic threat, IE = -0.107 [-0.180, -0.052]. The mediation of group-esteem threat, IE = -0.038 [-0.092, 0.004], and the indirect effect of realistic threat, IE = 0.038 [-0.035, 0.117], were not significant. For Cyprus, adherence to ingroup narratives also had a negative total indirect effect on trust, TIE = -0.122 [-0.216, -0.028]. One of the three specific indirect effects of adherence to ingroup narrative on trust was significant. This involved the mediation of group-esteem threat, IE = -0.078 [-0.154, -0.020]. The mediation of symbolic threat, IE = -0.017 [-0.057, 0.001], and the indirect effect of realistic threat, IE = 0.027 [-0.091, 0.020], were not significant. Similarly, for Croatia adherence to ingroup narratives also had a negative total indirect effect on trust, TIE = -0.063 [-0.118, -0.021]. One of the three specific indirect effects of adherence to ingroup narrative on trust was significant. This involved the mediation of group-esteem threat, IE = -0.075 [-0.128, -0.035]. The mediation of symbolic threat, IE = -0.005 [-0.035, 0.013], and the indirect effect of realistic threat, IE = 0.017 [-0.011, 0.053], were not significant.

Discussion

Our research showed that internalizing the ingroup's account of historical events related to the conflict leads to viewing the outgroup as a threat to the ingroup and, as such, a group that should not be trusted. More specifically, the results replicate our hypothesis that adherence to ingroup narratives would be related to more distrust towards the outgroup via heightened feelings of threat coming from the outgroup(s).

The course of relationships as was tested via the path models (i.e. adherence to ingroup narrative leading to greater perceived threats, leading to outgroup distrust) is in line with the ontogenetic perspective of social representations according to which children find out about their past victimization (Bar-Tal and Teichman 2005) by an outgroup at a very early age (see Psaltis 2015; Psaltis et al. 2015) and then internalize master narratives of collective victimization. This internalization gradually leads to a more coherent and abstract notion of realistic, symbolic and group-esteem threats which are mostly future oriented (Stephan et al. 2009).

We are, of course, aware that claims for causality cannot really be made given the cross-sectional type of our data, and we therefore encourage longitudinal and/or developmental research which would back up with evidence the proposed sequential order, i.e. one extending from adherence to narratives to perceived threat and distrust. Furthermore, we do not claim that this sequential order represents the only course of relationships between adherence to ingroup historical narratives and intergroup relations. Smeekes et al. (2017) have, for instance, demonstrated in one study that when people feel threatened in times of social change or transition, they could find a symbolic "shelter" through further adherence to narratives of continuity. This direction of causality is opposite to the one that was tested in the study presented in this chapter even though the nature of the associations remains constant (a positive relationship between perceived threat and adherence to ingroup's narrative).

A second finding of this study is that the mediated relationship between adherence to ingroup narratives and distrust was replicated in all three contexts. The only difference across contexts regarded the type of threat that significantly mediated the relationship. Symbolic threat emerged as a significant mediator in Serbia, and group-esteem threat in Cyprus and Croatia. A more in-depth analysis of probably the content of the narrative and the representation of the enemy would possibly explain the aforementioned differences. Such analysis forms a possible avenue of future research on the topic. Interestingly, realistic threat did not mediate the relationship between adherence to ingroup narratives and outgroup distrust in any of the contexts. We contend that this is because the interethnic conflicts in the three contexts are not characterized by violence at this point in time.

An extrapolation of the present findings is that the uncritical internalization of the historical narrative of the ingroup is counterproductive to the aim of conflict transformation in conflict societies. If the communities involved in post-conflict societies decided to resolve their differences through dialogue and negotiation, then the role of master narratives becomes destructive as it reinforces division, sectarianism and competition by escalating conflict and distrust. Contrary to what is often argued by the heritage, nationalist or romantic approach to nation building, the sense of self created is not one of security but one of a threatened and fragile self which is what Bar-Tal and Teichman (2005) called a "siege mentality". Identity construction on the basis of conflict narratives is thus not liberating as it might be argued by theoretical approaches or politicians who support the heritage approach. On the contrary, it is about constructing a fragile and threatened self which is distrustful of those with whom they need to co-operate to end violence, division or conflict.

Thinking about the ramifications of the present findings for history teaching, what could in fact be liberating is reflection on the structure and function of historical conflict narratives as social representations by both teachers and students. In this way, children, youth and adults can understand the consequences of the internalization of master narratives for conflict transformation.

To conclude, the heritage or the romantic identity building approach in history teaching can thus be criticised on all four grounds: pedagogical, epistemological, moral and political. Pedagogically, it is based on an outdated model of a transmission metaphor given that it is mostly delivered by educators as a communication type that Moscovici described as propaganda (Kello and Wagner (Chap. 8)). Epistemologically, it is based on naïve realism since it promotes the single truth of the nation, which is an outdated epistemological stance. Morally, the idea of manipulating, silencing or hiding parts of the past from students is unacceptable. Politically, it reinforces conflict instead of resolving it.

As Barton and Levstick (2004) argue, students have to examine the impact of telling any particular narrative, or any set of narratives, as well as the consequences of students' narrative simplifications. For the disciplinary approach, there is an important take-home message from the present findings: history teachers need to familiarize themselves with relevant social psychological research and have in their "toolbox" the main findings of research such as the present one. Given the well-established findings that master narratives pose a threat to the cultivation of the historical thinking of students (Carretero 2011; Lopez et al. 2012), the present should be read as adding support to the idea of moving from the disciplinary to an interdisciplinary approach (see Psaltis et al. 2017) to the study of historical culture and consciousness in the history classroom. The cultivation of a critical historical and reflective consciousness that recognizes the socially constructed nature of master narratives and their pernicious effects for conflict transformation is an essential element of such an approach that could be termed transformative history teaching. Finally, both first and second-order concepts of history teaching could be enriched by a better understanding of concepts that come directly from the social psychological field such as "threats", "social identity", "prejudice", "distrust", "conflict transformation" and "reconciliation" and above all "master narratives".

Notes

1. There were missing cases on some variables. Participants who had a missing value on any one variable tested were excluded from the sample. This led to a sample of $N = 427$ (Cyprus: $N = 112$; Serbia: $N = 161$; Croatia: $N = 154$). Results reported in this chapter are based on this sample.

References

Anderson, B. (1983). *Imagined communities: Reflections on the origin and spread of nationalism*. London: Verso.

Ashmore, R. D., Deaux, K., & McLaughlin-Volpe, T. (2004). An organizing framework for collective identity: Articulation and significance of multidimensionality. *Psychological Bulletin, 130*, 80–114.

Banjeglav, T. (2013). conflicting memories, competing narratives and contested histories in croatia's post-war commemorative practices. *Politička Misao, 49*(5), 7–31.

Bar-Tal, D., & Čehajić-Clancy, S. (2013). From collective victimhood to social reconciliation: Outlining a conceptual framework. In D. Spini, D. Čorkalo-Biruški, & G. Elcheroth (Eds.), *War and Community: Collective experiences in the former Yugoslavia*. New York: Springer.

Bar-Tal, D., & Salomon, G. (2006). Israeli-Jewish narratives of the Israeli-Palestinian conflict: Evolvement, contents, functions and consequences. In R. I. Rotberg (Ed.), *Israeli and Palestinian narratives of conflict: History's double Helix*. Bloonington: Indiana University Press.

Bar-Tal, D., & Teichman, Y. (2005). *Stereotypes and prejudice in conflict: Representations of Arabs in Israeli Jewish society*. Cambridge: Cambridge University Press.

Bar-Tal, D., Chernyak-Hai, L., Schori, N., & Gundar, A. (2009). A sense of self-perceived collective victimhood in intractable conflicts. *International Review of the Red Cross, 91*(874), 229–258.

Barton, K. C., & Levstik, L. S. (2004). *Teaching history for the common good*. Mahwah: Lawrence Erlbaum Associates.

Bekerman, Z., & Zembylas, M. (2011). The emotional complexities of teaching conflictual historical narratives: The case of integrated Palestinian-Jewish schools in Israel. *Teachers College Record, 113*(5), 1004–1030.
Bhabha, H. (1990). *Nation and narration*. London, UK: Routledge.
Bieber, F. (2002). Nationalist mobilization and stories of Serb suffering: The Kosovo myth from 600th anniversary to the present. *Rethinking History, 6*, 95–110.
Billig, M. (1995). *Banal Nationalism*. London: Sage.
Boym, S. (2001). *The future of nostalgia*. New York: Basic Books.
Branscombe, N. R., & Doosje, B. (2004). *Collective guilt: International perspectives*. Cambridge: Cambridge University Press.
Brown, R., & Čehajić, S. (2008). Dealing with the past and facing the future: Mediators of collective guilt and shame in Bosnia and Herzegovina. *European Journal of Social Psychology, 38*, 669–684.
Carretero, M. (2011). *Constructing patriotism. Teaching history and memories in global worlds*. Charlotte: Information Age Publishing.
Carretero, M., & Van Alphen, F. (2014). Do master narratives change among high school students? Analyzing national historical representations characteristics. *Cognition and Instruction, 32*(3), 290–312.
Carretero, M., Asensio, M., & Rodriguez-Moneo, M. (Eds.). (2012). *History education and the construction of national identities*. Charlotte: Information Age Publishing.
Carretero, M., Lopez, C., Gonzalez, M. F., & Rodriguez-Moneo, M. (2012). Students historical narratives and concepts about the nation. In M. Carretero, M. Asensio, & M. Rodriguez Moneo (Eds.), *History education and the construction of national identities* (pp. 153–170). Charlotte: Information Age Publishing.
Doosje, B., Branscombe, N. R., Spears, R., & Manstead, S. R. (1998). Guilty by association: When one's group has a negative history. *Journal of Personality and Social Psychology, 75*, 872–886.
Duyvendak, J. (2011). *The politics of home: Belonging and nostalgia in Western Europe and the United States*. Basingstoke, UK: Palgrave.
Ferro, M. (1984). *The use and abuse of history, or, how the past is taught to children*. London: Routledge.
Galtung, J. (2000). *Conflict transformation by peaceful means: The Transcend method*. United Nations.
Goldberg, T. (2013). "It's in my veins": Identity and disciplinary practice in students' discussions of a historical issue. *Theory & Research in Social Education, 41*(1), 33–64.
Goldberg, T., Baruch, B. B., & Porat, D. (2011). "Could they do it differently?": Narrative and argumentative changes in students' writing following discussion of "hot" historical issues. *Cognition and Instruction, 29*(2), 185–217.

Hammack, P. (2010). Identity as burden or benefit? youth, historical narrative, and the legacy of political conflict. *Human Development, 53,* 173–201.
Jetten, J., & Hutchison, P. (2011). When groups have a lot to lose: Historical continuity enhances resistance to a merger. *European Journal of Social Psychology, 41,* 335–343.
Jetten, J., & Wohl, M. J. A. (2012). The past as a determinant of the present: Historical continuity, collective angst, and opposition to immigration. *European Journal of Social Psychology, 42,* 442–450.
Jović, D. (2007). The slovenian-croatian confederal proposal: A tactical move or an ultimate solution? In L. J. Cohen & J. Dragović-Soso (Eds.), *State collapse in South-Eastern Europe: New perspectives on Yugoslavia's disintegration* (pp. 249–280). USA: Purdue University Press.
Liu, J. H., & Hilton, D. J. (2005). How the past weighs on the present: Social representations of history and their role in identity politics. *British Journal of Social Psychology, 44,* 537–556.
Liu, J. H., & László, J. (2007). A narrative theory of history and identity: Social identity, social representations, society and the individual. In G. Moloney & I. Walker (Eds.), *Social representations and identity: Content, process and power* (pp. 85–107). London, UK: Palgrave MacMillan.
Lopez, C., & Carretero, M. (2012). Identity construction and the goals of history education. In M. Carretero, M. Asensio, & M. Rodriguez-Moneo (Eds.), *History education and the construction of national identities* (pp. 139–150). Charlotte: Information Age.
Lowenthal, D. (1985a). *The past is a foreign country.* Cambridge: CUP.
Lowenthal, D. (1985b). *The heritage crusade and the spoils of history.* Cambridge: CUP.
Makriyianni, C., & Psaltis, C. (2007). History teaching and reconciliation. *Cyprus Review, 19,* 43–69.
Makriyianni, C., Psaltis, C., & Latif, D. (2011). History teaching in Cyprus. In E. Erdmann & W. Hasberg (Eds.), *Facing mapping, bridging diversity: Foundations of a European discourse on history education, part 1* (pp. 91–138). Germany: Wochen Schau Wissenschaft.
McCully, A. (2012). History teaching, conflict and the legacy of the past. *Education, Citizenship and Social Justice, 7*(2), 145–159.
Mirkovic, D. (2000). The historical link between the Ustasha genocide and the Croato-Serb civil war: 1991–1995. *Journal of Genocide Research, 2*(3), 363–373.
Moscovici, S. (1998). The History and actuality of social representations. In U. Flick. (Ed.), *The Psychology of the social,* (pp. 209–247). Cambridge: Cambridge University Press.
Narodne novine, [Official Gazete], 2000: Deklaracija o Domovinskom ratu [Declaration on the Homeland War], www.nn.hr, no. 102.
O'Neill, W. G. (2002). *Kosovo: An unfinished peace.* Boulder, Co.: Lynne Rienner.

Páez, D., Bobowic, M., & Liu, J. H. (2017). Social representations of the past and competences in history education. In M. Carretero, S. Berger, & M. Grever (Eds.), *Handbook of research in historical culture and history education, (pp. 491–510)*. UK: Palgrave Macmillan.

Papadakis, Y. (2008). Narrative, memory and history in divided Cyprus: A comparison of school books on the history of Cyprus. *History & Museum, 20*, 128–148.

Perikleous, L. (2010). At a crossroad between memory and thinking: The case of primary history education in the Greek Cypriot educational system, Education 3–13. *International Journal of Primary Elementary and Early Years Education, 38*(3), 315–328.

Perković, M., & Puljiz, V. (2001). Ratne štete, izdaci za branitelje, žrtve i stradalnike rata u Republici Hrvatskoj [War damages and the expenditure for the veterans and victims of the war in the Republic of Croatia]. *Revija za socijalnu politiku, 8*(2), 235–238.

Psaltis, C. (2012). Intergroup trust and contact in transition: A social representations perspective on the Cyprus conflict. In I. Markova & A. Gillespie (Eds.), *Trust and conflict: Representations, culture and dialogue* (pp. 83–104). London: Routledge.

Psaltis, C. (2015). Genetic social psychology From microgenesis to ontogenesis and sociogenesis…and back. In C. Psaltis, A. Gillespie, & A. N. P. Perret-Clermont (Eds.), *Social relations in human and societal development*. UK: Palgrave, Macmillan.

Psaltis, C. (2016). Collective memory, social representations of intercommunal relations and conflict transformation in divided Cyprus. *Peace and Conflict: Journal of Peace Psychology, 22*(1), 19–27.

Psaltis, C., Gillespie, A., & Perret-Clermont, A. N. P. (Eds.). (2015). *Human relations in human and societal development*. UK: Palgrave/Macmillan.

Psaltis, C., Lytras, E., & Costache, S. (2011). *History educators in the Greek Cypriot and Turkish Cypriot community of Cyprus: Perceptions, beliefs and practices*. Nicosia: UNDP-ACT.

Psaltis, C., McCully, A., Agbaria, A., Makriyianni, C., Pingel, F., Karahasan, H., Carretero, M., Oguz, M., Choplarou, R., Philippou, S., Wagner, W., & Papadakis, Y. (2017). Recommendations for the History Teaching of Intergroup Conflicts. COST IS 1205 Working Group. Retrieved 9 July 2017 from http://docs.wixstatic.com/ugd/89ca3b_a592bbe79ece4d218cbf9858928b5d10.pdf.

Reicher, S., & Hopkins, N. (2001). *Self and nation*. London: Sage Publications.

Rüsen, J. (2004). Historical consciousness: Narrative structure, moral function, and ontogenetic development. In P. Seixas (Ed.), *Theorizing historical consciousness* (pp. 63–85). Toronto, Canada: University of Toronto Press.

Sani, F., Bowe, M., & Herrera, M. (2008). Perceived collective continuity: Seeing groups as temporally enduring entities. In F. Sani (Ed.), *Self continuity: Individual and collective perspectives* (pp. 159–172). Hove: Psychology Press.

Seixas, P. (Ed.). (2004). *Theorizing historical consciousness.* Toronto: University of Toronto Press.

Sibley, C. G., Liu, J. H., Duckitt, J., & Khan, S. S. (2008). Social representations of history and the legitimation of social inequality: The form and function of historical negation. *European Journal of Social Psychology, 38,* 542–565.

Smeekes, A., & Verkuyten, M. (2013). Collective self-continuity, group identification and in-group defense. *Journal of Experimental Social Psychology, 49,* 984–994.

Smeekes, A., & Verkuyten, M. (2014a). Perceived group continuity, collective self-continuity and ingroup identification. *Self and Identity, 13,* 663–680.

Smeekes, A., & Verkuyten, M. (2014b). When national culture is disrupted: Cultural continuity and resistance to Muslim immigrants. *Group Processes and Intergroup Relations, 17,* 45–66.

Smeekes, A., & Verkuyten, M. (2015). The presence of the past: Identity continuity and group dynamics. *European Review of Social Psychology, 26*(1), 162–202.

Smeekes, A., McKeown, S., & Psaltis, C. (2017). Endorsing narratives under threat: Maintaining perceived collective continuity through the protective power of ingroup narratives in Northern Ireland and Cyprus. *Journal of Social and Political Psychology*

Stephan, W. G., Ybarra, O., & Rios Morrison, K. (2009). Intergroup threat theory. In T. Nelson (Ed.), *Handbook of Prejudice* (pp. 43–59). Mahwah, NJ: Lawrence Erlbaum Associates.

Subotic, J. (2013). Remembrance, Public Narratives, and Obstacles to Justice in the Western Balkans. *Studies in Social Justice, 7*(2), 265–283.

The United Nations International Criminal Tribunal for the Former Yugoslavia ("UN-ICTY") Croatia—1991–1995. Retrieved 15 July, 2017 http://www.icty.org/en/about/what-former-yugoslavia/conflicts.

Turner, J. C., & Reynolds, K. J. (2001). The social identity perspective in intergroup relations: Theories, themes, and controversies. In R. Brown & S. Gaertner (Eds.), *Blackwell handbook of social psychology* (Vol. 4, pp. 133–152). Intergroup processes Oxford, UK: Blackwell.

Van Alphen, F., & Carretero, M. (2015). The construction of the relation between national past and present in the appropriation of historical master narratives. *Integrative Psychological and Behavioral Science, 49*(3), 512–530.

Wertsch, J. V. (2007). Collective Memory. In J. Valsiner & A. Rosa (Eds.), *The Cambridge handbook of pociocultural psychology* (pp.625–644). Cambridge: Cambridge University Press.
Zittoun, T., Duveen, G., Gillespie, A., Ivinson, G., & Psaltis, C. (2003). The use of symbolic resources in developmental transitions. *Culture & Psychology, 9*, 415–448.
Živić, D., & Pokos, N. (2004). Demografski gubitci tijekom domovinskog rata kao odrednica depopulacije Hrvatske (1991–2001) [*Demographic losses during the homeland war as a determinant of depopulation in Croatia* (1991–2001)]. *Društvena istraživanja, 13*(4–5), 727–750.

AUTHORS' BIOGRAPHY

Charis Psaltis is an Associate Professor of Social and Developmental Psychology at the University of Cyprus. His research interests fall in the areas of genetic social psychology, social interaction in learning and cognitive development, social representations of gender, intergroup contact and intergroup relations in Cyprus and other post-conflict societies, development of national identities and history teaching and collective memory. He published papers in *Journal of Personality and Social Psychology, European Journal of Social Psychology, British Journal of Developmental Psychology, Culture & Psychology and Human Development*. Since 2014, he is a member of the Editorial Board of the *British Journal of Developmental Psychology* and since 2015 Associate Editor of *European Journal of Psychology of Education*. In April 2014, his book co-authored with Anna Zapiti *Interaction, Communication and Development: Psychological Development as a social process* was published by Routledge, and in 2015, his co-edited volume *Social Relations in Human and Societal Development* by Palgrave Macmillan.

Renata Franc is a Scientific Adviser at the Ivo Pilar Institute of Social Sciences and Full Professor of Social and Political Psychology at the University of Zagreb. Her research interests include social attitudes, values, intergroup relations and conflict, political participation and quality of life. Currently, she is a member of the research team on projects PROMISE (PROMoting Youth Involvement and Social Engagement: Opportunities and challenges for "conflicted" young people across Europe, EU H2020, 2016–2019) and CRO WELL (Croatian Longitudinal Study on Well-Being, Croatian Science Foundation 2015–2019). Since 2009, she is Editor-in-Chief of the Croatian international social sciences journal *Društvena istraživanja (Social research—Journal for general social issues)*. Most recently, she is a co-author of *The situation of children's and women's rights in Croatia—update* (UNICEF Office for Croatia 2015) and "Personal Security and Fear of Crime as Predictors of Subjective Well-Being," in D. Webb, E. Wills-Herrera (Eds.) *Subjective Well-Being and Security* (Springer, 2012).

Anouk Smeekes is an Assistant Professor of Interdisciplinary Social Sciences at the European Research Centre on Migration and Ethnic Relations (ERCOMER) at Utrecht University (the Netherlands). Her research in the field of Social Psychology focuses on historical representations, national identity, identity motivation, group-based emotions (national nostalgia) and intergroup relations. She published various papers on these topics in *British Journal of Social Psychology, Journal of Experimental Social Psychology, Personality and Social Psychology Bulletin, European Review of Social Psychology* and *International Journal of Intercultural Research*. Her Ph.D. dissertation published in 2014 titled "The presence of the past: Historical rooting of national identity and current group dynamics" won the Rae and Dr. Dan Landis Outstanding Dissertation Award of the International Academy for Intercultural Research (IAIR) in 2015.

Maria Ioannou is a Tutor at the University College Groningen, University of Groningen. Her research interests fall in the area of intergroup relations, intergroup contact and prejudice reduction. Her PhD thesis focused on comparing the effectiveness of direct and indirect types of intergroup contact between Greek and Turkish Cypriots in Cyprus. Part of this work was published in the journal *Group Processes & International Relations*. She is also interested in how scientific research can inform policies. The work she undertook while working in the civil society sector led to the co-authoring of a book publication entitled *Predicting Peace: The Social Cohesion and Reconciliation Index as a Tool for Conflict Transformation*.

Iris Žeželj is an Assistant Professor of Social Psychology at the University of Belgrade. Her research focuses on two areas: social cognition and intergroup relations. More specifically, she investigates memory biases, motivated cognition, attitude–behaviour relations, and ethnic, national and social identities in the post-conflict regions and the role of direct and online contact in prejudice reduction. Her research draws from a variety of methods, from laboratory, field experiments and social games, to interviews and focus groups, to large cross-cultural surveys, and tries to address real-life issues of ethnic, religious and gender discrimination. She published in *Social Psychology, British Journal of Social Psychology, Journal of Applied Social Psychology* and *Computers in Human Behavior*. She is currently co-editing a volume entitled *Social Identities in Western Balkans* by Palgrave Macmillan.

Open Access This chapter is licensed under the terms of the Creative Commons Attribution 4.0 International License (http://creativecommons.org/licenses/by/4.0/), which permits use, sharing, adaptation, distribution and reproduction in any medium or format, as long as you give appropriate credit to the original author(s) and the source, provide a link to the Creative Commons license and indicate if changes were made.

The images or other third party material in this chapter are included in the chapter's Creative Commons license, unless indicated otherwise in a credit line to the material. If material is not included in the chapter's Creative Commons license and your intended use is not permitted by statutory regulation or exceeds the permitted use, you will need to obtain permission directly from the copyright holder.

PART II

Social Psychological Perspectives of Perpetrators and Victims

Power Struggles in the Remembering of Historical Intergroup Conflict: Hegemonic and Counter-Narratives About the Argentine "Conquest of the Desert"

Alicia Barreiro, Cecilia Wainryb and Mario Carretero

INTRODUCTION

In this chapter, we examine laypeople's narratives about historical processes, collectively constructed, transacted, and transmitted in an effort to remember and make sense of past events involving conflicts between groups, and focus on the constitutive relations between hegemonic and counter-narratives. We rely on concrete examples of narratives about a specific process drawn from Argentine history, the "Conquest of the Desert," and examine what these narratives make visible, what they occlude and how they represent time, as a way to elucidate how the past is evoked, how the possibilities for a future are conceived, and how identities are negotiated and constructed. We focus, too, on the constitutive relations between hegemonic and counter-narratives. Our aim is to underscore some of the tensions and contradictions that arise in recollections and retellings of historical processes, as well as their implications for the construction of collective identities and intergroup relations.

A. Barreiro (✉) · C. Wainryb · M. Carretero
University of Buenos Aires, Buenos Aires, Argentina
e-mail: avbarreiro@gmail.com

The "Conquest of the Desert" implicated armed conflict as well as ongoing confrontation between groups. Thus, unavoidably, there are competing narratives about this historical process. The hegemonic narrative arose at the end of the 19th century to justify the territorial expansion and consolidation of the Argentine state in what used to be indigenous territory. This collective narrative is still expressed and supported by educational curricula and symbolic resources such as museums. The counter-narrative, traditionally endorsed by indigenous people, gained significant scholarly support only a few decades ago. The specific narratives we discuss in this chapter were gathered in a small Argentine city where descendants of the military men who had participated in the conquest and descendants of the immigrants who had occupied the conquered lands live together with descendants of the indigenous Mapuche people who used to occupy the land prior to the military campaign. Relying on these narratives, we consider the ways in which the hegemonic narrative becomes expressed in and supported by the exhibits of a local historical museum and the ways in which the counter-narrative supported by the local indigenous people stands in relation to the hegemonic narrative and constructs a complex group identity. To conclude, we reflect on the possibility of educational interventions aimed at reducing the tension between competing collective narratives and contributing to the development of intergroup dialogue and tolerance.

Laypeople's Narratives About the Common Past, Identity Construction, and Intergroup Relations

Laypeople's narratives about historical processes stem from collective past experiences and group images shared in their common everyday experience (Jodelet 2003). Appeals to collective memory (Halbwachs 1925/1992) become crucial to account for the way individuals remember history, that is, for how they remember a past that they did not themselves live. Hence, narratives about historical process are not created by individuals' direct experience, but are rather the "storage" of the collective memory of social groups, transmitted from one generation to the next one via the scientific production of historians, school teachings, mass media, and symbolic resources constructed by societies (Carretero 2011; Carretero and Kriger, 2011; Rosa 2006; Wertsch 2002). This everyday knowledge about the common past does not result only from transforming scientific knowledge into common sense knowledge; rather, it is a direct result of educational and school teaching interventions. Nevertheless, most people stop attending school some time at the end of their adolescence, but their knowledge about historical processes is kept alive in the collective memory and transmitted to future generations (Pennebaker et al. 2006).

Unsurprisingly, there are multiple versions about past events, depending on the varying perspectives and interests of the social or national groups implicated in the telling. This is important inasmuch as historical narratives influence how groups define their rights and duties, legitimize their political agreements, and adjudicate on the rightness or wrongness of their actions. Any account of the past has a political dimension, and all such accounts can be used to negate or legitimize the historical bases of claims made by social groups—claims that provide them with temporal continuity (Sibley et al. 2008). Hence, there necessarily is a constitutive tension between hegemonic narratives and counter-narratives. Hegemonic narratives convey the more stable, dominant, and consensual version of history; counter-narratives are defined by their opposition or resistance (whether explicit or implicit) to the dominant or hegemonic narratives. Thus, counter-narratives exist and make sense in relation to hegemonic narratives, and vice versa (Bamberg and Andrews 2004).

Common sense narratives about historical processes serve to support and defend a particular construction of social reality or to resist against hegemonic versions imposed by a powerful group. In our global world, multiple versions of reality coexist, and systems of knowledge are relatively heterogeneous and unstable; therefore, possibilities for critique, argumentation, and discussion abound (Barreiro et al., 2017). In general, people supporting hegemonic narratives are aware of the counter-version, and people who put forth counter-narratives are familiar with the hegemonic forms. In an important sense, and given the relational character of narratives, hegemonic and counter-narratives not only coexist side by side but penetrate each other, informing, arguing, and questioning. This complexity affects not only the narratives that are told; within both dominant and subjugated groups, individuals experience and reproduce these tensions. Hence, the conflicts between different— indeed, contradictory—versions of the same historical process can coexist in everyday life in the same social group, resulting in a state of *cognitive polyphasia* (Barreiro 2013; Duveen 2007; Jovchelovitch 2008; Moscovici 1961; Wagner et al. 2000). As will be discussed below, the state of cognitive polyphasia may be manifested at the collective level, such as in the construction of symbolic resources, as well as on the individual level, as expressed in the discourse of individual people.

Another way to think about the power struggles that become manifested in the construction of narratives about the past is to consider the process by which meanings are negotiated in dialogical relations among people and social groups. The social asymmetries of speakers often lead to certain representations not being recognized (Barreiro and Castorina 2016), thereby constraining the meaning-making processes. The meanings that prevail in this struggle between representational fields become positive representational elements included in the competing narratives. Other features—those that challenge and threaten the dominant perspective—are often excluded and become what has been labeled "*nothingness*" (Bang 2009; Barreiro and Castorina 2016), remaining as the dark or unacknowledged side of the positive elements represented in the narratives. This absence stems from a constructive process to cope with uncanny social objects or meanings. Nevertheless, those ignored elements of historical narratives perform a constitutive function in their genesis, as they can be constructed precisely because some elements are excluded.

Finally, it is also important to recognize that narratives about historical processes are relevant to identity development, especially to the construction of a sense of collective or group identity. Historical narratives tell group members who they are, where they are from, and where they are going (Sibley et al. 2008). In this way, individuals identify themselves as members of a group that has constructed an image of itself in the context of both collectively lived experiences and agreed-upon values. As has been abundantly shown, people's social identity is constructed based on the relative categorization and valuing of members of different social groups (Abrams et al. 2001; Ellemers et al. 2002; Tajfel and Turner 1986; Postmes and Branscombe 2010). In general, individuals strive to preserve a positive self-view and consider their ingroup more positively than the outgroups (Deaux and Martin 2003). Thus, individuals' understandings of social phenomena, such as historical events, depend more on how these events affect their sense of identity than on the actual facts or available evidence (Ellemers et al. 2002). Importantly, as social groups construct their own discourse about the social world, they also adapt to or resist other groups' discourse. To know the outgroup's discourse is to know how those individuals think of "us"; in other words, such discourse makes one aware of the existence of alternative representations of the self (Gillespie 2008). The representations of the different perspectives about ourselves are an important dialogical sub-part of our identity and allow individuals to deal with the plurality of representations about themselves. These alternative representations are attributed to other people and become evident when someone expresses the phrases "they think" or "they claim" or "they say."

Conflicting Narratives in Argentine Remembering of the "Conquest of the Desert"

The Conquest of the Desert was a military campaign carried out by the Argentine state at the end of the 19th century (1874–1885), wherein the military made inroads into territories that had been up to then inhabited by indigenous groups. This period of territorial expansion and national organization involved (and, indeed, relied on) the massacre and enslavement of indigenous communities. Thousands were exterminated and many more sold into slavery to the new landowners. Survivors were forced to negate or ignore their culture and assimilate to the conquerors' culture, effectively becoming invisible as a social group (Del Río 2005; Halperin Donghi 1995). Their invisibility persisted over many decades (Gordillo and Hisrch 2010; Valko 2012) as the Argentine national identity consolidated as largely "white" or "European" (Carretero and Kriger 2011).

In the last few decades, various indigenous communities in Argentina gained some recognition, including formal status for their group rights, even as they remained deeply affected by poverty, racism, and social exclusion (Sarasola 2010). Although counter-narratives first emerged from within the indigenous community, nowadays they have been legitimized by historiography and other scientific disciplines (e.g., Bayer 2010; Briones 1994; Halperin Donghi 1995; Novaro 2003). Indeed, scientific accounts have challenged the hegemonic version of the narrative about the "Conquest of the Desert" that is expressed in school textbooks and monuments—a narrative that portrays the Argentine military as heroically working to subdue the violent and uncivilized tribes, thereby contributing to the organization and consolidation of the Argentine state and nation. In its stead, this counter-perspective brought to the fore the massacre and abuses carried out by the military against indigenous groups.

The tension between conflicting narratives constitutes a state of cognitive polyphasia in the collective remembering of this historical process (Barreiro et al. 2016, 2017). The narrative about the glorious military campaign that consolidated Argentine sovereignty upon its current national territory works to create and support a sense of national identity (Carretero 2011); therefore, questioning such a narrative is deeply threatening. Nevertheless, there is also a collective awareness of the tragic history of the indigenous people, so individuals cannot simply deny these facts. Thus, both narratives become manifested in symbolic recourses such as history curricula, monuments, or names of streets, without maintaining a coherent relation between them. In this way, a state of cognitive polyphasia operates on Argentine collective memory, as a strategy to preserve their positive national identity and avoid collective guilt about their nation's actions, while at the same time recognizing the injustices suffered by indigenous people and representing a "politically correct" version of the national past (Barreiro et al. 2016). For example, many central provincial capitals throughout Argentina feature large equestrian statues commemorating General Roca, the chief commandant of the military campaign, that are ridden with graffiti saying "killer," "genocide," or "indigenous people are alive." Such vandalized monuments express the coexistence of two opposite versions of the past. Another example of the state of cognitive polyphasia is given by research (Barreiro et al. 2016; Sarti and Barreiro 2014) showing that although many Argentine adolescents and young adults are aware that indigenous people were massacred in the historical past, they fail to recognize the military campaign was carried out by the Argentine state and, erroneously, attribute it to "the Spaniards colonizers."

Importantly, the hegemonic narrative about the Conquest of the Desert denies not only the Argentine state's responsibility for the injustices suffered by indigenous people in the past, but also the existence of indigenous communities in the Argentine territory in the present, by constructing the story in such a way that one might think that all the indigenous people have been killed. Many studies (Gordillo and Hirsch 2010; Nagy 2014) have shown that the indigenous groups currently living in Argentina, and specifically in the province of Buenos Aires where more than 30% of the indigenous population resides, are still largely invisible. Moreover, the few symbolic recourses dedicated to recognizing the indigenous people, such as monuments or images in textbooks, tend to present their identity as homogenous and anachronistic.

Stereotypic representations of indigenous people constitute the basis for prejudice (Ungaretti et al. 2015; Ungaretti and Müller, forthcoming). Furthermore, inasmuch as individual members of indigenous groups today fail to comply with the expectations of what an indigenous individual should look or act like, such stereotypic representations are also used to deny the indigenous identity in the present day.

Constructing Group's Past in the Midst of Intergroup Conflict

From year 2013 to 2015, we carried out an ethnographic study to explore the varying narratives about the "Conquest of the Desert" in a small city, located in the southern region of the province of Buenos Aires. In this city, the descendants of the founding militaries and European immigrants who arrived at the beginning of 20th century to settle the "conquered" lands live alongside descendants of the indigenous Mapuche community who inhabited that territory before the conquest. In this chapter, we focus our analysis, first, on the hegemonic narrative as conveyed by the exhibitions of the local historical museum and, next, on the indigenous counter-narrative as registered during informal meetings and conversations with members of the local Mapuche community.

The Hegemonic Narrative Expressed in the Local Museum's Exhibits

The various rooms that articulate the exhibits of the local historical museum follow a traditional organization (Asensio and Pol 2012). Visitors are supposed to observe valued objects meant to reveal a narrative about the past, framed in terms of political events, world affairs, and national heroes. As is the case in many other Latin American historical museums (Gonzáles de Oleaga 2012), the hegemonic narrative in this local museum is presented as one-dimensional: Historical objects are presented as though they could narrate history in and of themselves. The sense of interpretation—which is essential to any historical texts—is not made visible to the visitor (Bennett 1998).

The sequence of the various rooms that constitute the exhibit is supposed to follow a chronological order. The exhibit begins with a room dedicated to pre-historical times, followed by another commemorating the indigenous people who inhabited the region. In this "indigenous room," visitors find a horse, tools used to make food, traditional indigenous cloths, some indigenous weapons, and several pictures of indigenous people dressed in traditional attire. The more antique objects exhibited there correspond to the time of the "Conquest of the Desert," but there is no explicit mention of such historical process in the exhibit. In addition to the enormous chronological gap between the previous room dedicated to pre-historical times and this one, the objects featured in this room include some pertaining to the end of the 19th century and others that refer to famous local indigenous people who died as recently as a few decades ago. In this sense, this room represents a time loop confusing past and present and joining very different moments of the local history. Across from the "indigenous room," visitors find a "colonial room" dedicated to the Conquest of America by Spaniards in the years 1492–1816, where the everyday life in the Argentine colony is depicted without any trace of indigenous people.

The sequence of the rooms in the museum seems to indicate a narrative wherein indigenous people inhabited the region after pre-historical times and until the arrival of the Spaniards, who colonized America. This narrative implicitly suggests that indigenous people disappeared because of the Spaniards' colonization. Unsurprisingly, this narrative is very similar to the one told by Argentine adolescents and adults (Barreiro et al. 2016; Sarti and Barreiro 2014), who hold the Spaniards responsible for the killing of the indigenous people while ignoring the role played by the Argentine nation-state.

While touring the "indigenous room" in the museum, we happened to observe a visit of a kindergarten classroom with their teacher.[1] Below we reproduce a fragment of our record of the teachers' explanations, which help illustrate the looping between past and present in the hegemonic discourse about indigenous culture, as well as the ensuing anachronic representation of indigenous identity:

> […] all these objects that we are seeing here show how many different things the indigenous people used to have and used to do. They used to have a flag, they used to take care of their children, they used to prepare their own food. They also used to have a thanksgiving ceremony that was called *nguillatun*, because they were a very grateful people.

In fact, all the objects and activities mentioned by the teacher still exist and are part of today's indigenous culture. However, the teacher's explanations were all articulated in the past tense, leading children to believe that indigenous people and their culture no longer exist.

This teacher's discourse as well as the sequence of rooms in the museum works so as to deny the existence of a people who still live in their very city and all across the country. Their existence becomes "nothingness," and their identity is constructed anachronically, fixed in the past without considering its possible and actual development through time. Then, given that today's indigenous people cannot be easily distinguished from the other inhabitants of Argentina because they look the same, wear the same clothing, and use the same technology, they are considered "not real indigenous people" and "opportunists who only care about their roots because they want to receive a pension or restitution money from the government" (Barreiro et al. 2016; Nagy 2014). In this way, the stereotype of the indigenous people supported by the hegemonic narrative contributes to continued and heightened prejudice against them.

Altogether, the local museum's exhibit promotes one version of history and presents it de facto as the only possible version. In this way, this local history museum (as many other similar museums throughout Argentina and other Latin American countries) legitimizes the hegemonic version of the past by showing it as the unquestionable and accurate reflection of achievement of scientific research (González de Oleaga 2012). The traditional museum artifice does not prompt visitors to question who decides what should be displayed, who speaks in the name of the nation, or what is told versus silenced (Macdonald 1998). These questions, however, are crucial to unveil and make visible the power conflicts expressed—or silenced—in the museum's exhibit.

Another interesting aspect of the museum is that it does not feature a room dedicated explicitly to the "Conquest of the Desert." Rather, the biggest and most central room is the one dedicated to the foundation of the city. What is left unsaid, however, is that the foundation of this specific city (and other similar cities) happened as a direct consequence of that historical process. In this room, visitors can observe a main red wall that proudly features three Remington rifles. And yet, there is no explanation concerning what these rifles were used for, or why they are so important for national and regional history. According to the indigenous counter-narrative, the deadly power of these guns made it possible for the Argentine military forces to carry out the genocide of their people. Thus, to proudly exhibit these guns may have the shocking effect of denying their condemnable role in the conquest and ensuing genocide.

It should also be noted that the construction of an exhibit dedicated to commemorating the guns used during the conquest implies a deeply insensitive and offensive attitude vis-à-vis the feelings of indigenous people who might visit the museum and encounter a room that celebrates the guns that killed their ancestors. This is not a minor oversight, given that the museum is located in (and tells the story of) a city that counts large numbers of indigenous people as their long-standing residents. In effect, this may work as yet another way in which the current existence of indigenous people is denied—inasmuch as no consideration is given to them as a possible audience. Perhaps in some ways, this both reflects and also tends to reinforce the hegemonic view that "all indigenous people were killed," which conveniently makes the need for justice and restitution unnecessary.

It is noteworthy that hegemonic narratives do not tend to include a dialogue with alternative representations. Rather, when a dominant social group becomes aware of the presence of an alternative representation, as might be the case with the ongoing existence of indigenous people, their members develop different *semantic barriers* (Gillespie 2008) in their discourse to defend their own representations, keeping them away from the dialogical exchange. Indeed, the use of the past tense in the teacher's discourse and the negation of the ongoing existence of indigenous people associated with the construction of an anachronic indigenous identity may be considered as instances of protective semantic barriers.

Finally, in analyzing the power of the official narrative as expressed in the museum's exhibits it is necessary to consider the way the national Argentine identity is presented. From an intergroup relation perspective, the narratives about "who we are" that constrain the formation of an imagined community are constructed in relation to narratives about "who they are." In this museum, the Argentine identity is presented across the various rooms as continuous and stable, beginning with the Spanish colony and until the foundation of the city where the museum is located. Thus, the essence of the Argentine identity is presented as arising after the "indigenous times." Furthermore, the Argentines, as a people, are considered as homogenous and as represented by homogenous social groups that still hold a dominant role in Argentine society: the militaries and the political class, all of whom deny the current existence of the ingenious community.

Counter-Narratives and Mapuche's Resistance

As mentioned above, in the last few decades various scientific disciplines disseminated in the lay population a counter-narrative about what happened during the "Conquest of the Desert." And yet, this counter-narrative is not new; it has been supported by indigenous communities since the end of the 19th century. Here, we present transcripts of records from our visit to the local Mapuche community. These help illustrate the counter-narrative upon which this community has constructed its identity and based their claims for justice and reparation against the Argentine state. We begin with a transcript from a formal document, given to us by one of the main representatives of the Mapuche community, which had been presented before the Indigenous Parliament (a group that comprises representatives from diverse indigenous communities):

> … I am the great-grandchild of the Chief of the Mapuches Pampa. In the year 1878, he was the first to suffer the brunt of the brutal Argentine invasion of the territories of our people, known euphemistically as the Conquest of the Desert […] The Argentine army, armed with the best weapons purchased abroad, decimated my people: men, women, and children. The survivors were spread around. Men were sent to jail or forced to do hard labor, women were sold or given away like property, some to the military, some as domestic workers to the wealthy families in the cities. Article 4 of the Treaty of June 14, 1873 stated: 'The national government makes a commitment to respect the lands occupied today by the tribes and to never invade them, so that they can live peacefully with the protection of the government'. But my people were sold into slavery. In this process we lost everything […] Today we are 200 families and we have come together, about 1000 people, and there are still many more spread around the country. How can we live with dignity and preserve our community without a land, when the promises and commitments made to us in the Treaty of June 14, 1873 have not been fulfilled?

The differences between the main contents expressed in this counter-narrative and its hegemonic counterpart discussed above are noteworthy. First, in this narrative the Conquest of the Desert is presented not as a war or conflict between groups with equal power and competing interests but as an unjust invasion of the indigenous lands carried out by the Argentine government. This invasion is thought of as unjust inasmuch as it had violated treaties entered into with the indigenous tribes—something not even acknowledged in the hegemonic version. Furthermore, this counter-narrative does not talk about a genocide or extermination of the indigenous people; rather, it tells the story as one involving a diaspora that resulted in the loss of the unity among indigenous groups, in the loss of their property and territories, and their being sold into slavery. It is worth noting that slavery was already illegal at the time, as it had been abolished in Argentina in 1813. Another element, less evident but not less interesting, is the usage of time in this narrative. The author of the text starts out by affirming his identity and his claims in the past, based on his being the descendant of the tribe's chief, the violation of previous treaties, and more broadly based on facts that took place over 100 years earlier. Nevertheless, he then moves on to the present, as he mentions the current and ongoing situation of indigenous families and even alludes to the future as he articulates the impossibility of imagining a life with dignity. In this way, the author appeals to the past in an effort to justify his present claims and explain the impossibility of a future for his people.

Also, this narrative presents past events as the direct cause of the present and ongoing social exclusion experienced by indigenous people in Argentine. In an important sense, the political implications of this narrative become quite evident: Inasmuch as this version makes visible to the Argentine people elements that were occluded from the hegemonic narrative, the Argentine government is called to admit past wrongdoings it had committed against the indigenous communities and find ways to provide reasonable restitution—thereby profoundly subverting the political and social status quo.

For the purpose of analyzing the constitutive relations between the counter-narrative and its hegemonic counterpart, it is important to understand how the former constructs the indigenous identity. As noted earlier, the author considers his identity based on his past and appeals to his being a direct descendant of the indigenous chief. But he also moves on to referring to "we" and "us" in order to articulate a continuity between "his" people that was decimated during the conquest and the ongoing experience of the indigenous community. In some respects, time seems to freeze, as indigenous people are presented as a homogenous group that is preserved over the centuries. This kind of rhetorical move has been identified as characterizing other historical accounts (Carretero and Van Alphen 2014), and in that respect, it may be a common feature of how groups constitute their group identity based on some sort of myth about their origins (Sibley et al. 2008). And yet, this direct and static relation between the indigenous people in the present and those of the past is not always preserved. On the contrary, the relation between the past "we" and the present "we" is often ridden with tensions, as shown in the following record of a meeting we held with a female member of the indigenous community during one of our visits.

> This woman started explaining that she taught traditional arts and pottery to members of her community, and then clarified: "well, I don't know if I taught them how to make pottery, I think they have it in their DNA, so they intuitively knew how to do it". Later, as she described her own life, she mentioned: "I chose to live in a house with an adobe floor because I wanted to find my identity, I had to have that experience. And my dad yelled at me, he said: 'I worked so hard to have a real floor, and you want to keep looking backwards'. But I feel that to move forward I have to keep looking backwards, I have to know what my identity is". And later in the conversation she explained that she teaches traditional pottery but she wants the experience of making pottery to have a real meaning; she wants her students to begin thinking up new designs that reflect their current experience and have meaning for them in the present. And she said: "… people always think that being part of the indigenous community means that one has to continue doing things the way they were done in the past, they don't understand that we exist today and that our art belongs in the present." And then she recalled that in preparing a piece of pottery for an assignment, one of her young students shaped the piece as 'Mickey Mouse' because this gave voice to something that was known and valuable to this girl in the present time. Her student's choice, she told us, gave her pause and left her pondering. Another member of the community who was present at that meeting intervened at that point and said "people are always surprised when we tell them we have cellphones, as though Indians[2] should just have boleadoras". Everyone burst out laughing.

At the beginning of this meeting, the art teacher defines the indigenous identity in terms of heredity (as she refers to "their DNA") and in relation to past traditions (as when she wanted a traditional adobe floor to feel connected to her traditional roots). The indigenous identity is thus constructed in an anachronic way, not unlike the way it was presented in the official version, as frozen in time. Nevertheless, this woman also articulates a more dynamic, less frozen, sense of identity, as when she wants her students to transform the traditional forms of art and make them their own, in the present. In this regard, she seems to convey that the sense of continuity with the culture and traditions of her ancestors does not prevent their transformation—as in her call for using traditional art methods to construct modern or current symbols.

In our view, the various discourses of members of the indigenous community seem to suggest the coexistence of two contradictory representations of their own indigenous identity—two representations that are in tension with one another. One is anachronistic, fixed in the past, and consistent with the prevalent hegemonic discourse. The other is a more dynamic version, one that permits members of the community to imagine different ways of being members of this community, ways that change over time. We propose that this state of cognitive polyphasia gives voice to two needs on the side of indigenous people. One is the need to constitute themselves as a social group, to be recognized by the other, and to legitimize their claims for justice against the Argentine state. In an effort to establish a linear continuity with their people from the past, as (in the way it would be articulated by the hegemonic narrative) "real indigenous people," they resort to taking in and adopting features of the alternative hegemonic representations. The other need is for their identities to reflect the fact that they live real lives in the present—lives that have modified their traditions; they need to think of themselves in less frozen ways, as members of an indigenous community who are entitled to modify themselves and be indigenous in some ways different from the ways their ancestors were indigenous. In some respects, then, their stories appropriate aspects of the alternative representations of the indigenous identity that are articulated by the dominant hegemonic narrative—this may serve for them to gain recognition as a community in the eyes of the dominant groups. At the same time, their stories also call for a newly elaborated version, their own perspective on their culture—a piece that has been invisible and, indeed, negated, within the hegemonic framework. As the two women burst out laughing when they say "people are always surprised when we tell them we have cellphones, as though Indians should just have boleadoras," their mocking of the alternative hegemonic representation reflects what Gillespie (2008) has labeled *bracketing*, a discursive strategy that conveys both acknowledgment and critical resistance. Nevertheless, their discourse makes it evident that while they recognize that version of themselves as not their own version but as the view that others have of them and mock it, they also, at times, grab on to and appropriate that representation, or pieces of it.

Conclusions

In this chapter, we have discussed the differences and similarities between the contents of hegemonic and counter-narratives related to the Conquest of the Desert and the tensions and conflicts between the two, as each version positions itself as the objective truth about what actually happened. The hegemonic narrative negates the conflict between the two groups in the present, by rendering the indigenous group invisible and nonexistent and by narrating their identity in anachronistic ways. As a result, it delegitimizes indigenous claims for recognition and reparation and works to protect and reproduce the social order. The counter-narrative explicitly postulates the existence of a conflict between the indigenous community and the Argentine state—a conflict that started out in the past and persists in the present, inasmuch as past wrongs have not been acknowledged and repaired, group rights have not been guaranteed, and injustices and exclusion persist in the present time.

And yet, we have also underscored that hegemonic and counter-narratives are not homogeneous and stable. Tensions and contradictions abound both between and within narrative discourses. Indeed, we have shown that specific narrative elements may serve distinct functions—whether it is to establish or challenge continuity, to resist characterizations suggested by alternative representations, or to avoid responsibility and deny claims for reparations. On the one hand, the hegemonic narrative promotes a positive view of the Argentine national identity by acknowledging the goodness of the original inhabitants ("they used to take care of their children, they used to prepare food… they used to be very grateful people") and attributing their extinction to the colonizing process initiated by the Spaniards (as manifested in their disappearance from the historical timeline in the museum) without ever acknowledging the actions of the Argentine state in the past and rendering invisible their existence in the present. On the other hand, the counter-narrative creates a continuity between past, present, and future by establishing its inevitable links with the Argentine state and features a noticeable tension between the need to assert their identification with their ancestors and gain recognition from the dominant group, while also allowing for change and transformation in their midst.

Our thinking about the process of remembering and narrating historical events allows us to draw implications for designing educational interventions aimed at modifying the extant narratives in such ways so as to promote the betterment of the indigenous communities in Argentina. It must first be noted that any such attempts at intervention cannot take place exclusively at the individual level because both hegemonic and counter-narratives are manifested and supported by collective symbolic resources. Hence, any intervention must attempt a broad or global transformation of how both past processes and the ongoing indigenous situation are discussed. Also, it would be critical to allow for multiple competing versions of events to coexist and dialogue, challenging, informing, and enriching one another. And yet, such transformation is not easy to accomplish inasmuch as alterations in collective narratives have direct impact on individual and group identity and are therefore resisted consciously and unconsciously.

In this vein, it is also important to note that we are not proposing an intervention at the informational or even conceptual level. Changes in collective narrative discourse are unlikely to come about merely as a result of new facts or evidence—it is the representation and interpretation of facts, the meanings made of facts that are in dispute. The notion of state of cognitive polyphasia suggests that people develop strategies to deal with conflicting information without changing their beliefs and interpretations. It is the state of polyphasia, rather than mere information, which must be addressed.

But how does one go about doing this? The goal is not necessarily to support or reinforce one or another version of historical events. Rather, it would be important to support students in acquiring and utilizing the skills of a lay historian: searching and selecting for sources of historical evidence, the systematic weighing and comparing of evidentiary facts, so as to construct hypotheses about the phenomenon at hand, and develop the willingness to critically revise their conclusions.

Notes

1. The social roles of all the people mentioned in this chapter had been slightly modified to preserve the anonymity of their identities.
2. Although "Indian" is not the acceptable term to refer to indigenous people because it builds on the mistaken assumption of the first Spaniards colonizers (i.e., that they had arrived to India) and denies their true identity, we did observe that members of the local indigenous community often use this term colloquially to refer to themselves without considering it offensive. It is, however, typically considered offensive or derogatory when used by non-indigenous people.

Acknowledgments This work has been supported by funding from the research projects PICT-2012–1594 and PICT-2014–1003 (FONCyT-Argentina), and a grant from the Latin American Studies, University of Utah.

REFERENCES

Abrams, A., Wetherel, M., Cochrane, S., Hoog, M., & Turner, J. C. (2001). Knowing what to think by knowing who you are: Self-categorization and the nature of norm formation, conformity and group polarization. In M. A. Hogg & D. Abrams (Eds.), *Intergroup relations. Essential readings* (pp. 270–288). New York: Taylor & Francis.

Andrews, M. (2004). Opening the original contributions. Counter-narratives and the power to oppose. In M. Bamberg & M. Andrews (Eds.), *Considering counter-narratives: Narrating, resisting, making sense* (pp. 2–6). Philadelphia: John Benjamins.

Asensio, M., & Pol, E. (2012). From identity museums to mentality museums: Theoretical basis for history museums. In M. Carretero, M. Asensio & M. Rodriguez Moneo (Eds.), *History education and the construction of national identities* (pp. 257–268). Charlotte, NC: Age Publishing.

Bamberg, M., & Andrews, M. (2004). Introduction to the book. In M. Bamberg & M. Andrews (Eds.), *Considering counter-narratives: Narrating, resisting, making sense* (pp. IX–X). Philadelphia: John Benjamin.

Bang, J. (2009). Nothingness and the human umwelt. A cultural-ecological approach to meaning. *Integrative Psychological and Behavioral Science, 43*, 374–392.

Barreiro, A. (2013). The appropriation process of the belief in a just world. *Integrative Psychological and Behavioral Sciences, 47,* 431–449.

Barreiro, A., & Castorina, J. A. (2016). Nothingness as the dark side of social representations. In J. Bangs & D. Winther-Lindqvist (Eds.), *Nothingness* (pp. 69–88). New Jersey: Transaction Publishers.

Barreiro, A., Castorina, J. A., & Van Alphen, F. (2017). Conflicting Narratives about the Argentinean 'Conquest of the Desert': Social Representations, Cognitive Polyphasia, and Nothingness. In M. Carretero, S. Berger & M. Grever (Eds.), *Palgrave Handbook of Research in Historical Culture and Education* (pp. 373–389). London, UK: Palgrave Macmillan.

Barreiro, A., Wainryb, C., & Carretero, M. (2016). Narratives about the past and cognitive polyphasia remembering the Argentine "Conquest of the Desert". *Peace & Conflict. Special Issue "Memory and Conflict", 22*(1), 44–51.

Bayer, O. (2010). *Historia de la crueldad argentina*. (History of the Argentinean cruelty). Buenos Aires: El Tugurio.

Bennett, T. (1998). Speaking to the eyes: Museums, legibility and the social order. In S. Macdonald (Ed.), *The politics of displays: Museums, science and culture* (pp. 25–36). London: Rutledge.

Briones, C. (1994). Con la tradición de todas las generaciones pasadas gravitando sobre la mente de los vivos. Usos del pasado e invención de la tradición. *RUNA, 21*, 99–129.

Carretero, M. (2011). *Constructing patriotism*. Charlotte, North Carolina: Sage.

Carretero, M., & Kriger, M. (2011). Historical representations and conflicts about indigenous people as national identities. *Culture & Psychology, 17*(2), 177–195.

Carretero, M., & van Alphen, F. (2014). Do master narratives change among high school students? A characterization of how national history is represented. *Cognition and Instruction, 32*(3), 290–312.

Deaux, K., & Martin, D. (2003). Interpersonal networks and social categories: Specifying levels of context in identity processes. *Social Psychology Quarterly, 66*(2), 101–117.

Del Río, W. (2005). *Memorias de la expropiación. Sometimiento e incorporación indígena en la Patagonia* (1872–1943). Ed. Universidad de Quilmes.

Duveen, G. (2007). Culture and social representations. In J. Valsiner & A. Rosa (Eds.), *The Cambridge handbook of sociocultural psychology* (pp. 543–559). Cambridge: Cambridge University Press.

Ellemers, N., Spears, R., & Doosje, B. (2002). Self and social identity. *Annual Review of Psychology, 53*, 161–186.

Gillespie, A. (2008). Social representations, alternative representations and semantic barriers. *Journal for the Theory of Social Behaviour, 38*(4), 375–391.

Gonzáles de Oleaga, M. (2012). Historical Narratives in the Colonial, National, Ethnic Museum of Argentina, Paraguay and Spain. In M. Carretero, M. Asensio & M. Rodriguez Moneo (Eds.), *History education and the construction of national identities* (pp. 239–256). Charlotte, NC: Age Publishing.

Gordillo, G., & Hirsch, S. (2010). La presencia ausente: invisibilizaciones, políticas estatales y emergencias indígenas en la Argentina. En G. Gordillo & S. Hirsch (Comps.) *Movilizaciones indígenas e identidades en disputa en la Argentina* (pp. 15–38). Buenos Aires: La Crujía.

Halbwachs, M. (1925/1994). *Les cadres sociaux de la mémoire*. Paris: Albin Michel.

Halperin Donghi, T. (1980/1995). *Una Nación para el Desierto Argentino*. Buenos Aires: CEAL.

Jodelet, D. (2003). Pensamiento Social e Historicidad. *Relaciones, 93*(24), 98–113.

Jovchelovitch, S. (2008). The rehabilitation of common sense. Social representations, science, and cognitive polyphasia. *Journal for the Theory of Social Behavior, 38*(4), 431–448.

Macdonald, S. (1998). Exhibitions of power and powers of exhibition: An introduction to politics of display. In S. Macdonald (Ed.), *The politics of displays: Museums, science and culture* (pp. 1–24). London: Routledge.

Moscovici, S. (1961). *La psychanalyse son image et son public*. París: PUF.
Nagy, M. (2014). *Estamos vivos. Historia de la comunidad indígena Cacique Pincén, provincial de Buenos Aires (siglos XIX–XX)*. Buenos Aires. Antropofagia.
Novaro, G. (2003). Indios" "Aborígenes" y "Pueblos originarios". Sobre el cambio de conceptos y la continuidad de las concepciones escolares. *Educación, Lenguaje y Sociedad, 1*, 199–219.
Pennebaker, J., Paez, D., & Deschamps, J. C. (2006). The social psychology of history: Defining the most important events of the last 10, 100, and 1000 years. *Psicología Política, 32*, 15–32.
Postmes, T., & Branscombe, N. (2010). Sources of social identity. En T. Postmes & N. Branscombe (Eds.), *Rediscovering social identity: Core sources*. Psychology Press.
Rosa, A. (2006). Recordar, describir y explicar el pasado, ¿qué, cómo y para el futuro de quién? In M. Carretero, A. Rosa, & M. F. Gonzáles (Eds.), *Enseñanza de la historia y memoria colectiva* (pp. 41–52). Buenos Aires: Paidós.
Sarasola, C. M. (2010). *De manera sagrada y en celebración: Identidad, cosmovisión y espiritualidad en los pueblos indígenas*. Buenos Aires: Biblos.
Sarti, M., & Barreiro, A. (2014). Juicios Morales y memoria colectiva: narrativas de jóvenes sobre la "Conquista del Desierto". In J. A. Castorina & A. Barreiro (Eds.), *Representaciones sociales y prácticas en la psicogénesis del conocimiento social* (pp. 141–156). Buenos Aires: Miño y Dávila.
Sibley, C., Liu, J., Duckitt, J., & Khan, S. (2008). Social representations of history and the legitimation of social inequality: The form of historical negation. *European Journal of Social Psychology, 38*, 542–568.
Tajfel, H., & Turner, J. C. (1986). The social identity theory of inter-group behavior. In S. Worchel & L. W. Austin (Eds.), *Psychology of intergroup relations*. Chicago: Nelson-Hall.
Ungaretti, J., & Müller, M. (forthcoming). Estudios sobre el prejuicio hacia diferentes grupos sociales. In A. Barreiro (Ed.), *La construcción del conocimiento social y moral: representaciones sociales, prejuicio y relaciones con los otros*. Buenos Aires: UNIPE.
Ungaretti, J., Etchezahar, E., & Barreiro, A. (2015). *Análisis de la escala de prejuicio sutil y manifiesto hacia indígenas*, poster presented at I Congreso Nacional de Psicología. Argentine: San Luis. [unpublished].
Valko, M. (2012). *Los indios invisibles del Malón de la Paz. De la apoteosis al confinamiento, secuestro y destierro*. Buenos Aires: Continente.
Wagner, W., Duveen, G., Verma, J., & Themel, M. (2000). "I have some faith and at the same time I don't believe in it"—cognitive polyphasia and culture change. *Journal of Community and Applied Social Psychology, 10*, 102–314.
Wertsch, J. (2002). *Voices of collective remembering*. Cambridge: Cambridge University Press.

Authors' Biography

Alicia Barreiro is a Professor at the University of Buenos Aires and FLACSO-Argentina. Besides, she is a Researcher at the National Council of Scientific and Technical Research. She studies moral and social development complementing developmental psychology approach with social representations theory, as well as collective memory and its role in determining the actual intergroup relations. She has published widely in international journals and published several book chapters. Recently, she co-authored with José Antonio Castorina and Floor Van Alphen "Conflicting Narratives about Argentinean 'Conquest of the Desert'. Representations, cognitive Polyphasia, and Nothingness" (Carretero, Berger and Grever, *Palgrave Handbook of Research in Historical Culture and Education*, Palgrave Macmillan forthcoming) and with José Antonio Castorina "*Nothingness as the dark side of social representations*" (Bang and Winther-Lindqvist, *Nothingness* pp. 69–88, Transaction Publishers 2016), and she edited the book "*La construcción del conocimiento social y moral: representaciones sociales, prejuicio y relaciones con los otros*" (Unipe, forthcoming).

Cecilia Wainryb is a Professor of Psychology at the University of Utah and the co-director of the Social Development Lab. Her research interests span moral, social and emotional development, and her work examines how children and adolescents construct meaning from moral transgressions and interpersonal and group conflict, and how such meanings contribute to the development of moral agency. She has studied these processes in community samples as well as with samples of youth growing up in the midst of war and political violence. Her studies combine interview data, narrative methods, conversation analyses and psychophysiological measures. She has published widely in international journals and has edited several volumes, including most recently "*Talking about right and wrong: Parent-child conversations as contexts for moral development*" (Cambridge University Press 2014, with H. Recchia) and "*Trauma, psychopathology, and resilience among child soldiers around the world*" (Routledge 2014, with P. Kerig).

Mario Carretero is a Professor of Cognitive Psychology at Autonoma University of Madrid, Spain, where he was Dean of the Faculty of Psychology, and Researcher at FLACSO, Argentina. He has carried out an extensive research on history education from both cognitive and sociocultural approaches. He has published in *Journal of the Learning Sciences* and *Cognition and Instruction*. His last books are *History Education and the Construction of National Identities* (2012) (co-ed.) and *Constructing Patriotism* (funded by the Guggenheim Foundation) (2011). He has been Santander Visiting Scholar at the David Rockefeller Center for Latin American Studies of Harvard University (2009) and Bliss Carnochan Visiting Professor at the Humanities Center of Stanford University (2011). His present research interests have to do with an interdisciplinary attempt to study history education issues as it can be seen in *Palgrave Handbook of Research in Historical Culture and Education* (2017) (co-edited along with S. Berger and M. Grever).

Open Access This chapter is licensed under the terms of the Creative Commons Attribution 4.0 International License (http://creativecommons.org/licenses/by/4.0/), which permits use, sharing, adaptation, distribution and reproduction in any medium or format, as long as you give appropriate credit to the original author(s) and the source, provide a link to the Creative Commons license and indicate if changes were made.

The images or other third party material in this chapter are included in the chapter's Creative Commons license, unless indicated otherwise in a credit line to the material. If material is not included in the chapter's Creative Commons license and your intended use is not permitted by statutory regulation or exceeds the permitted use, you will need to obtain permission directly from the copyright holder.

When History Teaching Turns into Parrhesia: The Case of Italian Colonial Crimes

Giovanna Leone

Introduction

The aim of this chapter was to highlight the importance and the consequentiality of a specific kind of history education that happens when teachers decide to openly narrate to their students the crimes committed by previous generations of their own group—crimes so far kept silenced and literally denied in the general social discourse. By applying to this teaching the discussion of Foucault (1983) on truth and social discourse, we propose to single it out from other kinds of teaching designed for learning about controversial issues (Leone 2012; Leone and Sarrica 2014). We think, in fact, that this kind of history education has to be distinguished from other kinds of difficult teaching on sensitive issues. Many times history teachers may be confronted with classrooms that could be divided by their own idea of what happened in the past. To quote only a couple of examples of this situation, imagine to be a teacher trying to explain Northern Ireland struggles in Dublin or in London (Barton and McCully 2012); or imagine to teach to your pupils the apparently innocent story of native Americans feeding starving newcomers disembarked from the Mayflower, being aware that this episode could be accounted for as an act of generosity or as the first moment of

G. Leone (✉)
Sapienza University of Rome, Rome, Italy
e-mail: giovanna.leone@uniroma1.it

a process leading to a terrible genocide (Kurtiş et al. 2010). But some other times, history teachers break down a silence about the facts that are not disputed, yet ignored by the large majority of society. Imagine, to quote an example of this other kind of issues, to teach to your French students that Vichy is a city historically known not only for its mineral water (Campbell 2006); or imagine, in a much more dangerous situation, to be a courageous teacher trying to convey to your Turk students the reasons why some historians call the mass killings of Armenians as genocide (Bilali 2013) Namely, according to Foucault's categorization of different kinds of social discourse aimed to convey truth, we propose that historical teaching that addresses not controversial past, but socially denied historical facts may be regarded as a specific case of *parrhesia:* a kind of social discourse that, addressing troubling issues, "chooses frankness instead of persuasion, truth instead of falseness or silence, (…) the moral duty instead of self-interest or moral apathy" (Foucault 2001, p. 19).

In the first part of the chapter, specificities of this kind of history education will be discussed. More in particular, theoretical expectancies on effects of this strategy of history education will be related to the discussion of Foucault on empowering consequences of *parrhesia*. In spite of the risk of aggressive or defensive reactions of listeners, *parrhesia* speaks, in fact, without fear a relevant yet inconvenient truth that, if eventually understood and accepted, may give to its receivers a better grasp on some important reasons accounting for the current features of their own lives.

Moreover, the consequences of this kind of historical education, which frankly unveils the past in-group wrongdoings to students, will be related to the socio-emotional model of needs of victims and perpetrators after the end of a massive social violence (Nadler and Shnabel 2008; Shnabel and Nadler 2015).

Finally, specificities of history education when it becomes a *parrhesiastic* communication will be understood taking into account how social denial may disempower historical awareness of descendants of perpetrators about relevant facts happened in their in-group past, facts that could allow them to better understand their current in-group and intergroup relations. Here, the concept of knowledge of historical facts has to be linked with the concept of historical thinking (Seixas and Peck 2004), which refers to the abilities school history teaching should provide students with, in order to enable them to approach historical narratives critically. Seixas and Peck (2004) distinguish six main elements composing this ability of historical thinking: significance, epistemology and evidence, continuity and change, progress and decline, empathy and moral judgment, and historical agency (Seixas and Peck 2004). Although obviously relying on all these elements in order to be effective, the use of *parrhesia* when teaching historical wrongdoings of the in-group covered up by a literal social denial (Cohen 2001) addresses in a specific way the dimensions linked to empathy and moral judgment. It has to be stressed that, in this description of Seixas and Peck (2004), empathy is evoked not as a psychological construct, yet as an ability to perspective taking that is historically based. It means that, although trying to "imagine" ourselves in the position of older generations when facing difficult choices, this kind of empathy is not based on "presentism," i.e., a cognitive short cut assuming that all people react in a similar way under different historical and cultural situations. On the contrary, this perspective taking is based "on a rich base of information about the fundamental structures and processes of everyday life during those (past) times" (Seixas and Peck 2004, p. 115), making it clear for students feeling empathy with past generations of the in-group that there are basic differences and changes between their life and life of their ancestors. Being empathic and aware of anachronistic abuses of imposing present-day moral standards to past situation, however, does not imply the impossibility to morally judge on past crimes. In fact, "exactly as with the problem of historical empathy, our ability to make moral judgment in history requires that we entertain the notion of an historically transcendent human commonality" (Seixas and Peck 2004, p. 115). Speaking fearlessly about moral transgressions committed by the in-group and then denied in the following social discourse, *parrhesia* specifically address this capability to recognize this urge to morally judge the past inherited by previous generations, without nourishing a relativism that disallows any condemnation, also when it is largely deserved.

In the second part of the chapter, results of a case study on contemporary history teaching about colonial crimes committed by the Italian Army during the Ethiopia invasion (1935–1936) will be presented, in order to observe how conveying this knowledge, although referring to remote facts, may produce considerable effects on present-day young Italians. This study explores how such a kind of historical teaching, narrating in-group misdeeds formerly denied in the social discourse, may help young descendants of perpetrators to better understand their current intergroup relations. According to the classic theoretical position of Ortega y Gasset (1930), in fact, historical knowledge referred to the group in which one happens to be born may be seen as a precious tool to improve awareness of one's own "historical pre-existence," i.e. of the past situations that account for present-day constraints in intergroup relationships. In this sense, when they help to explain current social conflicts some historical facts, although referred to remote past, may nevertheless be felt as "psychologically contemporary" (Lewin 1943).

The case study presented in this chapter could be seen as additional evidence that colonial crimes, similarly to all other contents eliciting controversial reactions of receivers, belong to this particular category of "psychologically contemporary" historical events. In fact, both the psychological past and the psychological future are simultaneous parts of the social perception of the situation existing at a given time. This classic theoretical remark of Lewin (1943) may be easily adapted to our times, when we read in newspapers that Islamic terrorists claim that their victims are "Crusaders," or when we quote recent comments of former London's Mayor and now Minister of Foreign Affairs of the UK, Boris Johnson, to Obama's advice that the UK is better off by staying in the European Union. Replying to this political speech of the US President, Boris Johnson attributed this opinion to Barak Obama's "ancestral dislike" for Britain as a result of his "part-Kenyan" heritage that made him hostile to his former colonizers. Apart from controversies stirred by these somehow appalling comments, the Mayor of London's political argument is a very good example of how much social perception of current international relations may be influenced by the psychological contemporaneity of the ancient ghosts of colonial violence (Volpato and Licata 2010).

Moreover, the exemplum given by the research discussed in the second part of this chapter explores risks yet great opportunities offered by the breaking of a long-lasting social silence on the past wrongdoings of a social group. The complete denial of colonial crimes committed by the Italian Army during the invasion of Ethiopia, in fact, makes the contemporary historical education on these facts deeply different from any other kinds of difficult history teaching. This case study, therefore, is presented not to discuss the specifics of Italian history, but to better understand what happens in situations when social silence is widespread across all other sources of information available to young generations and history teaching is the only way to frankly speak to them about the moral indignities of their group.

In this chapter, the idea that in these situations history education may turn into *parrhesia* is advanced. It is proposed that, when all the multiple sources contributing to build a social representation of history (family reminiscing and conversations, literature and arts, movies, media narratives, etc.) deny for a long time that historical events accounting for moral indignities of the in-group occurred, only historians may offer to young descendants of perpetrators a precious occasion to cope with this difficult knowledge of their in-group past.

However, an issue at stake for studying more in depth this specific kind of history education refers to the consequences theoretically expected when history teaching breaks such a long-lasting and widespread denial. If we consider as prominent the psychological need for a positive social identity (Tajfel 1982), avoidance of inconvenient facts could be expected as the best way of coping with a troubling past and each frank narrative may be seen, on the contrary, as a threat. According to this theoretical frame, psychological consequences of a frank history teaching about socially denied crimes are expected to be mainly negative. But if we understand acknowledgment of past responsibilities as a first unavoidable step for a real intergroup reconciliation (Vollhardt et al. 2014), then presenting descendants of perpetrators with a frank and truthful narrative of in-group wrongdoings may be seen on the contrary as the best choice to cope with this difficult past, since the lack of knowledge of past in-group responsibilities may be expected to threaten the harmony of current intergroup relations. According to this other theoretical frame, even if first psychological *reactions* in front of a clear narrative of in-group crimes could be expected to be ambivalent or fully negative, in the long run the breaking of an unrealistic denial could be expected to produce overall positive *consequences* for receivers, enabling them to better understand the history of their group.

This chapter deals with the issue of reactions and consequences of this specific kind of history education both theoretically and empirically. Although theoretical expectations and empirical evidence aspects are obviously intertwined, for clarity's sake theoretical points will be previously discussed, starting from Michel Foucault's considerations on the evolution of truth-speaking strategies used in classic Greek culture— strategies that could be seen as the root of modern attitudes toward the dilemma between facing or avoiding historical narratives conveying inconvenient historical indignities to young generations.

Michel Foucault on Parrhesia

In his problematization of different kinds of truth-speaking—that he saw as social activities to be studied not from an epistemological, but from a pragmatic point of view—Foucault proposed to categorize them according to their *effects on receivers*. More particularly, he singled out a specific kind of them that he named *parrhesia*, tracing back an old concept firstly proposed by classic Greek philosophers. According to its classic Greek root, the word *parrhesia* describes a kind of truth-speaking that, by openly and fearlessly conveying a disturbing knowledge, implies a risk for those telling it *(parrhesiastes)*. The *parrhesiastes* is a person who, being free to choose whether to do it or not, speaks a difficult truth in order to accomplish a sense of moral duty toward receivers. Moreover, the *parrhesiastes* chooses to speak frankly the truth regardless of any risk to himself. The *parrhesiastes* speaks so frankly and fearlessly the truth, because he appreciates advantages of this choice both for him and for his receivers. Referring to himself, communication being in Foucault's point of view an influential *social activity*, the *parrhesiastes* chooses to openly speak the truth in order to safeguard harmony between his words and his acts. Referring to receivers, Foucault maintains that the dangerous choice of truth-speaking challenges yet empowers them. In fact, such an uneasy truth may, if accepted, make receivers able to cope with some important evidence that they would have preferred to ignore.

Foucault argues that it is precisely its empowering effect that makes *parrhesia* different from other kinds of troubling communication, as, for instance, the aggressive ones. However, being effects of communication linked not only to source's intention, but also to receiver's capacity and will to understand, *parrhesia* may be better defined as a "communication game", leading to positive effects for receivers only when a cooperation of both speakers and listeners successfully occurs. Apart from reactions of receivers, however, *parrhesia* turns out to be always an expression of protection of the *parrhesiastes*, reinforcing their personal harmony between their words and their social actions. Regardless of its final outcomes, therefore, *parrhesia* is always a way of taking care of oneself, an action of *cura sui*. Taking all together these different aspects, *parrhesia* may be regarded therefore as a specific kind of education, since the authority of the *parrhesiastes* does not come from power or status, but only from his free moral choice—encouraging receivers to take care of themselves and to treat receivers of their own communication in a similar way (Foucault 1983).

In this chapter, I propose to apply Foucault's discussion on the utility of singling out *parrhesia* as a specific kind of truth-speaking, to describe the specific social activity by which history teachers decide to uncover for their students a moral indignity committed in the past by their group—a moral indignity so far kept *silent* and even *denied* in the general social discourse. Assuming the pragmatic point of view that frames Foucault's studies, we may consider history teaching that breaks down social silence on past in-group crimes as a specific communicative choice, inserted into the wider set of social and psychological processes eventually leading to intergroup reconciliation (Nadler et al. 2008). More precisely, it could be argued that the factual evidence provided by this specific kind of history teaching, provided when this same evidence is lacking in any other kind of social discourse, is essential for descendants of past perpetrators to fully acknowledge past historical responsibilities of their group (Vollhardt et al. 2014).

According to the theoretical model on different needs of perpetrators and victims after a massive intergroup violence (Nadler and Shnabel 2008; Shnabel and Nadler 2015), acknowledgment is foreseen as a difficult yet unavoidable step toward a sound intergroup reconciliation. When violence ends, in fact, perpetrators need to be reinserted in their community, avoiding the exclusion due to their wrongdoings. Victims, on the contrary, need to recover control on their own lives, after being helpless and unable to defend themselves. When the group of perpetrators fully accepts responsibilities for hurting their victims, it opens the door for meeting the needs of both victims and perpetrators, as described in the Nadler and Shnabel model (2008).

In spite of its clear-cut description of different needs of victims and perpetrators, however, this socio-emotional model of reconciliation does not address the issue of how long it could take for groups to arrive to face their past lack of morality—if perpetrators—or their lack of agency—if victims (Cajani and Leone 2015). Sometimes, the search for historical truth is straightforwardly linked to reconciliation processes: given, for instance, the famous example of the Truth and Reconciliation Committees in South Africa, where, at the presence of the local community and of its authorities, truthful narratives of violence were overtly negotiated between victims and perpetrators (Gibson 2006).

Apart from this specific cultural situation, however, an immediate and overt acknowledgment of violence rarely occurs in perpetrators' communication. In particular when victims are too weak or socially isolated, their voice is seldom heard. In these more frequent situations, silence on violence could take place for a long time in the social arena and go down the generations. It implies that the needs described by the Nadler and Shnabel model (2008; Shnabel and Nadler 2015), as directly associated with victims and perpetrators, may go down the generations too and affect the social and psychological needs of their descendants.

If we take into consideration both the model proposed by Nadler and Shnabel (2008; Shnabel and Nadler 2015) and the evidence of the possibility that often many years are needed for atrocities to be overtly recognized and officially narrated to descendants of perpetrators' group (Leach et al. 2013), we can agree on the idea that the same needs foreseen for perpetrators and victims may go down the generations, to influence descendants of victims and perpetrators too (Bilewicz and Jaworska 2013; Leone 2012).

It is clear that, when a long time elapses from the end of the violence to its full acknowledgment by perpetrators, the dilemma between avoidance and coping with this difficult truth begins to affect not only the current social discourse but also the historical teaching. At this point, we may ask ourselves whether it is necessary to draw a dividing line between history education that breaks down a long-lasting social silence on past violence enacted by the group and other kinds of difficult teaching on sensitive issues.

Parrhesia and Controversial Historical Issues in the Classroom

Past historical crimes of the group in which one happens to be born are one out of many controversial issues that could emerge during classroom discussions. However, unlike other sensitive issues (see, for instance, Goldberg 2013; Kello 2015; King 2009; Barton and McCully 2012), history teachers cannot skip or avoid them when narrating to students these periods of the past of their group. Apart from sensitiveness that every competent teacher could have to show when addressing difficult topics (Zembylas and Kambani 2012), in fact, history teachers are expected to inform their students about the more important facts that happened in their group story, since only this learning may give to these adults-to-be a real mastery about their "historical pre-existence" (Ortega y Gasset 1930), steering their future participation to the democratic life of their community. Without knowing relevant past events of one's own community, in fact, it is neither possible to judge on contemporary issues, nor to understand contemporary intergroup relations. Generally speaking, this makes intergroup violence a specific topic of history teaching (Sen and Wagner 2005) and, more particularly, teaching on past in-group crimes an essential social activity to foster effective democratic participation in the future life of students.

On the other hand, immediately after the end of violence perpetrators, together with other protagonists of violence such as victims or apathetic bystanders, often use *silence* among former foes as the first implicit communication concerning the past events. In the first moments after the violence settlement, in fact, silence may appear as a way to restore a sense of "normality" in everyday life. It enhances initial viable local life and allows perpetrators, apathetic bystanders and victims to continue to live side by side (Eastmond and Selimovic 2012).

However, this choice for silence could be more or less common among the multiple sources of information about the past of their own group that are available to young people, ranging from informal settings, such as family narratives, to media communication, literature, or fiction. An analysis of the Italian movies produced after WW2 could provide a striking example of it. Immediately after the end of the war, while silence and avoidance were often used in current social exchanges in order to avoid the high risks of a civil war between those who had adhered to Fascism and who had supported the resistance, the Italian neo-realistic cinema helped nevertheless to convey a representation of humiliation and moral blunting of the Italian people, thanks to movies directed by Rossellini and De Sica (De Caro 2014). However, in the majority of cases the solution of avoiding any open communication concerning violent past does not last, neither can it be enough to cope with violence's aftermaths. As time goes by, in fact, silence instead of being seen as a first viable solution becomes threatening and effortful.

Nevertheless, in some specific cultural situations, silence is not a transient solution. In these unhappy social situations, in fact, as time goes by, silence on past violence cannot be broken. Historians are forbidden to study this period of the in-group past, leaders are not referring to it when commenting on their decisions, and also more informal communication (such as family conversations, or artistic performances, or books, movies, or other fictional narratives) seems to ignore what happened. In these social situations, the transient silence immediately following the end of violence has turned into the highly detrimental states of *social denial*. Referring only to the narratives of perpetrators, denial may occur at different degrees, as a refusal: to admit the historical reality of violent facts *(literal denial)*; to recognize the moral responsibility of perpetrators for these facts *(interpretive denial)*; or to assume the practical consequences of acknowledging one's own responsibility for past violence *(implicatory denial)* (Cohen 2001).

There is no need to invoke obscure conspiracies, since many aspects account for the "banality" of the well-known phenomenon of social denials. As a matter of fact, we have already quoted some examples in previous pages, since we may often appreciate this phenomenon today in various contexts: the literal denial of the Armenian genocide (Hovannisian 1998; Bilali 2013); the covering up of French collaboration with Nazi occupation (Campbell 2006); the social amnesia about the Italian colonial crimes perpetrated during the occupation of Ethiopia (Leone and Sarrica 2012); the rhetoric of official discourses on Thanksgiving day, when US presidents avoid to remember the role of native Americans in episodes commemorated by this special day (Kurtiş et al. 2010), to quote only a few. Instead of well-organized manipulation, historical denials dominant in many social situations are often simply the result of "a gradual seepage of knowledge down some collective black hole" (Cohen 2001, p. 13). In these social situations, reconciliation is therefore linked to every intelligent effort performed by the members of the social group of former perpetrators to oppose such an easygoing and generalized seepage, choosing to narrate violence to younger generations instead of letting it disappear down some "black holes."

The choice to break down the social denial originates from a keen understanding of their detrimental consequences for perpetrators' descendants. With *literal* or *interpretive denial*, knowledge itself available to descendants of perpetrators is at stake—either because facts themselves are not recognized (literal) or because they are acknowledged, but their interpretation as violent acts is challenged (interpretive), as when violence is claimed to be a kind of self-defense, or the only way to prevent further escalations. Finally, with *implicatory denial*, what is denied or minimized are "the psychological, political, or moral implications that conventionally follow" (Cohen 2001:8) the knowledge of serious facts, linked to one's own group responsibilities for past atrocities and suffering.

We propose to call *"parrhesia"* only the history education that breaks down a *literal denial* so widespread across social sources of information and so long-lasting in time, to make history teachers the only possible *parrhesiastes* among all those who convey to young people a representation of their own historical past. Taken into account all the serious consequences of social denial, it is easy to grasp that it is not possible to challenge either interpretive or implicatory denial, when the mere knowledge of facts is not socially available. It allows us to better understand why the historical teaching that turns into *parrhesia*, although difficult and risky, may be also regarded as a meaningful empowerment for those who receive at last clear information about past historical indignities of their group.

Empirical Evidence of the Impact of Parrhesia

However, a basic requirement for this empowerment to be reached is the capacity of students to successfully cope with negative emotions, arising from the difficult historical truth that teachers decide to unveil. To make this point, we will take as an example a research on the case study of Italian university students' reactions to a clear historical description of Italian colonial crimes, formerly silenced and denied in current social discourse. The present-day European collective memories on colonialism, in fact, allow us to find many insightful examples of the different kinds of social denials (Cohen 2001). Sometimes it is possible to observe implicatory denials related to the difficulty of adopting political decisions that take into account the economic consequences of long-lasting exploitation of resources of colonized countries. At other times, an interpretive denial may be observed, when descendants of colonizers are still representing the colonial past of their countries to have been a kind of civilization instead than a systematic exploitation of other groups, implying structural and even direct violence (Galtung and Höivik 1971). In the case study of Italian colonial crimes against Ethiopians, victims having not gained enough power to impose on the research agenda the study of the history of violence they have suffered, until recent years a silence on these facts has been observed in history textbooks (Leone and Mastrovito 2010; Cajani 2013). This lack of historical information, amended only in the most recent manuals, is part of a wider social denial that, for more than seventy years, did not acknowledge these facts to have been proved as true. Moreover, a *historical myth* replaced factual knowledge, describing Italian soldiers as good fellows, unable of any kind of cruelty (Del Boca 2005). Due to the widespread intergenerational silence and the long-lasting social denial, when finally narrated in present-day textbooks, these historical facts—although historically well proven—may sound therefore surprising for young readers. In fact, in spite of recent advances in history teaching, researchers have found that these facts are generally ignored by Italian people, especially younger ones (Pivato 2007). Furthermore, an in-depth textual analysis of the recent Italian history textbooks including this information on past colonial war crimes against Ethiopians has shown that these historical facts are conveyed sometimes in a clear and detailed way, but sometimes in a more evasive one (Leone and Mastrovito 2010).

According to theoretical assumptions previously discussed, only clear historical narratives about these past war crimes can be defined as a kind of *parrhesia*, since only these texts accept the risk of evoking strong negative reactions from readers. On the contrary, evasive historical textbooks seem to pursue, although in a less open way, the same avoiding aims of previous social denial.

To better understand reactions and consequences of these two different strategies of history education, speaking more or less frankly on past in-group misconduct, an empirical study was organized (Leone and Sarrica 2014). This study explores, through a quasi-experimental procedure, the effects of two different kinds of text addressed to young Italian students, which convey either in a *parrhesiastic* or in an evasive way the war crimes that happened during the Italian invasion of Ethiopia (1935–1936).

Researchers explored the reactions of 67 Italian university students (average age: 23.51) who read two online versions (*parrhesiastic* vs. evasive) of a same historical text on crimes committed by the Italian Army during the colonial invasion of Ethiopia (1935–1936). This historical text was inserted in a self-administered questionnaire on social representation of Italian colonial past. Questionnaire controlled for previous knowledge of participants on these crimes and asked to self-assess emotions associated with Italian colonial past both before reading the text and again after reading it. The two bogus texts were built referring to the textbooks that are currently used in history teaching and are addressed to Italian high school students. Starting from the same text, the crimes committed against the Ethiopian group were described in a clear way in the *parrhesia* condition (e.g., saying that the Italian Army used poisonous gases formally forbidden by the Geneva protocol of 1925 during air strikes) or in a less open way in the evasive condition (e.g., saying only that the Italian Army used "unconventional weapons" during air strikes). Each participant was covertly videotaped when sitting alone in a room filling in the questionnaire and reading the text. This setting allowed to attribute directly observed first reactions to the reading and not to the actual presence of other people during the fulfillment of experimental tasks. Results were elaborated using statistical comparisons for quantitative data of the questionnaire and qualitative comparison of coding of first reactions during the text reading observed by three independent judges. Quantitative results of the questionnaire showed that as expected, in spite of recent changes in Italian history textbooks, all participants were ignorant about these past war crimes of their in-group. Referring to emotions that participants associated with the Italian colonialism, a statistical comparison of differences between self-assessed emotions scored before and after the information conveyed by the historical text showed that reading the *parrhesiastic* text affected experienced emotion more than the evasive text. Participants' identification with the in-group showed no significant interactions with the narrative's effects.

The original mix of paper-and-pencil tools and direct observations allowed to better grasp how the consequences of frank narratives differ from those of evasive ones. Interestingly, first reactions expressed during the reading were different in the two experimental conditions. They were covertly videotaped and coded according to the Facial Action System Coding (FACS) by three independent coders. Before debriefing participants were fully informed of all procedural details, in order to make them able to give or deny their consent to the elaboration of their data and videotapes. No one refused to be included in the elaboration.

A frame-by-frame analysis of videotapes of participants reading the historical text on Italian crimes allowed to grasp micro-expressions shown by their faces while reading the text and to code them according to the FACS. According to Ekman and colleagues, micro-expressions immediately following the exposure to a relevant stimulus are seven: surprise, fear, anger, happiness, disgust, sadness, and contempt. Together with these micro-expressions, faces closely scrutinized may show signs of mental activities: as, for instance, a frowning expression. These facial signs occurring together with micro-expressions are interpreted thanks to them. For instance, a frowning activity, occurring with a micro-expression of surprise, may suggest that the stimulus is difficult to grasp and arises doubts in the mind of the observed person. In spite of the fact that cultural norms on emotional expressions may amplify or reduce these movements of the facial muscles, being largely involuntary, these first facial expressions subsequent to relevant stimuli proved to be universal across cultures (Ekman et al. 2013).

This new kind of analysis, made possible by technological advances in videotaping, is based on the idea of Darwin (1965) that the expression of emotions is innate both for man and animals, since inherited as a natural reaction guiding our first efforts to cope with relevant stimuli. For instance, when a stimulus is important, new, and startling, eyelids are so wide-opened that white of the eye is showing above and below. This micro-expression of surprise seems to facilitate a closer look to this unexpected stimulus. In the expression of disgust, both upper and lower lips are raised and nose is wrinkled: This is the expression you make when you smell something bad or take a look on a very dirty room. It is easy to observe how the micro-expression of disgust resembles the first stages of the action of throwing up, when the body rejects a harmful food. Interestingly, these first micro-expressions are common to man and animals, corroborating Darwin's idea of a slow evolution of mankind from other animal species.

However, among the seven facial emotions designated by Ekman and colleagues in their groundbreaking research, only a first reaction is uniquely shown by man, i.e., contempt. While disgust may be expressed for all stimuli-provoking negative sensitive reactions (when seen, smelled, touched, etc.), contempt is shown on the contrary only to express a self-distancing from the behavior of another human being when it seriously deviates from commonly accepted moral norms.

It is not possible to discuss at length on this important remark provided by Ekman et al. (2013) about the insightful evidence originating from their research. I would only comment that their observations on the unique role of contempt among the first human reactions to emotion-provoking stimuli seem to ask again, starting from the new evidence offered by modern technologies, the old philosophical question about the wonders of "the moral within" man, seen in the famous quote of Kant as sublime and difficult to explain as the "starry heavens." In this chapter, it should be underlined that only participants assigned to the experimental condition of reading the *parrhesiastic* historical text showed a first reaction of contempt. Moreover, when self-assessing their own emotions associated with Italian colonialism, participants assigned to the *parrhesia* condition scored higher in all emotions, but not when self-assessing guilt (Leone and Sarrica 2014).

Different effects following evasive historical teaching or parrhesia could be grasped if we consider jointly micro-expressions of contempt showed while reading a historical text breaking down the social denial of in-group crimes on the one hand, and changes of emotions on Italian colonialism, self-assessed before and after reading this text, on the other hand. Only parrhesia, in fact, seems to enable young descendants of perpetrators to *take a critical distance from the historical responsibilities of previous generations*: immediately expressing an innate reaction of self-distancing (contempt) and recognizing through self-aware emotion of shame the need to repair the moral image of the Italian in-group (Allpress et al. 2014). On the contrary, guilt, which could be felt by these young participants born many years after these historical facts only associating their own responsibilities to those of previous generations (Branscombe and Doosje 2004), is *not* significantly affected by the *parrhesiastic* historical narrative.

Conclusion

Concluding these brief notes on situations when historical education turns into *parrhesia*, I think that it is important to pay attention to the differences between emotional reactions of participants described in the study that we used as an example of this field of research (Leone and Sarrica 2014). I propose that, all results taken together, clearer information provided in the *parrhesia* condition allowed participants to better regulate their emotional reactions (Frijda 1986), especially their self-conscious or moral emotions (Lewis 2008). The exemplum given in the research described in this chapter shows how these emotions may be seen not only as a barrier (Bar-Tal and Halperin 2013) yet, if well regulated, as a motivational resource (Frijda 1986) to get to know a formerly hidden aspect of one's own historical past.

Of course, not all historical sensitive issues require a *parrhesiastic* narrative, but those breaking a long-lasting social denial of past in-group faults. Only in this last case, in fact, psychological processes linked to first emotional reactions become crucial, since there is not a consolidated and widespread *historical culture* framing this knowledge, silenced since teacher's intervention. In such a situation, literal social denial (Cohen 2001) on past moral indignities of the group produces a lack of historical knowledge that makes *parrhesiastic* teaching a risky yet unavoidable communication move, since there is a need to break a social silence disempowering young generations' capacity to cope with the troubled past of the in-group they are born in. More in particular, referring to the dimensions that teaching should provide, in order to enable students to confront historical narratives critically (Seixas and Peck 2004), a parrhesiastic account of past in-group wrongdoings formerly silenced in the social discourse address at a same time historical perspective taking and empathic attitude toward the past, as well as capability to morally judge previous generations. On the one hand, straightforwardly filling a gap on basic information about relevant processes occurred in the past, a *parrhesiastic* teaching on socially denied in-group crimes allow its receivers to understand the history of their group referring firmly to factual evidence instead than to a delusive and fictional version of it. On the other hand, rooted in this rich base of truthful information, a moral judgment may follow, finally acknowledging ethic responsibilities of former generations.

In such a situation, the choice of using *parrhesia* (Foucault 1983) as a strategy of history education can allow perpetrators' descendants to cope at the same time with the two opposed aims of protecting the state symbology (Liu et al. 2014) and of advancing intergroup reconciliation processes (Nadler and Shnabel 2008; Shnabel and Nadler 2015).

Summing it up, it seems that the concept of *parrhesia*, i.e., of a specific kind of the truth-speaking communications generally used in the social discourse (Foucault 1983), could be fruitfully used also to better understand social and psychological processes linked to the case of a historical teaching that uncovers a formerly denied truth referred to the national past—a truth that could threaten both the social and moral identity of its receivers (Allpress et al. 2014), but that could also help young students to better understand the current historical position of their country.

In particular, moral group-based emotions expressed by students when told about these negative facts could be used as important *methodological cues*, in order to describe the main effects of these difficult historical narratives. On the one hand, according to a well-consolidated field of research (Frijda 1986), moral group-based emotions are predictive of the consequentiality of learning activities—since only important issues are able to provoke emotional reactions. On the other hand, moral group-based emotions may play also a relevant self-regulatory role, by inhibiting the well-proven tendency to in-group favoritism (Shepherd et al. 2013).

However, to better appreciate the different emotional reactions of students exposed either to controversial and difficult history teaching or to *parrhesia*, much more research is needed. These differences between students' reactions could be highly consequential for theoretical reasons—shifting our attention from defensive consequences of self-categorization processes to the intriguing issue of the self-regulatory role of group-based emotions. Certainly, reactions studied in this kind of studies are mostly referred to students in their young adulthood. Theoretical reasons could account to that, since in democracies young adults are expected to take their own place in the public forum to gradually substitute old generations. It is up to young adults, in fact, to decide to eventually continue or to change the political orientations of public actions, and this difficult choice could not be taken if a clear knowledge of facts happened during their "historical pre-existence" (Ortega y Gasset 1930) is lacking. But also reactions of participants belonging to other age groups could be extremely important to know and therefore more research is needed in this specific direction.

Moreover, and more importantly, discussing on these differences could also advance our understanding of psychological processes in the educational field. In particular, I would like to propose that studies on concrete cases when all other sources of information are silent and only history teachers break down a long-lasting social denial of past crimes of the group could be highly influential, since for younger generations of perpetrators' groups moral reparation is a basic social and psychological need as well as for their ancestors (Nadler and Shnabel 2008; Shnabel and Nadler 2015; Bilewicz and Jaworska 2013; Leone 2012). For educational purposes, understanding psychological reactions which regulate group-based emotions of young students, when their teachers make a clear knowledge of moral faults of in-group history finally available for them, can be a key element helping to explain how intergroup relations may not only stay hostile for a long time, but may also change and flourish again when generations change.

References

Allpress, J. A., Brown, R., Giner-Sorolla, R., Deonna, J. A., & Teroni, F. (2014). Two faces of group-based shame: Moral shame and image shame differentially predict positive and negative orientations to in-group wrongdoing. *Personality and Social Psychology Bulletin, 40*(10), 1270–1284. doi:10.1177/0146167214540724.

Bar-Tal, D., & Halperin, E. (2013). The nature of socio-psychological barriers to peaceful conflict resolution and ways to overcome them. *Conflict & Communication Online, 12*(2), 1–16.

Barton, K. C., & McCully, A. W. (2012). Trying to "see things differently": Northern Ireland students' struggle to understand alternative historical perspectives. *Theory & Research in Social Education, 40*(4), 371–408.

Bilewicz, M., & Jaworska, M. (2013). Reconciliation through the righteous: The narratives of heroic helpers as a fulfillment of emotional needs in Polish–Jewish intergroup contact. *Journal of Social Issues, 69*(1), 162–179.

Bilali, R. (2013). National narrative and social psychological influences in Turks' denial of the mass killings of Armenians as genocide. *Journal of Social Issues, 69*(1), 16–33.

Branscombe, N. R., & Doosje, B. (2004). *Collective guilt: International perspectives.* Cambridge: Cambridge University Press.

Cajani, L. (2013). The image of Italian colonialism in Italian history Textbooks for secondary schools. *Journal of Educational Media, Memory, and Society, 5*(1), 72–89.

Cajani, L., & Leone, G. (2015) How long it takes to face collective responsibilities: The case study of public awareness on crimes of Italian colonialism. In: *Social representation of history: Social psychological and historical approaches to their antecedents, evolution, and role in influencing identities and intergroup relations,* Pécs, Hungary, April 9–10th, 2015.

Campbell, J. (2006). Vichy, Vichy, and a plaque to remember. *French Studies Bulletin, 27*(98), 2–5.

Cohen, S. (2001). *States of Denial: Knowing about atrocities and suffering.* Cambridge: Polity Press.

Darwin, C. R. (1965). *The expression of emotions in man and animals.* Chicago: University of Chicago Press. (Original edition, 1872).

De Caro, G. (2014). *Rifondare gli italiani? Il cinema del Neorealismo Il cinema del Neorealismo (Building Italians anew? Neorealism cinema).* Milano: Jaca Book.

Del Boca, A. (2005). *Italiani, brava gente? Un mito duro a morire (Italians, good fellows? A myth that dies hard).* Vicenza: Neri Pozza.

Eastmond, M., & Selimovic, J. M. (2012). Silence as possibility in postwar everyday life. *International Journal of Transitional Justice,* ijs026, 6(3): 502–524. first published online October 12, 2012 doi:10.1093/ijtj/ijs026.

Ekman, P., Friesen, W. V., & Ellsworth, P. (2013). *Emotion in the human face: Guidelines for research and an integration of findings.* Burlington: Elsevier.

Frijda, N. H. (1986). *The emotions.* London, England: Cambridge University Press.

Foucault, M. (1983). *Discourse and truth: The problematization of Parrhesia. Six lectures given by Michel Foucault at the University of California at Berkeley* [also published in 2001 under the title *Fearless Speech*. Los Angeles: Semiotexte].
Galtung, J., & Höivik, T. (1971). Structural and direct violence: A note on operationalization. *Journal of Peace Research, 8*(1), 73–76.
Gibson, J. L. (2006). The contributions of truth to reconciliation: Lessons from South Africa. *Journal of Conflict Resolution, 50*(3), 409–432.
Goldberg, T. (2013). "It's in My Veins": identity and disciplinary practice in students' discussions of a historical issue. *Theory & Research in Social Education, 41*(1), 33–64.
Hovannisian, R. G. (1998). *Remembrance and denial: The case of the Armenian genocide*. Detroit: Wayne State University Press.
Kello, K. (2015). Sensitive and controversial issues in the classroom: Teaching history in a divided society. *Teachers and Teaching*, 1–19.
King, J. T. (2009). Teaching and learning about controversial issues: Lessons from Northern Ireland. *Theory & Research in Social Education, 37*(2), 215–246.
Kurtiş, T., Adams, G., & Yellow Bird, M. (2010). Generosity or genocide? Identity implications of silence in American Thanksgiving commemorations. *Memory, 18*(2), 208–224.
Leach, C. W., Zeineddine, F. B., & Čehajić-Clancy, S. (2013). Moral immemorial: The rarity of self-criticism for previous generations' genocide or mass violence. *Journal of Social Issues, 69*(1), 34–53.
Leone, G. (2012). May clarity about in-group crimes be a better choice, when narrating the story of past war to perpetrators descendants? In: *11th International Conference on Social Representations. Social Representations in Changing Societies*. Evora, Portugal, June 25–28, 2012.
Leone, G., & Mastrovito, T. (2010). Learning about our shameful past: A sociopsychological analysis of present-day historical narratives of Italian colonial wars. *International Journal of Conflict and Violence, 4*(1), 11–27.
Leone, G., & Sarrica, M. (2012). When ownership hurts: Remembering the in-group wrongdoings after a long lasting collective amnesia. *Human Affairs, 22*(4), 603–612.
Leone, G., Sarrica, M. (2014). Making room for negative emotions about the national past: An explorative study of effects of parrhesia on Italian colonial crimes. *International Journal of Intercultural Relations*, 1–13. doi:10.1016/j.ijintrel.2014.08.008.
Lewin, K. (1943). Defining the 'field at a given time'. *Psychological Review, 50*(3), 292–310.
Lewis, M. (2008). Self-conscious emotions: Embarrassment, pride, shame, and guilt. In M. Lewis, J. Haviland-Jones, & L. Feldman Barrett (Eds.), *Handbook of emotions* (3rd ed., pp. 742–756). New York: Guilford Press.

Liu, J. H., Onar, N. F., & Woodward, M. W. (2014). Symbologies, technologies, and identities: Critical junctures theory and the multi-layered nation–state. *International Journal of Intercultural Relations, 43,* 2–12.

Nadler, A., Malloy, T., & Fisher, J. D. (Eds.). (2008). *Social psychology of intergroup reconciliation: From violent conflict to peaceful co-existence.* New York: Oxford University Press.

Nadler, A., & Shnabel, N. (2008). Instrumental and socioemotional paths to intergroup reconciliation and the needs-based model of socioemotional reconciliation. In A. Nadler, T. E. Malloy, & J. D. Fisher (Eds.), *The social psychology of intergroup reconciliation* (pp. 37–56). New York: Oxford University Press.

Ortega y Gasset, J. (1930). *La rebelión de las masas* [The Revolt of the Masses]. Madrid.

Pivato, S. (2007). *Vuoti di memoria: usi e abusi della storia nella vita pubblica italiana [Memory lapses: Uses and misuses of history in Italian public life].* Roma-Bari: Laterza.

Seixas, P., & Peck, C. (2004). Teaching historical thinking. In A. Sears & I. Wright (Eds.), *Challenges and prospects for Canadian social studies* (pp. 109–117). Vancouver: Pacific Educational Press.

Sen, R., & Wagner, W. (2005). History, emotions and hetero-referential representations in inter-group conflict: The example of Hindu-Muslim relations in India. *Papers on Social Representations, 14,* 2.1–2.23.

Shepherd, L., Spears, R., & Manstead, A. S. (2013). 'This will bring shame on our nation': The role of anticipated group-based emotions on collective action. *Journal of Experimental Social Psychology, 49*(1), 42–57.

Shnabel, N., & Nadler, A. (2015). The role of agency and morality in reconciliation processes the perspective of the needs-based model. *Current Directions in Psychological Science, 24*(6), 477–483.

Tajfel, H. (ed) (1982). *Social identity and intergroup relations.* New York: Cambridge University Press.

Vollhardt, J. R., Mazur, L. B., & Lemahieu, M. (2014). Acknowledgment after mass violence: Effects on psychological well-being and intergroup relations. *Group Processes & Intergroup Relations, 17*(3), 306–323. doi:10.1177/1368430213517270.

Volpato, C., & Licata, L. (2010). Collective Memories of Colonial Violence. *Special issue of International Journal of Conflict and Violence, 4*(1): 4–10.

Zembylas, M., & Kambani, F. (2012). The teaching of controversial issues during elementary-level history instruction: Greek-Cypriot teachers' perceptions and emotions. *Theory & Research in Social Education, 40*(2), 107–133.

Author Biography

Giovanna Leone is Associate Professor of Social Psychology at Sapienza University of Rome, Italy, where she teaches Social Psychology and Communication, Political Psychology and Community Psychology. Full member of several national and international academic associations. MC Member of Italy in the COST European action IS1205 "Social psychological dynamics of historical representations in the enlarged European Union". Former coordinator of the Ethics Committee of AIP (Association of Italian Psychologists). Her main research interests include: social and collective aspects of autobiographical memory; ambivalent effects of over-helping, as observed in multicultural classrooms; relationships between changes of historical narratives on past intergroup violence and reconciliation. She published papers on Lecture Notes in Computer Science, International Journal of Conflict and Violence, International Journal of Intercultural Relations, Cognitive Processing, Journal of Language and Politics, Papers in Social Representations, Qualitative Research in Psychology, Human Affairs. She contributed to the first and second edition of the Cambridge Handbook of Sociocultural Psychology.

Open Access This chapter is licensed under the terms of the Creative Commons Attribution 4.0 International License (http://creativecommons.org/licenses/by/4.0/), which permits use, sharing, adaptation, distribution and reproduction in any medium or format, as long as you give appropriate credit to the original author(s) and the source, provide a link to the Creative Commons license and indicate if changes were made.

The images or other third party material in this chapter are included in the chapter's Creative Commons license, unless indicated otherwise in a credit line to the material. If material is not included in the chapter's Creative Commons license and your intended use is not permitted by statutory regulation or exceeds the permitted use, you will need to obtain permission directly from the copyright holder.

How to Teach about the Holocaust? Psychological Obstacles in Historical Education in Poland and Germany

Michal Bilewicz, Marta Witkowska, Silviana Stubig, Marta Beneda and Roland Imhoff

In 2000, a group of high-ranking political, religious and civil society leaders, educators, historians and survivors assembled in Stockholm and drafted the Stockholm Declaration about Holocaust education and remembrance (Assmann 2010). The declaration, signed by the representatives of 46 governments, included a pledge to "promote education, remembrance and research about the Holocaust, both in those of our countries that have already done much and those that choose to join this effort", as well as commitment to "promote education about the Holocaust in our schools and universities, in our communities and encourage it in other institutions" (Allwork 2015, p. 6). The most recent analysis of historical education in 135 nation states (Carrier et al. 2015) showed that in approximately half of

---

M. Bilewicz (✉) · M. Witkowska · M. Beneda
University of Warsaw, Warsaw, Poland
e-mail: michalbilewicz@gmail.com

S. Stubig
University of Cologne, Cologne, Germany

R. Imhoff
Johannes Gutenberg University, Mainz, Germany

these countries, Holocaust is part of teaching curricula—most frequently covered within history curricula, but also in human rights education, ethics, philosophy and general social studies. In Europe, knowledge about a Holocaust is directly taught in almost all national education systems (except of Moldova, Ukraine, Norway and Slovenia, where it is referred to only indirectly, and Iceland where the Holocaust is not part of the historical education).

Apart from committing themselves to encourage and spread education about the Holocaust, the signatories of the Stockholm Declaration about Holocaust education mentioned also current problems, such as racism, xenophobia, discrimination and antisemitism that could be eradicated by successful Holocaust education. Therefore, the aim of educating about the Holocaust is not only to provide knowledge about this prototypical genocide (Mazur and Vollhardt 2015), but also to change attitudes of young people in order to prevent antisemitism, to raise awareness about intergroup violence and to better understand consequences of prejudice, discrimination and processes of conflict transformation. This is why it is of crucial importance to evaluate how well these tasks are met by schools.

This chapter presents results of different empirical studies on the effects of Holocaust education in Germany and Poland.[3] Based on this research, we will outline the main obstacles in Holocaust education. Most of these obstacles are directly caused by interpreting the Holocaust on the grounds of students' national identities and ethnic membership, therefore potentially posing a national identity threat, leading to competitiveness in victimhood and negation of the newly acquired knowledge. Based on that criticism, we will also propose several ways of overcoming these problems. Based on relevant social psychological research, we would like to propose three different approaches towards Holocaust education: an approach based on empathy and regret (Imhoff et al. 2012), moral-exemplars approach (Bilewicz and Jaworska 2013; Čehajić-Clancy and Bilewicz 2016) and an approach based on local identities (Stefaniak and Bilewicz 2016; Wójcik et al. 2010). Combination of these strategies could form an alternative to the dominant Holocaust education approach that is based on national identities and ethnic membership salience.

Failures of Holocaust Education: The German Case

Currently, the Holocaust seems to be an omnipresent topic in German public discourse, which may be supported by the fact that on every single day there is an average of almost two prime-time television broadcasts on the topic of National Socialism and the Holocaust (Schmidt-Denter and Stubig 2011). At the same time, communication on National Socialism and the Holocaust within the family—as far as still available and not concealed—seems to follow homogenous patterns, characterized by stories of resistance, personal victimization and war suffering (Brockhaus 2008). These communication patterns and the continuous fading away of eyewitnesses reduce the relevance of family as an important source of knowledge for learning about National Socialism and the Holocaust. As research shows, German youth do not regard biographical points of reference in their families as important (Ahlheim and Heger 2002; Welzer 2004).

This makes formal school education the primary source of learning about National Socialism and the Holocaust. Indeed, in the study by Stubig (2015), 234 pupils from North Rhine-Westphalian high schools (9th to 12th grade) were asked about sources of their knowledge about National Socialism and the Holocaust. The majority of the pupils (63%) listed their school as the main source of knowledge on this topic, underlining especially the importance of history lessons. Among other relevant sources were television (10%) and family (10%). When the teenagers were asked about the trustworthiness of these different sources of knowledge, they pointed to history classes as to the most reliable source, whereas family and television were described as markedly less trustworthy (Stubig 2015). These findings show that pupils perceive their history lessons and school education as an important source of information about National Socialism and the Holocaust. By the same token, this suggests a remarkable responsibility put on the teachers designing classes on this topic.

It should be noted that teaching guidelines for history education in Germany are relatively vague in their recommendations for devising history lessons. This gives educators a lot of freedom in choosing their methods of teaching and designing classes. Although the topic is recommended to be introduced in history lessons in nineth grade (Ministerium für Schule und Weiterbildung des Landes Nordrhein-Westfalen 2007), German students are confronted with the topic of the Holocaust and National Socialism much earlier as it is also a central topic in literature, religion, politics, fine arts, social science, music and pedagogy classes (Stubig 2015). Another important aspect of education on National Socialism and the Holocaust that should be mentioned is the amount of time that teachers devote to this topic. In general, there seems to be a striking difference between the amount of time spent on teaching about National Socialism and the Holocaust and that devoted to other historical topics. Not only in North Rhine-Westphalia, but also in other German regions, twice as much time is dedicated to the topic of National Socialism and the Holocaust in comparison with remaining historical problems (Schmidt-Denter and Stubig 2011), adding to a period of intensive learning lasting at least two and up to six months (Stubig 2015). Yet, although the majority of teachers tend to devote a great amount of time to the issue of National Socialism and the Holocaust, there seems to be a considerable variance in the ways of teaching about this topic.

In the view of history teachers, the ultimate aim of history lessons about National Socialism and the Holocaust is to generate strong emotional reactions in youth (Henke-Bockschatz 2004; Brockhaus 2008; Keupp 2008; Kühner and Langer 2008). This claim rests on the assumption that intensive affective reactions (and even shock) increase empathy and social awareness, as well as the likelihood of accepting one's group moral responsibility, which then leads to a decrease in radical attitudes. All of this serves the ultimate goal of preventing a second Holocaust (Abram and Heyl 1996; Keupp 2008; Kühner and Langer 2008). This approach is present in a variety of didactic methods that, again, seem to differ from those applied to other historical topics (Schwendemann and Marks 2002). These methods focus especially on affective processes in contrast to the more traditional cognitive approaches (Brockhaus 2008; Schwendemann and Marks 2002) and may consist of textbook analyses, students' presentations, using video documentations and movies, visiting exhibitions and memorials or interviewing eyewitnesses (Brendler 1994; Heyl 1996). In particular, the latter methods seem to be especially effective in promoting emotional access to the topic of the Holocaust in an especially intense manner and are thus widely prevalent. Across a number of studies, German high school students report high levels of emotionality in reaction to teaching units on the topic (Brusten and Winkelmann 1992, 1994; Brendler 1997a, b; Cisneros 2008; Meier 1997; Schwendemann and Marks 2002).

Nevertheless, enthusiasm about this is not ubiquitous. Teachers repeatedly report problems during their lessons due to pupils' reactions to the topic, ranging from disinterest to defensiveness. Students' little knowledge about National Socialism and the Holocaust together with such negative reactions tends to cause feelings of frustration in teachers (Brockhaus 2008; Schwendemann and Marks 2002). Frequently, teachers try to overcome this situation by employing more emotionally shocking sources of information and may end up exaggerating, in terms of both quantity and quality (Brockhaus 2008; Heyl 1996; Schneider 2004).

The way in which pupils tend to be affected by Holocaust education may be described as a remarkable conundrum. Although the Holocaust is frequently found to be a historical episode that evokes the highest levels of interest and curiosity (Cisneros 2008; Stubig 2015) and receives much attention in terms of time and teaching intensity, students' level of knowledge on this topic seems to be surprisingly low (Brendler 1994; Schwendemann and Marks 2002; Zülsdorf-Kersting 2007). Pupils report strong feelings of shame and guilt when being confronted with this chapter of German past (Brockhaus 2008; Rommelspacher 1995), at the same time experiencing other affective states, such as feelings of being left alone accompanied by unresolved emotions of disgust, shock or anxiety (Brendler 1994; Glück and Wagensommer 2004; Rommelspacher 1995; Schwendemann 2004). This may be one of the possible solutions for the conundrum described. If pupils are indeed emotionally overburdened, a process of knowledge acquisition and information processing is likely to be inhibited by such strong emotions and high levels of arousal (Anderson 2007; Easterbrook 1959). Alternatively, it might lead to historical defensiveness that blocks any empathic response to the victims (Bilewicz 2016).

Apart from these emotional processes that may result in poor knowledge acquisition, Holocaust education may also have an impact on social identity development. Since the topic of National Socialism and the Holocaust is introduced in nineth grade, so in the early years of adolescence, pupils exposed to it tend to be in the most critical moment of their identity construction and therefore may experience an increased interest also in their national group's history. In a recent study (Stubig 2015), five classes of nineth-grade high school pupils in North Rhine-Westphalia were surveyed twice: before and after their teaching unit on the Holocaust. The survey examined their attitudes towards Europe, national attachment and pride, tolerance towards others, their opinion about national feelings, antisemitism, xenophobia and xenophilia. In the second survey, the pupils were also asked to evaluate the lessons they had attended—their aim and the methods used—as share the reactions these lessons evoked.

For most variables measured in the study, there was no significant difference between the survey administered before and after the lessons on National Socialism and the Holocaust. In stark contrast to the explicated aim of such an education, there were no observed improvements in attitudes towards Europe, increased tolerance, or decreases in neither xenophobia nor antisemitism. The teaching unit only had an effect on measures of national identification, as students declared less national pride and had less positive attitudes towards national feelings after Holocaust education programmes than before (Stubig 2015). While this might be seen as an intended effect, two details are remarkable here. First, these reductions in national pride were not accompanied by synchronous reductions in prejudice and outgroup negativity. Second, of all items that tapped into pride for different aspects of being German, the effect was mostly driven by aspects of national identity that could be construed as democratic, post-Nazism identity. As an illustration, after the lesson students were less proud with regard to "current democracy and the democratic constitution" or "the fall of the wall and the peaceful transition." In contrast, arguably more problematic sentiments such as "pride for German history", "pride for German soldiers' bravery in the world wars", "pride for Germany's standing in the world" and "pride for typically German virtues like diligence, discipline, and reliability" were not significantly reduced at single item level. It is well established that—compared to other nations—German adolescents show relatively low levels of national attachment and pride (Bar-On et al. 1997; Schmidt-Denter 2011; Smith and Jarkko 1998; Smith and Seokho 2006; Westle 1999), and the reported results (Stubig 2015) suggest that this may—at least partially—be a direct effect of Holocaust teaching. In the light of the many detrimental effects on nationalist pride throughout the literature (e.g. Golec de Zavala et al. 2013; Mummendey et al. 2001), this may serve as an indicator of educational success. At the same time, many developmental scholars argue that such national identification is an important part of a normal identity development. By asking "who am I" and defining self by one's affiliation to groups, young people construe their self-image which is experienced as a consistent self over past and future times (Fend 1991; Mayer et al. 2006). Constructing identity is the ability to reflect and problematize even negative aspects of self-image, which leads to a balanced identity achievement (Krejci 1995), whereas the elimination of identity aspects, like skipping national and historical acquisitions of self, might lead to difficulties in identity construction (Rommelspacher 1995). It is certainly open to debate whether adolescents as future citizens really need to form strong ties to their nation and thus establish a strong *national* identity. Independent of the outcome of this dispute, however, it seems remarkable that in the present context, the identification with democratic, post-fascist aspects of the national identity decreased over the course of Holocaust education, whereas identification with more problematic aspects like dominance and bravery did not.

Being asked about their experience of learning about National Socialism and the Holocaust in history lessons, pupils revealed their conviction about what they should have learned in this unit: next to acquisition of declarative knowledge which scored on first place, students secondly agreed in the idea that the aim of the unit on National Socialism and the Holocaust was to teach them how to think and talk about this topic in a socially desired manner (Stubig 2015). These results confirm statements of university students and pupils which attest appeals of consternation to their history lessons (Stubig 2015) and even expressed feelings of being indoctrinated (Brockhaus 2008). This result reveals a paradox in education on National Socialism and the Holocaust. While this topic is—according to the curriculum—meant to foster maturity and responsibility in social and political aspects of democratic life, factually it seems to leave students with the impression that the goal of history lessons is to teach or suggest pre-assembled communication patterns. Further research is required to verify the occurrence of such lesson outcomes.

FAILURES OF HOLOCAUST EDUCATION: THE POLISH CASE

Following the Declaration of Stockholm International Forum on the Holocaust signed by the President of Poland in 2000, education about the Holocaust has been an important element of Polish education system. Since 2005, the Holocaust Memorial Day (April 19) is officially observed in Polish school system. Holocaust education in the current educational programme is introduced at several stages as part of the core curriculum: in primary schools (Polish language; History and civics classes), lower-secondary school (Polish language; Civics) and upper-secondary school (History; Polish language; Civics). Many schools visit the death camps and other Holocaust memorial sites (e.g. Majdanek, Auschwitz, Polin Museum of the History of Polish Jews). This structure, together with existing textbooks and teaching curricula, provides bases for extensive coverage of Holocaust-related topics in the course of education (Szuchta and Trojański 2012). It is also mirrored in students' perception of school education as one of the most important sources of knowledge about the Holocaust and Jewish history (Bilewicz and Wójcik 2009). More than three-quarters of students from small towns in Poland declared that they learned about these topics in their schools. Family stories, tours or newspapers and books were indicated less often as sources of knowledge about Jewish history and the Holocaust. At the same time, teachers often do not know the international recommendations for teaching about the Holocaust and possible programmes and curricula (Węgrzynek 2006; Szuchta 2006). They also devote significantly less time to the topic of Holocaust than recommended (Szuchta 2013).

The last decades brought some positive developments in regard to the content of school lessons about the Holocaust. While under Communist rule students were taught about the Jewish tragedy as a facet of the Polish martyrdom, modern textbooks acknowledge the pan-European extent of the crime and its ethnic nature (see Ambrosewicz-Jacobs and Szuchta 2014). However, despite the progress in reducing the existing gap between historiography and education, great parts of the Holocaust history depictions remain unchanged even in the most modern Polish textbooks (Gross 2010). This particularly applies to historical discoveries about the Polish involvement in crimes against Jews that manifestly contravenes the collective memory framework of Poles as victims (but not perpetrators) of the WWII (Gross 2014). The very emotional public debate after the publication of the Jan Thomas Gross' book about the crime on the Jewish population of Jedwabne (Gross 2001) is a clear instance of difficulties in accepting unfavourable historical facts (Ambrosewicz-Jacobs and Szuchta 2014). These difficulties are obviously mirrored in the school education about the crime. The very rare attempts to evaluate the effectiveness of Polish teaching about Holocaust show its mediocre results in reducing ethnocentrism and antisemitism (Ambrosewicz-Jacobs and Szuchta 2014).

In order to test the effects of current Holocaust education in Poland, the Center for Research on Prejudice at the University of Warsaw conducted a survey that assessed three key outcomes of such education: factual knowledge about the Holocaust, understanding of historical relations between Poles and Jews and attitudes towards Jews. Above one thousand students from 20 high schools in the capital city of Poland participated in the study during their normal school activities (Witkowska et al. 2015).

The factual knowledge about the Holocaust was assessed with three questions concerning the Warsaw Ghetto Uprising, a revolt that took place in Nazi-occupied Warsaw as a form of resistance to the liquidation of the Jewish ghetto (by deporting last remaining Jews to Treblinka death camp by the German occupants). Participants were asked to indicate the exact year in which the uprising took place, the name of the main commander and whether the uprising was a military success. In order to check whether the level of students' knowledge about the history of Polish Jews diverges from the level of their general historical knowledge, the participants were also asked about the outcomes of other four Polish national uprisings. In order to assess students' understanding of the historical relations between Poles and Jews, we asked them to evaluate the amount of help offered by Poles to those Jews who were fighting in the Warsaw Ghetto or hiding on the "Aryan side" of the Polish capital. The answers were given on a five-point scale, from "The amount of help was definitely insufficient" to "The amount of help was definitely too extensive" with a midpoint statement—"The amount of help was just sufficient."

The attitudes towards Jews were tested with three different measures. A "feeling thermometer" captured the "temperature" of feelings towards Jews on a scale ranging from very cold, negative feelings to very positive, warm feelings. A scale of contact intentions assessed readiness to engage in contact with Jewish peers and to learn about Jewish culture. Finally, a social distance scale measured the acceptance of Jews in one's social environment—family, school and neighbourhood.

In order to test the effectiveness of Holocaust education, we asked students to provide information about their final grades in history and about the number of hours that have been devoted in their schools to the topic of the Warsaw Ghetto Uprising. Based on this information, we created two indicators measuring the impact of school education: accomplishment (grades) and extensiveness of the course (number of hours).

The data from the survey showed that one in four high school students did not know the most basic facts about the Warsaw Ghetto Uprising—26% of the participants did not know the exact year of its outbreak, 23% thought that the uprising was a military success and 44% were not able to select its commander's name from the list. However, the wrong answers to the questions concerning the history of Polish Jews did not stand out from the answers assessing the level of general historical knowledge, as 31% of the participants gave wrong answers to other questions about historical facts unrelated to the history of the Holocaust. When asked about the amount of Polish help offered to Jews, participants most often chose the answer "sufficient" (39%), whereas 22% considered the amount of Polish help as "slightly too extensive" or "definitely too extensive."

Within the section measuring attitudes, the students demonstrated considerable prejudice towards Jews—more than half of the participants (54%) declared cold, negative feelings. A similar pattern was obtained for the measure of contact willingness—the majority of the young Poles indicated that they would prefer not to have contact with people of Jewish origin. Almost half of the students said that they would react negatively to Jewish classmates (40%) or to Jewish neighbours (44%).

In order to determine how school education is related to knowledge and attitudes of students, we conducted a series of correlation analyses (see Table 1). The results showed that factual knowledge is practically unrelated to history school education; hence, those students who knew the correct answers are likely to have acquired their knowledge outside

Table 1 Correlation between knowledge, understanding of history, attitudes and school education among Warsaw students. Pearson correlation coefficients (r)

	Grade in history	Course extensiveness
Correct date of Warsaw Ghetto Uprising	0.03	−0.03
Correct name of Uprising ghetto commander	0.09**	−0.03
Knowledge about the outcomes of the Uprising	0.02	−0.02
Biased assessment of Polish role in the Uprising	0.08*	0.14**
Positivity of feelings towards Jews	0.09**	−0.07
Willingness to contact Jews	0.05	−0.07*
Acceptance of Jews in close environment	0.04	−0.02

*$p < 0.05$, **$p < 0.01$

the school environment. We observed only a weak correlation between the correct answers to the questions on factual knowledge and the participants' grades in history, and no relationship with extensiveness of teaching. Therefore, school's effectiveness in conveying knowledge about the Holocaust proved to be very low.

Interestingly, both extensiveness of school Holocaust education and students' grades seem to be significantly related to their idealized views of their national history. The more extensive the school teaching on the Holocaust was, the more likely the students were to perceive the amount of help offered by Poles to Jews as too big. A relatively weak relation was observed also in case of history grades: the students with good grades were more likely to perceive the amount of Polish help offered to Jews as too extensive, comparing to their peers with lower grades. Among the students with best grades, 26% believed that the amount of Polish help offered to Jews was more than sufficient, whereas among the students with worst grades this belief was shared by 20%.

The direct relationship between school education and attitudes towards Jews seems to be unclear and inconsistent (see Table 1). We observed no relation between the amount of Holocaust education and acceptance of Jews in the close social environment. School accomplishments were weakly related to attitudes towards Jews—the better grades the students achieved in history, the warmer feelings they declared towards Jews. The extensiveness of the teaching, in turn, was negatively related to willingness to have a contact with Jews; i.e., willingness was lower among students who had more classes devoted to the topic of the Holocaust. At the same time, we found that this negative effect of school teaching was rooted in the biased and idealized perception of Polish–Jewish wartime relations, i.e. the overestimation of Polish help offered to Jews. Students who had extensive course on the history of the Holocaust acquired convictions that their ancestors offered extensive help to Jews and this, in turn, deteriorated their attitudes towards Jews. Therefore, efforts made by schools to fight prejudice seem to be not only insufficient and inconsistent but even counterproductive: a biased school education about the Holocaust might increase negative attitudes towards Jews.

Psychological Obstacles: Historical Defensiveness and Aversive Emotions

The German and Polish examples presented above suggest that current forms of Holocaust education in Polish and German school programmes are, in fact, not effective in eradicating antisemitism and making students more tolerant. The only meaningful change is observed in loosening their identification and pride of national group membership. Apart from inappropriate school education and defensive approaches of governments, the failures of Holocaust education could be affected also by psychological processes involved in learning about negative history of one's national group.

Information about the perpetratorship (in case of Germans) or bystandership (in case of Poles) of fellow ingroup members during the Holocaust can severely threaten students' social identities. Among strongly identifying individuals, there is a pronounced desire to view their own nation in a positive manner (Tajfel and Turner 1979). In fact, explanations of the Holocaust history depend on the strength of students' national identification (Bilewicz et al. 2016), and they affect students' contemporary intergroup attitudes (Imhoff et al., in press). The review of studies performed in several national contexts showed that when people are confronted with a historical narrative about the crimes committed by their nation, they most commonly deny the facts and do not feel responsible, guilty or ashamed (Leach et al. 2013). People can use the whole system of emotion regulation in order to downregulate negative emotions resulting from such confrontations with history (Bilewicz 2016). For instance, after learning about ingroup members' misbehaviour during the Holocaust, one can avoid contact with Jews (as they become reminders of such negative past), detach from national history, question and criticize the source of information (e.g. teacher, textbook or historian) and engage in victimhood competition with Jews (e.g. by pronouncing German losses, such as Dresden bombings, or Polish victimhood during Warsaw Uprising or Katyn massacre). Finally, one can employ a biased structure of explanation or engage in conspiracy theorizing (e.g. different forms of Holocaust revisionism and denial). Such reactions are relatively common when people are faced with information about ingroup members' involvement in a genocide—either as perpetrators or as passive bystanders.

Another important question is as follows: What kind of emotions should be elicited by Holocaust education in countries characterized by the dominant collective memory of being a nation of perpetrators (e.g. Germany and Austria), collaborators (e.g. Ukraine, Latvia, Lithuania and Hungary) or passive bystanders (e.g. Poland) of the Holocaust[1]? Should teachers try to evoke highly aversive feelings of (group-based) guilt and shame as these are frequently believed to be antecedent of reparative tendencies? Or does such a strategy overburden students emotionally and therefore does not meet its goal of ultimately improving intergroup relations?

A plethora of research points to the allegedly positive outcomes of group-based guilt (Ferguson and Branscombe 2014). Guilt signals that an intergroup relationship is damaged and needs to be repaired (Branscombe et al. 2002), and is often connected to prosocial consequences such as reduced racism (Branscombe et al. 2007) and increased forgiveness (Hewstone et al. 2004). More specifically, guilt increases the motivation to make amends or to apologize (Brown et al. 2008; Imhoff et al. 2013; Tangney 1995). This has led several researchers to characterize guilt as a relationship-enhancing emotion that strengthens social bonds and attachment (Baumeister et al. 1995), thus playing a "pivotal role in alleviating group conflict" (Maitner et al. 2007, p. 224). Therefore, there are good reasons to indeed evoke negative emotions or even vicarious bad conscience for the deeds committed by Nazi Germans and their collaborators.

Although these examples seem to allow the straightforward conclusion that teaching strategies incorporating shaming or guilt induction are (even if ethically, psychologically and educationally questionable) indeed effective in promoting positive intergroup attitudes, the reality is more complex. In fact, it is conceivable that recipients merely learn (about) teachers' expectations and comply with their norms rather than internalizing this position. Moreover, they may even reject this message and demonstrate reactance to this perceived pressure to adopt a politically correct opinion. As has been argued for decades in the context of secondary antisemitism (Imhoff and Banse 2009), such teaching strategies might even backfire as the Jewish victims are likely to become potentially blamed for these aversive feelings of guilt and shame. Even though the original source of them was the teacher, students might easily start perceiving Jews as a lobby group standing behind such forms of education or might associate Jews with the negative classroom experience by which "every living and surviving Jew becomes the witness and the accused at the same time" (Broder 1986; p. 38, original in German, translation by authors). So, is it indeed true that certain confrontational ways of dealing with the Nazi past evoke guilt and reparation intentions at the explicit verbal level but create resentment at the implicit level?

Very much in line with such a proposition, reminding young German students of ongoing suffering of Jewish Holocaust victims led to higher self-reports of feelings of group-based guilt and greater claims of reparation intentions (Imhoff et al. 2013). The very same manipulation also led to a decrease in antisemitism compared to a baseline measurement three months earlier (Imhoff and Banse 2009). Taking the differentiation between public conformity and private acceptance vs. resentment seriously, however, led researchers in the same study to implement another manipulation: wiring up participants with the information that this will help the experimenter to detect untruthful responses (bogus pipeline). Very much in contrast to the group without a bogus pipeline, it did not decrease but increase antisemitic responding, making participants express more prejudices against Jews. This finding strongly suggests that some forms of confrontation will lead to conformity with whatever is perceived as desired but create reactance and prejudice increase on the implicit level.

Some studies suggest that precisely because guilt is such an aversive experience, it is associated with not only greater reparation intentions but also feelings of discomfort in face of victims or their descendants which suppresses the willingness to engage in interpersonal contact with them (Imhoff et al. 2012). This is why any guilt-inducing Holocaust education might not address its aims in improving current intergroup relations of Poles, Germans or Hungarians with Jews. It might in fact increase antisemitic responses among young people instead of constraining them. In order to overcome the aversive emotional guilt-driven reactions, as well as the historical defensiveness derived from national identities that are salient in traditional forms of Holocaust education, we would like to propose three alternative educational strategies based on recent social psychological research on post-genocide reconciliation. These three approaches are aimed at overcoming the defensiveness and emotional regulation stemming from strong national identities. In order to achieve such goal in Holocaust education, one should focus teaching on individual and local narratives instead of national-level ones.

Proposal 1. Regret Instead of Guilt. Empathic Education

Due to the aversive character of guilt (Imhoff et al. 2012), one could doubt about the use of this emotion in Holocaust education. Social psychological research shows however that milder forms of negative emotions, such as feelings of regret, could be associated not only with the self-reported intentions to engage in intergroup contact but also with money allegedly donated in one's name to the cause of promoting intergroup contact. Studies of collective regret (Imhoff et al. 2012) found that raising this emotion can increase contact-promoting actions among descendants of the perpetrator group (i.e. German high school students) as well as descendants of the bystander group (i.e. inhabitants of the Polish town Oświęcim, location of the Nazi death camp Auschwitz). Regret, as the same studies suggest, can be conceptualized as an empathic emotion that arises from a focus on the plight of the victims (e.g. "Jews were killed") rather than a focus on the cruelties of the perpetrators (e.g. "Germans killed Jews").

On a relatively abstract level, these findings therefore resonate with the effects ascribed to the American TV show "Holocaust" aired in German television in 1978. Attacked by many as a trivialization of history and applauded by many for not expressing an accusation of collective guilt against all Germans (Reichel 2004), many commentators agree that this personalized TV drama constituted a turning point in public German discourse about the Holocaust. Through identification with the portrayed Jewish family Weiss, many Germans, for the very first time, empathized with the Jews (Brandt 2003), and this slowly initiated an increasing awareness and a greater willingness to deal with the topic at all. Therefore, psychological studies and case studies of media effects seem to converge in their suggestion that creating chances to empathize with humanized victims might be less aversive and potentially more effective than creating a sense of vicarious guilt around the Holocaust.

Empathy-based Holocaust education has been proposed by both theorists (Riley 1998) and practitioners of Holocaust education (Facing History and Ourselves project; Schultz et al. 2001). For this purpose, a great educational resource for potential use could be wartime diaries (e.g. diaries of Anne Frank or Dawid Rubinowicz in case of primary school children or Calel Perechodnik's diaries in case of young adults) or testimonies (e.g. the Visual History Archive of the USC Shoah

Foundation). Such forms of education can overcome the national-collectivistic approach represented in many existing textbooks and school curricula (presenting the "whole nations" as actors, focussing on national leaders and military history).

The only risk in empathy-based education could concern students' psychological reactions to extreme acts of suffering. A recent study performed on a group of 854 young visitors to Auschwitz-Birkenau State Museum found that approximately 13% of them developed secondary post-traumatic stress disorder syndrome related to the visit in KL Auschwitz (Bilewicz and Wójcik 2016[2]). At the same time, these visitors improved their overall attitudes towards Jews and Jewish victims of the Holocaust (Wójcik and Bilewicz 2012). This study found that PTSD syndrome was particularly visible among young people that reacted to KL Auschwitz visit in a highly empathetic way—by including the Jewish victims into their structure of self. These findings suggest that empathy-based education in memorial sites, however effective in attitude change, has to be carefully prepared by the teacher or facilitator working with the students intensively prior to a visit in a memorial site.

Proposal 2: Employing Moral Exemplars

According to analyses of history textbooks used in Polish schools, the idea of Poles helping Jews during the Second World War is among the common ones conveyed in school teaching. At the same time, not enough attention has been devoted to avoid simplification and banalization of such heroic help, and to objectively present its instances, without omitting the broader context of Polish–Jewish relations which were complex and often violent (Ambrosewicz-Jacobs and Szuchta 2014; Szuchta 2013). That is why teaching about help offered to Jews happens to be misleading, which was demonstrated in the study of Polish high school students' historical knowledge presented in this chapter. Despite this failure in education, we believe that the more realistic and precise approach to wartime helping behaviour could provide an important opportunity for more meaningful Holocaust education.

The moral-exemplars model of reconciliation (Čehajić-Clancy and Bilewicz 2016) proposes that reliable depictions of heroic helpers can facilitate positive intergroup relations in post-conflict settings, among both victims and perpetrators, as well as bystanders. According to this model, heroic helpers stemming from the own national group or the adversaries in conflict could serve as moral exemplars, since they exhibited uniquely moral behaviour in comparison with their compatriots. In particular, the model suggests that presenting narratives about heroic helpers who decided to act morally and in opposition to the passive or active aggression of their group can restore impaired intergroup relations, by improving attitudes among descendants of historical perpetrators, victims and bystanders.

Research on Polish–Jewish youth encounter programme (Bilewicz 2007) showed that Holocaust-related topics present during such encounters suppressed positive effects of intergroup contact in improving mutual attitudes. However, narratives about moral exemplars proved to be effective in overcoming these obstacles. When the encounter was preceded by a meeting with a Polish heroic helper (i.e. a person awarded with the honorary title "Righteous among the Nations" for rescuing Jews), intergroup contact had a positive effect on young Poles' attitudes towards Israelis and Israelis' attitudes towards Poles. Documented stories of rescue (i.e. films, testimonies and photographs) catalysed also a positive effect of intergroup encounters between Bosniaks and Serbs in the context of the Bosnian War (Čehajić-Clancy and Bilewicz 2016). The exposure to such stories facilitated the positive effect of intergroup contact on beliefs in reconciliation and forgiveness.

Positive effects of moral-exemplars narratives were observed also outside of the intergroup contact setting. Interestingly, a study conducted in the context of the Armenian genocide demonstrated that an exposure to narratives about Turks who helped Armenians in 1915 increased Turks' willingness to engage in contact with Armenians and improved their attitudes towards them (Witkowska et al. 2016). Similar results were found in the context of the Second World War, where reminders of German heroic helpers, who rescued Jews during the Holocaust, proved to be effective in reducing the tendency of Germans to engage in temporal distancing from the Nazi past (Peetz et al. 2010).

Current empirical findings obtained in this area suggest that the use of heroic helpers' narratives—as long as it is free from simplifications and does not ignore the negative setting in which the heroic help took place (i.e. aggression or passivity of others)—may be an effective tool in reducing discomfort related to threatening past of one's group and may give a possibility of discussing difficult historical topics in the classroom.

Proposal 3: Working with Local Identities Instead of National Ones

Most of the existing Holocaust education curricula use the national or ethnic groups as key agents in the historical narrative. It is known, however, that most defensive reactions to the history of the Holocaust stem from strong national identities (for a review, see Bilewicz 2016). Empathy-based approach and moral-exemplars-based approach suggest that student's attention can be redirected to individualized stories that allow to personalize education about the Holocaust. In a process of personalization, students' national identities become less salient which allows them to gain a new perspective and makes them more open to outgroup members and new narratives (Miller 2002). At the same time, personalized education can lead to subtyping: students can change their attitudes towards a given person (e.g. Anna Frank or Dawidek Rubinowicz), while at the same time remaining prejudiced and insensitive about other members of victimized nation (Brown et al. 1999). To overcome this problem, we suggest another approach, based on the local history education that incorporates psychological theories of common ingroup identity (Gaertner et al. 1993) and place attachment theory (Lewicka 2008).

Moreover, the local history approach suggests that it may be beneficial to expose students to the history of the Holocaust in their local environment and thereby include Jews into the common local identity (e.g. Varsovians, Berliners, Galicians). In most of the current Holocaust education programmes, the main focus is put on several key historical locations, such as Auschwitz and Treblinka death camps or the Warsaw Ghetto. Such an approach does not engage local identities and leads to the perception of the Holocaust as a geographically distant event, especially for those students who live in the places where numerous Jewish communities existed prior to WWII and their historical presence and destruction remains unacknowledged.

Recently, various educational institutions have attempted to overcome this problem by implementing local history approach using interventions such as presenting the local Holocaust narratives as a part of the history of Budapest (Zachor Foundation in Hungary), reminding Germans about their lost Jewish neighbours with memorial cobblestones in their hometowns (*Stolperstein* project by Gunter Demnig) or increasing interest in local Jewish heritage in small Polish towns (School of Dialogue programme by Forum for Dialogue Foundation). Such projects are in line with the findings of environmental psychology demonstrating that an increased interest in local history can improve intergroup relations by generating more inclusive social identities (Lewicka 2008, 2012).

In the in-depth study of one of these interventions (School of Dialogue programme), Stefaniak and Bilewicz (2016) assessed the specific mechanism responsible for the effectiveness of local history programmes. They found that such programmes increase student's interest in history and, at the same time, provide them with historical knowledge about the Jewish past. This, in turn, creates a situation in which students more readily include Jews into their collective identity (as historical fellow residents of the same space), which ultimately leads to the improvement of attitudes towards Jews, and even greater curiosity to learn Jewish history.

The local history approach can clearly facilitate successful Holocaust education. It brings the victims to the scope of students' understanding by decreasing the geographical–temporal gap between themselves and the Jewish victims of the Holocaust. The Holocaust may become personally significant to students only after they are able to properly understand the scale of the historical losses endured by their community, as well as by their local culture. Without that, there is a risk of distancing from the Holocaust and perceiving it as a typical "somebody-else's problem." In general, common ingroup identity approaches, when used in the context of Holocaust education, were found to increase one's sense of responsibility for the past and lead to intergroup reconciliation (Kofta and Slawuta 2013; Wohl and Branscombe 2005).

Summary

German and Polish Holocaust education in its current form often does not fulfil its goals. A comparison of several nationwide surveys performed after 1989 showed a linear decrease of knowledge about the Holocaust in Polish population (Witkowska and Bilewicz 2014). This trend was observed in times when the country implemented Holocaust education in its curricula. Similarly, a survey performed 10 years after the massive public Holocaust education programme was implemented in Sweden found that more than 70% of Swedish teachers show vast ignorance about the Holocaust (Lange 2008).

Apart from failures in providing knowledge, Holocaust education was also ineffective in changing attitudes. The results of studies from Poland and Germany presented in this chapter show that current Holocaust education fails to reduce antisemitism and promote tolerance among students. The only measurable effects of such education were as follows: threatened national identities (Germany) and biased perception of the Holocaust history (Poland). Neither of them could be considered a desired outcome of Holocaust education.

As an alternative to dominant forms of Holocaust education, we propose three approaches that are not based on national identities, national-level emotions (guilt, shame, pride) and national-level responsibilities. First of them, empathic education, leads to greater focus on victims experiences and generates feelings of regret instead of collective guilt. The second, moral-exemplars approach, stresses the diversity of behaviours in times of the Holocaust presenting individual heroism as a counterpoint to the passivity or cruelty of others. Such way of education about the Holocaust allows to overcome essentialist and entitative perceptions of groups. The third approach, based on local identities, aims to include the victims into the common local identity, and to acknowledge the losses in the local Jewish population.

Holocaust education is often considered not only a part of historical education, but also an important experience that could prevent future crimes, cruelty and conflicts. The success of such endeavour lies in the ability of educators to utilize the psychological knowledge in their teaching about the Holocaust, in order to better understand potential obstacles and being able to overcome them.

Notes

1. Although it is clear that these three positions are merely constructions of collective memory, as in every nation there were individuals in perpetrator, collaborator, passive bystander, and victim role, whereas the process of genocide was transforming people and groups from one role to another (Bilewicz and Vollhardt 2012).
2. More than a half of these visitors could be classified as having intrusion-related symptoms, about a quarter developed avoidance symptoms and more than 10% showed hypervigilance symptoms.
3. This research was supported by the DFG-NCN Beethoven grant (2014/15/G/HS6/04589).

References

Abram, I., & Heyl, M. (1996). *Thema Holocaust. Ein Buch für die Schule.* Reinbek: Rewohlt.
Ahlheim, K., & Heger, B. (2002). *Die unbequeme Vergangenheit. NS-Vergangenheit, Holocaust und die Schwierigkeiten des Erinnerns.* Schwalbach: Wochenschau-Verlag.
Allwork, L. (2015). *Holocaust remembrance between the national and the transnational: The Stockholm international forum and the first decade of the international task force.* London: Bloomsbury Publishing.
Ambrosewicz-Jacobs, J., & Szuchta, R. (2014). The intricacies of education about the Holocaust in Poland. Ten years after the Jedwabne debate, what can Polish school students learn about the Holocaust in history classes? *Intercultural Education, 25,* 283–299.
Anderson, J. R. (2007). *Kognitive Psychologie.* 6. Auflage. Berlin: Spektrum.
Assmann, A. (2010). The Holocaust—A global memory? Extensions and limits of a new memory community. In A. Assmann & S. Conrad (Eds.), *Memory in a global age. Discourses, practices and trajectories* (pp. 97–117). London: Palgrave Macmillan UK.
Bar-On, D., Hare, A. P., Brusten, M., & Beiner, F. (1997). Den Holocaust 'durcharbeiten'? Ergebnisse einer vergleichenden Untersuchung an deutschen und israelischen Studierenden. In D. Bar-On, K. Brendler, & A. P. Hare (Eds.), *"Da ist etwas kaputtgegangen an den Wurzeln...": Identitätsformation deutscher und israelischer Jugendlicher im Schatten des Holocaust* (pp. 21–53). Frankfurt am Main: Campus.
Baumeister, R. F., Stillwell, A. M., & Heatherton, T. F. (1995). Personal narratives about guilt: Role in action control and interpersonal relationships. *Basic and Applied Social Psychology, 17,* 173–198.
Bilewicz, M. (2007). History as an obstacle: Impact of temporal-based social categorizations on Polish-Jewish intergroup contact. *Group Processes & Intergroup Relations, 10,* 551–563.
Bilewicz, M. (2016). The dark side of emotion regulation: Historical defensiveness as an obstacle in reconciliation. *Psychological Inquiry, 2,* 89–95.
Bilewicz, M., & Jaworska, M. (2013). Reconciliation through the righteous: The narratives of heroic helpers as a fulfillment of emotional needs in Polish–Jewish intergroup contact. *Journal of Social Issues, 69,* 162–179.
Bilewicz, M., & Vollhardt, J. R. (2012). Evil transformations: Psychological processes underlying genocide and mass killing. In A. Golec De Zavala & A. Cichocka (Eds.), *Social psychology of social problems. The intergroup context* (pp. 280–307). New York: Palgrave Macmillan.
Bilewicz, M., Witkowska, M., Stefaniak, A., & Imhoff, R. (2016). *The lay historian explains intergroup behavior: Identification and epistemic abilities as*

correlates of ethnocentric historical attributions. Manuscript submitted for publication.
Bilewicz, M., & Wójcik, A. (2009). Antysemityzm na gruzach sztetl: stosunek polskiej młodzieży do Żydów w miastach i miasteczkach południowej i wschodniej Polski. W: LM Nijakowski (red.), Etniczność, pamięć, asymilacja: wokół problemów zachowania tożsamości mniejszości narodowych i etnicznych, 153–167.
Bilewicz, M., & Wójcik, A. (2016). Visiting Auschwitz. Evidence of secondary traumatization of high-school students. Manuscript submitted for publication.
Brandt, S. (2003). Wenig Anschauung? Die Ausstrahlung des Films Holocaust im westdeutschen Fernsehen. In C. Cornelißen, L. Klinkhammer, & W. Schwentker (Eds.), *Erinnerungskulturen. Deutschland, Italien und Japan seit 1945* (pp. 257–268). Frankfurt am Main: Fischer.
Branscombe, N. R., Doosje, B., & McGarty, C. (2002). Antecedents and consequences of collective guilt. In D. M. Mackie & E. R. Smith (Eds.), *From prejudice to intergroup emotions: Differentiated reactions to social groups* (pp. 49–66). New York: Psychology Press.
Branscombe, N. R., Schmitt, M. T., & Schiffhauer, K. (2007). Racial attitudes in response to thoughts of White privilege. *European Journal of Social Psychology*, *37*, 203–215.
Brendler, K. (1994). Die Holocaustrezeption der Enkelgeneration im Spannungsfeld von Abwehr und Traumatisierung. *Jahrbuch für Antisemitismusforschung*, *3*, 303–340.
Brendler, K. (1997a). Vorwort. In D. Bar-On, K. Brendler, & A. P. Hare (Eds.), *"Da ist etwas kaputtgegangen an den Wurzeln...": Identitätsformation deutscher und israelischer Jugendlicher im Schatten des Holocaust* (pp. 7–9). Frankfurt am Main: Campus.
Brendler, K. (1997b). Die NS-Geschichte als Sozialisationsfaktor und Identitätsballast der Enkelgeneration. In D. Bar-On, K. Brendler, & A. P. Hare (Eds.), *"Da ist etwas kaputtgegangen an den Wurzeln...": Identitätsformation deutscher und israelischer Jugendlicher im Schatten des Holocaust* (pp. 53–105). Frankfurt am Main: Campus.
Brockhaus G. (2008). "Bloß nicht moralisieren!" – Emotionale Prozesse in der pädagogischen Auseinandersetzung mit dem Nationalsozialismus. *Einsichten und Perspektiven*, *1*, 28–33.
Broder, H. M. (1986). *Der Ewige Antisemit. Über Sinn und Funktion eines beständigen Gefühls*. Frankfurt am Main: Fischer.
Brown, R., González, R., Zagefka, H., Manzi, J., & Čehajić, S. (2008). Nuestra culpa: Collective guilt and shame as predictors of reparation for historical wrongdoing. *Journal of Personality and Social Psychology*, *94*, 75–90.
Brown, R., Vivian, J., & Hewstone, M. (1999). Changing attitudes through intergroup contact: The effects of group membership salience. *European Journal of Social Psychology*, *29*, 741–764.

Brusten, M., & Winkelmann, B. (1992). The understanding of the Holocaust and its influence on current perspectives of German youth. *Soziale Probleme, 3*, 1–27.

Brusten, M., & Winkelmann, B. (1994). Wie denken deutsche Studenten in "West" und "Ost" nach der Wiedervereinigung über den Holocaust. In D. Diner & F. Stern (Eds.), *Tel Aviver Jahrbuch für deutsche Geschichte. Nationalismus aus heutiger Perspektive* (pp. 461–486). Gerlingen: Bleicher Verlag.

Carrier, P., Fuchs, E., & Messinger, T. (2015). *The International status of education about the Holocaust: A global mapping of textbooks and curricula*. Paris: UNESCO Publishing and Georg Eckert Institute.

Čehajić-Clancy, S., & Bilewicz, M. (2016). Fostering reconciliation through historical moral exemplars in a post-conflict society. Manuscript submitted for publication.

Cisneros, D. (2008). Unterricht aus Lehrerperspektive. *Einsichten und Perspektiven, 1*, 44–51.

Easterbrook, J. A. (1959). The effect of emotion on cue utilization and the organization of behaviour. *Psychological Review, 66*(3), 183–201.

Fend, H. (1991). Identitätsentwicklung in der Adoleszenz. Lebensentwürfe, Selbstfindung und Weltaneignung in beruflichen, familiären und politisch-weltanschaulischen Bereichen. Entwicklungspsychologie der Adoleszenz in der Moderne (Bd. 2). Bern: Huber.

Ferguson, M. A., & Branscombe, N. R. (2014). The social psychology of collective guilt. In C. von Scheve & M. Salmela (Eds.), *Collective emotions* (pp. 251–265). New York: Oxford University Press.

Gaertner, S. L., Dovidio, J. F., Anastasio, P. A., Bachman, B. A., & Rust, M. C. (1993). The common ingroup identity model: Recategorization and the reduction of intergroup bias. *European Review of Social Psychology, 4*, 1–26.

Glück, E. M., & Wagensommer, G. (2004). Erinnern ist mehr als Informiertsein. In W. Schwendemann & G. Wagensommer (Eds.), *Erinnern ist mehr als Informiertsein. Aus der Geschichte Lernen (2)* (pp. 97–109). Münster: LIT-Verlag.

Golec de Zavala, A., Cichocka, A., & Bilewicz, M. (2013). The paradox of in-group love: Differentiating collective narcissism advances understanding of the relationship between in-group and out-group attitudes. *Journal of Personality, 81*, 16–28.

Gross, J. T. (2001). *Neighbors: The destruction of the Jewish community in Jedwabne, Poland*. Princeton: Princeton University Press.

Gross, M. H. (2010). Rewriting the nation: World War II narratives in Polish history textbooks. In I. Silova (Ed.), *Post-socialism is not dead: (Re)reading the global in comparative education* (pp. 213–246). Bingley: Emerald Group Publishing Limited.

Gross, M. H. (2014). Struggling to deal with the difficult past: Polish students confront the Holocaust. *Journal of Curriculum Studies, 46,* 441–463.

Henke-Bockschatz, G. (2004). Der "Holocaust" als Thema im Geschichtsunterricht. Kritische Anmerkungen. In W. Meseth, M. Proske, & F. O. Radke (Hrsg.), *Schule und Nationalsozialismus. Anspruch und Grenzen des Geschichtsunterrichts* (S. 9–32). Frankfurt a. M.: Campus.

Hewstone, M., Cairns, E., Voci, A., McLernon, F., Niens, U., & Noor, M. (2004). Intergroup forgiveness and guilt in Northern Ireland: Social psychological dimensions of 'The Troubles'. In N. R. Branscombe & B. Doosje (Eds.), *Collective guilt: International perspectives* (pp. 193–215). Cambridge: University Press.

Heyl, M. (1996). "Erziehung nach Auschwitz" und "Holocaust Education" – Überlegungen, Konzepte und Vorschläge. In I. Abram & M. Heyl (Eds.), *Thema Holocaust. Ein Buch für die Schule* (pp. 61–164). Reinbek: Rewohlt.

Imhoff, R., & Banse, R. (2009). Ongoing victim suffering increases prejudice: The case of secondary anti-Semitism. *Psychological Science, 20,* 1443–1447.

Imhoff, R., Bilewicz, M., & Erb, H. (2012). Collective regret versus collective guilt: Different emotional reactions to historical atrocities. *European Journal of Social Psychology, 42,* 729–742.

Imhoff, R., Bilewicz, M., Hanke, K., Kahn, D. T., Henkel-Guembel, N., Halabi, S., et al. (in press). Explaining the inexplicable: Differences in attributions for the Holocaust in Germany, Israel and Poland. *Political Psychology.*

Imhoff, R., Wohl, M. J. A., & Erb, H. (2013). When the past is far from dead: How ongoing consequences of genocides committed by the ingroup impact collective guilt. *Journal of Social Issues, 69,* 74–91.

Keupp, H. (2008). Editorial. *Einsichten und Perspektiven, 1,* 4–5.

Kofta, M., & Slawuta, P. (2013). Thou shall not kill… your brother: Victim–perpetrator cultural closeness and moral disapproval of Polish atrocities against Jews after the Holocaust. *Journal of Social Issues, 69,* 54–73.

Krejci, J. (1995). Die Suche nach einer neuen nationalen und europäischen Identität bei Deutschen, Tschechen und Polen. Frankfurt a. M.: Peter Lang.

Kühner, A., & Langer, P. (2008). Wie Geschichte zum Thema wird. "Holocaust Education" aus sozialpsychologischer Perspektive. *Psychosozial, 114,* 131–141.

Lange, A. (2008). *A survey of teachers' experiences and perceptions in relation to teaching about the Holocaust.* Stockholm: Living History Forum.

Leach, C. W., Bou Zeineddine, F., & Čehajić-Clancy, S. (2013). Moral immemorial: The rarity of self-criticism for previous generations' genocide or mass violence. *Journal of Social Issues, 69,* 34–53.

Lewicka, M. (2008). Place attachment, place identity, and place memory: Restoring the forgotten city past. *Journal of Environmental Psychology, 28,* 209–231.

Lewicka, M. (2012). *Psychologia miejsca.* Warsaw: Wydawnictwo Naukowe Scholar.

Maitner, A. T., Mackie, D. M., & Smith, E. R. (2007). Antecedents and consequences of satisfaction and guilt following ingroup aggression. *Group Processes & Intergroup Relations, 10,* 223–237.

Mayer, U., Pandel, H. J., Schneider, G., & Schönemann, B. (Hrsg.). (2006). *Wörterbuch Geschichtsdidaktik* (S. 90–91). Schwalbach: Wochenschau Verlag.

Mazur, L. B., & Vollhardt, J. R. (2015). The prototypicality of genocide: Implications for international intervention. *Analyses of Social Issues and Public Policy* (Advanced online publication).

Meier, C. (1997). Debatte: Goldhagen und die Deutschen. *Internationale Zeitschrift für Philosophie, 1,* 119–123.

Miller, N. (2002). Personalization and the promise of contact theory. *Journal of Social Issues, 58,* 387–410.

Ministerium für Schule und Weiterbildung des Landes Nordrhein-Westfalen. (2007). *Kernlehrplan für das Gymnasium—Sekundarstufe I (G8) in Nordrhein-Westfalen. Geschichte.* Frechen: Ritterbach.

Mummendey, A., Klink, A., & Brown, R. (2001). Nationalism and patriotism: National identification and out-group rejection. *British Journal of Social Psychology, 40,* 159–172.

Peetz, J., Gunn, G. R., & Wilson, A. E. (2010). Crimes of the past: Defensive temporal distancing in the face of past in-group wrongdoing. *Personality and Social Psychology Bulletin, 36,* 598–611.

Reichel, P. (2004). *Erfundene Erinnerung: Weltkrieg und Judenmord in Film und Theater.* Munich/Vienna: Carl Hanser Verlag.

Riley, K. L. (1998). Historical empathy and the Holocaust: Theory into practice. *International Journal of Social Education, 13,* 32–42.

Rommelspacher, B. (1995). *Schuldlos - Schuldig? Wie sich junge Frauen mit Antisemitismus auseinandersetzen.* Hamburg: Konkret-Literatur-Verlag.

Schmidt-Denter, U. (2011). *Die Deutschen und ihre Migranten. Ergebnisse der europäischen Identitätsstudie.* Weinheim: Juventa.

Schmidt-Denter, U., & Stubig, S. (2011). *Holocaust Education: Lehrplanrecherche, TV-Recherche und Untersuchungen.* (Forschungsbericht Nr. 35 zum Projekt "Personale und soziale Identität im Kontext von Globalisierung und nationaler Abgrenzung"). Cologne: Universität.

Schneider, W. L. (2004). Die Unwahrscheinlichkeit der Moral. Strukturen moralischer Kommunikation im Schulunterricht über Nationalsozialismus und Holocaust. In W. Meseth, M. Proske, & F. O. Radke (Eds.), *Schule und Nationalsozialismus. Anspruch und Grenzen des Geschichtsunterrichts* (pp. 205–234). Frankfurt am Main: Campus.

Schultz, L. H., Barr, D. J., & Selman, R. L. (2001). The value of a developmental approach to evaluating character development programmes: An outcome study of facing history and ourselves. *Journal of Moral Education, 30,* 3–27.

Schwendemann, W. (2004). Didaktisches Chaos oder alles im Griff? Aspekte einer Erziehung nach und über Auschwitz. In W. Schwendemann & G. Wagensommer (Eds.), *Erinnern ist mehr als Informiertsein. Aus der Geschichte lernen (2)* (pp. 33–47). Münster: LIT-Verlag.

Schwendemann, W. & Marks, S. (2002). Unterrichtsthema "Nationalsozialismus" in einer Hauptschule – Ergebnisse einer Pilotstudie (Schülerbefragungen). *Im Gespräch: Hefte der Martin Buber-Gesellschaft, 3,* 62–77.

Smith, T. W., & Jarkko, L. (1998). *National pride: A cross-national analysis* (GSS Cross-national Report No. 19). Chicago: National Opinion Research Centre/ University of Chicago.

Smith, T. W., & Seokho, K. (2006). National pride in comparative perspective: 1995/96 and 2003/04. *International Journal of Public Opinion Research, 18,* 127–136.

Stefaniak, A., & Bilewicz, M. (2016). Contact with a multicultural past: A prejudice-reducing intervention. *International Journal of Intercultural Relations, 50,* 60–65.

Stubig, S. S. (2015). *Die Wirkung des Geschichtsunterrichts zu Nationalsozialismus und Holocaust auf die Identität von Jugendlichen.* Aachen: Shaker.

Szuchta, R. (2006). Nauczanie o Holokauście – zalecenia programowe a praktyka szkolna. In A. Żbikowski (Ed.), *Nauczanie o Holokauście* (pp. 75–83). Pułtusk: ASPRA-JR.

Szuchta, R. (2013). *Czego uczeń polskiej szkoły może się dowiedzieć o Holokauście na lekcji historii dziesięć lat po "dyskusji jedwabieńskiej".* Unpublished manuscript.

Szuchta, R., & Trojański, P. (2012). *Jak uczyć o Holokauście: Poradnik metodyczny do nauczania o Holokauście w ramach przedmiotów humanistycznych w zreformowanej szkole.* Warsaw: Ośrodek Rozwoju Edukacji.

Tajfel, H., & Turner, J. C. (1979). An integrative theory of intergroup conflict. *The Social Psychology of Intergroup Relations, 33*(47), 74.

Tangney, J. P. (1995). Shame and guilt in interpersonal relationships. In J. P. Tangney & K. W. Fischer (Eds.), *Self-conscious emotions: The psychology of shame, guilt, embarrassment, and pride* (pp. 114–139). New York: Guilford Press.

Welzer, H. (2004). "Ach Opa!" Einige Bemerkungen zum Verhältnis von Tradierung und Aufklärung. In W. Meseth, M. Proske, & F. O. Radke (Eds.), *Schule und Nationalsozialismus. Anspruch und Grenzen des Geschichtsunterrichts* (pp. 49–64). Frankfurt am Main: Campus.

Westle, B. (1999). *Kollektive Identität im vereinten Deutschland. Nation und Demokratie in der Wahrnehmung der Deutschen.* Opladen: Leske + Budrich.

Węgrzynek, H. (2006). Prezentacja Holokaustu i dziejów Żydów w aktualnych podręcznikach historii. In A. Żbikowski (Ed.), *Nauczanie o Holokauście* (pp. 13–74). Pułtusk: ASPRA-JR.
Witkowska, M., & Bilewicz, M. (2014). Czy prawda nas wyzwoli? Przełamywanie oporu psychologicznego w przyjmowaniu wiedzy o Holocauście. *Zagłada Żydów. Studia i materiały, 10*, 805–822.
Witkowska, M., Bilewicz, M., & Čehajić-Clancy, S. (2016). *Fostering intergroup contact after historical atrocities. An approach based on moral exemplars.* Unpublished manuscript.
Witkowska, M., Stefaniak, A., & Bilewicz, M. (2015). Stracone szanse? Wpływ polskiej edukacji o Zagładzie na postawy wobec Żydów. *Psychologia Wychowawcza, 5*, 147–159.
Wohl, M. J., & Branscombe, N. R. (2005). Forgiveness and collective guilt assignment to historical perpetrator groups depend on level of social category inclusiveness. *Journal of Personality and Social Psychology, 88*, 288–303.
Wójcik, A., & Bilewicz, M. (2012). Oświęcim inaczej. Raport z badań. [Auschwitz in a different way. Research report]. Warsaw: Center for Research on Prejudice.
Wójcik, A., Bilewicz, M., & Lewicka, M. (2010). Living on the ashes: Collective representations of Polish-Jewish history among people living in the former Warsaw Ghetto area. *Cities, 27*, 195–203.
Zülsdorf-Kersting, M. (2007). *Sechzig Jahre danach: Jugendliche und der Holocaust. Eine Studie zur geschichtskulturellen Sozialisation.* Münster: LIT-Verlag.

Authors' Biography

Michał Bilewicz is an Associate Professor of Psychology at the University of Warsaw, where he chairs the Center for Research on Prejudice. His research concerns social psychology of intergroup relations, particularly the problems of post-conflict reconciliation, the aftermath of mass violence and hate speech. As vice-president of the Forum for Dialogue, he was involved in creating teaching materials about multi-ethnic history and novel educational methods. He was co-chairing the Working Group on collective emotions and reconciliation within the COST IS1205 research network, and he currently serves as Governing Council member of the International Society of Political Psychology. He published numerous articles, e.g., in Psychological Inquiry, International Journal of Conflict and Violence, Group Processes and Intergroup Relations and European Journal of Social Psychology. He is a member of Editorial Boards of European

Journal of Social Psychology, International Journal of Intercultural Relations and Journal of Community and Applied Social Psychology.

Marta Witkowska is a doctoral candidate at the Department of Psychology at the University of Warsaw. She works within NCN-DFG research grant Beethoven on the role of psychological motivations in historical representations. Her current research concerns the role of moral exemplars in reconciliation (portrayals of heroic helpers in times of genocide). Apart from psychological research, she is also active in antidiscriminatory education (e.g. Human Library project in Radom). She published several chapters and articles about the holocaust education in Poland and potentials for alternative education.

Silviana Stubig is a Senior Lecturer at the Department of Psychology at the University of Cologne. Her research concerns issues of Pedagogical Psychology and Developmental Psychology. Her doctoral dissertation dealt with the topic of Holocaust Education in German classes and was published in 2015. Actual research projects concentrate on smartphone usage in learning contexts.

Marta Beneda completed an MA in Psychology at the University of Warsaw in 2016 and is currently pursuing an MA in Social and Developmental Psychology at the University of Cambridge. Since 2013, she has been a part of the Centre for Research on Prejudice at the University of Warsaw where she has been engaged in several projects focused on the social psychology of intergroup relations. Her main research interests include the role of historical narratives in intergroup reconciliation and forgiveness, prejudice reduction and the role of social and cognitive processes in gender development.

Roland Imhoff is Chair for Social and Legal Psychology at the Johannes Gutenberg University (JGU) Mainz, Germany, and a board member of the Center for Interdisciplinary Forensics at the JGU Mainz. His research interests lie in the areas of social psychological approaches to intergroup conflict and history, stereotypes and prejudice, ideology and conspiracy thinking as well as sexual orientation and methodological and measurement issues. Exploring and pushing the boundaries of his field, he has been part of inter- and transdisciplinary research centres with economists, legal scholars, medical scholars, sociologists, historians and other disciplines. He has published papers in Journal of Personality and Social Psychology, Psychological Science,

Perspectives on Psychological Science, Psychological Assessment, Emotion and European Journal of Social Psychology, among others. Since 2011, he is a member of the Editorial Board of the Archives of Sexual Behavior.

Open Access This chapter is licensed under the terms of the Creative Commons Attribution 4.0 International License (http://creativecommons.org/licenses/by/4.0/), which permits use, sharing, adaptation, distribution and reproduction in any medium or format, as long as you give appropriate credit to the original author(s) and the source, provide a link to the Creative Commons license and indicate if changes were made.

The images or other third party material in this chapter are included in the chapter's Creative Commons license, unless indicated otherwise in a credit line to the material. If material is not included in the chapter's Creative Commons license and your intended use is not permitted by statutory regulation or exceeds the permitted use, you will need to obtain permission directly from the copyright holder.

PART III

Textbook and Teacher Perspectives in Post-transition and Post-conflict Societies

History Teaching as 'Propaganda'? Teachers' Communication Styles in Post-Transition Societies

Katrin Kello and Wolfgang Wagner

THE POLITICS OF HISTORY TEACHING

Based on studying history curricula in Germany, UK and the Netherlands in the nineteenth and twentieth centuries, Arie Wilschut concludes that

---

The work on this chapter was facilitated by the Estonian Science Foundation project ETF9308 ('Geographies of Media and Communication in a Transition Country'), Estonian Ministry of Education and Research (IUT grant 20–38), the European Regional Development Fund (Centre of Excellence in Cultural Theory, CECT), and ESF COST Action IS1205 ('Social psychological dynamics of historical representations in the enlarged European Union').

K. Kello (✉)
University of Tartu, Tartu, Estonia
e-mail: Katrin.Kello@ut.ee

W. Wagner
Johannes Kepler University, Linz, Austria

© The Author(s) 2017
C. Psaltis et al. (eds.), *History Education and Conflict Transformation*,
DOI 10.1007/978-3-319-54681-0_8

> Generally speaking, we can distinguish three factors influencing the content and form of history curricula: politics and society; pedagogical and psychological considerations; and academic history itself. [...] However sensible it seems to take pedagogical and psychological considerations and insights concerning the developing child into account, they cannot be decisive when it comes to the formulation of general aims of history teaching. The course history teaching should take can only be directed by politics and society, which will have to decide whether or not to respect the standards of scholarly history (Wilschut 2010, p. 717).

This statement sets the stage for this chapter. Wilschut points both to the dynamic nature of the contexts of history teaching and to the fact that the particular constellation of the factors is to some extent open to interpretations. The constellation can change quite quickly even in the same country, and history educators even in the same time and space can perceive the relative weights of contextual factors quite differently (see Kello 2016). Educators face a multiplicity of understandings and expectations from the different fields, and often they need to navigate between contradictory understandings and expectations. There is a continuous discussion and dialogue between the fields over aims, contents and functions of history teaching (Wilschut 2010).

In lay and political representations, serving national identity and patriotism is still perceived as the main function of history teaching in many countries. However, since its beginnings, the school subject has always served what Carretero and Bermudez (2012) call 'enlightened' approach aiming at the more general education of the students. The compatibility of the 'patriotic' and 'enlightened' tasks depends on how the latter are understood. 'Educating students', if conceived as transmitting information without much reflection, need not interfere with the patriotic aims. In contrast, 'critical enlightened' history teaching demands recognition of divergent experiences and perspectives, critical (self-)reflection and contesting celebratory myths and narratives (Carretero and Bermudez 2012).

The present chapter is set on the backdrop of such variety of understandings and expectations of history as a school subject. We take a look at different positions that history teachers take towards their subject and its contexts using material from in-depth interviews with Estonian and Latvian history teachers. Viewing the history classroom as a communicative space, we discuss how the three styles of communication—*diffusion*, *propagation* and *propaganda*—as proposed in *Social Representation Theory* (Moscovici 2008) can be used to characterise styles of history teaching.

COMMUNICATION SPACES IN HISTORY TEACHING

Teacher's Action Space

There are many ways how a particular teacher can position themselves with regard to the aims and functions of history teaching. The curriculum is often not a sufficient landmark for the orientation of teachers, textbook authors and other educators because, as with any text, it needs interpretation based on some external framework. Even if the national curriculum has legal force, it is not usual for it to be thoroughly law-like. Neither are lawyers normally there to help users read it. Often, in order to gain a broader acceptance, either it is generic, or it contains 'something for everybody' (cf. Simpson and Halse 2006), presuming that the teacher or textbook author makes his or her own choices and sets his or her own emphases. Not to mention that from a quite practical point of view the teachers need to choose foci and decide on time allocations *here and now*.

Individual teacher's positioning is probably most obvious in the case of socially and politically sensitive and controversial issues that are connected to different social memories and political interests. In the case of such issues, it becomes particularly visible that history teachers are positioned as mediators between different fields or perspectives (academy, science, politics, different nations, different worldviews or ideologies, etc.), or between different group-bound social memories. Teacher positions are shaped by their location, both perceived and actual, on the landscape. Teachers' representations of their subject reflect both their social positions and their individual perceptions. On the one hand, the teacher's action space is made up of 'objective' or 'external' limitations such as national final examinations or the teacher's ethnolinguistic belonging. On the other hand, their action space is made up of more subjective, dynamic and situational things such as pedagogical repertoire, epistemological position, self-confidence and sense of professional autonomy and legitimacy that are connected to their image of the social, political and academic space that surrounds history teaching.

In Fig. 1, we distinguish relevant 'external' contexts from the perspective of history teaching. Teachers' positions towards the different

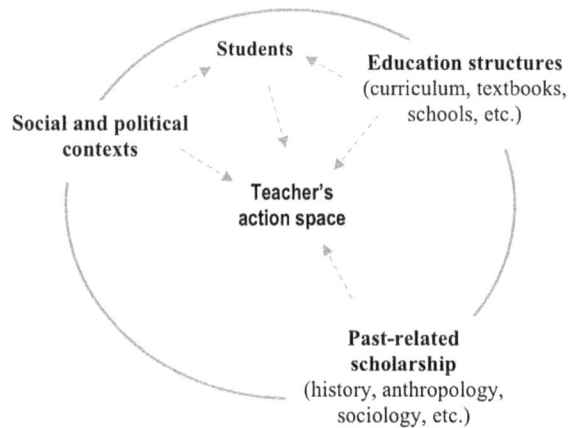

Fig. 1 Contextual dimensions of the history teacher's action space

kinds of contexts include their own positions on the social, mnemonic and political landscape, as well as their conceptions of those fields' influences on their students and classrooms. Of course, each of the three contexts merge influences from the other two. Curricula and textbooks, for instance, merge sociopolitical influences with considerations from pedagogical psychology and with inputs from academic research about the past; social and political representations of the past receive inputs from both school and academy, whereas academic scholars are obviously also influenced by beliefs and experiences from their primary and secondary socialisation. What is important in the present context is the interconnectedness of the fields and the absence of a stable hierarchy between them. If hierarchies appear, they are dynamic constellations, changing in time and space and perceived differently by different actors.

Communication Styles as Social Representations

For further analysis of orientations in teaching history, we draw on *Social Representation Theory*. By social representations, we understand coordinated patterns of thinking, communication and behaving that exist among actors in social groups relative to issues or imaginary or real objects, which become relevant in certain situations (e.g. Jovchelovitch 2007; Moscovici 2008; Wagner and Hayes 2005). A social representation equally includes what individual members of a group think about an issue, how they communicate about it and how they behave towards others and towards the things related to an issue. In other words, representations are in action as much as they are in thinking (Wagner 2015).

In his study on psychoanalysis, Moscovici (2008) made the important point that representations are social not only due to in-group members sharing in their contents, but also by the very fact that different representational *contents* are contingent on *styles* of communication. To explicate this, he used three bodies of newspapers. Firstly, newspapers addressed to the French society as a whole, i.e. to a heterogeneous readership, followed a relatively neutral *diffusion*—or better: *dissemination*—of the new science of psychoanalysis in the fifties. This style did not evaluate what was communicated, but offered content irrespective of potential contradiction. Another style was used by the communist press. Moscovici called the communication style *propagandistic* as it flatly rejected psychoanalysis as harmful. It was a highly evaluative way of communication and assessed any news with regard to its implications for communist ideology and political progress. In fact, workers and members of the Communist Party took a critical and ideologically inspired stance that echoed their papers' propagandistic style and rejected psychoanalysis as a bourgeois ploy against dialectical materialism. Third, there was the *propagation* style of the catholic press that took a pragmatic approach by appropriating some and silencing other aspects of the new psychology to serve the church's moral message.

Moscovici's analysis demonstrates how styles of communication are not imposed on, or independent of, representations of psychoanalysis. Rather, they are an integral part of the latter. In his view, social representations not only exist *for* the purpose of communication, so to say *before* it, but are created, shaped and elaborated *by and through* communication in groups. The discourse related to a social object, that is the interests and motivations of group members and the affective and cognitive resources brought forward, jointly determines and characterises the content and form of the representation. We consider the integrative character of social representations to be pivotal in theorising. If we want to understand how local worlds, conflicts (Psaltis 2016), school textbooks (Sakki 2010) and other social objects take shape, the concrete form of communal communication must be part and parcel of the representation and the object that it addresses (Duveen 2008a, b; Wagner et al. forthcoming). In history teaching, the style of teaching not only conveys a message about epistemology, i.e. about the ways how knowledge about the past comes about, but also constitutes the history narrative in terms of its content.

In 'traditional history teaching', teachers will represent the past in a way that is determined by some kind of ideology, usually of nationalist origin, but it could also be Marxist–Leninist as in the case of Soviet history teaching. Maintaining the image of a valuable in-group by way of a celebratory past from the perspective of a certain group does not allow presenting alternative narratives on an equal footing to the self-serving version. This style of teaching is clearly propagandistic: favouring a self-serving version of history at the expense of alternative views with the aims of influencing the students' future action.

In contrast, if involved in critical history teaching, the teacher will employ contents that contest national myths and deconstruct celebratory narratives. A critical and multiperspective approach to history motivates students to consider alternatives to their own views, which may have been or are currently dominant with an adversary or even inimical groups or countries. This approach proceeds by offering complementary historical interpretations, weighing their evidence and accepting them as possible alternatives to the students' 'indigenous' perspective. This involves critical self-reflection as well as learning to respect alternatives to one's own position. The goal of communication is raising an emancipatory and tolerant consciousness of others' life worlds, rights and values. Such communication style does not defend a specific historical interpretation, but offers several side by side. In some respects, this approach reminds of the term of 'diffusion'.[1]

'Propaganda' and 'dissemination' can be seen as two opposite ends of a continuum. We conceive 'propagation' as the intermediate space between the two poles (Fig. 2).

Spanning a range of possible teaching approaches, 'propagation' can be seen both as a milder form of propaganda and as a more standpoint-based (or 'biased') version of dissemination. It can appear as critical identity work such as when offering support to the student identity building together with critical reflection on narratives traditionally used by the students' in-group. However, it can also appear in a form much closer to propaganda, if an in-group-serving selection is made from academically adequate knowledge. This kind of 'propagation' would not be pure 'propaganda', as the chosen accounts themselves would not be knowingly distorted. But it would be closer to 'propaganda' than to

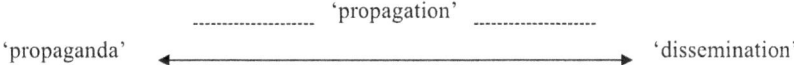

Fig. 2 'Propagation' as spanning a continuum between 'propaganda' and 'dissemination'

'dissemination', since alternative views and critical reflection on the selection criteria would not be made available. 'Propagation' can also appear as teaching close to the 'dissemination' end when no in-group-serving concessions are made, but the account is modified to show consideration for the students' assumed needs and feelings, for example, by leaving out some violent details. Not because the perpetrators were from the in-group—this would be a 'propagandistic' motivation—but because the teacher does not regard them age appropriate. That is to say, the unavoidable content selection can be more or less 'propagandistic'. Anyway, no account of the past can include 'everything', and pedagogy precludes 'pure dissemination' (cf. Fig. 1).

Crucially for the present context, the distinction between communication styles focuses on the teachers' intentions, motivations and the limits set by their action space. This is particularly relevant for the dissemination end of the scale, as it is clear that teachers can only 'disseminate' what they *perceive* as an appropriate scholarly representation, not some scholarly state of the art as such. Even if there may be teachers who knowingly teach 'pure propaganda', seeing themselves as state servants 'just doing the job', rather than serving 'enlightenment' (cf. Kello 2016), we assume that the two forms of communication, 'propaganda' and 'dissemination', rarely exist in present-day Europe.

History Classroom as Communicative Space

A history classroom can thus be imagined as a communicative space where the teacher can more or less consciously choose between communicative styles and teaching strategies. Viewing the classroom as such space highlights pedagogical restrictions *on* as well as *deriving from* teacher's communication style choices. At the same time, depending on the teacher's pedagogical preference, there are several ways how both ends of the scale, i.e. 'propaganda' and 'dissemination', can manifest themselves in terms of general approaches to history teaching (Fig. 3).

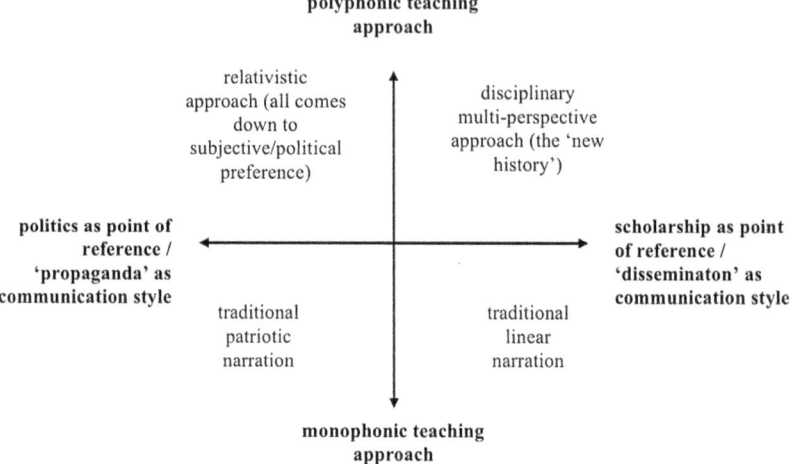

Fig. 3 Opposite styles of propaganda and dissemination cross-cut by two opposite approaches in history teaching

For example, a 'dissemination' approach can appear as a traditional, linear—but scholarship based—narrative as well as a critical and multi-perspective (polyphonic) way of history teaching. The polyphonic way, in turn, need not be necessarily scholarship based, i.e. a disciplinarily oriented multiperspectivity that includes weighing different accounts in the light of available evidence. It can also appear as a relativistic 'anything goes' approach according to which differences between accounts come down to little more than differences between subjective truths and the politics utilising them.

In the following, we first give a brief overview of the historical contexts from which our empirical examples come from. Then, we proceed to Estonian and Latvian history teachers positions viewed through the lens of the theoretical considerations just described.

Historical Contexts: Social Memory and Teaching of History in Estonia and Latvia

Estonia and Latvia are two post-Soviet countries that have experienced several ruptures and historical transitions over the course of the twentieth century. The main highlights have been their declaration of national independence in 1918, followed by respective Wars of Independence and an era of independent Estonian/Latvian Republics from 1920 to 1939; Soviet Occupation from 1939/1940 to 1941; German Occupation from 1941 to 1944/1945; and again Soviet era until re-establishment of the nation states in 1991. The latter era can be divided into Stalinist and post-Stalinist eras, separated by Stalin's death in 1953. The former period was marked by terror, arrests of intellectuals, civil servants, politicians, as well as mass deportations of civilians to Siberia in 1941 and 1949. The post-Stalinist era was marked by 'Khrushchev's thaw', 'Brezhnev's stagnation' and Gorbachev's glasnost and perestroika.

During the Soviet era, workforce immigration resulted in large Russian-speaking communities in Estonia and Latvia, often having a different perspective towards both past and present history and politics, as compared to the indigenous populations. Hence, it is not surprising that historical conflicts are perceived as providing the clearest social division lines in both countries, leading to them being utilised to legitimate both the more evident language based and the more implicit socio-economic (e.g. Kaprāns and Zelče 2011; Kus et al. 2013). In fact, a part of the Estonian and Latvian public suspect that the 'Russian schools' teach 'incorrect' or even hostile 'Russian' interpretations to their students. At the same time, previous research has found that history teachers of Russian-speaking students perceive their task as smoothing sharp edges and enhancing students' understanding of the existence of different conceptions and positions and the absence of one absolute truth (e.g. Lauristin et al. 2011).

These are important aspects of the local contexts of history teaching in both countries—teachers from different 'camps' perceive the public expectations clearly differently. On the one hand, more is 'allowed' for majority teachers as they are not suspected of lacking loyalty to the country in case they take a critical view towards a dominant national perspective (Kello 2016). On the other hand, teachers from a 'minority camp'—both in ethnic terms and those who personally disagree with a dominant narrative—perceive their 'state servant' role when being history teachers more emphatically (Kello and Wagner 2014). Those who disagree, either from ethnic majority or from ethnic minority, are more aware of their precarious position in between different conceptions, institutions and communities.

At the same time, several 'layers' of discourse (or more broadly: social representation) related to history teaching are present and alive in Estonia and Latvia, stemming from different eras and world views. Between the two World Wars, history teaching there followed general trends of European history teaching, meaning that a, for that time, 'normal' combination of general education (horizon broadening) and patriotic teaching aims was applied. During the Soviet era, history teachers were also expected to transmit a pre-defined set of values as before WWII, just that the survival and battles of 'working people' replaced those of Estonian/Latvian people, and national values were replaced by Soviet 'communist' values (e.g. Ahonen 1992; Symcox and Wilschut 2009). From a general education perspective, history teaching was expected to educate students and to enhance their analytical thinking, ability to see causal connections and other skills like summation and narration. However, propaganda in history teaching was not retouched during the Soviet era. In the early 1990s, just after re-establishment of the independent Estonian and Latvian Republics (1991), a patriotic perspective more or less dominated in the countries' history teaching (e.g. Kivimäe 1999). During the 1990s however, this trend was combined with increasing influences from the history teaching communities of Western Europe. Two organisations were of particular significance, the European Association of History Educators (*Euroclio*) and the Council of Europe, which both disseminated ideas about multiperspective and constructivist history teaching by learning and teaching materials, teacher training, national curricula and national final examinations (e.g. Oja 2004; Klišāns 2011). Besides promoting multiperspective and constructivist teaching approaches, such influences led to withdrawal of national identity- and patriotism-related aims of history teaching on which we will focus on in the following section.

Between 'Propaganda' and 'Dissemination'—Discursive Representations of History Teaching

The 'Public' Level: How Teachers Represent What Is Expected, Appropriate and Possible

As we noted, since the 1990s, identity has been mentioned only fleetingly in national curricula and more constructivist influences have been added, with regard to both student learning and historical knowledge. The most explicit identity-related goals in the history curriculum have since then been worded with reference to an undefined 'students own' community rather than any particular (e.g. Estonian ethnic national) one. For example, in Estonian history curriculum from 1996, the students' identities were referred to in a generic manner, compatible with diverse nationalities: 'the student [...] shall relate themselves to their home, native country, Europe, and the world' (Estonian Government 1996). In 2002, the curriculum was a bit more explicit by replacing 'native country' with 'Estonia'—the list of things the students were expected to relate was now 'place of origin, Estonia, Europe and the world'). Also, a sentence saying that 'the student [...] shall define themselves as a member of their nation[ality]' was added (Estonian Government 2002). Since 2002, also 'national and cultural identity' have been mentioned as important aims in the context of history teaching (Estonian Government 2002, 2011a, b, 2014a, b).

Such wordings create an 'illusion of consensus' (Simpson and Halse 2006)—they can be agreed with from both multicultural and ethnic–nationalist positions. On the one hand, the curriculum could be presented to the West as promoting tolerance and multiperspectivity. On the other hand, in the curricular support materials ethnic and nationalist positions were found more explicitly (e.g. in Õispuu 2002).[2]

In fact, as elsewhere, there is some division between social and professional representations regarding the aims and essence of history teaching. Among the broader public, a traditional identity, patriotism and/or factual knowledge-oriented representation of history teaching prevails (Kello and Harro-Loit 2014), whereas in professional and official *explicit discourse*, the traditional identity- and patriotism-related representation seems to be pushed back, while lingering no less powerfully under the surface (Kello and Wagner 2014). For reasons that we will explain shortly, this division seems to be more pronounced in Estonia than in Latvia.

When Estonian history teachers talked about their aims and intentions when teaching the subject, they usually enacted either a 'traditional enlightened' or a 'critical enlightened' representation (knowing, understanding and being able to analyse the past and present events, sometimes also developing a more generally critical mind). Interestingly, identity-related aims were mentioned only in few cases: the analysis of the spontaneously mentioned main aims in 26 Estonian interviews revealed that only two Russian-speaking teachers, working at the same school and involved in organising local history and identity-related out-of-school activities, mentioned enhancing their students' local or

Estonian identity among their main aims as history teachers (Kello 2010).[3] Considering the long history and global resilience of identity and patriotism building aims of history teaching, the rarity of such aims and intentions in spontaneous discourse was quite conspicuous. All the more so, as these same aims were implied in teachers' comments on the importance of teaching national history (Kello and Masso 2012) and teachers agreed with the importance of these aims when asked explicitly (Kello and Wagner 2014).

Looking closer, it seems that these aims are important for the teachers—just that they are not explicitly acknowledged in so-to-say explicit professional discourse about the subject's *aims*. The explicitly acknowledged objectives are rather cognitive ones such as knowledge and thinking skills, plus interest in history. Identity and patriotism seem to belong to a separate bundle. Therefore, as long as one talks about the academic or more cognitive bundle and is not reminded about 'identity bundle', they just don't come into mind. They simply do not fit so well into the interlinked range of 'enlightened' aims that most Estonian teachers offered spontaneously (Kello 2010, 2014; Kello and Wagner 2014). Not just in Estonia but also elsewhere the enlightened and disciplinary discourses are stronger among history educators. Schüllerqvist (2015) points out how it is even inappropriate to talk about other than 'critical enlightened' aims of history teaching in certain circles: there seem to be separate conferences for those history educators interested in political- or citizenship-related aims of the school subject, and conferences attended by 'disciplinarists' who don't acknowledge them. In a similar line, the interviewer's influence can be assumed: a representative of the academy may have encouraged more 'enlightened', rather than 'patriotic' representations, particularly at the beginning of the interview.

Secondly, outright indoctrination (which is connected to the notions of identities and patriotism) might have been perceived as a taboo, particularly against the backdrop of Soviet history teaching, which was perceived as overly ideological.

Thirdly, at least in Estonia, identity and patriotism are sensitive and possibly awkward topics not only among history educators, but more broadly as well. Positions related to (ethnic, national) identity are politically and socially laden, and there seems to be no really safe way to express relevant positions.

Notwithstanding, identity-related aspects of history teaching may be taken for granted as implicit aims, as part of teaching the local past naturally, without explicit effort and without addressing any particular group. In fact, this is the way identity-related aims are addressed in Estonian national curriculum: 'In the process of solving historical problems [...] [the students'] national and cultural identity, tolerance and positive attitude to the values of democracy develop' (Estonian Government 2002, similarly 1996, 2011, 2014). As can be seen, the curriculum mentions these things rather in passing, cautiously, so there is a lot of space for individual interpretations by the teachers—more space than in the case of the more cognitively oriented aims.

This explanation is also supported by the teachers' comments on the statement *The current teaching of history is too 'self-centred'—concentrating on the Estonian and European past produces young people with narrow worldviews.* Although some of the teachers admitted that current history teaching in Estonia was too self-centred (ethno- or Euro-centric), most of them did not oppose the focus, either supporting Estonia- and Europe-centred history teaching with pedagogical or ideological arguments (thus negating excessive self-centredness), or considering such a state inevitable. The 'self-centredness' was justified by the necessarily limited teaching time and, thus, the inevitability of choosing some kind of a focus in history teaching, as well as with reference to the pedagogical principle that teaching should commence with what was closest to the student. Connected to this was the argument that history teaching is first and foremost about understanding oneself and learning about oneself and that in support of this goal Estonian and European history is the most important (see more in Kello and Masso 2012).

> On what else should we concentrate? [...] if you don't know about your own country's history, then what sense does it make to talk about anything else. (Jaanika)

It is also interesting that those few teachers who agreed that there was too much teaching of Estonian history were never ethnic Estonians. In addition, the fact that minority teachers happened to be those who felt that Russia or other neighbouring countries were neglected in the curriculum shows how much the teachers own sociocultural and ethnic position influences how s/he perceives the curriculum (Kello and Masso 2012).

In Latvia, former history curricula seem to have followed similar trends as in Estonia. For example, the curricula for 'Latvian and world history' from 2006 state rather cautiously that history teaching should enhance students' understanding of 'family, place of origin, [and] Latvia as significant values in their own and other people's lives' and 'the development of a European identity, and support the growth of a responsible and tolerant member of the democratic society of European Union' (Latvian Government 2006). However, since in Latvia school history teaching has long been the object of 'high politics' (e.g. Klišāns 2011) and 'Latvian history' has been mandated in a top-down way by the government and parliament as a separate subject (Latvian Government 2010, 2011), direct political influences are visible in the curricula. Referring to an alleged lack of factual knowledge among young people, nationalist politicians have supported mandating Latvian history as a separate subject, apart from European and world history. Thus, since 2010 Latvian lower secondary curriculum for 'Latvian history' mandates that among other things Latvian history teaching should enhance students 'sense of belonging to the Latvian state and patriotism' (Latvian Government 2010, 2011, 2014).[4] In Estonian curriculum, the term 'patriotism' is present since 2011, but still only in the general section of social subjects curricula, not history as such, and as part of a longer list of 'universal values': 'freedom, human dignity, equality, honesty, caring, tolerance, responsibility, justice, patriotism and respect for themselves, others and the environment' (Estonian Government 2011a, b, similarly 2014a, b).

There are also other contextual differences that explain why in 2010, Latvian history teachers referred to their patriotic tasks more often and more explicitly than their Estonian peers. Above all, the different political situation is one reason why Latvian ethnic majority teachers perceived the political expectations more vividly than their Estonian majority colleagues: Latvia's political landscape is more fragmented and ethnically charged as compared to Estonia (Nakai 2014). This automatically gives somewhat more importance to history interpretations as issues of party politics in Latvia (e.g. Cheskin 2013). In addition, the economic crisis of 2008 hit Latvia harder, and the following workforce emigration wave was more visible in Latvia as compared to Estonia. This caused more attention to the country's future and might have turned the teachers' attention more to their task in convincing students to connect their future visions with their home country as an aspect of 'patriotism'.[5] Thus, whereas ethnic minority teachers' context perception is always more vivid as they perceive their 'state servant' role more clearly, a similar difference due to different political contexts seems to hold when Latvian and Estonian majority teachers are compared.

While the following statement by Rahel might be representative of majority Estonian history teachers' position, Lija represents a general feeling that is left from the Latvian interviews.

> [...] in my opinion, nobody demands anything of the history teacher. [...] Does the society or the parent or the headmaster demand anything? Well, who? [...] Rather, it's myself [...] I demand of myself as of a teacher. [...] No-one controls what they [the students – KK] get from me. [...] It's myself who demands and in better cases they also are able to demand, saying I want to know, well, I want to orientate myself [in the facts – KK] a bit. In fact, it's between me and them. Who controls it? Isn't it true? (Rahel)

> I don't feel that one would demand of me as a teacher of history, yes, somehow at the present moment to teach a *wrong* history or somehow present the facts in a way that conforms to the state's ideology. That's not so. But of course, one can feel something, something a bit. [...] the first couple of years that I worked as history teacher, Latvia was a EU, NATO candidate, unequivocally we very much stressed exactly these questions, attempting to form a positive opinion of EU as well as NATO. So yes, there is something the teacher stresses [...]. But that's more depending on the initiative of the teacher. I wouldn't say that we are influenced ideologically *very* much. (Lija)

Such a difference doesn't mean that there is necessarily much less 'ideological bias' in the social and political contexts in Estonia as compared to Latvia. Rather it shows that such a bias might be less explicitly visible in everyday public discussions for reasons mentioned above.

It can thus be hypothesised that there is a difference between what kinds of representations allow themselves readily to be formulated in lay versus professional discourses in different political contexts and in different situations. In some situations, history teachers are more often and more explicitly reminded of their patriotic tasks than in other situations. In Estonia, as compared to the general public, a 'patriotic' representation of history teaching seems to be somewhat less readily available in the professional and official discourse where the central aims are defined in a 'critical enlightened'—i.e. 'dissemination'—vein, compatible with the orientation towards academic historiography of many history teachers. In Latvia where the situation has been similar in many regards—the historical background of the country, the development of history curricula since the early twentieth century, the academic history-based education of most history teachers—some recent contextual differences seem to have made identity-related aims spontaneously more available in spontaneous professional discourse, too.

The 'Individual' Level: How Intended 'Dissemination' May Turn into 'Propaganda'

Consistently with the dominant professional and curricular rhetoric, most interviewees *agreed* with the idea that it is import to introduce multiple interpretations to students, rather than 'one truth'. In practice, however, they admitted that the core of their teaching was imparting some central grid of knowledge. Even teachers who valued discussions and interpretations could be afraid of them as challenging their lessons plans. Thus, many interviewees expressed the view that lower secondary school was rather the place where students should acquire some basic factual knowledge. Later this minimal repertoire—as far as the students remembered it—could be used for a more analytical approach. The following was a rather typical comment with which even most discussion- and interpretation-oriented teachers seemed to agree:

> [...] an average student does indeed learn just generally acknowledged positions and evaluations. Those that are in the textbook – and that's that. [...] I would wish more, yes. But I have to work from the person's abilities. (Anne)

A polyphonic and critical history teaching was represented as depending on the teacher's ability to include those *in addition* to imparting the core facts and on the pressures of curricular time combined with the students' abilities.

Some interviewees expressed a frustration with the various stereotypes their students had adopted from the growing diversity of accessible sources—in these cases, students were represented as neither able to argue their views, nor able to recognise the lacunae in their arguments. However, developing students' thinking and argumentation in order to counter these flaws was not represented as always realistic considering the above-mentioned limitations.

In fact, several teachers were afraid that their students could learn 'wrong' lessons from a too 'polyphonic' teaching:

[…] the more able ones who have their own opinions about history, they take facts […] to support their *own* view, and leave everything else aside. (Jaanika)

This did not always cause the teachers to drop their attempts of a critical and nuanced teaching. But still a multiperspective teaching was restrained by an image—or reality—of students who were not seen as able to deal with it. However, the alternative to such teaching style was not necessarily a neutral, academically dry narration. As we will see from the following example, a 'disseminative' ideal could easily turn into a 'propagandistic' practice.

According to a teacher whom we call Meeri, the teacher balances between all what she knows and her student's reception ability. For example, as a historian the teacher may be aware of different interpretations and facts connected to an event or a person, but shouldn't reveal them to the students, if they could understand it 'the wrong way'. Also, the students shouldn't be overtaxed with information. This is of course a generic pedagogical task—maths and biology teachers face the same problem. But in the case of history teaching the 'patriotic aspect' is added.

Referring to a communicative counter-memory that was kept alive during the Soviet era among ethnic Estonians in spite of Soviet history distortions, but which included distortions and idealisations of the pre-WWII era of its own, she noted that

> […] during the Soviet era, people viewed Konstantin Päts, Laidoner, other statesmen [from the pre-WWII Estonian Republic – KK] as something holy and untouchable […] But if we look at later research [since 1990s – KK], if we read studies […] [they don't seem so infallible any more – KK]. Of course, I don't tell all of it to the students. There needs to be some small reservation or limit. But for myself… [she doesn't think of history as something dogmatic – KK]. (Meeri)

Meeri's statement can be interpreted as referring to a necessity to avoid that students understand something 'in the wrong way' politically. She herself had come from the Soviet-era counter-memory tradition which had shaped her values and world view. So perhaps she regarded those Soviet-time idealistic representations as difficult to unchain from a love for the country and patriotic feelings which she also wanted to pass on to her students. She may have felt that she should spare her students of the disappointment she herself had experienced when learning of newer studies about the statesmen. Or perhaps she was simply afraid that de-idealising pre-war-era statesmen would enhance a common disaffection with politics and politicians among her students, which would be detrimental from a citizenship education perspective.

Indeed, Meeri added that she was not in the position 'to present the information in another light, because the critical mind of the students hasn't developed sufficiently yet'. However, at the same time among her main aims as history teacher she also had the aim to teach students to approach things critically, not taking everything at face value. In fact, she noticed a contradiction between her critical thinking aims and the position reflected in the quotation above, and looked for a way to reconcile the positions in the interview.

Her solution was to represent history teacher as balancing between what we could call 'truth' and 'pragmatism'. On the one hand, she said, students should get the opportunity to decide on their own positions. But on the other hand it is a question of the teacher's gut feeling where to draw the line.

Meeri said she would sometimes bring examples of different perspectives towards an event, but she would also say, which version should be memorised. Thus, Meeri's position wasn't a univocally 'propagandistic' one in Moscovici's terms. But according to her representation of her teaching she often did resort to such practice and had no real problem with this fact.

Why, however, did a patriotic approach seem like such an evident alternative to a more critical one even to an academically informed teacher? One explanation was offered already above—'propagandistic' values and practices may lurk under 'enlightened' ideals and discourses. Another explanation resides in an uneasy answer to the essential question: what is the scholarly accepted knowledge that should be 'diffused' in the first place?

The Essential Question—What to Disseminate

According to a teacher we call Andrus, it was important that the students develop an appreciation of academic research as the most trustworthy source of historical knowledge—as opposed to, for example, journalistic or political sources. For him, teaching trust in professional historians and their objectivity was related to teaching 'relativity of relativism'.

> I value the historian's profession very much [...] I'm very disdainful of politicization. [...] That's constant work: first to shake them so-to-say, so that they would take the blinders off their eyes and take on a critical attitude. And then at some point they need to be shaken to realise that, come on, there are limits to criticism somewhere; there are some things one doesn't need to argue about. Somewhere trust enters the play also. *Question:* Trust for historians? *Answer:* Yes. And trust for methods as well as for people. And for professionalism. (Andrus)

However, in the real world, historians' work is of varied quality, particularly when it comes to history textbooks (in case authored by academic historians in the first place). In concise overviews like the school textbook format demands, even academic historians easily slip out of their professional distanced observer roles, writing more like representatives of their social memory community. This is especially evident in the case of issues that don't belong to their professional research topics, and that are important, acute, sensitive from the perspective of their social memory community. So it's not the case that a history teacher can trust a historians' representation without hesitation.

> [...] they say: 'What to believe?' I say: 'Believe documentary sources: photos, films, numbers of losses, etc.' But already, let's say, a journalist – there's also a fact, but there's also a journalistic opinion. The same often applies for a historian – there's a fact, but there's also her/his opinion. (Eliana)

In the interviews, some of the teachers focused on historians' position-boundedness, painting a rather individualistic picture of textbook production:

> These are two out of 6 billion people who have announced their point of view there. [...] Yes, they have worked on this issue for a long time, but they are common people. (Viktoria)

Presenting historians as normal people with their own subjective predispositions was useful in order to distinguish between an 'official' stance versus historians' personal views as represented in the textbook, as well as to 'reconcile' Russian students with the 'ethnic Estonian' position reflected in the texts. However, aside of the fact that textbook authors often do represent some broader groups (or, indeed, the 'powerful') and that textbooks are co-production of the authors named on the cover *and* various structures from the curriculum to the concrete publisher's practices, one could ask whether such view does not bear the danger of encouraging students' relativism towards historical knowledge, reducing historical knowledge to a matter of individual opinion. With no clear division line between academic knowledge (production), on the one hand, and individual, social or political representations, on the other, it was more difficult to answer students' questions about whom or what to trust:

> Yes they do say 'you are lying, how do you know'. And well, if I lie, then let it be so. […] we have different positions about different events and now it's your task […] to form your own opinion about it. What do *you* believe? […] I say for example that I think this way, but this is my opinion and it doesn't have to be your opinion and it isn't the opinion of many other historians. (Jaanika)

In fact, teachers who were more tolerant of openness maintained that they attempted to leave as much open to the students as possible—discussion itself and the ability to listen to different opinions is what is important. It may be useful if a student learns textbook facts, but s/he does not need to be dissuaded, and the 'truth'—the decision to which perspective to stick—can be left open (Kello 2016).

Of course, teachers need more help in offering difficult epistemological explanations in simple, age and ability appropriate ways. Another relevant point here is that there are different 'payers' of the 'pipers' who compete in 'calling the tune' in the field of history teaching. In case the curriculum provides no clear answer—which it often does not in a democratic society—whom the teacher perceives as the main 'payer' becomes decisive. Whose expectations—academy? society? parent? politics?—are perceived as posing the most legitimate demands to the general education school history teaching? Recent issues like the ones mentioned in an above quotation by the Latvian teacher Lija (accession to EU and NATO), in particular, are treated in academically deep and neutral ways neither in schoolbooks, academic history nor in even scientific publications broadly available to teachers. Rather, these are current and politicised topics mentioned only fleetingly on last pages of history textbooks. Teachers are quite alone when deciding on what would be the neutral information to 'disseminate'—even if they really want to 'disseminate' rather than 'propagate'.

A teacher's ideal could be that there was some 'concrete stance'—or helpful guidance to the teacher—which would be an academically sound one and not a political prescription. This, as elucidated by Wilschut (2010) whom we quoted in the beginning of this chapter, is, however, difficult to achieve. So in case of inherently biased and politicised issues there is perhaps indeed no better solution than leaving them to the 'lonely' teacher to decide (groping alone in the darkness, as one teacher put it), rather than risking that biased prescriptions would be produced as a result of some public negotiations (for example, see the volume by Nakou and Barca 2010).

Conclusion: Dilemmata of 'Enlightened' Teaching

We started this chapter with the observation that societies that experienced a recent transition from a Soviet style to a Western democratic style government provide a fruitful ground for observing the dilemmata of history teaching. Every new country and its government needs to justify and emphasise its newly found political orientation and foundational myth (Liu and Hilton 2005; Wagner et al., forthcoming) as well as observe the tolerant 'enlightened' perspective that accepts that other regions in the world have a right to their own evaluation of historical events, persons and notions in inter-generational transmission of identity and loyalty. This is particularly dilemmatic if, as in the Baltic states, there exists a considerable minority of Russian pre-transition immigrants who have their own historical values and perspectives. This institutional frame, together with the teachers' interests, motivations and memories, makes navigating the 'sea of history' in teaching fraught with risky cliffs.

Under any preconditions, a really neutral dissemination of a relevant variety of facts and perspectives can only be achieved for a limited number of issues. Even if being modest and attempting to present some more relevant and well-known perspectives to the students, the twin problems of 'location' and 'sufficiency' remain: finding a tentative balance and 'location of openness' between the positions presented. Each student's perception of what is taught is idiosyncratic to a certain extent. A point at which a class has dealt 'sufficiently' with a topic, that is at which point there has been 'sufficient polyphony' or 'sufficient investigation', cannot be determined once and for all. What has been exhaustive processing for one student may well leave another feeling confronted with different perspectives, without having an appropriate 'apparatus' with which to handle the difficult issues (cf. Lee 2010, p. xii). Thus, the choice between making a structure of facts clear to *most* students, and discussing interpretations with some brighter ones, can be felt as a dilemma by the teacher. Both, in cases of sensitive and less 'hot' topics it rather seems to be a matter of either the teacher's gut feeling or of some societal/collective consensus at that particular point in time.

The teachers often seem to regard 'different perspectives' as different *evaluations* of the same facts, rather than as the more substantive *meaning* of the facts, i.e. the different contextualisations of, and relations among, the facts. In the interviews, only a few teachers represented the choice of facts to be studied as possibly problematic. Disregarding the perspective dependence of the selection process, however, may render invisible the inherent bias in some entrenched interpretations and master narratives. There may be a similar problem with the position that we can escape today's evaluations and interests in dealing with the past.

To be sure, we don't advocate for 'pure dissemination' in history lessons. Besides the state's interest in emphasising its own political perspective, also teachers showing and not hiding a moral stance seems inevitable in many cases, for example even the very obvious pursuit of enhancing ethnic tolerance in students and supporting understanding of some certain other perspective (as opposed to a more 'technical' and distanced dealing with different perspectives). What we would like to warn against is that such a stance could turn into teaching pre-defined 'lessons from past', i.e. propagating a certain narrow, perhaps even a propagandistically pre-defined set of 'lessons'.

As studies by McCully, Barton, Reilly and their colleagues have shown, for the reason that Northern Irish history teachers often attempt to refrain from contentious contemporary issues Northern Irish students do not always relate what they have learnt at school to their personal identity-based positions. Students from both communities are aware of the *existence* of an academic, neutral and balanced approach to the past that is different from their own (e.g. Barton 2012; Reilly and McCully 2011). However, school history teaching neither challenges their existing in-group narratives nor provides an alternative to the divided identifications: 'schools are so concerned not to challenge diverse identifications that they fail to provide—or even to enable—the kind of shared identity that might contribute to overcoming the region's conflict' (Barton 2012, p. 99). One could push even further, asking whether there is not some need for patriotic narratives in the students, be it a nation or a religion or something third towards which this patriotism is directed. So even if on academic grounds we would leave out a number of still too 'hot' issues, wouldn't they find these narratives elsewhere—then, however probably in a much less analytical and critical context that even the most traditional school history teaching.

This chapter presents an integrated view on an educational issue—history teaching—in the theoretical context of a social psychological theory. It takes an empirical—not normative—position towards history teaching as practice. The Theory of Social Representations is particularly useful when applied to real-life societal contexts where individual behaviours become a collective pattern as is the case with communication styles in teaching.

In the field of social representation research, there have been several proposals to re-apply Moscovici's model to communicative situations other than mass media—for example, as characteristic to different group and affiliation types (Duveen 2008b), or as various ways of dealing with knowledge and conflict (Psaltis 2005). The main difference compared to our approach is that in the other proposals—as indeed in Moscovici (2008)—'propagation' is seen as a style in its own right rather than as a continuum between the two poles of 'dissemination' and 'propaganda'. For the present purpose, we do not go into a more thorough discussion of this issue. On the other hand, the pedagogic practice is so much constrained by various commitments and convictions on different levels that it is indeed characterised by at least one crucial feature of propagation as defined by Moscovici, namely by a constant consideration of what would be the appropriate account for a particular audience. True, in a democracy, in history teaching that follows a disciplinary ideal this is usually not done based on a pre-defined set of beliefs as in the case of the catholic press studied by Moscovici: pedagogic convictions vary from educator to educator. But constraints deriving from societal values, moral convictions and beliefs about the student needs will always shape the content selection and teaching style. A teacher is in our view crucially interested in what message is received, in terms of avoiding confusion as well as of the world view. The model of communication styles used in the present chapter helps to grasp the fluctuation of teaching between communication styles, interrelations between teaching ideals and practice, and teacher dilemmata between various expectations, aims and ideals.

Notes

1. When analysing diffusion as media communication style, Moscovici (2008) mentions characteristics—such as the need to entertain an inherently indeterminable, heterogeneous audience—that do not translate into history teaching in the present context. We do not delve into these details here. What applies here is one crucial aspect of Moscovici's concept of diffusion, namely the communicator's disinterest in what kind of 'aggregate representation' of an object is received by the audience.
2. Of course, the implicit importance of patriotism can also be seen from thematic choices such as the relative importance of own country's history, as compared to other regions, which is the case with most history curricula in the world.
3. Here and henceforth, we refer to the first author's interviews with 39 Estonian and 14 Latvian history teachers between 2007 and 2011 (see sample and method description in Kello 2014 or Kello 2016). Other analyses of the same data have been published in Kello 2010, Kello and Harro-Loit 2012, Kello and Masso 2012, Kello and Wagner 2014 and Kello 2016. We use the same pseudonyms as in previous publications to refer to the interviewees.
4. In contrast, Latvian upper secondary history curriculum which wasn't in focus of the political debates is written in a very disciplinary style, and includes only one identity related aim "to promote a multifaceted development of the student as a member of democratic and civic society via studying Latvian, European and world history processes" besides various disciplinary aims (Latvian Government 2013).
5. Yet another explanation is the timing of the interviews. Several of the Latvian interviews were conducted during or soon after a week in November which included celebrations of several important anniversaries relating to the founding of the Latvian state: *Lāčplēsis* Day on November 11th, commemorating the defeat of the West Russian Volunteer Army in the Latvian War of Independence in 1919, and Latvian Independence Day (1918) on November 18th. Several interviewees discussed their position on, or role as history teachers in, the celebrations.

References

Ahonen, S. (1992). *Clio Sans uniform. A study of the post-Marxist transformation of the history curricula in East Germany and Estonia, 1986–1991*. Helsinki: Suomalainen Tieteakatemia.

Barton, K. (2012). School history as a resource for constructing identities: Implications of research from the United States, Northern Ireland, and New Zealand. In M. Carretero, M. Asensio, & M. Rodríguez-Moneo (Eds.),

History education and the construction of national identities (pp. 93–107). Charlotte, NC: Information Age Publishing.

Carretero, M., & Bermudez, A. (2012). Constructing histories. In J. Valsiner (Ed.), *The Oxford handbook of culture and psychology* (pp. 625–646). Oxford: Oxford University Press.

Cheskin, A. (2013). Exploring Russian-speaking identity from below: The case of Latvia. *Journal of Baltic Studies, 44,* 287–312.

Duveen, G. (2008a). Introduction. In *Serge Moscovici: Psychoanalysis—Its image and its public* (pp. xi–xvii). Cambridge, UK: Polity Press.

Duveen, G. (2008b). Social actors and social groups: A return to heterogeneity in social psychology. *Journal for the Theory of Social Behaviour, 38,* 370–374.

Estonian Government. (1996). Ajalugu. Lisa 13 Eesti põhi- ja keskhariduse riikliku õppekava juurde [History. Appendix 13 to Estonian national curriculum for basic and upper secondary education, Estonian]. *Riigi Teataja* 65–69, September 27, 2087–2094.

Estonian Government. (2002). Vabariigi Valitsuse 25. jaanuari 2002. a määruse nr 56 "Põhikooli ja gümnaasiumi riiklik õppekava" lisa 15: Ajalugu [Appendix 15 (History) to Regulation no 56, January 25, 2002 "National curriculum for basic and upper secondary schools", Estonian]. Retrieved February 26, 2016, from https://www.riigiteataja.ee/akt/162998.

Estonian Government. (2011a). Vabariigi Valitsuse 6. jaanuari 2011. a määrus nr 1 (avaldatud 14.01.2011) "Põhikooli riiklik õppekava" Lisa 5: Ainevaldkond "Sotsiaalained" [Appendix 5 (Social subjects) to Regulation no 1, January 6, 2011 (published January 14, 2011) "National curriculum for basic schools", Estonian]. Retrieved February 26, 2016, from https://www.riigiteataja.ee/akt/114012011001.

Estonian Government. (2011b). Vabariigi Valitsuse 6. jaanuari 2011. a määrus nr 2 (avaldatud 14.01.2011) "Gümnaasiumi riiklik õppekava" Lisa 5: Ainevaldkond "Sotsiaalained" [Appendix 5 (Social Subjects) to Regulation no 2, January 6, 2011 (published January 14, 2011) "National curriculum for upper secondary schools", Estonian]. Retrieved February 26, 2016, from https://www.riigiteataja.ee/akt/114012011002.

Estonian Government. (2014a). Vabariigi Valitsuse 6. jaanuari 2011. a määrus nr 1 "Põhikooli riiklik õppekava" Lisa 5 (muudetud sõnastuses, avaldatud 29.08.2014): Ainevaldkond "Sotsiaalained" [Appendix 5 (Social subjects) to Regulation no 1, January 6, 2011 (published January 14, 2011) "National Curriculum for Basic Schools" (revised wordings, published August 29, 2014), Estonian]. Retrieved February 26, 2016, from https://www.riigiteataja.ee/akt/129082014020?leiaKehtiv.

Estonian Government. (2014b). Vabariigi Valitsuse 6. jaanuari 2011. a määrus nr 2 Gümnaasiumi riiklik õppekava" Lisa 5 (muudetud sõnastuses, avaldatud 29.08.2014): Ainevaldkond "Sotsiaalained" [Appendix 5 (Social

Subjects) to Regulation no 2, January 6, 2011 "National Curriculum for Upper Secondary Schools" (revised wordings, published August 29, 2014), Estonian]. Retrieved February 26, 2016, from https://www.riigiteataja.ee/akt/129082014021?leiaKehtiv.

Jovchelovitch, S. (2007). *Knowledge in context: Representations, community and culture.* London: Routledge.

Kaprāns, M., & Zelče, V. (2011). National identity, history and social memory. In B. Zepa & E. Kļave (Eds.), *Latvia. Human development report 2010/2011. National identity, mobility and capability.* (pp. 39–51). Riga: Advanced Social and Political Research Institute of the University of Latvia.

Kello, K. (2010). Milleks koolis ajalootunnid? Aine eesmärgid õpetaja taotluste peeglis [Why teach history at school? The aims of history teaching as reflected in teachers' intentions, Estonian]. *Haridus [Education: Journal for Estonian Educational Publications]* 4, 31–38.

Kello, K. (2014). *The functions and contexts of general education history teaching: Social and professional representations in Estonia and Latvia.* Tartu: University of Tartu Press.

Kello, K. (2016). Sensitive and controversial issues in the classroom: Teaching history in a divided society. *Teachers and Teaching: Theory and Practice, 22,* 35–53.

Kello, K., & Harro-Loit, H. (2012). Recognising dilemmas in history teaching—a tool for increasing teacher's autonomy. In J. Mikk, M. Veisson, P. Luik & Frankfurt am Main et al. (Eds.), *Lifelong learning and teacher development. Estonian studies in education 4* (pp. 113–129). Bern: Peter Lang Verlag.

Kello, K., & Harro-Loit, H. (2014). How should the past be treated in Estonian schools? Constructions of history teaching in an Estonian teachers' newspaper. *Journal of Baltic Studies, 45,* 397–421.

Kello, K., & Masso, A. (2012). The spatial foci of history teaching. Individual views of Estonian history teachers. *Spaces and Flows: An International Journal of Urban & ExtraUrban Studies, 2*(4), 31–48.

Kello, K., & Wagner, W. (2014). Intrinsic and extrinsic patriotism in school: Teaching history after Estonia's critical juncture. *International Journal of Intercultural Relations, 43*(part A), 48–59.

Kivimäe, J. (1999). Re–writing Estonian history? In M. Branch (Ed.), *National history and identity. approaches to the writing of national history in the North–East Baltic region nineteenth and twentieth centuries.* Helsinki: Finnish Literature Society.

Klišāns, V. (2011). National and European history in Latvia's schools. In E. Erdmann & W. Hasberg (Eds.), *Facing-mapping-bridging diversity: Foundation of a European discourse on history education* (pp. 109–114). Schwalbach/Ts.: Wochenschau Verlag.

Kus, L., Liu, J., & Ward, C. (2013). Relative deprivation versus system justification: Polemical social representations and identity positioning in a post-Soviet society. *European Journal of Social Psychology, 43*, 423–437.
Latvian Government. (2006). Ministru kabineta noteikumi Nr. 1027: Noteikumi par valsts standartu pamatizglītībā un pamatizglītības mācību priekšmetu standartiem [Regulation no 1027: Regulation on the National Standard of Basic Education and Standards of Basic Education Subjects, Latvian]. *Latvijas Vēstnesis, 204* (3572), Dec 22, 2006.
Latvian Government. (2010). Ministru kabineta noteikumi Nr. 968: Grozījumi Ministru kabineta 2006. gada 19. decembra noteikumos Nr.1027 'Noteikumi par valsts standartu pamatizglītībā un pamatizglītības mācību priekšmetu standartiem'[Regulation no 968: Revisions to the Regulation no 1027, Dec 19, 2006, on the National Standard of Basic Education and Standards of Basic Education Subjects, Latvian]. *Latvijas Vēstnesis, 167* (4359), Oct 21, 2010.
Latvian Government. (2011). Ministru kabineta noteikumi Nr. 325: Grozījumi Ministru kabineta 2006. gada 19. decembra noteikumos Nr.1027 'Noteikumi par valsts standartu pamatizglītībā un pamatizglītības mācību priekšmetu standartiem'[Regulation no 325: Revisions to the Regulation no 1027, Dec 19, 2006, on the National Standard of Basic Education and Standards of Basic Education Subjects, Latvian]. *Latvijas Vēstnesis, 69* (4467), May 5, 2011.
Latvian Government. (2013). Ministru kabineta noteikumi Nr. 281: Noteikumi par valsts vispārējās vidējās izglītības standartu, mācību priekšmetu standartiem un izglītības programmu paraugiem [Regulation no 281: Regulation on the National Standard of General Upper Secondary Education, Subject Standards and Example Programmes, Latvian]. *Latvijas Vēstnesis, 107* (4913), June 5, 2013. Retrieved February 26, 2016, from http://likumi.lv/doc.php?id=257229.
Latvian Government. (2014). Ministru kabineta noteikumi Nr. 468: Noteikumi par valsts pamatizglītības standartu, pamatizglītības mācību priekšmetu standartiem un pamatizglītības programmu paraugiem [Regulation no 468: Regulation on the National Standard of Basic Education, Basic Education Subject Standards and Example Programmes, Latvian]. *Latvijas Vēstnesis 165* (5225), August 22, 2014. Retrieved February 26, 2016, from http://likumi.lv/doc.php?id=268342.
Lauristin, M., et al. (2011). *Integratsiooni monitooring 2011 [Integration monitoring, Estonian]*. Tartu: AS Emor, SA Poliitikauuringute Keskus Praxis, Tartu Ülikool.
Lee, P. (2010) Series introduction: International review of history education, vol. 6. In I. Nakou & I. Barca (Eds.), *Contemporary public debates over history education* (pp. xi–xvi). Charlotte, NC: Information Age Publishing.

Liu, J. H., & Hilton, D. J. (2005). How the past weighs on the present: Social representations of history and their role in identity politics. *British Journal of Social Psychology*, 44, 537–556.

Moscovici, S. (2008). *Psychoanalysis—Its image and its public*. Cambridge, UK: Polity Press.

Nakai, R. (2014). The influence of party competition on minority politics: A comparison of Latvia and Estonia. *Journal on Ethnopolitics and Minority Issues in Europe*, 13, 57–85.

Nakou, I., & Barca, I. (Eds.). (2010). *Contemporary public debates over history education*. Charlotte, NC: Information Age Publishing.

Õispuu, S. (2002). Metoodilisi soovitusi ainekäsitluseks ajaloodidaktika juhtküsimuste kontekstis [Methodical recommendations for subject teaching in the context of history didactical key issues, Estonian]. In E. Sepp & H. Peet (Eds.), *Abiks õpetajale: ajaloo õpetamisest [Teacher's handbook: On teaching history]* (pp. 23–47). Tallinn: Riiklik Eksami- ja Kvalifikatsioonikeskus.

Oja, M. (2004). The graduation examination in the context of major changes in teaching history in Estonia during the last decade. In M. Roberts (Ed.), *After the wall. History teaching in Europe since 1989* (pp. 201–211). Hamburg: Körber Stiftung.

Psaltis, C. (2005). Communication and the construction of knowledge or transmission of belief: The role of conversation type, behavioral style and social recognition. *Studies in Communication Sciences*, 5(2), 209–228.

Psaltis, C. (2016). Collective memory, social representations of intercommunal relations, and conflict transformation in divided Cyprus. *Peace and Conflict: Journal of Peace Psychology*, 22(1), 19–27.

Reilly, J., & McCully, A. W. (2011). *Abstract: Critical thinking and history teaching in a contested society: The potential influence of social cognitions*. American Educational Research Association Annual Meeting, New Orleans. American Educational Research Association. Conference contribution. http://eprints.ulster.ac.uk/18137/.

Sakki, I. (2010). *A success story or a failure? Representing the European integration in the curricula and textbooks of five countries*. Helsinki: University of Helsinki.

Schüllerqvist, B. (2015). *History education without nation?—Problematic positions in the international debate on the status and future of history in school*. Paper presented at NOFA 5 Conference at University of Helsinki, May 27–29, 2015.

Simpson, I., & Halse, C. (2006). Illusions of consensus: New South Wales stakeholders' constructions of the identity of history. *Curriculum Journal*, 17, 351–366.

Symcox, L., & Wilschut, A. (2009). Introduction. In L. Symcox & A. Wilschut (Eds.), *National history standards: The problem of the canon and the future of teaching history* (pp. 1–11). Charlotte, NC: Information Age Publishing.

Wagner, W. (2015). Representation in action. In G. Sammut, E. Andreouli, G. Gaskell, & J. Valsiner (Eds.), *The Cambridge handbook of social representations* (pp. 12–28). Cambridge, UK: Cambridge University Press.

Wagner, W., & Hayes, N. (2005). *Everyday discourse and common sense—The theory of social representations*. Basingstoke: Palgrave-Macmillan.

Wagner, W., Kello, K., & Rämmer, A. (forthcoming). Making social objects: Social representation theory. In A. Rosa & J. Valsiner (Eds.), *The Cambridge handbook of sociocultural psychology* (2nd ed.). Cambridge, UK: Cambridge University Press.

Wilschut, A. H. J. (2010). History teaching at the mercy of politicians and ideologies: Germany, England, and the Netherlands in the 19th and 20th centuries. *Journal of Curriculum Studies, 42*, 693–723.

Authors' Biography

Katrin Kello is a Researcher at University of Tartu, Institute of Social Studies. She has an M.A. in History and a Ph.D. in Media and Communications. She is interested in perceptions of educational policies among teachers and students, teachers' professional identities, social memory, history politics, history teaching and social representation theory. Her Ph.D. thesis was on teacher positions and understandings of history teaching, together with its social and political contexts, in Estonia and Latvia. Currently, she studies representation processes in school history textbooks. She has published in *Journal of Baltic Studies, International Journal of Intercultural Relations* and *Teachers and Teaching: Theory and Practice*.

Wolfgang Wagner is a Professor emer. of Social and Economic Psychology at Johannes Kepler University, Linz, Austria. He is interested in theoretical and empirical work on societal psychology, social and cultural knowledge, popularization of science, intergroup relationships and social representation theory. He authored and edited several books. "Everyday Discourse and Common Sense" (Palgrave), authored together with Nicky Hayes, has become a standard on the Theory of Social Representations. He is a co-editor, associate editor and board member of several scholarly journals.

Open Access This chapter is licensed under the terms of the Creative Commons Attribution 4.0 International License (http://creativecommons.org/licenses/by/4.0/), which permits use, sharing, adaptation, distribution and reproduction in any medium or format, as long as you give appropriate credit to the original author(s) and the source, provide a link to the Creative Commons license and indicate if changes were made.

The images or other third party material in this chapter are included in the chapter's Creative Commons license, unless indicated otherwise in a credit line to the material. If material is not included in the chapter's Creative Commons license and your intended use is not permitted by statutory regulation or exceeds the permitted use, you will need to obtain permission directly from the copyright holder.

A Clash of Communication? Intervening in Textbook Writing and Curriculum Development in Bosnia and Herzegovina After the War of 1992–1995

Falk Pingel

Various institutions and players participate in consultations on international textbook and curriculum revision: ministries of education, pedagogical-oriented as well as subject-oriented academic institutes, teacher associations and international organizations. Although all of them may agree on the common aim to contribute to the reform of education systems, they often differ in specific objectives and strategies of how to reach the common aim. They are used to act in different contexts such as political, educational or scientific environments, which are imprinted by specific traditions and attitudes of negotiating and problem-solving. In this respect, particularly political and scientific approaches may differ or even exclude each other. Whereas political bargaining is searching for legitimate compromise, science builds on a truth-finding process aiming at an intersubjective objectivity (Habermas 1984).

F. Pingel (✉)
Georg Eckert Institute, Braunschweig, Germany
e-mail: fpingel@gmx.de

This chapter deals with advantages and limits of communication and negotiation strategies stakeholders in textbook and curriculum revision chose to cope with the problem of how to follow their own agenda and to cooperate with partners in reaching the common goal.

These issues will be inquired taking as an example the year-long consultations on textbook and curricula reform, which took place after the war of 1992–1995 in Bosnia and Herzegovina (henceforth BaH). Although one deals here with consultations between different stakeholders within a country—and not between different states—also features normally characteristic of international revision projects are included in the Bosnian case. The international community played a crucial role in the whole process, and some of the Bosnian players acted as if they were opponents in an international context because they rejected the official concept according to which BaH represents a united society and one state.

Changing Patterns of International Textbook Revision

Traditionally, international textbook research and revision has been performed as a school-subject-oriented analysis followed by joint recommendations agreed upon by the involved partners in a project. Analysis and recommendations evaluated the breadth and depth as well as correctness and compliance of the issue at stake with results of academic research and referred mainly to content issues. Although leading documents on objectives and methods of textbook revision touched upon the pedagogical and psychological dimensions of textbook research from its very beginnings, official bi- or multilateral national commissions as well as academic projects often play down or almost neglect the pedagogical aspects and psychological implications of textbooks and curricula as instruments of teaching and learning. The scientific correctness has been regarded as a proof for the intended objectivity and political neutrality of findings and recommendations for revision (Faure 2015; Pingel 2010a).

The broad pedagogical and sociological debate about the impact of globalization, the emerging knowledge society and a rapidly changing world order since the 1980s questioned this traditional model and fostered trends to pay more attention to the context and conditions which frame the use pupils and teachers make of curricula and teaching material. UNESCO as one of the leading agencies for the improvement in educational structures worldwide underscored this trend when the organization developed its report "Learning to be" (Faure et al. 1973), which propagated the concept of lifelong learning. The report strove to make education experts in UNESCO's member states aware of the need for learning processes that are open to changing environments. The traditional teacher-centred way of instruction should be altered into classroom environments that support democratic communication structures and develop pupils' activities and participatory learning. When referring to UNESCO's long-standing engagement in education towards international understanding, the report expressly takes into account Piaget's "genetic psychology" as a scientific approach to the intended new education model (Pingel 2016). Yet, born in the time of rapprochement after the height of the Cold War and fostered through the breakdown of the bipolar world order after the dissolution of the Soviet bloc, the new model of an interactive consensual, democratic education process was severely shattered through ongoing or new conflicts springing up particularly in Africa and South Asia as well as in some of the former socialist countries, BaH being one of them. Experts in education policy and economy—often affiliated with international organizations—directed international attention to the devastating effects violent conflicts have on education. They underscored that history and civic education have been abused for legitimizing conflict and fostering adversary images and negative stereotyping of the "other" (Seitz 2004; Smith and Vaux 2002; Bush and Saltarelli 2000). With the adoption of the "Education for All Dakar Framework for Action" (UNESCO 2000) in the year 2000, UNESCO made "quality education" its overall concept concentrating on regions affected by severe undernourishment and protracted armed conflict. The turn to internal conflicts in the revision of curricula and teaching material—instead of almost exclusively dealing with wars between states as in the past—and the new emphasis on learning processes pushed the question to the fore which role education has in strengthening or weakening social cohesion in conflict or post-conflict societies. It was UNESCO's "International Bureau of Education" (Piaget was its director from 1929 to 1968), which first expressly addressed the topic in a substantial publication in 2004 dealing with the role of education in conflict-ridden societies in Europe, Asia, the Middle East, Latin America and Africa (Tawil and Harvey 2004). However, it took almost a decade before theories of learning and social psychology have been applied as well in a publication dealing with textbook revision (Perikleous and Shemilt 2011). It was not by chance that this time an NGO (the Association for Historical Dialogue and Research) was the publisher reflecting the increasing role civil society initiatives play in developing educational strategies aiming at fostering the understanding for peaceful conflict resolution in education.

The Need for Symmetry: Seeking Balance and Recognition

With the significant involvement of NGOs, the need for establishing balance, symmetry and mutual recognition within revision projects has come to the fore. In the traditional model of politically induced and often also financed and approved bi- or multinational commissions, the political authorities set the formal ramifications of a project including the content areas which should be dealt with and sometimes also the qualifications which should be represented in the commission if the authorities themselves did not appoint members. Thus, the general working procedures are defined by sovereign governmental institutions with equal standing. Scholarly analysis then guarantees the objectivity of the working process and the political neutrality of recommendations. In contrast, NGO-geared groups can be composed of lay persons, academics, politicians with quite different social statuses, qualifications and working experiences. As no supervising political authority exists, group members have to elaborate procedures and content areas themselves. Whatever the qualifications and political views of participants in a project are, they must be seen as equivalent and of equal value lending the same argumentative power to all sides involved.

Social psychology theories have emphasized that symmetric relations between partners in problem-solving activities are a basic requirement for fostering cooperative attitudes and innovative thinking (Shultziner 2010; Kelman 2009; Rouhana and Kelman 1994). Piaget has delivered the most profound explanation based on experiment and theoretical analysis as Gerard Duveen has shown referring to the children's transition from pre-operational to operational thinking. According to Piaget, "symmetric relations" are needed to stimulate productive, innovative knowledge and to create an environment of cooperation rather than "constraint" (Duveen 2002), as constraints may be seen any kind of authoritative impediments that hinder free and open thinking. In fact, adults are more flexible in responding to constraints and may even challenge restrictions set by authorities, but such reactions would create a climate of fighting for superiority and symmetry-impeding competition.

A cooperative basis must be agreed upon as a starting point if issues of clashing collective identities are at stake and multiple perspectives and opposing views are represented within a project. As a rule, members of revision commissions are well minded, willing to cooperate and to overcome mistrust and biased views which help to find a common basis. However, groups with adversarial, clearly defined self-characterizations as they occur in situations of protracted civil war, strong ethnic nationalism and unequal power relations perceive each other as in-group and out-group and tend to reinforce their exclusive group identities in encounters with their "adversaries" (Amir 1976; Turner et al. 1987; Tajfel and Turner 1986). In this case, short-term dialogical encounters between the groups may not help to overcome stereotype and mistrust as could be expected according to a simple application of the contact hypothesis. Further research on the contact hypothesis has shown that the reduction in stereotypes is not only a matter of correct information and reasonable intellectual argumentation in joint meetings. Encounters must be accompanied by positive emotions leading to acknowledgement and recognition of the "other". Situations of practical cooperation must be created that show that all parties involved depend on each other in order to produce a common result (Oskamp 2000; Brewer and Miller 1988).

The social and epistemological dimensions of learning inextricably underlie the controversial dialogue between the parties with the aim to reach a common understanding of the conflict at stake. The late Israeli professor of social psychology, D. Bar-On, has devoted year-long research and practical group work with the aim to establish symmetry of communication between persons and groups with different, even contrasting experiences and historical backgrounds. In contact with children of holocaust survivors and Nazi perpetrators, he created a dialogical method based on biographical storytelling, which should lay foundations for a dialogue on equal footing (Bar-On 1995). He transferred his method to encounters between Israelis and Palestinians with the aim to jointly develop teaching material about the Israeli–Palestinian relationship which could be used in Israeli as well as Palestinian schools (Adwan et al. 2012; Bar-On and Kassem 2004). Telling each other's life stories has the function to distract attention from the dividing political dimension. So to speak, it individualizes and humanizes politics. It shows how the political dimension influences human lives. Personal experiences cannot be refuted: they are neither right nor wrong. Their narrative structure deviates from the model of binary logic. Life stories show how and why group members act under the impact of heavy political constraints. This is an experience member of both sides share. Mutually listening to life stories brings about empathy and furthers trust and recognition of the "other". Whereas Bar-On's approach is influenced by psychoanalytical thinking, experimental social psychological research has also underscored the positive effects of empathy and described perspective taking exactly as what has taken place in Bar-On's groups, namely to "increase the perception that a common humanity and destiny is shared with the other group" (Brown and Hewstone 2005:293). Biographical storytelling is just a means to make people ready for what Pettigrew has defined as "self-disclosure": to open oneself to others (Pettigrew 1998). Biographical storytelling stands at the beginning of Bar-On's projects, accompanies them at each phase and paves the way for the proper historical and pedagogical work on the teaching material. Bar-On has called this approach TRT (= To Reflect and Trust) (Bar-On et al. 2000). The TRT concept is not easily applicable because it presupposes the involvement of psychologically trained moderators, prolongs the group's work and claims from the participants to bring in their own personality, to present their personal experiences to persons who are regarded as enemies by the majority of one's own society. Usually, its application is restricted to small groups, and it is mostly used by NGO-driven projects. It can hardly be applied in official expert commissions.

Besides Bar-On's special approach, W. Fisher and others have formed a more general theory of narrative communication as a counter-model to binary argumentative logic (Fisher 1984). The stories' coherence and the sincerity of the narration and the narrator create confidence and allow the listeners to relate themselves to the experiences of the "other".

Whereas the biographical approach strives to generate empathy and positive feelings within a project from the very beginning and to take out politics as long as possible, J. Rothman (1997) has developed a contrasting model of dialogical identity conflict resolution containing four phases. It starts expressly with a confrontational "antagonism phase" during which participants exchange their conflicting political views. When participants come to the conclusion that a continuation of the political debate would not produce any common results, they are asked to rationally define their own positions and interests, to compare them with the ones of the adversary and so develop step by step an understanding of possible common goals and to work on solutions. He calls his model according to the four steps ARIA (= Antagonism, Resonance,

Invention, Action). Rothman's model surely comes closer to normal working procedures of official revision commissions though they use it informally or implicitly rather than systematically and consciously. It builds more on rational argumentation and reason than on personal trust and empathy.

BOSNIA AND HERZEGOVINA: FROM POLITICAL NEGOTIATIONS TO AN EXPERT DIALOGUE

When textbook and curriculum revision began in BaH, neither local authorities nor the International Community (= IC)[1] had much systematic knowledge at hand of how to steer such a process. It was not even clear whether one could regard this as an internal Bosnian process not considerably different from normal changes of educational conditions as they happen in any country from time to time, or whether the example of international textbook and curricula commissions could serve as an appropriate paradigm to set the structure for the intended Bosnian reform. In fact, it was something in between. To understand this situation, I have to shortly recall the political conditions in BaH after the conclusion of the Dayton Peace Accords in 1995.

BaH has been divided into two political entities, the Serb Republic with its own ministry of education and the Federation of Bosnia and Herzegovina. The latter consists of 10 cantons with local governments in addition to the government of the Federation. Yet, the Federation's ministry of education has only a coordinating role between the cantonal education ministries and its room for manoeuvre is always contested. Thus, education foremost played a negative role in the peace regulations. In order to pay respect to the strive for cultural autonomy of the so-called constituent peoples of BaH—the Serbs, Croats and Bosniaks[2]—the education system was entirely federalized. Soon after the war, broadly speaking, three different streams of education were formed: a Serb oriented in the Serb Republic, a Croat oriented in the Croat majority cantons and a Bosniak stream in the Bosniak majority cantons, amongst them the capital Sarajewo. Whereas the Serb and Croat systems adopted content patterns and even textbooks from Serbia and Croatia, respectively, which were tainted with exclusive nationalism and denied the historical as well as current legitimacy of BaH as a distinct political unit, the Bosniak cantons developed a narrative of Bosnian unity since the Middle Ages which displayed a positive image of Islam and Ottoman legacy but also embraced Serbs and Croats and paid respect to their respective religious beliefs such as Christian orthodoxy and Catholicism.

The IC has been commissioned to control the implementation of the peace regulations. Its most powerful organ is the "High Representative" (= HR) who acts on behalf of the IC and has the right to interfere in all matters—including withdrawal or imposition of legislation as well as dismissal of staff—that are not in compliance with the Dayton Accords. In the years following the war, the IC concentrated their support for the reconstruction of the education system on rehabilitation of destroyed schools and administration buildings. Only at the end of the 1990s, the IC became aware that the Bosnian educational authorities had constructed curricula and textbooks, which fostered ethnic hatred and feelings of cultural superiority and partly neglected the status of BaH as an independent state. As a countermeasure, the IC initiated a process of curriculum and textbook reform. In the following, I can only shortly refer to the complex political ramifications of this process, which has already been described in detail (Torsti 2011; Karge and Batarilo 2009; Pingel 2009). Instead, I concentrate on group relations within the commissions and working groups which tried to find a consensus on how to construct educational material acceptable to the constituent peoples of BaH in spite of their different cultural, religious and political concepts.

The Bosnian case has a special position within the plethora of contextual constraints that shape textbook consultations of various kinds as developed by Bentrovato (this volume). One may even doubt whether it can be subsumed under the notion of "conciliatory" textbook work. Particularly in its initial state, it can rather be compared with forced international interventions such as the occupying powers executed in Germany when they withdrew Nazi textbooks and curricula and exerted strong control over the developments of new ones after the end of the Second World War.

Although the two entity ministers and the Croat deputy education minister of the Federation signed a joint agreement on textbook revision, the process would have never got into motion if the IC would not have insisted on its implementation. Furthermore, the first step was interventionist, purely negative and without an alternative for the Bosnian stakeholders. UNESCO officials partly protected by soldiers visited schools, checked textbooks and screened passages which were regarded "inappropriate" to fostering the living together of the three constituent peoples. Thus, the revision process was shaped by top-down power relations at its very beginning. Nevertheless, IC and ministries followed a double strategy. The process itself was conducted by local experts with the only small representation of the IC. IC, local authorities and stakeholders in education worked together in commissions and project groups, but when agreement could not be reached or results not be implemented, the IC has always the power—and the HR has used it—to impose needed measures. Therefore, it was not easy to install a feeling of consensual processing at working levels in such an unequal power structure although this is essential if education reform should be accepted by local stakeholders, in particular teachers, pupils and parents. To comply with the IC's proposals could always be interpreted as compromising with the stronger partner.

Textbook commissions were set up for the subjects of language and literature, history, geography, the environment and society as well as religion. When the consultation process started, participants mostly followed a political agenda and saw themselves as representatives of the local ministries which had nominated them. Against the intentions at least of the IC, the starting phase can be characterized as mostly antagonistic in a double meaning. The majority of the Bosnian members showed sceptical or even dismissive attitudes towards the IC. The IC propagated a multicultural approach which was—and often still is—not well understood by most of the Bosnian members—scholars from pedagogical universities and senior teachers mostly—who were not familiar with this concept and regarded it a threat to their cultural identities. They were not well informed by their ministries about procedures and aims of the commissions and entered them mostly with the feeling that the IC is about to threaten their independence in shaping their own curricula and teaching material. However, the division between IC and Bosnians did not contribute to strengthen inner-Bosnian cohesion, because the Bosnians were united in their negative attitudes towards the IC only in order to maintain their ethnically separated education systems. Thus, the commission was characterized by an international–local (or Bosnian) antagonism as well as the inner-Bosnian division between the representatives of the three constituent peoples. In the first phase, the main dividing line ran between locals and internationals because the Bosnians were united in their efforts to torpedo the IC's intentions. Yet, they had at least to agree to those revision measures which were conditioned by the observation of the Dayton Accords and therefore could not be rejected. Consequently, only a minimal understanding could be achieved meaning to take out obvious negative, discriminating and disparaging representations without being able to replace rejected statements through positive formulations. Under these conditions, creative and productive cooperation could not be developed and group relations did not change considerably. This meagre result complies with Hoffman's critique of Rothman's method that it would not foster but rather "stifle creativity" because common, but minimal goals are defined at an early stage after the articulation of dissent and opposing views so that no procedure of recognition is being installed (Hoffman 2004).

It took about 2–3 years of work to de-politicize to a certain extent the commissions and arouse a kind of common expert understanding. The continuation of commission work over several years without great changes in the membership contributed to creating an in-group feeling as textbook and curricula experts in school disciplines. This made members more independent from the ministries and reduced attitudes to defend their assumed ethnic particularity. One could say that the second phase according to Rothman's model had been reached. Participants started to recognize characteristics of themselves in the "others" without feeling obliged to identify with them. The distinction between in- and out-group became less important and did no longer shape the dialogue. The longer the process lasted, the less the role of the IC was contested, since the institutional framework had been set, the goals of revision in principle accepted, organizational support and expertise provided by the OSCE (Organization for Security and Co-Operation in Europe) and experts from outside even welcomed. In the longer run, the expert status took the role of a superordinate category that embraced almost all commission members and lowered the impact of political-ethnic sub-categories. Mytko (2013) refers to the same effect and quotes Warden (2011) who made the same observation in a project conducted in Moldova, a country which is linguistically and culturally divided in a similar way as BaH. Warden corroborates that many of the history professionals were driven "by a desire to promote pedagogical change, affirm their identity as professionals, and belong to a professional community" (Warden 2011:242). Warden "found that professional identity was important" (Mytko 2013:29).

In addition and in parallel to the commissions, the IC organized training seminars for teachers, curriculum experts and textbook authors to make them familiar with new concepts and help implement the commissions' results. At the beginning, seminar members were handpicked by the ministries; later on, they were accepted on the basis of applications showing their expertise in the field. This selection process broadened the recruiting basis and again underscored the significance of expert knowledge.

Only at a third stage positive results could be achieved. IC and local authorities agreed on a new format of the commissions' procedures and goals. Instead of criticizing and screening already published books and approved curricula, commissions were instructed to develop general guidelines for the writing of—future—textbooks and curricula that should acknowledge the country's multi-ethnic composition without stimulating feelings of superiority or inferiority. This task stimulated a sense of cooperation, forward-looking invention and ownership. The debate was creative and dedicated to the cause at stake. A personalization of contact and individuation of members of the "other group" could be particularly observed in the disciplinary subgroups. One could say that in the end a process of decategorization of their relationship took place (Brewer and Miller 1988).

The guidelines published in the official gazette of BaH in January 2007 had a notable impact on textbook authors who have become more sensitive to contentious issues such as the representation of the constituent peoples or the break-up of Yugoslavia. Particularly, authors have included more tasks, questions, sources and illustrations than in older books in order to develop pupils' critical thinking and interpretative abilities (Karge 2008).

The cooperative approach was intensified through a special commission given the task to develop a "common core curriculum", i.e. to define all contents and methodologies the existing curricula of the cantons and entities have in common. This aim reminded members of this commission on commonalities of Yugoslav times which were positively connoted. This triggered a controversial discussion amongst the Bosnian members: Should the commission only define commonalties of the existing curricula or also determine what should be in common in future and so go beyond the curricula currently in force? Although some participants fervently argued that the commission should be creative and innovative and would have a mandate to put forward future curriculum changes to the ministries in order to enlarge commonalties, the majority rejected this proposal. Nevertheless, the common core curriculum that was approved in 2003 documented common features of BaH's diverse curricula landscape for the first time after the war. It enhanced the working capacities and self-respect on the Bosnian side and eased the new constructive approach to textbook revision leading to the Guidelines.

The more a working group or commission brought political objectives and opinions to the fore in consultations, the more members were driven in their statements by social identity patterns in contrast to their personal, individual identity (Sedikides and Brewer 2001). Language plays a key role in defining one's social, ethnic or religious identity in BaH. When the political unity broke apart in the war, also the common South Slavic language was no longer accepted as one language with different variants according to ethnicity. Instead, the Slovenian, Croat, Serb and Bosniak variants are now defined as separate languages. Consequently, the common core sub-commission on the three languages of BaH had severe problems to accept that all the three languages are taken into account in the curriculum and are represented in literature classes. Communication accommodation theory shows that speech acts transmit not only an argument but also a social message about the group to which the speaker wishes to belong (Giles and Coupland 1991). Different languages are strong signifiers of different group affiliations and are used in BaH to mark group distinctiveness. As linguistic experts, the sub-commission members' expertise lay exactly in keeping up this distinctiveness so that political and professional dimensions became more or less inseparable. It was a problem of social communication for the experts to admit that the Bosnian languages are mutually understandable and to acknowledge the "other's" languages as teaching content vis-à-vis their own group members. Therefore, seeing themselves as disciplinary experts did not help to bridge the social and political gaps within this sub-commission as in the other disciplinary sub-commissions. They could agree on a common core only at the very end of the consultations although more forced by time pressure than activated by their own conviction. Astonishingly, having reached a positive result in the end this had also a positive effect on group relations within the sub-commission. Members openly showed their pride in the successful finalization of their work, congratulated each other. Finally, the outcome created feelings of empathy and individualization.

According to an opinion poll, a clear majority of teachers was in favour of the common core curriculum. Also, the common core curriculum was remembered more often than other, more profound innovations such as the framework law on education or the textbook commissions (Karge and Batarilo 2009). However, after the common core curriculum had been secured by the first country-wide framework law on secondary and primary education in 2003, instead of building on this moderate, positive result, the IC soon lost interest in it, did not insist on developing it further as originally planned but changed its educational agenda in order to implement latest European standards which were no longer content oriented—like all the existing curricula in BaH—but competency based. The common core curriculum became less important. The new pedagogical concept was unknown to most teachers and textbook authors. It needed intensive training which could only be offered by the IC and takes a long time to reach a critical mass of teachers (Pantić et al. 2011). From the point of modernization, the altered agenda could be justified but it failed to foster ownership, engagement and understanding of the reform on the Bosnian side.

Not only in this case, are local interests sacrificed to a superficial modernization favoured by the IC. The experience of joint actions such as in the core curriculum commission could be much more important for the acceptance of reform and cooperation between the ethnic groups than the implementation of up-to-date internationally acknowledged pedagogy. However, such considerations did not reach the minds of the IC.

Yet, not only inconsistencies of the IC's policy hindered educational reform to advance. The implementation and formal acknowledgement of the commissions' results needed local by-laws. Not all of the local ministries were willing to adopt appropriate cantonal laws so that these were, in the end, partly imposed by the HR. The cooperative consensus reached at working level could not always also be installed at governmental level. Here, the argumentation remained political so that every side defended its own concept and compromised only if power relations forced them to do so. At governmental level, reform work remained a power play and did not turn into an expert dialogue. The common goal was only used as a means to pursue the aims of one's own group.

Two different and often incomprehensible communication strategies meet in multinational and multicultural textbook and curriculum revision because the expert-oriented scientific debate is almost inevitably accompanied by a political meta-discourse. As conceived in its ideal form by the German philosopher Jürgen Habermas (1984), the scientific dialogue corresponds to the paradigm of an exchange of rational arguments in order to reach a common understanding free from any kind of external interests. Objectivity is secured through intersubjective rationality. According to the German sociologist Niklas Luhman (2005), political argumentation represents a counter-paradigm to truth-oriented scientific communication. It aims at legitimation of decision-making and action. If textbook revision goes beyond pure analytical work based on scientific methodology and intends to revise education material, the political dimension comes in. Therefore, both streams of communication often interact in textbook and curriculum revision projects. Revision projects apply different strategies to cope with this problem. Often, political issues are treated by the chairs before presented to the whole group. The PRIME group of Israeli and Palestinian teachers sometimes split up in their respective "national" groups in order to deal separately with political issues that stand in the way of reaching a common understanding (Pingel 2010b). In the Bosnian case, a clear-cut distinction between both streams could only seldom be reached so that the analytical work was often interrupted by statements which were meant to defend the ethnically tainted education policy of one's own group.

External Intervention versus Internal Empowerment

The IC propagated multiculturalism as the lead concept for reforming education in BaH (A Message 2002). The multicultural concept has for most of the IC a persuasive power. Particularly, the Europeans conceive the Ottoman and also to a certain extent the Hapsburg Empire—which occupied Bosnia in 1878 and annexed in 1908—as a multicultural entity suiting the ethnic and religious mix-up of BaH. Thus, they think that they would just take up this old multicultural tradition—also applied by Socialist Yugoslavia—when introducing their modern concept of multiculturalism. However, they underestimate the long tradition of ethnic and religious compartmentalization during Ottoman and partly also Hapsburg times which was only superficially covered by Tito's "brotherhood and unity" but never forgotten or totally abolished. On the contrary, ethnic nationalism taken over from the European powers in the course of the nineteenth century translated the cultural characteristics such as language, religion and behavioural patterns connected with them into a concept of political sovereignty which was alien to the form of living together under foreign domination that represented the Bosnian experience since the late Middle Ages up to the end of the First World War (Sundhausen 2003). "Multiculturalism" meets neither Bosnia's remote past, nor the Yugoslav experience; it has no equivalence in the local languages and could hardly be understood as an indigenous term that should provide the Bosnians with "ownership"; rather, it was easy to be denounced by local politicians as a foreign concept imposed on the region to establish an egalitarian culture and society.

The problematic reputation the Bosnian District of Brcko has with most politicians and educationalists in BaH proves how difficult it is to break the barriers of ethnic-cultural separatism. Brcko forms a separate political unit under the surveillance of the HR. Brcko was not integrated into the Serb-dominated Republic because of its mixed population. Brcko schools use a blend of Croat, Bosniak and Serb curricula, and teachers work with textbooks from all political units. All the three South-Slav languages are used in the classroom. Although the local authorities, parents and pupils accept the Brcko education system, it is not regarded as a future model and viable alternative to ethnic separation outside of the district. Rather, it falls here under the dictum as being implemented by the IC in spite of the support it enjoys with the local population. Representatives of the education ministries were not even willing to take part in excursions to Brcko in order to study how the system works. They showed no interest in implemented multiculturalism in their country.

As the commissions' and ministers' meetings alternatively took place in Sarajewo, the Croat part of Mostar and Banja Luka, the capital of the Serb Republic, representatives of the IC proposed several times to jointly visit cultural highlights of these places in order to acknowledge cultural achievements of the three constituent peoples. This was also rejected. Also out of school activities with pupils from different ethnicities occurred only rarely. Some international organizations conducted seminars of this kind, but for most of the participants, these were unique and short-time encounters that hardly have a sustainable effect. When pupils come back to their normal, ethnically shaped environment, they fall back to their previous positions, even if they changed opinions about the "other" during the seminar (Pettigrew 1985).

Local and international NGOs, foundations and international organizations such as UNESCO, United Nations Development Programme, Council of Europe conducted a great number of projects dealing with the broad area of peace education in parallel to but often not coordinated with the official textbook revision activities. However, it is difficult to measure their influence on educational practice because most of them were not systematically evaluated. Many projects act on a short-term basis and follow different agendas. For teachers, it is often not transparent which project to follow. Long-term perspectives and clear agendas are, however, conducive to the success of reform (Stedman and Rothchild 1996; Downton and Wehr 1997).

Although this chapter mainly deals with history education, it is worthwhile to also look at civic education in order to better evaluate strategies of the IC vis-à-vis local interests. The citizenship education projects run by the international organization Civitas have produced a well-documented impact on curriculum change and teaching methods. This organization tries to reach local educational authorities' agreement for conducting projects. It has been able to integrate teaching material and curricular guidelines into official curricula (Batarilo 2008) and could disseminate its approach to a considerably wider range of pupils than many other organizations. The programs include social community work, the improvement in school facilities and training of students on how to efficiently participate in school councils. Civitas reaches a great number of students in all political units of the country—the report of 2015 mentions 35,000 addressees every year for the program "Project Citizen" (News from the Center for Civic Education 2015). From time to time, projects are evaluated (Summary of Research 2000). Nevertheless, the Executive Director of Civitas BaH reported about problems to establish positive working relations with the educational authorities contending in an evaluation seminar that official "institutions are often unable or unwilling to engage citizen participation in local processes, and citizens, in turn, are hesitant to trust and engage in those very institutions" (Frouzesh 2005; see also Soule, n.y.). Moreover, Civitas is one of the few organizations which work on the same program and follow a coherent agenda over a long-time span. Providing continuity, coherence, involvement of authorities and students' participation in practical school and communal activities, Civitas has probably found the most effective way to train students and teachers and brought about a curricular change towards democracy and civic education replacing the Yugoslav pre-military education. Civitas had to approach all the cantonal and entity ministers. One can say that Civitas was successful in establishing a common core for the diverse civic curricula in BaH.

Most of the NGOs and international organizations are not able to apply such a concerted bundle of coordinated processing capacity, content-oriented curricular elaboration and social engagement of students and teachers. The Greek NGO Center for Democracy and Reconciliation in South-Eastern Europe, for example, still has problems to disseminate its Joint History Project teaching material in BaH because of unwilling local authorities and teachers sceptical to innovations coming from outside of the country and not yet approved by the education ministries.

In contrast to Civitas which established working relations to local educational authorities from the very beginning of their project, the Center first elaborated the material in cooperation with a group of scholars and teachers and then tried to get the authorities' support for teaching it. Its teaching material is mostly used by those—now more than 1000—teachers from Balkan countries, Turkey and Cyprus who have participated in special training seminars (Fajfer 2013). Even if most of them show positive reactions, ripple effects are often still missing.

Surveys and evaluation studies show that the majority of teachers do not simply reject innovative steps towards peace education and intercultural understanding, but they feel dependent on support from their authorities, parent organizations and school boards (Magill 2010). According to a survey conducted in the year 2008, teachers are satisfied with the formal modernization of textbooks (Karge and Batarilo 2009). They enjoy clear multi-coloured design with images, photographs and shorter texts. However, they have problems to teach content areas that do not fit into the up to now official line of emphasis on ethnic difference. Teachers feel uneasy to refer to commonalties of the three constituent peoples in history or to teach new issues such as the recent war of 1992–1995 and the break-up of Yugoslavia. Nevertheless, the majority spoke out for dealing with these topics in textbooks. Teachers and secondary school students (addressed in a smaller pilot study of the same project conducted by Karge and Batarilo 2009) wished to get more information about the consequences of the war for the current situation in BaH. This is quite a rational result, in contrast to the often heated emotional public debates. The questionnaires were answered, and the interviews conducted during an in-service seminar on textbook reform. It may well be that teachers showed more openness to innovation in an environment where they feel being free from the context of normal school life.

Flexible International Strategies of Change Versus the Perseverance of Disciplinary Local Knowledge

As we have seen, cooperative attitudes in textbooks revision are mainly based on the acknowledgement of participants' expertise (mostly in the case of official, politically induced commissions) and/or on recognition of personality and sincerity. With which qualifications do members of the IC contribute to this process? Their professional background influences their reputation in commissions and negotiation strategies. Only the heads of the educational departments of UNESCO and OSCE—the IC lead organizations for education in the time period dealt with here—were professional educationalists or textbook specialists, respectively, for a relatively short period. Most of the staff involved in the commissions had received higher education although with quite different subject backgrounds. They were often specialized in social work or international relations. Many of them have worked for international organizations for a number of years but normally under short-time contracts, on different places with different organizations in various fields of intervention. Their greatest professional advantage is the acquisition of a flexible knowledge about intervention strategies in underdeveloped and conflict-ridden regions. They have acquired this knowledge mostly on the job. It builds on experience with little theoretical reflection. Their knowledge is not country specific and needs to be moulded according to the specific local needs. For example, before the OSCE took over the mandate for education, it had worked in the field of human rights issues, security policy and had helped to prepare and oversee elections. OSCE took over education without considerably enlarging its staff which was mostly transferred from the election section to the newly founded education department. To what an extent staff members get familiar with local characteristics of the issues at stake depends very much on their own initiative. Most of them have not received systematic training. The objectives of intervention are set by the agenda of the organization which they are part of. As a number of international organizations are represented in the IC, their strategies, objectives and financial means must be coordinated to speak with one voice to their local counterparts. Yet, the obligation to follow the organizations' specific agendas often counts more than the responsibility for working on a common goal.

    The IC staff, therefore, brings in different strategies of intervention which already have been used in different regions and proved as generally applicable but not yet tested at the concrete site of operation. The internationally acquired knowledge meets with local, long-time professional practice in the commissions. Both could complement each other. However, given the power imbalance this unequal encounter tends to create mistrust and scepticism against the "other's" wisdom. The internationals suspect the locals to stick to their outdated and no longer applicable past experience, whereas the locals fear to be overwhelmed by content and methodology that does not fit into their context which the internationals do not know sufficiently. The power imbalance is supplemented by an asymmetry of knowledge which the locals often translate into an inferiority–superiority relationship. This supports mistrust and scepticism rather than developing mutual trust and cooperative attitudes. Yet, there are ways to mitigate these ruptures. The majority of the OSCE staff is made up by locals. Whereas the internationals hold mainly leading positions, most of the locals work in the many OSCE field offices (these were 14 during the height of the reform in the first decade of the twenty-first century) and are in almost daily contact with local practitioners and stakeholders. Over the years, they have acquired specific local knowledge and established positive working relations. Their reporting back to the main office and their possible intervention in the commissions' deliberations can serve as a buffer and transmitter between the local–international imbalances.

On the Way to a "Narrative Transformation"?

After approximately a decade of intense reform activities in primary and secondary education, the IC reshuffled its capacities. Different factors were to be taken into account. Firstly, the focus of international aid moved from the Balkans in general and BaH in particular to other regions of still open or new conflicts such as the Middle East, Africa and, later on, to Eastern Europe. The Balkans was, by and large, pacified. The OSCE education department has been downsized and now concentrates its efforts on capacity building. It no longer directly interferes in curriculum or textbooks matters. The reform agenda of the first decade of the twenty-first century has helped to install the necessary legislation in all sectors of education. It removed offensive material from schools, curricula and teaching devices. It has laid foundations for the development of multi-perspectival teaching material and modernized curricular structures. Despite these notable achievements, it did not fundamentally change the divided education system according to ethnicity, culture, language and religion. Most of the cooperative structures developed by the IC through commissions, working groups, ministers meetings did not survive the reform phase. Nevertheless, the many projects conducted by the IC and international as well as local NGOs have introduced open learning methods to a wide range of teachers and curriculum experts, strengthened parents' and pupils' participation in democratic school management and created innovative teaching material. However, although such activities continue, they still reach only a minority and have not yet changed the official mainstream narratives and textbook representations. The hiatus continues to exist between the ongoing official policy of separation and emphasis on ethnic difference on the one hand and engaged NGOs and innovative experts on the other hand. As long as the electorate in the Serb Republic and the Croat majority cantons favours parties that stand for ethnic separatism, a real breakthrough towards the recognition of a mixed society without intellectual, cultural and religious borderlines is hardly to be expected. One may concede that the reform work has created a "transformative potential" as it is called by Bentrovato (this volume), but this potential has only partly been activated up to now. One may doubt whether the innovative local forces have become strong enough to fully awake this potential in future or whether the traditional political institutions will exert their power to denounce it and to keep it small.

NOTES

1. The International Community comprises the representatives of member states of the *Peace Implementation Council* and international organizations actively rebuilding BaH.
2. "Bosnian" refers to the whole of BaH or all its citizens; "Bosniak" is the self-designation of BaH's Muslim population who so create their own ethnic identity vis-à-vis the "Croats" and "Serbs".

REFERENCES

Adwan, S., Bar-On, D., & Naveh, E., Peace Research Institute in the Middle East (Eds.). (2012). *Side by side. Parallel histories of Israel-Palestine*. New York: The New Press.

A Message to the People of Bosnia and Herzegovina. Education Reform. (2002, November 21). (in English, Bosniak, Croat and Serb language).

Amir, Y. (1976). The role of intergroup contact in the change of prejudice and ethnic relations. In P. A. Katz (Ed.), *Towards the elimination of racism* (pp. 245–308). New York: Pergamon.

Bar-On, D. (1995). Encounters between descendants of Nazi Perpetrators and Descendants of Holocaust Survivors. *Psychiatry,58*(3), 225–245.

Bar-On, D., & Kassem, F. (2004). Storytelling as a way to work-through intractable conflicts: The German-Jewish experience and its relevance to the Palestinian–Israeli context. *Journal of social Issues,60*(2), 289–306.

Bar-On, D., Kutz, S., & Wegner, D. (Eds.). (2000). *Bridging the gap*. Hamburg: Körber Foundation.

Batarilo, A. (2008). *Civic education in Bosnia and Herzegovina. The inclusion of civic education into official curricula*. Sarajewo, unpublished report.

Brewer, M. B., & Miller, N. (1988). Contact and cooperation: When do they work? In P. Katz & D. Taylor (Eds.), *Eliminating racism: Profiles in controversy* (pp. 315–326). New York: Plenum.

Brown, R., & Hewstone, M. (2005). An integrative theory of intergroup contact. *Advances in Experimental Social Psychology,37*, 255–343.

Bush, K. D., & Saltarelli, D. (2000). *The two faces of education in ethnic conflict. Towards a peacebuilding education for children*. Florence: United Nations Children's Fund, Innocenti Research Centre. Retrieved August 22, 2016, from https://www.unicef-irc.org/publications/pdf/insight4.pdf.

Downton, J., Jr., & Wehr, P. (1997). *The persistent activist: How peace commitment develops and survives*. Boulder, CO: Westview.

Duveen, G. (2002). Construction, belief, doubt. *Psychologie & Société,5*, 139–155.

Fajfer, L. (2013). Reconnecting history—The joint history project in the Balkans. In K. V. Korostelina, & S. Lässig (Eds.), *History education and post-conflict reconciliation. Reconsidering joint textbook projects* (pp. 140–154). London: Routledge.

Faure, R. (2015). *Netzwerke der Kulturdiplomatie. Die internationale Schulbuchrevision in Europa, 1945–1989* [Networks of cultural diplomacy. International textbook revision in Europe, 1945–1989]. Berlin: Walter de Gruyter.

Faure, E., Herrera, F., Kaddoura, A.-R., Lopes, H., Petrovsky, A. V., Rahnema, M., et al. (1973). *Learning to be. The world of education today and tomorrow*. Paris and Toronto: UNESCO and Ontario Institute for Studies in Education.

Fisher, W. R. (1984). Narration as human communication paradigm: The case of public moral argument. *Communication Monographs,51*, 1–22.

Frouzesh, S. (2005, April). Civic education in divided societies: Using civic education materials to build a democratic political culture. Summary of focus group. Retrieved April 20, 2016 form www.civiced.org/pdfs/research/FocusGroupSummary.pdf.

Giles, H., Coupland, J., & Coupland, N. (1991). Accommodation theory: Communication, context, and consequence. In H. Giles, J. & Coupland, N. Coupland (Eds.), *Contexts of accommodation* (pp. 1–68). New York: Cambridge University Press.

Habermas, J. (1984). *Theory of communicative action* (Thomas McCarthy Trans.). Boston: Beacon Press.
Hoffman, M. (2004). Peace and conflict impact assessment methodology. *Berghof handbook for conflict transformation*. Retrieved August 22, 2016, from http://www.berghof-handbook.net.
Karge, H. (2008). *20th century history in textbooks of Bosnia and Herzegovina: An analysis of books used for the final grades of primary school.* Sarajewo: OSCE Mission to Bosnia and Herzegovina.
Karge, H., & Batarilo, K. (2009). Norms and practices of history textbook policy and production in Bosnia and Herzegovina. In A. Dimou (Ed.), *"Transition" and the politics of history education in Southeastern Europe* (pp. 307–335). Göttingen: Vandenhoeck & Ruprecht.
Kelman, H. C. (2009). A social-psychological approach to conflict analysis and resolution. In D. Sandole, S. Byrne, I. Sandole-Staroste, & J. Senehi (Eds.), *Handbook of conflict analysis and resolution* (pp. 170–183). New York: Routledge.
Luhmann, N. (2005). *Risk: A sociological theory (Communication and Social Order)*. Chicago: Aldine Transactions.
Magill, C. (2010). *Education and fragility in Bosnia and Herzegovina*. Paris: International Institute for Educational Planning in cooperation with UNESCO, INEE, University of Ulster. Retrieved April 20, 2016, from http://unesdoc.unesco.org/images/0019/001910/191060e.pdf.
Mytko, G. (2013). *Peacebuilding in the Balkans through history education reform.* (Master's thesis). University of Leiden. Retrieved August 22, 2016, from https://openaccess.leidenuniv.nl/bitstream/handle/1887/24162/Thesis%20Final%20Draft%20Mytko.pdf?sequence=1.
News from the Center for Civic Education. Students showcase projects in Bosnia and Herzegovina (2015, May 26). Retrieved August 20, 2016, from http://www.civiced.org/e-news/?p=1581.
Oskamp, S. (Ed.). (2000). *Reducing prejudice and discrimination. The Claremont symposium on applied social psychology.* Mahwah, NJ: Erlbaum.
Pantić, N., Wubbels, T., & Mainhard, T. (2011). Teacher competence as a basis for teacher education: Comparing views of teachers and teacher educators in five Western Balkan countries. *Comparative Education Review,55*(2), 165–188.
Perikleous, L., & Shemilt, D. (Eds.). (2011). *The future of the past. Why history education matters.* Nicosia: The Association for Historical Dialogue and Research.
Pettigrew, T. F. (1985). The contact hypothesis revisited. In M. Hewstone & R. Brow (Eds.), *Contact and conflict in intergroup encounters* (pp. 169–195). Oxford: Blackwell.

Pettigrew, T. F. (1998). Intergroup contact theory. *Annual Review of Psychology,49,* 65–85.

Pingel, F. (2009). From ownership to intervention—Or vice versa? Textbook revision in Bosnia and Herzegovina. In A. Dimou (Ed.), *"Transition" and the politics of history education in Southeastern Europe* (pp. 251–305). Göttingen: Vandenhoeck & Ruprecht.

Pingel, F. (2010a). *UNESCO guidebook on international textbook research and textbook revision.* 2nd, rev. and extended ed., Braunschweig and Paris: Georg Eckert Institute and UNESCO.

Pingel, F. (2010b). Geschichtsdeutung als Macht? Schulbuchforschung zwischen wissenschaftlicher Erkenntnis- und politischer Entscheidungslogik [The power of interpreting history. Textbook research between science and politics]. *Journal of Educational Media, Memory, and Society,2,* 93–112.

Pingel, F. (2016). Textbook revision programme: History, concepts, and assumptions. In A. Kulnazarova, & C. Ydesen, (Eds.), *UNESCO without borders. Educational campaigns for international understanding* (pp. 13–31). New York: Routledge.

Rothman, J. (1997). *Resolving identity-based conflict in nations, organizations and communities.* San Francisco, CA: Jossey-Bass.

Rouhana, N. N., & Kelman, H. C. (1994). Promoting joint thinking in international conflicts: An Israeli-Palestinian continuing workshop. *Journal of Social Issues,50,* 157–178.

Sedikides, C., & Brewer, M. C. (Eds.). (2001). *Individual self, relational self, collective self: Partners, opponents, or strangers?.* Philadelphia: Psychology Press.

Seitz, K. (2004). *Education and conflict. The role of education in the creation, prevention and resolution of societal crises. Consequences for development cooperation.* Stuttgart: Deutsche Gesellschaft für Technische Zusammenarbeit (GTZ).

Shultziner, D. (2010). *Struggling for Recognition. The psychological impetus for democratic progress.* New York: The Continuum International Publishing Group.

Smith, A., & Vaux, T. (2002). *Education, conflict and international development.* Report commissioned by the UK Department for International Development.

Soule, S. (n.d.). *Beyond communism and war. The effect of civic education on the democratic attitudes and behavior of Bosnian and Herzegovinian Youth.* Calabasas, CA: Center for Civic Education.

Stedman, S., & Rothchild, D. (1996). Peace operations: From short-term to long-term commitment. *International Peacekeeping,3*(2), 17–35.

Summary of Research: Project Citizen in Bosnia and Herzegovina (2000). *Project citizen in Bosnia and Herzegovina.* Retrieved August 20, 2016 from http://www.civiced.org/papers/research_bih_summary.html.

Sundhausen, H. (2003). Staatsbildung und ethnisch-nationale Gegensätze in Südosteuropa [State building and ethnic-national antagonism in Southeastern Europe]. *Aus Politik und Zeitgeschichte,* B 10–11, 3–9.

Tajfel, H., & Turner, J. C. (1986). The social identity theory of intergroup behavior. In S. Worchel & W. G. Austin (Eds.), *Psychology of intergroup relations* (pp. 7–24). Chicago: Nelson-Hall.

Tawil, S., & Harley, A. (Eds.). (2004). *Education, conflict and social cohesion.* Geneva: UNESCO International Bureau of Education.

Torsti, P. (2011). How to deal with a difficult past? history textbooks supporting enemy images in post-war Bosnia and Herzegovina. In T. Abba (Ed.), *Education in Eastern Europe, Central Eurasia, South Asia and South East Asia* (pp. 65–86). London: Routledge.

Turner, J. C., Hogg, M. A., Oakes, P. J., Reicher, S. D., & Wetherell, M. S. (1987). *Rediscovering the social group: A self-categorization theory.* New York: Basil Blackwell.

UNESCO (2000). *The Dakar framework for action. education for all: Meeting our collective commitments.* Adopted by the World Education Forum, Dakar, Senegal, 26–28 April 2000. Paris: UNESCO. Retrieved August 22, 2016 from http://unesdoc.unesco.org/images/0012/001211/121147e.pdf.

Warden, E. (2011). The "Mock Reform" of history education in Moldova: Actors versus the script. *Comparative Education Review*,55(2), 231–251.

Author Biography

Falk Pingel Ph.D., is an Associated Research Fellow at the Georg Eckert Institute for International Textbook Research in Braunschweig/Germany. He was for many years the Institute's Deputy Director. Since his retirement in 2009, he is a consultant on issues of textbook and curriculum research and revision to governmental and academic institutions as well as international organizations. He has been particularly involved in projects dealing with the representation of conflicting identities, for example in South Africa, the Middle East and East Asia. In 2003/2004, he was the first Director of the OSCE's Education Department in Sarajewo/Bosnia and Herzegovina. Falk Pingel also taught contemporary history as well as theory and didactics of history at Bielefeld University. Amongst his publications is the UNESCO Guidebook on International Textbook Research and Textbook Revision (Braunschweig/Paris, 2010^2). He co-edited (in conjunction with U. Han, T. Kondo and B. Yang) History Education and Reconciliation. Comparative Perspectives on East Asia, (Frankfurt/M, 2012).

Open Access This chapter is licensed under the terms of the Creative Commons Attribution 4.0 International License (http://creativecommons.org/licenses/by/4.0/), which permits use, sharing, adaptation, distribution and reproduction in any medium or format, as long as you give appropriate credit to the original author(s) and the source, provide a link to the Creative Commons license and indicate if changes were made.

The images or other third party material in this chapter are included in the chapter's Creative Commons license, unless indicated otherwise in a credit line to the material. If material is not included in the chapter's Creative Commons license and your intended use is not permitted by statutory regulation or exceeds the permitted use, you will need to obtain permission directly from the copyright holder.

Textbook Narratives and Patriotism in Belarus

Anna Zadora

This chapter analyzes history textbooks narratives in a specific context: Belarus—a post-totalitarian and authoritarian state. School history teaching has always been a powerful instrument for patriotism and identity building. Political authorities tend to control the school history textbook writing and the transmission of sentiment of loyalty to the motherland (Noizet and Caverni 1978). History teaching is often used for identity-building processes, because history is relating to the continuity and stability, fundamental notions for identity building according to social psychologists, historians and sociologists (Erikson 1950, 1959; Dubar 2000; Wodack 2004; Weber 1995; Gellner 1983).

This chapter will provide a chronological analysis of the evolution of history textbooks writing in Belarus and the transmission of patriotism discourse through the history textbooks through the prism of the construction of the dividing line between "us": patriots, belonging the nation and the "other": "the strangers" (Cote and Levine 2002; Michaud 1978).

A. Zadora (✉)
University of Strasbourg, Strasbourg, France
e-mail: anna_zadora@hotmail.com

History textbooks narratives and patriotism model in Belarus are constantly changing and balancing between openness to global tendencies, European heritage, democracy on the one hand, and isolation, links with Russia and totalitarian tendencies on the other hand. This fact explains why the extremely fluctuant and contradictory official discourse on patriotism, identity devotion to the country transmitted by the educational system and especially by history textbooks is not socially efficient, because this discourse is deprived of a fundamental characteristic—stability. Textbooks in Belarus were rewritten considerably (radical change of the identity and history matrix) three times from 1988 to 1994, and after 1994, the history textbooks globally remain loyal to Soviet and Russian-orientated tradition (Loukashenko 2003), but are still rewritten every two years. In this context, textbooks cannot be a stable instrument in identity and patriotism matrix building. The major opposed traditions in history interpretation, patriotism and identity building are nationalist tradition on the one hand and Soviet-styled and Russian-orientated on the other hand. The terms "Soviet" and "Russian-orientated" are used as synonymous. Even during the Soviet period the dominant Republic, the "oppressor," the obstacle for the national development of Soviet republics was Russia.

Historiography and Patriotism

The definition of patriotism is deeply connected to the concept of nationalism. French writer R. Gary maintains: "Patriotism is the love for the 'us' and nationalism is the hate of 'the other'" (Kaufmann 2014). Patriotism as a set of allegiances, loyalties, the emotion of "national pride" and "a sense of shared national identity" (Nussbaum 1996) and emotional attachment for a country is orchestrated by state actors with the objective to maintain and legitimate social order, the frontier between "us" and "the other." Architects of patriotism model, mainly sovereign states, make extensive use of history to promote those historical narratives that embody the politically correct teleology of the state. It has been suggested by many scholars (Bassin 2012) that the historiographies of the new independent states, like Belarus, engaging in nation-building process of a new sovereign state continue to be essentially monolithic and monopolized by political power. In different contexts, but especially in transition contexts (from Soviet totalitarian regime to democracy under perestroika and shift to authoritarianism after perestroika), governments are too ready to use history education to promote a new sense of nationhood through a "ready-made" vision of history and national identity and frontiers between "us" and "the other" (Hajjat 2012). School history textbooks as instruments of ideological transmission and nation building are closely monitored by the state (Schissler 2005).

The idea of patriotism commonly refers to the discourse on links between members of the nation and a sense of a nation as a cohesive whole separated from "the other," "the foreigner," "the stranger" (Wodack 2004). Patriotism, sense of attachment to the motherland, which is constructed in interaction and relation with "others," requires mental (Erikson 1959) and physical borders (Hajjat 2012). Scholars who insist on the discursive mechanism of identity and patriotism building maintain that "border is an artefact of dominant discursive process that have led to the fencing off chunks of territory and people from one to another" (Foucher 2007). Notions or even organizations like the EU are defined as a "bounded communicative space" (Sierp 2014). Identity building is a "spacialization" and "territorialization" of allegiance matrix, and the management of the sense of belonging to a nation, its territory and identity, passes "upon its territorial management" (Rey and Saint-Julien 2005).

Emotional and psychological components in building links to a nation should also be highlighted. It is part of human behavior for individuals to aspire to a valorizing collective identity within a group, belonging to which confers on them certain characteristics favorized by the group in question (Reicher 2001). Thus, the affective component plays a very important role in the mobilization and appropriation of discourse on history and patriotism (Braud 1996). Emotions engendered by belonging to a group play a structural role in self-categorization and identification (Mackie 2009).

The Context of Belarusian Historiography

In Soviet times (from 1919 to 1991), the history of Belarus did not exist, either as an autonomous academic discipline or as a school subject. The first and only school textbook on the History of the Soviet Socialist Republic of Belarus (SSRB) was published in 1960 in Russian and went through eleven editions, remaining the only educational support on the subject until 1992. For every edition of this textbook, the number of printed books was 9000 copies (for a country with 9,000,000 citizens), which is an indication of the minor place accorded to the

History of Belarus as a school discipline during the Soviet period. From 1947 to 1991, the history of Belarus was incorporated into the curriculum of the history of the U.S.S.R., and only 27 h per year were devoted to it at the last year of the secondary school. For the Soviet historiography, the history of Belarus begins only in 1917. Belarus was able to start and consolidate its existence as a nation-state only within the framework afforded by the Byelorussian Soviet Socialist Republic (BSSR), a part of the USSR. Thus, Belarusian government is a Soviet creation, and the Belarusian people is fundamentally a Soviet people. The history of Belarus is accordingly the history of the BSSR.

Government policy on History Textbooks in the Belarusian Soviet Socialist Republic prescribed the denial of an independent Belarus and an independent Belarusian history (Abetsadarski 1968). The history of Belarus was merged into Soviet history. Identity politics transmitted through history textbooks aimed at the construction of a Soviet identity above all other identities. In Soviet period, patria-motherland was the URSS.

The most important historical event for patriotism and identity building for the Soviet period was the Second World War and the sacred victory over Nazism.

The following sentences quoted from the only history textbook on Belarus published during the Soviet period are an illustration of the extent to which Belarusian history was viewed as no more than a constituent part of Soviet history, inasmuch as a fundamental tenet of Soviet historiography was its articulation of the Second World War as the central event in the history of the USSR: "From the first days of the occupation, workers in Soviet Belarus began the People's War. Brigades of partisans were created everywhere. Their number increased daily. The organizer and leader of the partisan movement was the Communist Party" (Abetsadarski 1968). The semantic and stylistic construction of the text is revealing. Short sentences and a dogmatic tone meet the objectives of Soviet propaganda: to point out that the information provided by the textbooks is an ultimate and indisputable truth.

The Soviet patriotism and identity model was simple, binary: the "us"—Soviet people—and the "other"—Nazi enemy, and after the war, by extension the enemy was the Western world.

Textbooks on the history of Belarus became a propaganda tool underlining the superiority of the Soviet Communist model as against the Western capitalist model. History as an academic discipline was itself used as an important tool in the construction and legitimization of the

Soviet totalitarian state, claiming a specific place for it in world politics. The victory in the Second World War, called "the holy of holies" (Tumarkin 1995) was presented as a proof of the superiority of Soviet society over Western society.

PERESTROIKA AND THE NEW PATRIOTISM MODEL

In the post-Soviet bloc, the period known as "Perestroika (1985–1991)" was a crucial moment for the building of states and their national identities. New political parties appeared to challenge the political monopoly of the Communist party of the USSR, claiming the right of the Soviet republics to an independent history, historiography and an independent future. Since the break-up of the Soviet Union, the majority of post-Soviet countries have tended to articulate historical consciousness in opposition to Soviet and Russian interpretations of the past, seeking for European roots in their histories. For Belarusians, the USSR and Russia changed their category: from the "us" they become the "other" (Zaiko 1999).

In post-Soviet Belarus, political authority elected in 1994 started the search for the legitimacy through new national identity and patriotism building, as any new political authority regardless of the political regime.

Soviet history writing changed completely during perestroika in all Soviet Republics, where history was used as a legitimizing authority for profound social change, the creation of an independent state in 1990, the establishment of a new sociopolitical system and the shaping of a new national identity matrix (Zaprudnik 1993). Under perestroika, numerous publications appeared in the media relating to the link between education, history teaching, this national renaissance and new patriotic allegiance: "Education—the Only Way to a National Renaissance," "Give History Back to the People," "History Education as a Source of a National Identity" (Lindner 1999). The first school programs on the history of Belarus were inspired by the National Front program, as was the new Constitution of the independent Belarus, which claimed that "the Belarusian people has a long history which can be traced back many centuries" (http://www.pravo.by). The coat of arms and "nationalist" flag dating back to the era of the Grand Duchy of Lithuania, regarded by Belarusian nationalists as the "Golden age" of the Belarusian nation, were introduced after the proclamation of independence in 1991. New patriotism model appealed to new historical references like the Grand

Duchy of Lithuania, a state existed from the thirteenth to eighteenth centuries (Sahanovitch 2001).

Under perestroika, the communist period was frequently described in terms of invasion and occupation in historical work, but even in school textbooks (Sidartsou 1993). For the histories of the post-Soviet countries, Russia plays the role of "the other," the "convenient" enemy to which it is possible to attribute all errors and all failures. During perestroika in all the post-Soviet countries, all contacts with Russia and Russians began to be described in terms of disaster. Russians were qualified as invaders, and all territorial divisions, whether unions or annexation, are described in very negative terms. The positive elements provided by annexation to the Russian Empire or the Soviet Union (administrative modernization, access to the infrastructure of the economy of a great empire) were ignored.

The gradual gaining of autonomy and the institutionalization of the history of Belarus as an academic discipline and school subject are also linked to perestroika. Until 1992, the total number of hours devoted to history of Belarus in school curricula was 27; in 1992, this number was 152 (education. gouv.by).

The curriculum of the history of Belarus in a secondary school of 1991 emphasizes the fundamental changes in the teaching of history affecting content, methodology, structure and teaching. For the first time, issues of national consciousness were discussed in the school history curriculum, and new teaching principles such as historical humanism, democracy, and the rejection of dogmatism and stereotypes were introduced.

The books were supposed to educate patriots devoted to independent Belarus and awaken critical thinking skills, which was a novelty pedagogically speaking compared with Soviet-era thinking.

It was a new form of patriotism model, not dogmatic as under Soviet time, but pluralistic and critical. Pluralism as one of the most important requirements of a democratic society was an important element of perestroika politics of history textbooks.

Under perestroika, textbook authors and experts stressed the need to present multiple perspectives on historical events in the textbooks. Pluralistic tendencies are strongly reflected in the books of this period. The introduction that opens Ouladzimir Sidartsou and Vital 'Famine's textbook, published in 1993, clearly states the authors' pedagogical point of view (Sidartsou 1993). Through the manual V. Sidartsau aspires "to explain the contradictory process of the development of our society, help students to become aware of the history of Belarus as our history and as part of our everyday lives today" (Sidartsou 1993, 4). The authors invite young readers to study "the role of historical figures, to reflect on their actions" and "to put themselves in the place of historic characters to understand their motivations (Sidartsou 1993, 4)." The author draws attention to the diversity of opinion on the historical facts analyzed in the book: "Different points of view are represented in the textbook. You can accept them or defend your own opinion; however you should keep a respectful attitude towards those who have a different opinion from yours." "I recommend that students take an active part in debates on controversial issues in order to learn how to defend their points of view" (Sidartsou 1993, 5). The author encourages reflection on historical events and personalities, and their book does not contain indisputable dogmas.

The experts who gathered at the beginning of the 1990s at the National Center for Textbooks of the Ministry of Education debated on the modalities of revision of the totalitarian Soviet period, which was a major step toward democratization. The condemnation of the Soviet heritage and the search for European roots in Belarusian history was a very important trend in the writing of history textbooks.

During perestroika the attempt of transformation from totalitarian Soviet system into on open and democratic society, the Second World War was subject to thorough historical reinterpretation. The myth of the crucial role played by the Communist Party in the victory was debunked, as was the myth of the struggle of the whole people against the Nazis: The whole people did not fight on the side of the Red Army and the partisans (Weiner 2002). Historians revealed instances of collaboration and crimes committed by partisans. Soviet-era glorification of the Second World War was significantly toned down. Europe became the part of "us": Belarus aspired to identify with Europe and the USSR and Russia became the "other" (Zaprudnik 1993).

The particular attention paid to the Great Duchy of Lithuania, to which the Belarusian lands belonged between the twelfth and sixtieth centuries, was the result of a search for a valid historical alternative to the idea of the Belarusian nation as a constituent part of the Soviet totalitarian state advanced by Soviet-era historiography. History of Belarus is a history of incorporations into empires, divisions, annexations. It is not easy to find glorious elements, which explain why perestroika historiography mobilized the Great Duchy of Lithuania as an independent and glorious period.

In textbooks published in 1993, particular emphasis was placed on the Grand Duchy of Lithuania and on the wars between the Grand Duchy of Lithuania and Muscovy during thirteenth and fourteenth centuries as a historical proof of resistance to "eternal" Russian domination. Even the titles of the chapters underlined the link between Belarusian and European and world history: "Belarusian Culture in the Context of European Civilization," "The Great Patriotic War in the Context of the Second World War." The perestroika period used the same ideological weapons as the Soviet times propaganda: promoting positive identity matrix and glorious past. It is natural for individuals to want to join a group, which gives them a positive personal identity (Erikson 1959). The search for "the oldest and most glorious possible" history (Berger 1999) characterizes the majority patriotism models; the post-Soviet countries are not an exception. Perestroika offered an identity and patriotism model different from Soviet model. It was not more Soviet glorious references like the victory at the Second World War perestroika, but this model was very positive and glorious with other victories: victory over Muscovy during the Grand Duchy of Lithuania period.

Re-Sovietization of History and Identity Politics

The year 1994 witnessed a major shift in the liberalization of Belarusian society. The political forces that came to power in 1994 forged their victory by promising a people in disarray that they would restore the Soviet legacy, fraternal ties with Russia and the welfare state. The new government began to use methods inherited from Soviet leaders and differing from democratic methods. A referendum in May 1995 focused on changing state symbols, union with Russia and the status of the Russian language as the state language. After the 1995 referendum, nationalist symbols were again replaced by those of the Soviet era. The majority of the electorate voted for union with Russia and two state languages in Belarus: Russian and Belarusian. The referendum institutionalized a return to the Soviet era. This legalized Sovietization also affected history writing and teaching and official policy on Belarusian national identity. An edict of the President of Belarus Alexander Loukashenko of August 16, 1995, stated: "given the results of the referendum, it is necessary to replace the books published between 1992 and 1995 with new textbooks" (Loukashenko 2000). Concerned to defend the Soviet legacy, history textbooks seen by the president as having a nationalistic content were condemned to be replaced by books that better met the aspirations of the new political authorities, who took the Soviet heritage as the basis of their political legitimacy and patriotism matrix.

The intervention of the political authorities in textbook writing provoked heated debates in society. Discussions in the academic and general press reflected the negative attitude of teachers and the intelligentsia toward the hardening of control on and manipulation of school history teaching (Lindner 1999). The round table on history textbooks organized by the Belarusian historical review was a response to the decision to remove all textbooks published between 1992 and 1995. Authors and teachers strongly criticized state intervention in textbook rewriting. The author Mikhas' Bitch criticized the authoritarian ban on books edited in 1993: "The history curriculum was openly debated and discussed in 1991 and 1992. Where were the people who are now raising their voices to criticize our textbooks in 1992?" (Mikhas' Bitch, Archives of National Center for Textbooks of the Ministry of Education of Belarus).

Politics of History and Identity Under Political Censorship

In the mid-1990s, the creation of the State Commission for the Control of School Literature in the Field of the Humanities and Social Sciences, called into being by a presidential order of August 24, 1995, and answering directly to the Presidential Administration, marked a new stage in Belarusian politics of history textbooks (Lukashenko 2000). This structure responded to the aspiration of the Belarusian political authorities to bring the writing of school history under their control. Countless mechanisms introduced in the procedure of textbook publishing stifled any attempt to go against the official government conception of history. The purpose of the Commission is to monitor and directly control textbook writing. Thus, the Commission remains the ultimate judge of textbook manuscripts. Before being monitored by the Commission, however, a manuscript must pass many stages of correction and review.

At first, a manuscript is read by two experts at the Institute of Education of the Ministry of Education. The experts appointed by the Institute check the didactical and ideological quality of the work. If the manuscript corresponds to the pedagogical requirements of a textbook and is not openly opposed to official ideology, it obtains approval in the first instance. A manuscript can be subjected to number of criticisms, and the author is obliged to make corrections in response to the experts' objections. The secretariat of the Ministry can send the manuscript for "improvement" many times until it is accepted by the Commission. The next step is expert analysis and deliberation within the Section of History textbooks of the Ministry of Education. The Section verifies whether the work corresponds to the official curriculum, the didactical characteristics of the manuscript and the ideology expounded by the author in his book. The manuscript is submitted to new experts, and if there are points to rework, it is returned to the authors for corrections. The officials of the Ministry of education know which points to "polish" so that the manuscript can be analyzed first by the Presidium of the Academic Council of the Ministry of Education and then by the Commission. Points relating to political history, the Soviet period and the Second World War are considered to be sensitive. After the approval of the Section of the Ministry, the manuscript is submitted to the examination of the Presidium of the Academic Council of the Ministry of Education. Its members are appointed by the Ministry of Education, and it is chaired by the Minister of Education. Before deliberation in the Council, the manuscript is submitted to the experts of the Commission, and although it does not form part of official procedure, their opinion carries much weight during deliberations. It is the Academic Council which gives the greatest number of negative verdicts to manuscripts. This makes sense, because the next step is the Commission, which takes a final decision on manuscripts, so they must correspond to official ideology by the time they reach this stage. The Commission controls politically important school subjects such as world history, geography and the literature and history of Belarus. These are the most controversial and politicized academic disciplines, so the political authorities control how they are taught with particular vigilance. The file concerning each manuscript considered by the Commission includes nearly ten expert conclusions, the authors' responses to the corrections made on the basis of objections and the reports of all the meetings of all the bodies that have analyzed the manuscript. The Commission issues the final verdict. If the script gets the approval of the Commission, the Ministry sends the manuscript to the publisher (only state publishing houses can publish school textbooks) specifying the number of copies to be printed.

Social Consequences of Politics of History Textbooks in Belarus

The preeminence of Soviet historiography over other discourses in Belarus is an exception in the post-Soviet area. According to numerous research projects devoted to historical, identity and patriotism discourse and history textbooks in the post-Soviet countries, Belarus is the only country not to describe relations with Russia and the Soviet period in negative terms. Belarus is the only former Republic of the USSR which experienced a turning point in its historiography in the mid-1990s. If the historical narrative of Belarus at the time of perestroika was formed in opposition to Soviet and Russian imperial discourse, the mid-1990s marked a return to a Soviet interpretation of history.

Political control of the writing of school textbooks is reflected in mistakes, contradictions and omissions affecting the quality of the books. The rewriting of the school textbooks resulted in a contradictory amalgam between nationalist, Russian-orientated and Soviet-style references. Nationalist references have no open place in public discourse and are pushed to the margins of the system of political discourse and school education without, however, being completely eradicated. Indeed, the Soviet and nationalist conceptions of the historical development of the Belarusian people are inherently incompatible with one another.

Political control of the writing of school textbooks is reflected in mistakes, contradictions and omissions affecting the quality of the books. P. Loïka's textbook was considerably rewritten under political pressure. The editorial surface of the chapters devoted to the Russian–Belarusian war of the fourteenth–sixteenth centuries was reduced. The section titles were changed in order to "soften" its nationalist emphasis. The Battle of Orsha that pitted Russian and Belarusian troops against each other in the Grand Duchy of Lithuania (GDL) has already been mentioned as a major revelation of the historiography of perestroika and an important chapter of eight pages in textbooks of 1993 (Loïka 1993). However, in the 2002 edition, the same author has not been able to introduce a reference to this battle, which occupies an important position in Belarusian nationalist lore, in the body of the manual, although he still presents it briefly, as follows, in a chronological table at the end of the book:

> 1512–1522: War between G.D.L. and Muscovy. 1514, 8 September: the Battle of Orsha. The victory of the army of G.D.L. (Loïka 2005)

This shift is characteristic of the rewriting of school history: Nationalist references have no place in public discourse and are pushed to the margins of the system of political discourse and school education without, however, being completely erased.

The Soviet heritage is imposed by the political authorities as a dominant discourse. In textbooks on the Soviet period, the very term "totalitarian" is deleted and replaced by the euphemism "the Soviet administrative system" as a result of a direct Belarusian Presidential prohibition expressed during a meeting with textbook authors (Lukashenko 2000). Some authors even completely rehabilitate the Soviet period. For them, "the magnitude of J. Stalin" is indisputable, V. Lenin was a "political genius" and Soviet reprisals were necessary because they "allowed the U.S.S.R. to achieve staggering results" (Trechtchenok 2005). Another textbook author asserts that "the huge and unrealistic figures of the number of victims of political reprisals published during the last decade by nationalists is nothing but a myth, whose purpose is to discredit the socialist system" (Novik 2010). Other authors partially bow to political pressure. Thus, analyzing the 1917 revolution in the 1993 edition of their textbook, the authors O. Sidartsou and V. Famine use the term "the events of 1917," while in subsequent editions, we find the "October Revolution" formulation, which is a sort of compromise between the Soviet tradition, where this event was known as "the great October Socialist Revolution," and the nationalist tradition, for which they are "the events of October 1917."

The re-Sovietization of policy on history teaching can also be seen in a return to the sacralization of the Second World War as the fundamental event of Belarusian history. In 2004, when Belarus celebrated the sixty anniversary of victory in the Second World War, a special course on this event was introduced for students in the final year of high school and the first year of university. A new textbook was published as a didactical support for these courses. The title of the book is revealing, *The Great Patriotic War of the Belarusian people in the context of the Second World War*, which is an attempt to link Belarusian and world history. The content does not reflect the posted affiliation. The textbook presents a Soviet version of the war and barely evokes the crimes of Soviet leaders and the complex issue of collaboration, and reduces the role of the Allies in the victory to a minimum. The Molotov–Ribbentrop Pact and its secret protocol are mentioned, but without explanation: "On August 23, 1939, a German-Soviet agreement of non-aggression was signed (the Molotov–Ribbentrop Pact). At the same time a secret protocol was signed" (Kovalenia 2004). In the same textbook, a preface written by the Belarusian president (who has a degree in history) reads:

> Some pseudo-academics try to rewrite the history of the Great Patriotic War, diminishing the role of our grandfathers and rehabilitating traitors, collaborators, and slaves of the Nazis. Young people are the main target of these lies. I have confidence in your clear minds and the honesty that allow you to distinguish between truth and falsehood. The living memory of the past will help us to build the future. To know the history of our homeland is a sacred duty of every citizen. Patriotism is the foundation of the courage and heroism with which the Belarusian people has survived all its wars and defended its independence. (Kovalenia 2004, 35)

This quotation proves that the interpretation of the Second World War as a glorious and victorious event is a source of pride for the people of Belarus. No alternative vision is tolerated. The Holocaust issue is not totally absent from the textbooks, but its explanation is minimalized. The term Holocaust is used in the single textbook for the special course on the Great Patriotic War *The Great Patriotic War of the Belarusian people in the context of the Second World War* in one short sentence: "The Holocaust is the extermination of the Jewish population of Europe by the Nazis during the Second World War" (Kovalenia 2004). Even on the maps showing the sites of ghettos, extermination camps and killing sites in Belarus and in the Soviet Union, no spatial link is established with Europe or the Soviet Union. In the textbook for the special course on the War, in spite of the maps of Europe showing the sites of camps, the text does not explain the geopolitical dimensions of the Holocaust, but rather presents the event only insofar as it affected Belarus.

Moreover, while the textbooks edited under perestroika aimed to promote civic education, a pluralistic presentation of historical interpretation and critical thinking skills, current textbooks follow the educational traditions of Soviet totalitarianism. Students are not encouraged to think. The number of assignments and questions accompanying chapters is extremely small compared to the books of perestroika. Homework is often reduced to a mechanical committing to memory of "dogmatic truths." In a textbook edited in 2002 at the end of the chapter on the U.S.S.R. in the 1930s, we find the following question: "Why political reprisals became possible in the U.S.S.R.?" (Novik 2010). In order to be able to answer this question properly, students are in fact forced to make apologies for Soviet reprisals, as the author does in his text. The authoritarian turn that Belarus has taken since the mid-1990s explains the similarities between Soviet and current textbooks. Political logic that orchestrates the production of school literature has the same objective as during the Soviet period: to legitimize a political regime, where textbooks become tools of propaganda aimed at legitimizing an authoritarian regime claiming historical links with Russia and rejecting openness to global tendencies.

Belarus's Democracy Index rating continuously ranks as the lowest in Europe. The country is labeled as "Not Free" by Freedom House, "Repressed" in the Index of Economic Freedom, and is rated as by far the worst country for press freedom in Europe in the 2013–2014 Press Freedom Index published by Reporters Without Borders, where Belarus is ranked 157th out of an overall total of 180 nations. For these reasons, the country is referred to as the "Last Dictatorship in Europe." In this particular context, the education system plays a fundamental role in legitimizing the Belarusian regime.

It is interesting to recall the results of research into the assessment of the system of education that the sociology laboratory "Novak" conducted in March 2010. Positive assessment of the education system by 44.4% of the people interviewed was widely discussed by experts in the article "The Belarusian school makes robots" published on "www.naviny.by," a Belarusian Web site. A. Vardamatski, Director of the Laboratory of Sociology, "Novak," Y. Ramantchuk, president of the analytical center "Strategy," A. Kazuline, former Minister of Education, were deeply impressed by the difference between expert opinion and public opinion on the Belarusian education system. According to experts, the education system has achieved its goal that according to A. Kazuline is "to produce people who need nothing and are not interested in the sociopolitical processes in the country." In the opinion of Y. Ramantchuk, "Belarusians do not need education in society; there is no link between the level of education and the quality of life of a person." A. Vardamatski believes that "the current government does not require citizens capable of thinking." (www.naviny.by). This survey proves the idea of an imposed low level of education which corresponds to the identity and project power promoted by political authority and realized through its politics of history textbooks.

The current Belarusian political authorities aspire to disseminate a Soviet, Russian-orientated version of Belarusian national identity and patriotism model in the interests of justifying their own legitimacy, and they need an interpretation which can be accepted without discussion by the population. In this specific context, any interpretation of national identity and patriotism must be as simplistic and dogmatic as possible. The result of mixing Soviet and nationalist references in history textbooks is weak and contradictory books, unfit to be consistent and stable referents for the construction of national identity, for fostering a sense of belonging to a national community, and for justifying the place of a nation in the global system.

References

Abetsadarski, L. (1968). *The history of the Soviet socialist Republic of Belarus.* Minsk: Popular instruction.
Archives of National Center for Textbooks of the Ministry of Education of Belarus.
Bassin, M. (Ed.) (2012). *Soviet and Post-Soviet Identities.* Cambridge: University Press.
Berger, S. (1999). *Writing national histories. Western Europe since 1800.* London: Routledge.
Braud, P. (1996). *L'émotion en politique [Emotions in politics].* Paris: Presses de Sciences Po.
Cote, J., & Levine, C. (2002). *Identity formation, agency, and culture: A social psychological synthesis.* NY: Erlbaum Associates.
Dubar, C. (2000). *La crise des identités [Crisis of identities].* Paris: PUF.
Erikson, E. (1950). *Childhood and society.* Victoria: Penguin Books.
Erikson, E. (1959). *Identity and lifecycle.* New York: International Universities Press.
Foucher, M. (2007). *L'obsession des frontières [Obsession of frontiers].* Paris: Perrin.
Gellner, E. (1983). *Nation and nationalisme.* New York: Cornell University Press.
Hajjat, A. (2012). *Les frontières de l'identité nationale [Frontiers of national identity].* Paris: La Découverte.
Kaufmann, J.C. (2014). *Identités, la bombe à retardement [Identities, the time bomb].* Paris: Textuel.
Kovalenia, A. (2004). *The great patriotic war of the soviet people (in the context of the Second World War), school textbook.* Minsk: State University.
Lindner, R. (1999). *Historiker und Herrschaft [Historians and power].* München: R. Oldenbourg Verlag.
Loukashenko, A. (2000). *The Problems of textbooks. Teachers' journal,* № 55, April.

Loukashenko, A. (2003). *The historical choice of Belarus*. Minsk: State University Press.
Loïka, P. (1993). *History textbook Belarus for the 7th year*. Minsk: Popular instruction.
Loïka, P. (2005). *History textbook Belarus for the 7th year*. Minsk: Popular instruction.
Mackie, D. M. (2009). Intergroup emotion theory. In T. D. Nelson (Ed.) *Handbook of prejudice, stereotyping, and discrimination* (pp. 285–308). New York: Psychology Press.
Michaud, G. (1978). *Identités collectives et relations inter-culturelles [Collective identities and intercultural relations]*. Bruxelles: Éd. Complexe.
Noizet, G., & Caverni, J.-P. (1978). *Psychologie de l'évaluation scolaire [Psychology of school evaluation]*. Paris: P.U.F.
Novik, Y. (2010). *Textbook history of Belarus for the 11th year*. Minsk: Popular Instruction.
Nussbaum, M. (1996). *For love of country?*. Boston: Beacon Press books.
Reicher, S. (2001). *Self and nation*. London: Sage.
Rey, V., & Saint-Julien Th. (dir.) (2005). *Territoires d'Europe. La différence en partage [Territories of Europe. Shared difference]*. Lyon: ENS Éditions.
Sahanovitch, H. (2001). *Ten years of Belarusian historiography (1991–2000). Critical review of Belarusian history*, vol. 8.
Schissler, H. (dir.). (2005). *The nation, Europe, and the world: textbooks and curricula in transition*. New York: Berghahn Books.
Sidartsou, O. (1993). *Textbook history of Belarus for the 9th year*. Minsk: Popular Instruction.
Sierp, A. (2014). *History, memory, and Trans-European identity*. London: Routledge.
Trechtchenok, Y. (2005). *Gistoryia Belarusi [The history of Belarus]*. Mogilev: University of Mogilev Press.
Tumarkin, N. (1995). *The living and the dead: The rise and fall of the cult of World War II in Russia*. New York: Basic Boks.
Weber, M. (1995). *Économie et société: tome 2 [Economy and society: vol. 2]*. Paris: Plon.
Weiner, A. (2002). *Making sense of war: The second World War and the fate of the Bolshevik revolution*. Princeton: Princeton University Press.
Wodack, R. (ed.) (2004). *The discursive construction of national identity*. Edinburgh : University Press.
Zaiko, L. (1999). *Natsionalnye interesy Belarusi [National interests of Belarus]*. Minsk: Skakoun.
Zaprudnik, J. (1993). *Belarus. At crossroads in history*. Boulder: Westview Press.

Author Biography

Anna Zadora is an Associate Professor and Researcher at University of Strasbourg and a member and an expert of numerous international research networks (Georg Eckert Institute, European Consortium for Political Research, European Science Foundation). Anna Zadora's research is focused on identity; nationalism; memorial, social and political transformation of the post-Soviet space; historical consciousness; educational systems; history; and identity teaching. She published a book on education identity and textbooks in Belarus, *Entre Europe et Russie, la Biélorussie des manuels scolaires*, L'Harmattan, 2016, and papers in Education and Society, *Journal of War and Culture Studies, Revue d'Etudes Comparatives Est-Ouest, L'homme et la société, Carrefours de l'éducation.*

Open Access This chapter is licensed under the terms of the Creative Commons Attribution 4.0 International License (http://creativecommons.org/licenses/by/4.0/), which permits use, sharing, adaptation, distribution and reproduction in any medium or format, as long as you give appropriate credit to the original author(s) and the source, provide a link to the Creative Commons license and indicate if changes were made.

The images or other third party material in this chapter are included in the chapter's Creative Commons license, unless indicated otherwise in a credit line to the material. If material is not included in the chapter's Creative Commons license and your intended use is not permitted by statutory regulation or exceeds the permitted use, you will need to obtain permission directly from the copyright holder.

PART IV

Pedagogical Approaches to History Teaching and Reconciliation

The Official, The Empathetic and The Critical: Three Approaches to History Teaching and Reconciliation in Israel

Tsafrir Goldberg

NARRATIVES, CURRICULUM AND RECONCILIATION

Studies of social representations and intergroup conflict often stress the role of collective narratives and historical accounts in prolonging and legitimizing conflict. Collective narratives stress in-group victimization and righteousness, vilifying the adversary (Hilton and Liu 2008; Liu et al. 2014). Collective historical charters and symbols are used in mass performative occasions such as parades in ways that antagonize out-groups and enhance group cohesion (Liu et al. 2014). Adversaries de-legitimize out-group narratives and indulge in self-legitimizing collective narrative that justify their side's engagement in conflict and limit the chance of reconciliation (Bar-Tal and Salomon 2006; Bar-Tal and Halperin 2011). Studies of curricular materials—such as history textbooks—point to biased and in-group serving representation of the conflict, out-group members and adversaries (Firer et al. 2004; Kiezel 2008; Podeh 1948).

T. Goldberg (✉)
University of Haifa, Haifa, Israel
e-mail: tgoldberg@edu.haifa.ac.il

In spite of the importance attributed to historical narratives and the acknowledgment of institutionalized history teaching, few studies actually explored the effects of teaching and curricula on learners' intergroup attitudes in conflict-ridden societies. A notable exception is Barton and McCully's (2010) work on the effects of a dual-perspective critical inquiry history curriculum on Protestant and Catholic Northern Irish youth. It appears this curriculum promoted students complex understanding of the other's perspective through an internally persuasive dialogue. Perhaps naturally, while they showed understanding to both sides, learners used curricular contents mainly to enhance and legitimize their in-group standpoint.

History Teaching and Intergroup Attitudes in the Israeli Context

In the Israeli context, few studies were conducted about the effects of history teaching on intergroup relations. Of these, the majority documented the (very rarely implemented) empathetic Dual-Narrative suggested by Bar-On and Adwan (2006). Eid (2010) showed Israeli–Arab students found the Jewish narrative emotionally unacceptable, while Eini ElHadaf (2011) reported that Israeli–Jewish learners appreciated the opportunity to engage with the Palestinian perspective, but they also tended to dismiss it as "emotional and unobjective." On a parallel trajectory, Cohen (2013) claimed that Jewish adolescents studying about the holocaust increased their awareness of minority rights. Arab students and teachers who studied about the holocaust demonstrated increased empathy toward Jews (Abu-Ria 2014; Shoham et al. 2003). Findings, which seem to contradict impressions that holocaust education (especially in its informal activities), promoted xenophobic attitudes (Feldman 2002).

As for other teaching approaches, Kolikant and Pollack (2009, 2015) showed that critical work with conflicting historical sources enabled productive intergroup encounter during online co-construction of historical accounts. Jewish participants managed to contain the threat posed through their Arab participants' assertions by adopting an impartial "academic" role afforded by the critical inquiry approach. With reference to the conventional teaching approach, Peled-Elhanan (2012) made the claim that Israeli-authorized textbooks desensitize young Jewish–Israelis to Palestinian suffering. Analyzing the one-sided, neutralized representation of Israel's role in the conflict, she assumes it leads Jewish–Israeli soldiers to uncompassionate behavior, though she does not supply empirical evidence for the claim. None of the studies compared the effects of competing teaching approaches on intergroup attitudes and interaction in a systematic empirical way. The study described below sought to fill this lacuna. I will present findings and conclusions from the various publications which emanated from it (Goldberg 2014a, b; Goldberg and Gerwin 2013; Goldberg and Ron 2014).

The Curricular Pendulum and Competing Teaching Approaches

During the first decade of the new millennium (2000–2010), history curriculum in Israel has shown contrasting features of innovation and regression, leading to the production of varied and competing curricular materials about the Israeli–Palestinian conflict (Goldberg and Gerwin 2013; Goldberg and Ron 2014). On the one hand, this is the period in which Sami Adwan and Dan Bar-On, along with a group of Jewish–Israeli and Palestinian teachers, formulated a dual-narrative textbook (Adwan and Bar-On 2004). Teaching with this curriculum was based on mutual acknowledgment and affirmation, nonjudgmental listening and perspective-taking (Bar-On and Adwan 2006). In the same decade, the higher-order thinking reform in Israeli education called for promotion of critical thinking and disciplinary practices (Zohar 2009). In history subject, a new curriculum appeared, calling for engagement in historiographical controversies (Israeli Ministry of Education 2008a). Curriculum introduced new and sensitive topics such as the debate on the responsibility for the Palestinian refugee problem (Domke et al. 2009; Israeli Ministry of Education 2008b; Stern et al. 2007).

On the other hand, these innovations elicited strong reactions and a conservative backlash. A new education minister attempted to ban the teaching of the Palestinian perspective in Israeli schools (Kashti 2009, 2010). The history subject superintendent issued guidelines to present a "clear explanation of the Palestinian exodus" stressing "Palestinian and Arab leaders' responsibility." While noting the existence of debate on the causes and responsibility for the refugee question, the superintendent's site offered a set of sources stressing Israeli righteousness as a basis for teaching the historical controversy on the topic (Yaron 2009, 2010). Officials and conservative politicians issued vehement publicized denunciations of multiple perspective teaching. However, it appears that quite a few Jewish–Israeli teachers still insist on teaching the Palestinian narrative along the Israeli one (Blumenfeld 2015; Goldberg, submitted). Their commitment to helping their students forms an informed and complex understanding of the conflict in the face of students and officials' hostility situating such teachers as "risk takers" (Kitson and McCully 2005).

These vacillations created in fact at least three competing (though not simultaneous or equally supported by authorities) curricular approaches for teaching the history of the Israeli–Palestinian conflict: the later official approach, which stressed a single clear narrative, with a conventional textbook-oriented teaching, and a stress on in-group (Israeli) righteousness; the empathetic dual-narrative approach, which stressed perspective-taking and nonjudgmental acknowledgment of both sides' narratives; and the educational reform for higher-order thinking approach, which stressed critical disciplinary thinking and engagement in historical controversy evaluating and synthesizing conflicting historical accounts of both sides.

The above curricula demonstrate different features of engagement with the past, which should lead to different effects according to research on collective narratives and intergroup conflict. The official single narrative appears to replicate tendencies for self-justifying and exonerating cognitions and for intergroup attribution bias, which protract and normalize conflict (Bar-Tal and Halperin 2011; Doosje and Branscombe 2003; Roccas and Berlin 2015). The empathetic dual-narrative approach creates conditions for mutual affirmation and for intergroup empathy, reducing competitive victimhood and rejection of threatening out-group perspectives and promote reconciliatory attitudes (Čehajić-Clancy et al. 2011; Vollhardt 2013). The critical disciplinary thinking approach is assumed to curb bias and exonerating cognitions (Roccas et al. 2006), help learners take a critical stance to self-legitimizing narratives, and promote ability to contain complexity and disagreement (McCully 2011).

Comparing the Effects of Competing Curricula of Conflict

This variety of teaching approaches offered an opportunity for tracking the effects of teaching the history of intergroup conflict in a comparative empirical method. Using the competing curricula, three parallel teaching units were created, focusing on the Jewish–Arab war of 1948 and the birth of the Palestinian refugee problem ("Independence War" in Israeli terminology and the "Naqba" [catastrophe] in Palestinian terms). Hundred and seven Jewish and 82 Arab–Israeli high school students (aged 16–18) were randomly allocated to study the topic using one of the three teaching units (genders, ethnicities and political affiliations[1] distributed equally between conditions). Learning in all three approaches lasted about 45 min, consisting of a preparatory presentation, reading aloud of text and individual assignments. Participants studied the unit in their hometowns, guided by a research assistant who was a native speaker of their mother tongue and all materials were adapted to learners' native language. Two weeks prior to and immediately after this learning intervention, participants wrote short compositions, in response to questions about the causes of the war, of the ensuing Palestinian exodus and about responsibility for the Palestinian refugee problem. The narrative participants wrote allowed us to track their preconceptions and changes in the perceived responsibility of their in-group for the harmful outcomes.[2] Along with the compositions, learners filled a mode of social identification questionnaire (Roccas and Berlin 2015), which taps individuals' level of chauvinistic glorification and patriotic attachment to their nation.[3] Social identification is assumed to impact acceptance of collective responsibility. Conservative policy makers also claimed that encounter with out-group narratives would undermine national identification. Learners also filled questionnaires about intergroup attitudes such as interest in the other's perspective of the conflict (Bar-Tal and Halperin 2011)[4] and defense of in-group narratives (Klar and Baram 2016).[5] For detailed description of procedure, materials and measures, see Goldberg and Ron (2014) and Goldberg (2014a, b).

We shall now outline the various effects that history teaching approaches had on intergroup attitudes, perceptions of the conflict (mainly in-group responsibility for conflict-related harm) and intergroup interaction.

Rejection, Interest and Responsibility: Effects of History Teaching on Intergroup Attitudes

Official Rejection and Empathetic Interest: Effects on Interest in the Other's Perspective

History teaching approach had a significant impact on learners' interest in the other side's perspective (See Table 1). As Goldberg (2014b, p. 459) shows, repeated-measures ANOVA revealed an interaction effect of time and condition ($F(2.163) = 6.33$, $p = 0.02$, $\eta^2 = 0.05$). In the conventional single-narrative teaching approach, learners' interest in

Table 1 Means and standard deviations for defense of in-group narrative (DIN), interest in the other's perspective (IO) perceived in-group responsibility (IR), glorification (GLO) and attachment (ATT) by condition and national group

Condition	National group	DIN pre	DIN post	IO pre	IO post	IR pre	IR post	GLO pre	GLO post	ATT pre	ATT post
Conventional authoritative	Jewish	3.50 (1.14)	3.50 (1.14)	3.20 (1.20)	3.21 (1.28)	2.47 (2.25)	2.20 (2.14)	3.24 (0.85)	3.20 (0.88)	4.19 (0.71)	4.19 (0.82)
	Arab	4.01 (0.61)	4.04 (0.53)	3.88[a] (0.82)	3.57[b] (0.96)	0.93 (1.88)	1.09 (1.77)	3.68 (0.58)	3.62 (0.63)	4.41 (0.56)	4.53 (0.49)
Empathetic narrative	Jewish	3.49 (0.77)	3.42 (0.75)	3.42 (0.75)	3.45 (1.02)	3.22 (2.09)	2.43 (2.10)	3.12 (0.81)	3.11 (0.71)	4.18 (0.73)	4.17 (0.71)
	Arab	3.80 (0.64)	3.89 (0.65)	3.76[a] (1.01)	4.20[b] (0.75)	0.66 (1.33)	1.46 (1.95)	3.22 (0.55)	3.32 (0.553)	4.19 (0.78)	4.45 (0.61)
Critical disciplinary	Jewish	3.54 (0.87)	3.48 (0.82)	3.54 (1.15)	3.58 (1.27)	1.66 (2.25)	2.24 (2.00)	3.12 (0.71)	3.15 (0.93)	4.11 (0.78)	4.14 (0.83)
	Arab	4.03 (0.43)	4.16 (0.72)	4.00 (0.70)	4.05 (0.77)	0.79 (1.61)	0.31 (1.00)	3.61 (0.49)	3.69 (0.76)	4.46 (0.71)	4.57 (0.55)

Source Goldberg (2014a), p. 460
Note Standard deviations appear in parentheses below means
[a, b] Letters in superscript indicate significant difference at the level of $p < 0.05$

the other's perspective decreased, while in the empathetic dual-narrative condition it increased. In the critical condition, interest in the other's perspective remained comparatively stable. An interaction effect was also found for time, condition and national group ($F(2.163) = 4.79$, $p = 0.03$, $\eta^2 = 0.04$). It showed that the effect of approach on interest in the other's perspective was more pronounced among Arab participants. This may be due to the fact their perspective was not represented in the conventional single-narrative approach, which was based on Israeli official narrative (Goldberg 2014b, p. 460).

These results show that history teaching approach can increase (or decrease) the motivation to take out-group perspectives, an aspect of intergroup empathy be predictive of conflict resolution (Gehlbach 2004). Empathetic engagement with both in-group and out-group narratives had significant positive effect on minority members, perhaps due to their stronger need for acknowledgment and affirmation (Shnabel et al. 2009). Minority members studying the conventional single (majority) narrative experienced a pronounced decline in interest in the majority perspective, apparently in defensive reaction to the silencing of their voice (Yonah 2008).

Repeated-measures ANOVAs revealed no significant interaction effects of time and condition (or time, condition and national group) on modes of social identification and defense of in-group narratives (Fs$(2.173) = 0.08-0.65$, p's > 0.15). None of the teaching approaches caused a significant change in learners' glorification and attachment modes of social identification or their defense of in-group narratives. Nor did the effects of teaching approaches differ significantly. Thus, we can see that, regardless of teaching method, studying the other's perspective on a major historical issue in the conflict did not undermine individuals' identification with their group (whether in the form of patriotic attachment or chauvinistic glorification). It also showed that general commitment to in-group narrative did not falter due to encounter with out-group narrative.

Accepting Responsibility and Curbing Bias? History Teaching Effects on Perception of In-Group Responsibility

Perceived in-group responsibility (and the frequently accompanying collective guilt) is associated with reconciliatory intergroup attitudes. While the conventional single-narrative approach had no effect on learners' perception of in-group responsibility, the other two alternative history teaching approaches had contradictory effects on Arab and Jewish learners. In the empathetic dual-narrative approach, perceived in-group responsibility decreased among Jewish and increased among Arab participants. In the critical condition, perceived in-group responsibility increased among Jewish participants, a pronounced difference in direction and degree from the change occurring in the empathetic dual-narrative condition. We should note that change within each condition was not significant (Goldberg 2014b). The effect on Arab participants may show the power of affirmation in answering the needs of a weaker party in a conflict, as proposed above (Shnabel et al. 2009). However, the inverse effect on Jewish participants is yet to be explained. Nonjudgmental, mutually affirmative exposure to the Palestinian narrative, which stressed Jewish responsibility, should lead Jewish learners to accept, rather than reject, responsibility as it did with their Arab peers.

The comparatively increased acceptance of responsibility by majority members in the critical disciplinary approach contradicts normal assumptions about "confirmation bias," which should have led participants to reject the information. However, results align with Roccas et al. (2006) and McCully's (2011) assumptions. It also hints that "impartial" academic practice, as a path for intergroup dialogue, is more accessible to majority members. A finding parallels to Kolikant and Pollack's (Kolikant and Pollack 2009) work on Jewish and Arab learners' online dialogue.

What were the factors that facilitated or impeded acceptance of in-group responsibility. A bivariate correlation was computed with all

Table 2 Bivariate correlations between liberal political affiliation, initial interest in other and responsibility following learning

		Responsibility following learning	*Responsibility change*
Conventional authoritative	Political affiliation	0.48**	0.20
	Interest in other	0.25	0.29*
Empathetic narrative	Political affiliation	0.15	0.12
	Interest in other	0.44**	0.41**
Critical disciplinary	Political affiliation	0.09	−0.04
	Interest in other	0.17	−0.08

*Significant at the 0.05 level
**Significant at the 0.01 level

relevant factors, and two factors were found to have a significant correlation with acceptance of responsibility (See Table 2). Learners' interest in the other side's perspective was associated with their perception of in-group responsibility. Teaching approach moderated this relation, which was found to be strongest in the empathetic dual-narrative approach and negligible in the critical disciplinary approach (Goldberg 2014a). This may be related to the stress of the empathetic dual-narrative approach on taking the other's perspective. An undertaking assumed to be highly dependent on individuals' interest in the other's perspective.

Teaching approach also moderated the impact of political affiliation on responsibility. In general, political partisanship and polarization cause selective adoption of information and entrenchment, thwarting the effect of engagement with new information or with challenging perspectives (Bar-Tal and Halperin 2011; Bennett and Iyengar 2008). However, looking at the effect of political affiliation on in-group responsibility within each teaching approach, we find wide variations. Following the learning intervention, a more liberal political affiliation was associated with higher perceived in-group responsibility only in the conventional and empathetic conditions ($r = 0.60$, $p < 0.001$, $r = 0.31$, $p < 0.05$, respectively), while in the critical condition the relation was nonsignificant ($r = 0.10$, $p = 0.48$). To ascertain moderation effect, a structural equation modeling AMOS 21 software was used to compare a model, in which the association of political affiliation with perceived responsibility differed across conditions, to a model in which a cross-condition equality constraint was imposed over the regression weights (Kline 2011, p. 286; Rigdon 1998). Bootstrapping was performed over the model using 1000 iterations. The first model showed good fit indices (NFI = 0.98, CFI = 0.99, RMSEA = 0.03), while an alternative model in which critical disciplinary and conventional single-narrative conditions were constrained to be equal gave a significantly lower fit (NFI = 0.77, CFI = 0.72, RMSEA = 0.17; ΔNFI = 0.23, $\chi^2 = 6.91$, $p < 0.01$).

In the conventional teaching approach the effect of political affiliation on acceptance of responsibility increased following learning, while in the critical disciplinary condition it decreased (prior to the learning intervention the relation of political affiliation to responsibility in the conventional condition was $r = 0.21$, $p = 0.14$; while in the critical condition $r = 0.28$, $p = 0.04$). We may infer that conventional teaching enhances the political bias while the critical approach curbs it.

As we have shown, history teaching approach affected (and moderated the associations of) interest in the other side's perspective and perceived in-group responsibility, both of which are assumed to promote reconciliatory attitudes. Reconciliatory attitudes should influence intergroup interactions. Consequently, we found teaching approach has indeed affected actual intergroup interaction as represented by Jewish and Arab learners' deliberation of the conflict's history and resolution.

How We Learn and How We Talk: Effects on Intergroup Interaction

Following the first, individual learning study, participants were invited to participate in a follow-up study about the same topic, involving intergroup encounter and dialogue. Some 130 of the participants of the individual learning study proceeded to engage in dyadic intergroup discussion about the Jewish–Arab conflict. Participants were matched by teaching approach, supplied with the materials they studied in the individual learning study and instructed to discuss and reach joint decisions as to the responsibility and solution for the Palestinian refugee problem. Decisions, or points of disagreement in cases of impasse, were to be recorded in writing, to promote commitment to the task and approximate a negotiation situation. Discussions were conducted in Hebrew (a language both groups speak and understand but Jews speak considerably more fluently) facilitated and recorded by participants, transcribed and analyzed. For a detailed description of procedure, materials and measures, see Goldberg and Ron (2014) and Goldberg (2014a).

Transcripts were analyzed to track intergroup equality of status or dominance in discussion, a precondition of intergroup encounter success (Pettigrew 1998) and the general atmosphere of discussion in terms of opposition and collaboration, as a measure of intergroup behavior, rather than simply intergroup attitudes (Pettigrew 2008).

Dominance was analyzed along the lines adopted by Maoz (2001). We analyzed dominance in the use of time and in the control of discussion. For dominance over time, we computed for Jewish and Arab participants in each pair the percentage of their words out of the total number of words uttered in discussion. For control of discussion, we coded all instances in which a participant gave instructions, changed the topic, initiated procedures or asked intrusive questions. Discussion style or atmosphere was analyzed using a shortened version of Bales' (1976) Interaction Process Analysis to assess discussion style. We coded each discussant's utterance in relation to the other discussant's previous utterance as Rejection, Opposition, Compliance or Elaborative agreement. Discussion outcome was assessed on the basis of discussants agreement (or impasse) on a joint answer as to each of the two questions they discussed.

An MANOVA performed over domination of discussion time and control of discussion with teaching approach as between-subjects factor revealed a small multivariate effect for teaching approach ($F(6) = 2.48$, $p = 0.028$, $\eta^2 = 0.12$) (Goldberg and Ron 2014, p. 14). As Table 3 shows, discussions carried out among participants who studied in the empathetic dual-narrative condition featured a significantly lower Jewish dominance of discussion time than a control and the conventional-authoritative conditions. The critical disciplinary condition featured a significantly lower Jewish dominating behavior in discussion than the control and the conventional-authoritative conditions (Goldberg and Ron 2014). In both cases, it appears the exposure to both sides' perspectives promoted a more egalitarian discussion atmosphere. A condition considered essential for successful intergroup encounter (Pettigrew 1998).

This atmosphere apparently led to more collaborative deliberation of the conflict, both in terms of process and in terms of outcome. The proportion of elaborative (in contrast to oppositional) utterances was higher among groups of learners who studied in the two multi-perspective teaching approaches (see Table 4). Collaborative discussion atmosphere, as indicated by the proportion of agreement to opposition utterances, predicted the frequency of achieving a joint decision on historical responsibility (Estimate(B) = 3.22, β(S.E.) = 1.17 (0.42), Wald = 7.76, $p = 0.005$). Consequently, critical disciplinary teaching had a significant positive effect on the frequency of joint decisions on historical responsibility. The conventional single-narrative teaching approach had a significantly negative effect on the frequency of finding joint solutions to refugee problem as compared to the critical disciplinary approach and to a control group (Goldberg and Ron 2014; Goldberg in press).

Perceived in-group responsibility (which was affected, as mentioned above, by teaching approach) also promoted more collaborative deliberation atmosphere. Having calculated each discussants proportion of agreement and opposition utterances, we could check the relation of a discussants perceived in-group responsibility for the harsh outcomes of the conflict with the acknowledgment of such responsibility in discussion

Table 3 Mean Jewish–Arab difference scores for the dominance of discussion time and control of discussion by condition

Condition	Jewish–Arab words difference (%)		Jewish–Arab controlling instances difference	
	Mean	SD	Mean	SD
Control	34.1	28.0	9.7	12.7
Conventional authoritative	28.3	28.3	6.4	9.0
Empathetic narrative	8.8	29.8	3.0	8.6
Critical disciplinary	22.4	27.2	0.03	5.2

Source Goldberg and Ron (2014, p. 14)

Table 4 Mean percentage of agreement and opposition utterances by condition and frequency of agreement on solution for the refugee problem, by condition

Condition	%Opposition		%Elaborative agreement		Frequency of agreement on solution for the refugee problem
	M	SD	M	SD	
Conventional authoritative	38.90	22.10	20.05	16.63	38.5% (5)
Empathetic narrative	28.68	21.71	27.50	13.13	69.2% (9)
Critical disciplinary	**18.32**	**9.85**	**36.39**	**20.29**	**86.7% (13)**

Adapted from Goldberg and Ron (2014, p. 14), Goldberg (2016)

and with out-group peer opposition and agreement in discussion (see Table 5 for means and bivariate correlations). Jewish participants' acknowledgement of in-group responsibility was inversely correlated with Arab peers' opposition ($r = -0.35$, $p < 0.01$).

Jewish participants' perceived responsibility was associated with more frequent agreement utterances, and acknowledgment of responsibility among Jewish discussants, which led in turn to more collaborative reactions from Arab participants (see Fig. 1). The relation was not symmetrical (Arab participants did not increase in-group responsibility due to encounter with historical perspectives, nor did they impact Jewish participants collaboration). This actor–partner interaction aligns with the assumptions as to the effect of the stronger party's acknowledgment of

Table 5 Descriptive statistics and bivariate correlations of IGR and proportion of agreement, rejection, opposition and compliance utterances (% of total utterances), by ethnic group

	M	SD	Jewish IGR	Arab IGR	Jewish expressed IGR	Arab expressed IGR	Jewish agree	Arab agree	Jewish reject	Arab reject	Jewish oppose	Arab oppose	Jewish comply
Jewish perceived responsibility	2.38	1.99											
Arab perceived responsibility	1.08	1.75	0.04										
Jewish acknowledged responsibility	2.97	1.98	0.36**	0.15									
Arab acknowledged responsibility	0.82	1.61	0.28	0.32*	0.04								
Jewish agree	29.38	22.48	0.31*	−0.06	0.21	−0.01							
Arab agree	25.08	23.44	0.42**	−0.04	0.23	0.28*	0.29*						
Jewish reject	19.16	24.54	−0.38**	−0.19	−0.07	−0.05	−0.44**	−0.26					
Arab reject	18.18	21.05	−0.30*	−0.25	−0.05	−0.19	−0.36**	−0.28*	0.79**				
Jewish oppose	29.04	25.56	−0.04	0.31*	−0.05	−0.03	−0.45**	−0.14	−0.36**	−0.24			
Arab oppose	31.13	27.64	−0.26	0.19	**−0.35****	0.10	−0.08	−0.51**	−0.16	−0.26	0.33*		

(continued)

Table 5 (continued)

	M	SD	Jewish IGR	Arab IGR	Jewish expressed IGR	Arab expressed IGR	Jewish agree	Arab agree	Jewish reject	Arab reject	Jewish oppose	Arab oppose	Jewish comply
Jewish comply	25.75	22.37	0.10	−0.11	0.11	−0.17	−0.02	0.18	−0.23	−0.22	−0.37**	−0.10	
Arab comply	23.86	17.34	0.16	0.05	0.12	−0.25	0.12	−0.15	−0.26	−0.32*	−0.04	−0.45**	0.16

*Correlation is significant at the 0.05 level (two-tailed)
**Correlation is significant at the 0.01 level (two-tailed)

Arab participant

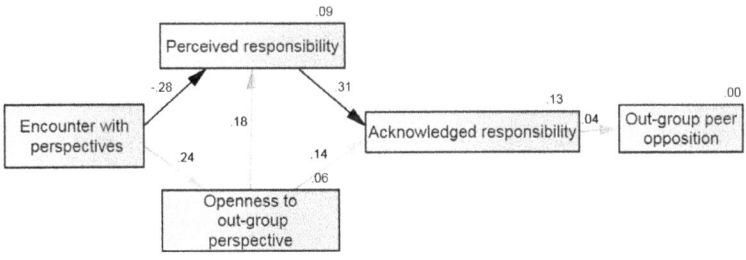

Jewish participant

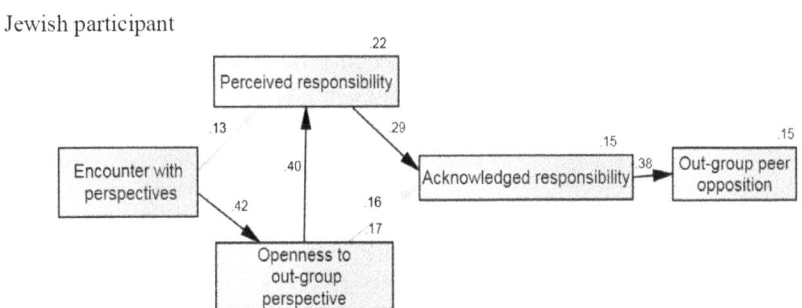

Fig. 1 Path diagram for the effects of teaching approach on responsibility and interest in out-group perspective on acknowledgement of responsibility and out-group partner reaction

responsibility on weaker party's reconciliatory attitudes (Shnabel et al. 2009).

Discussion

We now attempt to sum up the various findings as to the effects of history teaching approaches on intergroup attitude, perception of in-group responsibility and actual intergroup interaction. Conventional single-narrative teaching reduced interest in the other's perspective, while empathetic dual-narrative teaching increased it, especially among Arab learners. Teaching approaches also moderated the effect of interest in the other's perspective and political affiliation on perceived in-group responsibility. Critical disciplinary teaching curbed these biasing influences, while conventional single narrative, for example, enhanced political affiliation's hold on acceptance of responsibility. We should note teaching approaches did not undermine or even affect learners' social identification or frequency of acceptance of threatening out-group perspectives.

Consequently, conventional teaching also had significant negative effect on intergroup deliberation of the conflict and its history, in terms of egalitarian discourse, collaborative atmosphere and joint decision making. Teaching approaches also moderated the effects of individual attitudes on intergroup discussion. The (negative) effect of in-group glorification and defense of in-group narratives on intergroup interaction were markedly stronger in the conventional single-narrative teaching.

These findings align to a large degree with Liu et al.'s (2014a, b) and Barton and McCullys (2010) claims as to the effects of exclusive historical narratives on intergroup attitudes and relations. It appears that conventional history teaching curriculum's representation of the conflict through a single narrative, even when it contains some self-critical information, might be detrimental to intergroup relations. The way learners engage with the information is apparently just as important as the information itself. Such findings align with social psychological research on the effects of critical thinking prompts and affirmation (Čehajić-Clancy et al. 2011; Roccas et al. 2006; Vollhardt 2013). In this respect, both the critical and the empathetic teaching methods harbor greater promise for improving intergroup relations if used systematically. It is therefore quite alarming that both Israeli and Palestinian sides attempt to discourage such teaching methods (Goldberg and Gerwin 2013; Rohde 2014).

However, as, at least on the Israeli side, "risk takers" go on teaching both sides' perspectives (Goldberg, submitted) whether empathetically or critically, it is worth reflecting on their complex effects. The findings on the positive effects of empathetic dual-narrative teaching on Israeli–Arab learners' perspective-taking motivation are reassuring and stand in contrast to former findings (Eid 2010; Rohde 2013). Arab learners may have perceived the teaching of both narrative as Jewish acknowledgment of the Palestinian narrative and the Israeli responsibility it stresses. An acknowledgment assumed to answer the unique needs of the weaker party in asymmetric power relations (Shnabel et al. 2009). Jewish participants' tendency to reduce perceived in-group responsibility may be a reaction to the fact the Palestinian narrative contained no expressions of empathy with Jewish suffering or humanizing views of Jews, assumed necessary by Schnabel et al.'s needs based on model of reconciliation. The empathetic approach also curbed the negative effects of Jewish participants' glorification mode of social identification and defense of in-group narratives on actual intergroup collaborative discussion. It may be that perspective-taking helps the dominant groups' members overcome the push of in-glorification sentiments toward dominating discussion and antagonizing out-group members.

The effects of the critical disciplinary on Jewish participants in terms of perceived in-group responsibility, and lowered domination of discussion, align to some degree with Kolikant and Pollack's (2009) findings that Jewish participants collaborated better with Arab partners when assuming a more detached academic role. Findings also substantiate Barton and McCully's (2010) claims as to the positive effects of the critical inquiry curriculum and extend them from the realm of internal dialogue to the realm of actual intergroup interaction. As we noted, the critical disciplinary approach appears to curb the influence of political affiliation on in-group responsibility. This offers a hope of breaking through the entrenchment and rejection of information, caused by political polarization.

We should take the above conclusions cautiously. First, the sample is quite small, and the intervention was short and extracurricular. Another factor limiting the generalizability of findings is the voluntary nature of the sample, which could cause a self-selection bias, hinted by a higher proportion of liberal affiliated learners compared to national average. However, we should bear in mind that self-selection occurred in most intergroup encounters studies. In favor of the method, we should note this study is the only one currently known to the author in Israel (and actually for that matter also abroad) in which students were randomly allocated to teaching conditions, allowing for empirical comparisons with the conventional teaching approach. Allocation to groups was also performed within each school, thereby curbing to some degree the strong effect of school culture and values.

The implications of the studies seem quite straightforward. Teaching multiple perspectives has a potential to serve the goals of increasing intergroup perspective-taking motivation and improving intergroup deliberation of conflict. This outcome does not risk learners' national identification and esteem, a risk, which apparently may have detained educators and decision makers from engaging in such teaching. However, the prospects for such initiative current political climate in Israel do not seem promising. It may actually be that current decision makers find reduced motivation for out-group perspective-taking a positive outcome of the conventional teaching approach.

Notes

1. Political affiliation was reported on a 3-point scale; right wing, center, liberal left.
2. In-group responsibility was coded on a 6-point scale from none to exclusive, based on the number of responsible parties mentioned.
3. The Glorification mode of national identification measure was the mean score of agreement (on a scale from 1 to 5) to seven items (item example: "Other nations can learn a lot from us," Cronbach's $\alpha_{pre} = 0.73$, $\alpha_{post} = 0.79$). The Attachment mode of national identification measures was the mean score of agreement (on a scale from 1 to 5) to eight items (item example: "It is important for me to contribute to my nation," Cronbach's $\alpha_{pre} = 0.88$, $\alpha_{post} = 0.89$).
4. Based on the mean score of agreement (on a scale from 1 to 5) to nine items (item example: "The History of the Jewish–Arab Conflict we grew up on is, in the end, the most accurate" Cronbach's $\alpha_{pre} = 0.81$; Cronbach's $\alpha_{post} = 0.88$).
5. Based on the mean score of agreement (on a scale from 1 to 5) with five items depicting interest in various ways of learning about the other side's perspective of the Jewish–Arab conflict, from news article to dialogue group (item example: "Participate in a joint Jewish–Arab activity related to the conflict" Cronbach's $\alpha_{pre} = 0.86$; Cronbach's $\alpha_{post} = 0.87$).

References

Abu-Ria, T. (2014). *Empathy and change of attitude of Arab high school students towards the other following academic and experiential study of the holocaust.* (Hebrew. Unpublished Master's thesis). Haifa: University of Haifa.

Adwan, S., & Bar-On, D. (2004). Shared history project: A PRIME example of peace-building under fire. *International Journal of Politics, Culture, and Society, 17*(3), 513–521.

Bales, R. F. (Ed.). (1976). *Interaction process analysis.* Chicago: University of Chicago Press.

Bar-On, D. & Adwan, S. (2006). The psychology of better dialogue between two separate but interdependent narratives. In R. I. Rotberg (Ed.), *Israeli and Palestinian narratives of conflict: History's double helix* (pp. 205–224). Bloomington, IN: Indiana University Press.

Bar-Tal, D., & Halperin, E. (2011). Socio-psychological barriers to conflict resolution. In *Intergroup conflicts and their resolution: Social psychological perspective* (pp. 217–240). New York: Psychology Press.

Bar-Tal, D., & Salomon, G. (2006). Israeli–Jewish narratives of the Israeli–Palestinian conflict: Evolvement, contents, functions and consequences. In R.

I. Rotberg (Ed.), *Israeli and Palestinian narratives of conflict: History's double helix* (pp. 19–46). Bloomington, IN: Indiana University Press.

Barton, K. C., & Mccully, A. W. (2010). "You can form your own point of view": Internally persuasive discourse in Northern Ireland students' encounters with history. *Teachers College Record, 112*(1), 142–181.

Bennett, W. L., & Iyengar, S. (2008). A new era of minimal effects? The changing foundations of political communication. *Journal of Communication, 58*(4), 707–731.

Blumenfeld, R. (2015, April 1). Teachers who are not afraid to teach about the naqba: The refugees did not just evaporate. *Walla Newssite.* Retrieved January 20, 2016 from http://news.walla.co.il/item/2842641.

Čehajić-Clancy, S., Effron, D. A., Halperin, E., Liberman, V., & Ross, L. D. (2011). Affirmation, acknowledgment of in-group responsibility, group-based guilt, and support for reparative measures. *Journal of Personality and Social Psychology, 101*(2), 256–270.

Cohen, E. (2013). *Identity and pedagogy: Shoah education in Israeli state schools.* Brighton, MA: Academic Studies Press.

Domke, E., Urbach, C., & Goldberg, T. (2009). *Building a state in the Middle East* [Bonim medina baMizrach HaTichon]. Jerusalem, Israel: Zalman Shazar Center.

Doosje, B., & Branscombe, N. R. (2003). Attributions for the negative historical actions of a group. *European Journal of Social Psychology, 33*(2), 235–248.

Eid, N. (2010). The inner conflict: How Palestinian students in Israel react to the dual narrative approach concerning the events of 1948. *Journal of Educational Media, Memory, and Society, 2*(1), 55–77.

Eini-ElHadaf, Y. (2011). Jewish adolescents coping with two historical narratives. In T. Litvak Hirsch & G. Zeitlin (Eds.), *Junctions- ways of psychological-social reflection on Hebrew society* (pp. 108–113). BeerSheva: BeerSheva University Press.

Feldman, J. (2002). Marking the boundaries of the enclave: Defining the Israeli collective through the Poland 'experience'. *Israel Studies, 7*(2), 84–114.

Firer, R., 'Abd al-Razzāq 'Adwān, S., & Pingel, F. (2004). *The Israeli-Palestinian conflict in history and civics textbooks of both nations.* Hahnsche.

Gehlbach, H. (2004). Social perspective taking: A facilitating aptitude for conflict resolution, historical empathy, and social studies achievement. *Theory & Research in Social Education, 32*(1), 39–55.

Goldberg, T. (2014a). *"Do you think listening to our perspective …helps?": Impact of different approaches to teaching of the Jewish—Arab conflict on engagement in binational dialogue about its resolution* ["At Hoshevet she lehakshive lagirsa shelanu…ze ozer?": Hashpaat gishot shonot lehoraat hahistoria shel hasikhsukh hayehudi-aravi al nihul diyun du leumi"]. Tel Aviv: Tami Steinmetz Center for Peace Research.

Goldberg, T. (2014b). Looking at their side of the conflict? Effects of single versus multiple perspective history teaching on Jewish and Arab adolescents' attitude to out-group narratives and in-group responsibility. *Intercultural Education, 25*(6), 453–467. doi:10.1080/14675986.2014.990230.

Goldberg, T. (2016). Touching the roots or undermining national heritage: Studying single and multiple perspectives of a formative historical conflict. In C. van Boxtel, M. Grever, & S. Klein (Eds.), *Sensitive pasts? Questioning heritage education*. Oxford: Berghahn Books.

Goldberg, T. (submitted). Between trauma and perpetration: Psychoanalytical and social psychological perspectives on difficult histories in the Israeli context. *Theory and Research in Social Education*.

Goldberg, T., & Gerwin, D. (2013). Israeli history curriculum and the conservative—liberal pendulum. *International Journal of Historical Teaching, Learning and Research, 11*(2), 111–124.

Goldberg, T., & Ron, Y. (2014). 'Look, each side says something different': The impact of competing history teaching approaches on Jewish and Arab adolescents' discussions of the Jewish–Arab conflict. *Journal of Peace Education, 11*(1), 1–29.

Hilton, D. J., & Liu, J. H. (2008). Culture and intergroup relations: The role of social representations of history. In R. M. Sorrentino & Y. Susumu (Eds.), *Handbook of motivation and cognition across cultures* (pp. 343–368). London: Academic Press.

Israeli Ministry of Education. (2008a). *Guidelines to history textbook authors*. (Hebrew. personal correspondence).

Israeli Ministry of Education. (2008b). *History curriculum for the Jewish secular high schools, part B*. Retrieved January 20, 2016 from http://cms.education.gov.il/EducationCMS/Units/Mazkirut_Pedagogit/History/TochnitLimudimvt/TalTashah.htm.

Klar, Y., & Baram, H. (2016). In DeFENCE of the in-group historical narrative in an intractable intergroup conflict:An individual-difference perspective. *Political Psychology, 37*(1), 37–53. doi: 10.1111/pops.12229.

Kline, R. B. (2011). Convergence of structural equation modeling and multilevel modeling. In M. Williams & W. P.Vogt (Eds.), *The SAGE handbook of innovation in social research methods*. New York: Sage Publications.

Kashti, O. (2009, July 22). Israel bans use of Palestinian term 'Nakba' in textbooks. *Haaretz* (daily newspaper). Retrieved January 20, 2016 from http://www.haaretz.com/israel-bans-use-of-palestinian-term-nakba-in-textbooks-1.280515.

Kashti, O. (2010, September 27). Education ministry bans textbook that offers Palestinian narrative. *Haaretz* (daily newspaper). Retrieved January 20, 2016 from http://www.haaretz.com/print-edition/news/education-ministry-bans-textbook-that-offers-palestinian-narrative-1.315838.

Kiezel, A. (2008). *Enslaved history: Critical analysis of general history curricula and textbooks 1948–2006* [Historia Meshu'abedet: Nituakh bikorti shel,tochniot limudim behistoria 1948–2006]. (Hebrew) Tel-Aviv, Israel: Mofet.
Kitson, A., & McCully, A. (2005). 'You hear about it for real in school'. Avoiding, containing and risk-taking in the history classroom. *Teaching History, 120,* 32–37.
Kolikant, Y. B., & Pollack, S. (2009). The asymmetrical influence of identity: A triadic interaction among Israeli Jews, Israeli Arabs, and historical texts. *Journal of Curriculum Studies, 41*(5), 651–677.
Kolikant, Y. B., & Pollack, S. (2015). The dynamics of non-convergent learning with a conflicting other: Internally persuasive discourse as a framework for articulating successful collaborative learning. *Cognition and Instruction, 33*(4), 322–356.
Liu, J. H., Fisher Onar, N., & Woodward, M. W. (2014a). Symbologies, technologies, and identities: Critical junctures theory and the multi-layered nation–state. *International Journal of Intercultural Relations, 43, Part A*(0), 2–12. doi:http://dx.doi.org/10.1016/j.ijintrel.2014.08.012.
Liu, J. H., Sibley, C. G., & Huang, L. (2014b). History matters: Effects of culture-specific symbols on political attitudes and intergroup relations. *Political Psychology, 35*(1), 57–79.
Maoz, I. (2001). Participation, control, and dominance in communication between groups in conflict: Analysis of dialogues between Jews and Palestinians in Israel. *Social Justice Research, 14*(2), 189–208.
McCully, A. (2011). The contribution of history teaching to peace building. In G. Salomon & E. Cairns (Eds.), *Handbook on peace education* (pp. 213–223). London: Taylor & Francis.
Peled-Elhanan, N. (2012). *Palestine in Israeli textbooks: Ideology and propaganda in education.* London: Tauris.
Pettigrew, T. F. (1998). Intergroup contact theory. *Annual Review of Psychology, 49(1),* 65–85.
Pettigrew, T. F. (2008). Future directions for intergroup contact theory and research. *International Journal of Intercultural Relations, 32,* 187–199.
Podeh, E. (1948). *The Arab–Israeli conflict in Israeli history textbooks.* Westport: Bergin & Garvey.
Rigdon, E. E. (1998). Structural equation modeling. In G. A. Marcoulides (Ed.), *Modern methods for businessresearch* (pp. 251–294). Mahwah, NJ: Lawrence Erlbaum Associates Publishers.
Roccas, S., & Berlin, A. (2015). Identification with groups and national identity. In P. Schmidt, J. Seethaler, J. Grimm, & L. Huddy (Eds.), *Dynamics of national identity: Media and societal factors of what we are routledge'*] (pp. 22–43). New York: Routledge.

Roccas, S., Klar, Y., & Liviatan, I. (2006). The paradox of group-based guilt: Modes of national identification, conflict vehemence, and reactions to the ingroup's moral violations. *Journal of Personality and Social Psychology, 91*(4), 698–711. doi:10.1037/0022-3514.91.4.698.

Rohde, A. (2013). Learning each other's historical narrative: A road map to peace in Israel/Palestine? In K. V. Korostelina, & S. Lässig (Eds.), *History education and post-conflict reconciliation: Reconsidering joint textbook projects* (pp. 177–191). London: Routledge.

Rohde, A. (2014). *The texts of "the others" – an Israeli-Palestinian textbook project on the history of the Middle East conflict* (Summary report). The Georg Eckert Institute for International Textbook Research.

Shnabel, N., Nadler, A., Ullrich, J., Dovidio, J. F., & Carmi, D. (2009). Promoting reconciliation through the satisfaction of the emotional needs of victimized and perpetrating group members: The needs-based model of reconciliation. *Personality and Social Psychology Bulletin, 35*(8), 1021–1030.

Shoham, E., Shiloah, N., & Kalisman, R. (2003). Arab teachers and holocaust education: Arab teachers study holocaust education in Israel. *Teaching and Teacher Education, 19*(6), 609–625.

Stern, Y., Kashti, O., & Mualem, M. (2007, July 23). Tamir: Arab narrative should get a place in the educational system–ministry of education authorizes teaching about the Nakba in Arab schools. *Haaretz* (Daily newspaper). Retrieved January 20, 2016 from http://www.haaretz.co.il/misc/1.1428005.

Vollhardt, J. R. (2013). "Crime against humanity" or "Crime against Jews"? Acknowledgment in construals of the holocaust and its importance for intergroup relations. *Journal of Social Issues, 69*(1), 144–161.

Yaron, M. (2009). *History superintendent's requested corrections to the textbook: Building a state in the Middle East* (Hebrew. Personal correspondence).

Yaron, M. (2010). *History superintendent site: Topics for teaching in the senior high school*. Retrieved January 20, 2016 from http://cms.education.gov.il/EducationCMS/Units/Mazkirut_Pedagogit/History/hativa_elyona/helek_b/nosee_b_bonim.htm.

Yonah, Y. (2008). The Palestinian minority in Israel: When common core curriculum in education meets conflicting national narratives. *Intercultural Education, 19*(2), 105–117.

Zohar, A. (2009). *Report on education for thinking (Pedagogical Horizon) 2006–2009: Outline insights and recommendations* [Dokh al hinukh leHashiva (Ofek Pedagogy) 2006–2009] (Hebrew). Jerusalem: Israeli Ministry of Education; Publications Department.

Author Biography

Tsafrir Goldberg is a lecturer in the Faculty of Education in University of Haifa, Israel. His research focuses on the relations of history teaching, Iidentity and intergroup relations. He led research projects on the teaching of the Jewish–Arab conflict and its impact on leaners identity, intergroup attitudes and intergroup interaction, on history teaching and Islamophobia and on teachers' attitudes towards difficult histories. He is involved in teacher education and curricular reform.

Open Access This chapter is licensed under the terms of the Creative Commons Attribution 4.0 International License (http://creativecommons.org/licenses/by/4.0/), which permits use, sharing, adaptation, distribution and reproduction in any medium or format, as long as you give appropriate credit to the original author(s) and the source, provide a link to the Creative Commons license and indicate if changes were made.

The images or other third party material in this chapter are included in the chapter's Creative Commons license, unless indicated otherwise in a credit line to the material. If material is not included in the chapter's Creative Commons license and your intended use is not permitted by statutory regulation or exceeds the permitted use, you will need to obtain permission directly from the copyright holder.

History Teaching to Promote Positive Community Relations in Northern Ireland: Tensions Between Pedagogy, Social Psychological Theory and Professional Practice in Two Recent Projects

Alan McCully and Jacqueline Reilly

Introduction

Prior to the Belfast (Good Friday) Agreement (1998), Northern Ireland (NI) experienced 30 years of violent political conflict, which was widely but simplistically portrayed as a religious conflict; while the protagonist communities were broadly labelled Catholic and Protestant, these religious labels signify political, cultural and national identity preferences and objectives. The label Catholic is associated with mainly Nationalist or Republican and Irish identities, with a reunification of the island of Ireland as an objective. The label Protestant is associated with mainly Unionist or Loyalist and British identities, with NI remaining part of the United Kingdom (UK) as an objective. The Good Friday Agreement

---

A. McCully (✉) · J. Reilly
Ulster University, Coleraine, Northern Ireland
e-mail: aw.mccully@ulster.ac.uk

1998, recognising both groups and establishing a consociational devolved government, led to a greatly reduced level of violence, but the two communities remain polarised in many ways. This polarisation persists in a segregated education system with a large majority of pupils attending schools, which are classed as *Controlled* (mainly Protestant pupils) or *Maintained* (mainly Catholic pupils) with a small and very slowly growing integrated sector attended by approximately 7% of pupils (Furey et al. 2016, p. 3). A major focus of government continues to aspire to improvement in community relations, with a range of policy documents produced since 1998 leading to the *Shared Future, Together Building a United Community* strategy (Northern Ireland Government 2013) backed up by a raft of legislation. The latter seeks to ensure equality and requires that service providers and public sector organisations fulfil a duty to promote good relations.

Since the outbreak of violence in NI in 1968, educators have responded in three ways to bring about a more peaceful society: by seeking to break down this segregated education system and creating common schools; by accepting segregation as a reality and fostering meaningful contact between institutions to break down barriers; and by pursuing societal change through curriculum innovation irrespective of whatever school structures are in place. These approaches have evolved and overlapped, as the political situation has moved towards post-conflict, but essentially all three strategies currently continue to be visible (Gallagher 2004, pp. 119–135; 2016).

The curriculum in NI remains one that is predominantly organised through established subject disciplines, but since the introduction of statutory provision in the 1990s (revised in 2007) it contains overarching objectives which aspire to bettering community relations, thus implicitly contributing to group reconciliation (Smith 2005; CCEA 2007). These objectives impact on all subject teachers, but have particular implications for teachers of history, which is included in the NI Curriculum at primary level in Key Stages 1 and 2 (ages 5–11 years) as part of the learning area 'The World Around Us' and also at secondary level in Key Stages 3 and 4 (ages 11–16 years) as a discrete subject; all pupils study history to the end of Key Stage 3 (age 14). While their established role continues to be defined by the disciplinary rigour of their subject, history teachers are also expected to acknowledge their potential as educators to facilitate greater societal understanding and attitudinal change in young people (Richardson and Gallagher 2011; McCully 2012). Consequently, curricular and pedagogical innovations have been advocated to advance the subject's social utility, often supported by external funding for specific projects. Two such recent projects, *Facing Our History, Shaping the Future* (FOHSTF) and *Teaching Divided Histories* (TDH), are featured in this work. FOHSTF, funded variously by the International Fund for Ireland, the NI Office of the First and Deputy First Minister and the Irish Department of Foreign Affairs since 2013, provides free training for teachers and student teachers as well as workshops and residential courses for pupils. In its first phase, up to 2013, 280 teachers and student teachers attended FOHSTF training sessions and 1400 students in secondary schools experienced project workshops and residential courses (ETI 2013, p. 2). TDH is funded by the European Regional Development Fund under PEACE III. It also provides free training for teachers (internationally as well as in NI), and digital resources, lesson plans, teaching and evaluation materials are available to download from the website. In all, 84 teachers from 24 schools on both sides of the Irish border attended TDH training between 2011 and 2014 to prepare them to work with students in the 14- to 15-year-old age group (Gannon 2014, p. 7).

Education addressing community relations in Northern Ireland has been extensively researched, yet interestingly, individual academic disciplines at tertiary level have tended to concentrate on different areas. Educationalists have focused on curriculum issues, associated resources and pedagogy, while social psychologists have mainly explored the dynamics, effects and implications of cross-cultural contact on young peoples' attitudes and behaviour. Thus, potentially fertile areas for interdisciplinary collaboration between history educators and social psychologists may have been neglected. This chapter examines the aspirations of the NI Curriculum (with a focus on history) to contribute to greater community understanding and the expectation, as illustrated by FOHSTF and TDH, that history teaching, and teachers, should accept a major responsibility for this. The stances of the two projects are examined to ascertain the implications for approaches teachers might take and the potential benefits of a more explicit relationship between history teaching and social psychology concepts and theories are explored.

History Teaching and Community Relations

Attention has been frequently drawn to the negative use of history in conflict situations. The promotion by a dominant group of a partisan historical narrative has often been used to support an ideological position which bolsters that group's political control at the expense of those deemed 'suspect' or 'inferior' (Bush and Saltarelli 2000; Smith and Vaux 2003; Davies 2004; Cole 2007). History teaching has thus often been associated with shaping the development of particular forms of national identity, particularly in newly independent states (e.g. Korostelina 2010). Consequently, history teaching is highlighted as an aspect of educational policy, which needs to respond positively if sustainable peace is to be achieved (Smith and Vaux 2003; Cole 2007). Therefore, educational reformers in contested contexts have acknowledged that reaching consensus on an agreed common narrative is highly problematic and instead have argued for history teaching which adheres to the subject's disciplinary process, thus giving students access to the provisional and contested nature of historical knowledge (McCully 2012). Drawing on the work of the Schools' Council History Project (Shemilt 1980) established in the 1970s, it is argued that a history curriculum that opens the past up to the consideration of different interpretations, provided that these are underpinned by valid historical evidence, can provide a greater understanding of the nature of conflict and challenge prevailing ideological certainties, which are often biased in divided societies. It can open up possibilities for greater mutual understanding by acquiring insight into the thinking of the 'other' and develop critical faculties, which, in turn, might help move society beyond conflict, thus contributing to reconciliation. However, the advocacy for enquiry-based multi-perspective history has tended to run ahead of research studies that confirm its efficacy in bringing personal and group transformation. This may result from a conviction by progressive educators that a constructivist approach, where students actively engage in historical enquiry, analysing, evaluating and interpreting sources in order to develop historical interpretations, offers a clear pathway in situations where emotive positions are deeply held, whether in favour of or against biased conclusions. However, there is a small body of empirical research with young people that does (tentatively) indicate positive outcomes from an enquiry approach (Barton and McCully 2005, 2010, 2012; Goldberg 2013; Kolikant and Pollack 2015).

As early as the 1970s, innovative teachers in NI saw the potential to use evidential enquiry and perspective-taking to prise open students' restricted understandings of the past by challenging partial accounts acquired in families and communities. When the first statutory common curriculum was introduced in 1991 (three years before the first cease-fires brought an initial pause to endemic violence and seven years before the Good Friday Peace Accord), it was notable that the proposals offered by the working party set up to advise on history were largely accepted by teachers from both unionist and nationalist backgrounds. This was despite deep societal divisions and an education system, which reflected these divisions. The history curriculum at secondary level (compulsory for ages 11–14) harnessed the disciplinary framework to the study of key events from Ireland's past. Students were asked to study periods of history deemed essential for understanding the history of Ireland, but importantly, these were placed within wider British and European contexts (DENI 1991). The document argued for 'breadth, balance and coherence; that multiple interpretations of events be presented in a balanced way, with equal attention to the experiences and perspectives of both communities'. Teaching from a disciplinary base presents pedagogical challenges, and teachers have varying degrees of understanding of what is required in implementing this in practice. Apart from the challenges of dealing with contentious issues and having to take into account the potential influence of their own community allegiances, they also have to get beyond the mere transmission of historical knowledge to encourage critical thinking among their students (Smith 2005, pp. 148–150; Kitson 2007). Despite this, there is evidence—from academic research and government inspection reports—that, in the main, teachers value the aims of the curriculum and, despite shortcomings, have tried to approach Irish history in a fair and even-handed way (Education and Training Inspectorate 2006; McCombe 2006).

As already indicated, research into the impact of historical learning resulting from the 1991 history curriculum in Northern Ireland suggests that it has had some positive outcomes (Barton and McCully 2005, 2010, 2012). These papers were based on data collection involving interviews with 253 students, in groups of 2 or 3, from 11 different schools representative of a variety of demographic, social and educational contexts. Findings indicated that the enquiry approach was welcomed by young people. It had fostered criticality and had some success in helping them make sense of the range of interpretations of the past they encounter inside and outside school. However, significant limitations were also identified. Despite recognising the more balanced and discursive nature of school history when studying Ireland's past, most students' thinking was nevertheless clearly influenced by their respective community perspectives. This raises questions as to the emphasis of current practice on historical understanding as the basis for challenging partisan history. This, and other work (McCully 2005; Bell et al. 2010), suggests that young people often have strong emotional ties to particular cultural and political positions, which may hinder critical thinking processes, particularly when encountering sensitive historical material. Hence, teachers may need to take greater heed of the affective dimension of cognition, which is so strongly associated with national and cultural identity, and adapt their teaching approaches accordingly. However, little attention, to date, has been paid to the potential contribution of theories of social cognition, which may have something to offer in terms of understanding and addressing these issues.

Research outputs have influenced subsequent curriculum developments. When the curriculum was revised in 2007, nine years after the Belfast (Good Friday) peace accord, the enquiry dimension within history was consolidated further and the focus on the subject's social utility in a post-conflict context was strengthened. For example, it is a statutory requirement of the current provision that teachers explore with students the impact of history on their sense of identity, culture and lifestyle, its role in influencing stereotypes and the way the past can be used and abused in contemporary politics (CCEA 2007). More explicitly than before, these changes recognise that young people's understanding of the past influences their experiences and views in the present, which seems to suggest that there is a potential for social psychological theories and concepts to be incorporated into the curriculum. Before probing the two curriculum initiatives, FOHSTF and TDH, in terms of content relating to social psychological concepts, first it is necessary to examine the potential relationship between social psychology, social cognition and history teaching in divided societies at a theoretical level.

Social Psychology, Social Cognition and History Teaching

A range of potentially relevant and established social psychological theories can be identified as relevant to history teaching in a divided society, including social categorisation and Social Identity Theory (Tajfel and Turner 1986), stereotype threat (e.g. Steele 1997) and attribution theory (Heider 1958).

Categorisation has been dubbed 'the cognitive foundation of all forms of prejudice' (Brown 2010, p. viii). Using an information processing analogy, one of the prime strategies used for the purpose of avoiding information overload is categorisation, which allows us to understand the environment rather more easily than if we had to evaluate each stimulus individually to identify it. Categorisation in terms of social cognition, then, is nothing more than the brain taking useful short cuts to understanding. Yet this universal cognitive process has huge implications for those teaching in subject areas such as history, because of its close associations with prejudice via stereotyping and with Social Identity Theory (Tajfel and Turner 1979), which has been widely applied to research in NI.

Social Identity Theory research over the last three decades has produced evidence of potential interest to teachers of history and other disciplines where identity issues may be significant. It is now well established that individuals simultaneously hold multiple social identities, may develop new identities and can embrace superordinate identities. In NI, the possible utility of a Northern Irish superordinate identity for reducing sectarian attitudes has long been discussed (Trew 1998). Recent census data (NISRA 2011) indicate that this identification is on the increase although it must be remembered that those espousing a Northern Irish identity might still simultaneously maintain a strong affiliation to traditional British or Irish national identities.

As a result of research in contested spaces, it is argued that a 'hot' rather than a banal form of national identity (Billig 1995) is actively constructed (Stevenson and Muldoon 2010) although as Skey (2009) points out these are neither fixed nor discrete, and Jones and Merriman (2009) have suggested 'everyday nationalism' as an alternative, more dynamic term combining banal and hot elements. In such circumstances, it is clear that the same contextual information (such as historical events) may be construed by different groups (including political actors) to support more than one claim to national identity. It is also clear that humans categorise as much as possible, so they also categorise themselves and other people into groups (social categorisation), they identify with some groups but not others (social identification) and they compare groups that they belong to with those that they do not (social comparison), often in a way that bolsters their own identity.

Thus, social identity and categorisation are closely related to the development of stereotypes and that negative stereotypes of out-groups are a fairly inevitable result. Moreover, such stereotyping tends to be automatic in character; that is, the individual has minimal if any awareness and/or control over it. Stereotyping is also pervasive and notoriously resistant to change (e.g. Geeraert and Yzerbyt 2007). There has been a wealth of research on identity, stereotypes, prejudice, and these theories have not only been tested but also used to develop interventions aimed at reducing prejudice. The contact hypothesis (Allport 1954), based on the idea that getting to know members of out-groups would challenge negative stereotyping and, hence, 're-individuate' members of the out-group, has led to decades of research culminating in evidence that one important reason for the positive effect of contact is reduction in the anxiety commonly experienced when in the presence of the out-group (Hewstone 2003).

It would seem then that there is a great deal of theory and evidence about social cognition, which paints a mixed picture of the prospects for changing prejudiced attitudes. If identity formation, and thinking about in-groups and out-groups, is so pervasive, automatic, resistant to change, speedy and unconscious, one might be tempted to conclude that there is little teachers can do to reduce prejudice in contested social contexts. And yet we have noted above evidence from history classes in NI that some pupils can and do develop sound historical understandings in parallel with their own strong community identities and that attitudes may change as a result (Barton and McCully 2005, 2010, 2012). If one of the implicit aims of history education in NI is prejudice reduction, then some of the more recent developments in the understanding of social cognition might inform practical measures to intervene in these processes.

Two of these areas are 'stereotype threat' and Situational Attribution Training. The former has been shown to influence performance when an individual believes that they will perform poorly at a task because of their make-up or background. However, Johns et al. (2005) found that by teaching about stereotype threat, 'Knowing is half the battle' or in other words this effect could be counteracted. This might be of interest to history teachers where some pupils might feel disadvantaged when studying history that is perceived to be that belonging to 'the other'. Acknowledging this at the outset might help to ensure that those pupils who would benefit from learning about less familiar historical perspectives do so, rather than simply accept that these perspectives are too difficult for them to understand and accept.

Situational Attribution Training (e.g. Stewart et al. 2010) in educational settings had been developed on the basis of attribution theory. This addresses how we decide whether an individual's actions are due to context or to their own characteristics (disposition) and relates to stereotyping, as negative acts are more often attributed to situation for in-group members and to disposition for out-group members. Experiments have shown that automatic stereotyping can be reduced by repeatedly choosing situational explanations over dispositional ones for behaviours. This work took place in controlled conditions over a lengthy period, but in principle, situational explanations of actions resonate with contemporary arguments relating to empathetic understanding in history. Rather than asking young people to 'imagine you are' someone in the past, they should be encouraged to try to understand why individuals acted the way they did in the circumstances pertaining at the time (Lee and Shemilt 2011).

The principal point of this section is to argue that as theories and evidence in relation to the social cognition processes involved in prejudice become better understood, so too does understanding of how best to intervene in these processes. We now turn to examine two recent innovations in history teaching in NI designed to contribute to better intergroup relations. The aim is to analyse to what extent they may have been informed by social psychological theories and concepts, and how they might be better informed in this regard.

Facing Our History, Shaping the Future and Teaching Divided Histories: A Critical Analysis

As FOHSTF and TDH are designed to support history teaching's wider remit and have explicitly targeted the social utility of history teaching as a central aim, arguably, they signpost possibilities for dialogue between educators and psychologists. FOHSTF is an offshoot of the Boston-based organisation, *Facing History and Ourselves*. FOHSTF has evolved from the Facing History philosophy, which began with Holocaust education and the power of human agency to bring change if 'bystanders' can be transformed to 'upstanders' in opposition to social injustice. Internationally, the work of Facing History has been adapted in a number of conflict-affected contexts including South Africa and Rwanda to address the legacies of conflict, but its approach has also been criticised, particularly with regard to its role as a conduit for disciplinary understanding of history (Schweber 2004). TDH is a local NI initiative; its philosophy is rooted in the belief that the use of moving image and digital technologies to develop creative and critical skills can 'liberate and empower' young people to engage practically with issues of conflict and division (Nerve Centre 2014).

Similarities and differences in the ways social psychological concepts and terms are applied within the two project rationales and documents will be analysed through a social psychological lens as well as from the perspective of a history educator and researcher who is convinced of his subject's contribution to wider societal transformation from conflict, but also of the vital need to preserve its historical disciplinary integrity. This allows an exploration of the potential tensions arising from the ways in which the projects are related to the curriculum, and how history educators involved in such projects might incorporate social psychological terms and concepts in their teaching.

Unsurprisingly, given the importance of gaining access to schools, the literature of both projects strongly flags up their relevance to the statutory curriculum and their utility in fulfilling its objectives. For example, FOHSTF describes itself as 'fully aligned' to the revised NI History Curriculum, noting that it is particularly suitable for pupils at Key Stage 3 (KS3 is for pupils aged eleven to fourteen years) and is noted also to be compatible with citizenship classes and suitable for cross-curricular and whole school approaches consistent with the Department of Education's *Community Relations Equality and Diversity* (CRED) Policy

(DENI 2011). The project is therefore clearly aligned to the curriculum, and this is reinforced by a schematic which explicitly lays out a detailed (term by term over the three years) overview of how the project might be implemented at KS3, with how each element of the statutory requirements is addressed.

In contrast to the FOHSTF project, TDH initially focuses largely on the local context of NI with references to civil rights in the USA and a concluding section on international comparisons. The website (http://nervecentre.org/education/teaching-divided-histories) details six modules each with six lessons, covering the Civil Rights movement, the Conflict, Pathways to Peace, the Easter Rising, the Somme and International Conflict and extensive support material is available for each. Again, the project is explicitly linked to the KS3 curriculum in a schematic, with history identified as a core area, but also appeals are made to teachers of English, media and citizenship (and to teachers in the border regions of the Republic of Ireland). Its wider remit for preparing young people as 'contributors to society' (CCEA 2007) is through teacher training to enable them 'to use moving image and digital technologies within the classroom to liberate and empower young people to engage practically with issues of conflict and division'. Both projects envisage history education as having a social purpose in a divided society and therefore might be expected to employ aspects of social psychology.

On examination, both FOHSTF and TDH were found to employ terminology drawn from or related to Social Identity Theory. Associated most strongly with Tajfel (2003), as previously noted this is one of the most widely used frameworks for social psychological research in NI (Garry and McNicholl 2015). First, investigating the philosophy underpinning FOHSTF a key aim is that 'Facing History helps pupils learn to combat prejudice with compassion, indifference with participation, and myth and misinformation with knowledge' (http://www.fohstf.co.uk/#/about/4550679310). It seeks to do this by establishing its key ideas, first through studying the Holocaust, then focusing on the partition of Ireland and its consequences. Pupils embark on a journey, beginning 'by exploring questions of the individual and society -who am I? What makes my identity? Where has it come from? How much do I choose and how much is given to me?' This consideration of social identity is a fairly fundamental social psychological concept, which is then used as a basis for considering 'we and they'. Why and how do we as humans include and exclude? How does this play out in our lives? What is the role of prejudice and stereotyping, and what happens when this turns to active discrimination?' Again the concepts of social categorisation, stereotyping and prejudice are core concepts for social psychologists. The foundations thus laid, the emphasis appears to shift towards the historical, looking at the Holocaust and identifying how these concepts played out, and how choices were affected by identity, introducing the idea of 'bystanders and upstanders'. Judgement, legacy and memory feature next and the social psychology content seems less prominent, reappearing in the final, 'Choosing to participate' phase, where prevention of exclusion, prejudice and violence are the focus.

The Education and Training Inspectorate report (ETI 2013) on the project notes positively the application of the project's principles to the context of Irish history in the curriculum (the long-term and short-term causes and consequences of the partition of Ireland). However, from a history educator's perspective Schweber's reservations on Facing History's efficacy, both in relation to historical disciplinary efficacy and in relation to effecting attitudinal change, merit consideration (Schweber 2004). The report's evaluation concentrates on teachers, finding that their ability to teach controversial and sensitive issues had been enhanced and that they had greater understanding of the role of history education in divided societies. None of the above terms emanating from social psychology are evident in the report, although the inspectors note that the effects on pupils included enhanced conflict resolution skills and cross-community friendships. The report concludes that 'very effective methodologies were used to develop the young people's understanding of both themselves and of others, and extend their capacity for engaging with others in the reconciliation process' (ETI 2013, p. 4). Other documentation available on the implementation of FOHSTF displays a similar dearth of reference to the social psychological concepts which appear from the general description to underpin the approach. This suggests that any conflict resolution skills and cross-community friendships that have been fostered by teachers are not explicitly related to the social psychological concepts, which are evident in the project rationale, but not its implementation or evaluation.

Turning to TDH, its stated aim for teachers is to provide them with 'the confidence, skills and specific resources and support that enables them to explore contentious history and identity in the classroom'. In addition to local networks, it is intended that participants should share resources, experiences and expertise internationally with an emphasis on the promotion of shared societies and the enabling of young people to explore common experiences of conflict and peacebuilding. Alongside the explicit links to the curriculum standard terminology drawn from social psychology is evident, with the concepts of identity, prejudice, discrimination all being referenced. However, subsequently, there is little evidence of the terms being used in ways consistent with social psychological concepts.

For example, TDH presents identity as strongly related to political groupings rather than as an individual and multifaceted construct, as in the Module 2 'Questions and answers' teaching resource where teachers are advised that in an activity where students are asked to create a table stating what a Nationalist and a Unionist is, '*Nationalist should be defined as a person (some students may mention that Nationalists are usually Roman Catholic) who favours political independence for a country/a union with the Irish Republic. Unionist should be defined as a person who favoured the maintaining of the political and cultural union with Great Britain (some students may mention that a Unionist in Northern Ireland was usually of the Protestant religion)*'. Similar advice is offered in relation to comparing a Republican, who differs from a Nationalist by willingness to use 'any means necessary' to achieve a united Ireland, and a Loyalist, who differs from a Unionist by willingness to 'engage in violence' to maintain the union with Britain. Nationalist and Unionist political identities are thus clearly aligned with religion and Republican and Loyalist political identities clearly associated with violence. In the context of the lesson, which is titled 'Key players in the conflict', it might be argued that this binary representation is appropriate, but from a social psychological perspective this approach is unlikely to lead to reflective engagement with the concept of identity as a complex and nuanced issue. Indeed, the research of Barton and McCully (2012, pp. 399–400) drew attention to the dangers of a binary approach and the need for teachers to recognise the complexity of perspectives in the past.

In a balanced and reflective internal evaluation report (Gannon 2014), there is recognition that TDH has brought together a group of history teachers who are 'risk-taking ... with a passion for history and a personal commitment to peace and reconciliation' (Gannon 2014) and that young people have engaged with sensitive history and gained some insight into the 'other' community. Yet the author also acknowledges that the technological dimension tends to drive the learning with a danger that digital media production 'distracts from the process of critical analysis' (Gannon 2014). A textual analysis indicates that the single narrative presented of Northern Ireland's recent past in project materials is a balanced one, but it fails to problematise issues in a way that facilitates genuine historical enquiry. This is supported by the evaluation report, which concludes that the project's potential to fulfil its social objectives is heavily reliant on the intuitive skills of its leading practitioners. Greater exposure to applied social psychology may help to broaden the base of teacher expertise.

In summary, from the perspective of the social psychologist, both projects might be accused of drawing on, yet failing to exploit, the potential for improved intergroup relations, which might be achieved by history teaching incorporating an approach more explicitly informed by social psychology. For example, the multiple and complex nature of social identities appears relatively unexplored in TDH, while in FOHSTF, prejudice is to be fought with compassion, by the individual. Both approaches are, however, consistent with the Northern Ireland Curriculum, which clearly has a focus on the development of the individual pupil. FOHSTF (and to a lesser extent TDF) provides teachers with tools to realise the social utility of their discipline. However, the social roots and multidimensional nature of the phenomena implied by the terms used seem neglected. Social psychologists have long argued, for example, that individual prejudice is symptomatic of wider social issues rather than interpersonal ones and therefore, as Billig (1976) noted many years ago, requires a social analysis.

Moreover, there is little evidence that recent theoretical developments in social psychology have been incorporated into either of the two projects explored. Dovidio et al. (2010) note that in the wake of the Holocaust, social psychological attention was initially largely directed at identifying personality and individual differences related to prejudice, discrimination and related behaviours. This moved on over time to theories based on functional relations between groups as illustrated by social categorisation and social identity. This progression, from viewing prejudice and discrimination as a result of individual dysfunction, then as a result of normal intergroup processes and on to a more multidimensional understanding which takes into account dynamic aspects, opens up many avenues for research. This may eventually enable more effective approaches to prejudice reduction, to which the projects examined aspire.

From the perspective of the history educator, both projects also raise questions around the respective demands of disciplinary authenticity and social utility made on teachers by a curriculum aspiring to prepare young people to be contributors to a society with deep divisions. For example, how far should teachers, even when committed to bettering community relations, be cognisant of principles of social psychology in their teaching of history? If, as is argued by one of the authors of this chapter, disciplinary integrity necessitates that it is not the role of history teaching to engage directly in aspects of prejudice reduction (McCully 2012) then has social psychology a part to play? The answer is yes, in that history teaching with social purpose should challenge the certainty of identity positions shaped by uncritical versions of the past, inherited from the community. To do so would benefit from insights into individual need and the social psychological processes which are so pertinent to community relations. We suggest that a number of tensions may emanate at least in part from how community relations orientated funders evaluate proposed projects in this area in relation to the NI Curriculum. We argue that history educators would benefit from a deeper understanding of the potential and limitations of the relationship between history teaching and social psychology theory in the context of a divided society. This would enable them to better understand history's potential and limitations in contributing to positive community relations and help them to make connections with other areas of the curriculum, including citizenship education, where contemporary attitudes can be clarified.

Conclusion

This preliminary analysis raises a number of tensions in relation to using history education as a tool to improve community relations in NI, between the curriculum, funding bodies, project designers and history teachers. First, the Revised Curriculum quite correctly focuses on pupil outcomes. In other words, its aims are pitched at individual level. A focus on the individual is not congruent with current thinking in social psychology, but harks back to post-war attempts to correct dysfunctional individual attitudes. Funding bodies in conflict-affected societies are often positively disposed towards projects which are explicitly linked to curriculum objectives directed towards peacebuilding and which incorporate relevant theoretically based terminology. Project designers often compete for funding and may take the curriculum into account when developing proposals and also use terminology borrowed from social psychology to produce a convincing proposal, but the social psychological elements may not be reflected in project implementation. History teachers, rather than social psychologists, are tasked with delivering the projects and must not only satisfy project evaluators and school inspectors, but also must meet curriculum objectives, teach sensitive and controversial issues, enable pupils to achieve good exam results and on top of all this, hope to improve community relations. Facing such demands teachers, whose training and professional identity are wrapped up in a subject specialism, are likely to retreat to the comfort of disciplinary rigour. Exposure to current ideas in social psychology and greater collaboration with social psychologists might encourage risk-taking to push the boundaries of history's social utility, even when guarding its disciplinary integrity.

References

Allport, G. W. (1954). *The nature of prejudice*. Reading, Mass.: Addison-Wesley.

Barton, K. C., & McCully, A. W. (2005). History identity and the school history curriculum in Northern Ireland: An empirical study of secondary students' ideas and perspectives. *Journal of Curriculum Studies, 37*(1), 85–116.

Barton, K. C., & McCully, A. W. (2010). "You can form your own point of view": Internally persuasive discourse in Northern Ireland students' encounters with history. *Teachers' College Record, 112*(1), 142–181.

Barton, K. C., & McCully, A. W. (2012). Trying to "see things differently": Northern Ireland students' struggle to understand alternative historical perspectives. *Theory and Research in Social Education, 40*(4), 371–471.

Bell, J., Hansson, U., & McCaffrey, N. (2010). *The troubles aren't history yet*. Belfast: Community Relations Council.

Billig, M. (1976). *Social psychology and intergroup relations*. London: Academic Press.

Billig, M. (1995). *Banal nationalism*. London: SAGE.

Brown, R. (2010). *Prejudice: It's social psychology*. Chichester: Wiley-Blackwell.

Bush, K. D., & Saltarelli, D. (2000). The two faces of education in ethnic conflict. *United Nations Children's Fund, Innocenti Research Centre, Florence, Italy*. Retrieved July 23, 2016, from http://www.unicef-irc.org/publications/pdf/insight4.pdf.

Cole, E. A. (2007). Introduction: Reconciliation and history. In E. A. Cole (Ed.), *Teaching the violent past: History education and reconciliation* (pp. 1–28). Plymouth: Rowman and Littlefield Publishers Inc.

CCEA (Council for Curriculum, Examinations and Assessment). (2007). *History Curriculum Key Stage 3*. Belfast: CCEA (2007). Retrieved July 23, 2016, from http://www.nicurriculum.org.uk/docs/key_stage_3/areas_of_learning/statutory_requirements/ks3_history.pdf.

Davies, L. (2004). *Education and conflict: Complexity and chaos*. London: Routledge.

Department of Education, Northern Ireland. (1991). *Teachers for the 21st Century: A review of initial teacher training, consultative paper*. Bangor Northern Ireland: DENI.

Department of Education, Northern Ireland. (2011). *Community relations equality and diversity*. Bangor: DENI. Retrieved July 23, 2016, from http://www.ycni.org/downloads-publications/CRED/01-CRED-Policy.pdf.

Dovidio, J., Hewstone, M., Glick, P., & Esses, V. (2010). Prejudice, stereotyping and discrimination: Theoretical and empirical overview. In J. Dovidio, M. Hewstone, P. Glick & V. Esses (Eds.), *The SAGE handbook of prejudice, stereotyping and discrimination* (pp. 3–29). London: SAGE Publications Ltd.

Education and Training Inspectorate (ETI). (2006). *History matters: Report on the extent to which the teaching of history in post-primary schools helps prepare young people to live in Northern Ireland's divided and increasingly pluralist society*. Bangor: DENI.

Education and Training Inspectorate (ETI). (2013). *Facing history and ourselves—The corrymeela project: Second interim evaluation*. Bangor: DENI.

Facing our History Shaping the Future (FOHSTF) (2015). Retrieved June 2, 2016, from http://www.fohstf.co.uk/#/the-approach/4550813929.

Furey, A., Donnelly, C., Hughes, J., & Blaylock, D. (2016) Interpretations of national identity in post-conflict Northern Ireland: A comparison of different school settings. *Research Papers in Education*. Retrieved June 2, 2016, from doi:10.1080/02671522.2016.1158855.

Gallagher, T. (2004). *Education in divided societies*. Basingstoke: Palgrave Macmillan.

Gallagher, T. (2016). Shared education in Northern Ireland: School collaboration in divided societies. *Oxford Review of Education, 42*(3), 362–375.

Gannon, M. (2014). *Teaching divided histories: Teachers' experiences of using digital media in teaching about recent northern ireland history*. Internal paper, Londonderry: Teaching Divided Histories.

Garry, J., & McNicholl, K. (2015). *Understanding the 'Northern Irish' identity*. Paper presented as part of the Knowledge Exchange Seminar Series (KESS), Parliament Buildings, Stormont, Belfast, 13 May 2015. Retrieved July 23, 2016, from http://www.niassembly.gov.uk/globalassets/documents/raise/knowledge_exchange/briefing_papers/series4/northern_ireland_identity_garry_mcnicholl_policy_document.pdf.

Geeraert, N., & Yzerbyt, V. Y. (2007). How fatiguing is dispositional suppression: Disentangling the effects of procedural rebound and ego-depletion. *European Journal of Social Psychology, 37,* 216–230.

Goldberg, T. (2013). "It's in my veins": Identity and disciplinary practice in students' discussions of a historical issue. *Theory & Research in Social Education, 41*(1), 33–64.

Heider, F. (1958). *The psychology of interpersonal relations.* New York: Wiley.

Hewstone, M. (2003). Intergroup contact: Panacea for prejudice? *The Psychologist, 16*(7), 352–355.

Johns, M., Schmader, T., & Martens, A. (2005). Knowing is half the battle: Teaching stereotype threat as a means of improving women's math performance. *Psychological Science, 16,* 175–179.

Jones, R., & Merriman, P. (2009). Hot, banal and everyday nationalism: Bilingual road signs in Wales. *Political Geography, 28*(3), 164–173.

Kitson, A. (2007). History education and reconciliation in Northern Ireland. In E. A. Cole (Ed.), *Teaching the violent past: History education and reconciliation* (pp. 123–154). Lanham, MD: Rowman and Littlefield.

Kolikant, Y. B.-D., & Pollack, S. (2015). The dynamics of non-convergent learning with a conflicting other: Internally persuasive discourse as a framework for articulating successful collaborative learning. *Cognition and Instruction, 33*(4), 322–356.

Korostelina, K. (2010). War of textbooks: History education in Russia and Ukraine. *Communist and Post-Communist Studies, 43*(2), 129–137.

Lee, P., & Shemilt, D. (2011). The concept that dares not speak its name: Should empathy come out of the closet? *Teaching History, 143,* 39–49.

McCombe, J. (2006). *School history and the introduction of local and global citizenship into the Northern Ireland curriculum: The views of history teachers.* Unpublished PhD thesis, University of Ulster.

McCully, A. (2005). Controversial issues, citizenship and history. In G. Mills (Ed.), *Teaching sensitive and controversial issues in history* (pp. 34–43). Nottingham: History Teacher Education Network.

McCully, A. (2012). History teaching, conflict and the legacy of the past. *Education, Citizenship and Social Justice, 7*(2), 145–159.

Nerve Centre. (2014). *Teaching divided histories.* Retrieved July 23, 2016, from http://www.nervecentre.org/teachingdividedhistories.

Northern Ireland Government. (2013). *Together: Building a united community.* Retrieved July 23, 2016, from https://www.executiveoffice-ni.gov.uk/articles/together-building-united-community.

Northern Ireland Statistical Research Agency (NISRA). (2011). *2011 Census* Retrieved July 23, 2016, from http://www.nisra.gov.uk/Census/2011Census.html.

Richardson, N., & Gallagher, T. (2011). *Education for diversity and mutual understanding: The experience of Northern Ireland.* Oxford: Peter Lang.

Schweber, S. (2004). *Making sense of the Holocaust*. New York: Teachers' College Press.
Shemilt, D. (1980). *History 13–16 evaluation study*. Edinburgh: Holmes McDonald.
Skey, M. (2009). The national in everyday life: A critical engagement with Michael Billig's thesis of banal nationalism. *The Sociological Review, 57*(2), 331–346.
Smith, A., & Vaux, T. (2003). *Education, conflict and international development*. London: Department of International Development.
Smith, M. E. (2005). *Reckoning with the past: Teaching history in Northern Ireland*. Lanham: Lexington Books.
Steele, C. M. (1997). A threat in the air: How stereotypes shape intellectual identity and performance. *American Psychologist, 52*, 613–629.
Stevenson, C., & Muldoon, O. (2010). Socio-political context and accounts of national identity in adolescence. *British Journal of Social Psychology, 49*(3), 583–599.
Stewart, T. L., Latu, I. M., Kawakami, K., & Myers, A. C. (2010). Consider the situation: Reducing automatic stereotyping through situational attribution training. *Journal of Experimental Social Psychology, 46*(1), 221–225.
Tajfel, H. (2003). Emotional prejudice, essentialism and nationalism—The 2002 tajfel lecture. *European Journal of Social Psychology, 33*(6), 703–717.
Tajfel, H., & Turner, J. (1979). An integrative theory of intergroup conflict. In W. G. Austin & S. Worchel (Eds.), *The social psychology of intergroup relations* (pp. 94–109). Monterey, CA: Brooks-Cole.
Tajfel, H., & Turner, J. C. (1986). The social identity theory of inter-group behavior. In S. Worchel & L. W. Austin (Eds.), *Psychology of intergroup relations*. Chicago: Nelson-Hall.
Trew, K. (1998). The Northern Irish identity. In A. J. Kershen (Ed.), *A question of identity* (pp. 60–76). Aldershot: Ashgate.

Authors' Biography

Alan McCully is a Senior Lecturer at Ulster University. His research interests are in the fields of teaching history and citizenship education in divided societies. Particularly, his work has focused on the interface between history learned in schools and that encountered in families and communities, and on the pedagogy of teaching sensitive and controversial issues. Current work includes comparative studies in the two jurisdictions in Ireland. He has published in peer-reviewed journals such as *Educational Review, Compare, Teachers' College Review* and *Journal of Curriculum Studies*.

Jacqueline Reilly is a Senior Lecturer in Education at Ulster University. Her research interests lie broadly within the area of education for social justice and encompass education for local and global citizenship, human rights education and training, and peace education, particularly with a focus on issues of identity and divided societies. She is currently exploring the potential of social psychology to contribute to history teaching in divided societies and the experiences of ethnic minority students in such contexts. She has published papers in peer-reviewed journals such as *Compare: A Journal of International and Comparative Education*, *Journal of Peace Psychology*, *Comparative Education* and *Journal of Social Issues*.

Open Access This chapter is licensed under the terms of the Creative Commons Attribution 4.0 International License (http://creativecommons.org/licenses/by/4.0/), which permits use, sharing, adaptation, distribution and reproduction in any medium or format, as long as you give appropriate credit to the original author(s) and the source, provide a link to the Creative Commons license and indicate if changes were made.

The images or other third party material in this chapter are included in the chapter's Creative Commons license, unless indicated otherwise in a credit line to the material. If material is not included in the chapter's Creative Commons license and your intended use is not permitted by statutory regulation or exceeds the permitted use, you will need to obtain permission directly from the copyright holder.

Formal and Non-formal Reform Efforts of History Teaching in Cyprus: Openings and Closures for Dangerous Memories and Reconciliation Pedagogies

Michalinos Zembylas and Hakan Karahasan

One of the most significant tensions in efforts to deal with past historical traumas and promote reconciliation in education is what to do with people's *memories*. Should people *forget* past traumas of their communities in order to construct new, anti-essentialist identities that are not locked in past (group) identities? Or should they remember? 'Is it good, is it healthy, to do so? Is it better to forget and move on?' asks Bourguignon (2005, p. 64). This debate forces educators to confront many haunting issues, not the least of which is the relationship among education, memory and history. However, this debate is not just about *whether* children should be taught to remember the past, but rather about *how* the past is interpreted (Streich 2002). Given that historical legacies and memories

M. Zembylas (✉)
Open University of Cyprus, Nicosia, Cyprus
e-mail: michalinos.zembylas@gmail.com

H. Karahasan
Near East University, Nicosia, Cyprus

embedded in collective identities cannot be simply wished away, and past historical traumas continue to shape identities and structures in the present (Booth 1999), this issue may be rephrased as follows: How can educators use past historical traumas *pedagogically* to re-socialize children in a manner that is not locked into predefined scripts and collective memories (Hill 2000)?

A central concept we utilize in this chapter to respond to this question is the notion of memory as *dangerous*, that is, memory as disruptive to the status quo, which is the hegemonic culture of strengthening and perpetuating existing group-based identities (Ostovich 2002, 2005). Social Identity Theory (Tajfel and Turner 1986) and Self-Categorization Theory (Turner 1999) teach us that people are motivated to evaluate their in-group as better, superior and worthy. This motivation is grounded in the assumption that group-based identities are essentialized, static and tribalistic, because they are built on the notion of separating 'us' (the 'good') from 'them' (the 'bad') (Hill 2000). Dangerous memories are potentially subversive to those identities and may create new narratives and identities that do not retain essentialism. Needless to say, there is not a particular kind or source of memory that is dangerous per se (Ostovich 2002, 2005). The *danger* is in the practice of remembering the past in new ways that are disruptive to taken-for-granted assumptions about a group's identity; such ways establish new understandings of personal and collective identities that enable solidarity and conflict transformation. The question that is of concern, then, is: How can there be education spaces that encourage dangerous memories and contribute to conflict transformation, especially when hegemonic powers work tremendously hard to sustain essentialized memories?

As noted by Psaltis, Carretero and Cejahic-Clancy in Chap. 1, theoretical models of conflict transformation emphasize the importance of understanding the processes that enable the transformation of conflict from its destructive forms into a more productive one which is recognized as part of everyday struggles to negotiate power in socially just ways. The purpose of this chapter is to explore the potential of history teaching in formal and non-formal education spaces to facilitate conflict transformation processes, focusing in particular on the role of dangerous memories and reconciliation pedagogies. For this reason, we discuss openings and closures for the facilitation of conflict transformation in recent efforts for educational reform of history teaching in the Greek Cypriot and Turkish Cypriot educational systems in divided Cyprus. Our aim is to outline some insights from this endeavour—insights that may help history educators recognize the potential of dangerous memories and reconciliation pedagogies in conflict transformation.

This chapter is divided into four parts. First, a discussion on memory, history and identity sets the theoretical ground for addressing how dangerous memories could facilitate conflict transformation. Second, a brief review of recent formal reform efforts on history teaching is provided in the Greek Cypriot and Turkish Cypriot educational systems to show the challenges of promoting dangerous memories. Third, the work of NGOs working with both Greek Cypriot and Turkish Cypriot teachers shows some openings for reconciliation pedagogies and dangerous memories. This chapter ends with a broader discussion of the role that could be played by reconciliation pedagogies to promote dangerous memories through both formal and non-formal education efforts.

Dangerous Memories and Conflict Transformation

Memory plays a major role in structuring national identity (Kansteiner 2002) and sustaining a sense of self in and through the communities in which individuals belong and relate to others (Epstein 2001; Middleton and Edwards 1990). The connection between memory and identity raises two important issues: first, it highlights the political and emotional value of collective memories because past representations are preserved through social and ideological practices such as commemoration sites and rituals; second, the connection between memory and identity suggests that memory is created in interaction between and among people in social and political contexts (Conway 2003; Middleton and Edwards 1990; Olick 1999; Zerubavel 1996). Developments in social psychology over the last several decades show how social identity processes are crucial not only in maintaining positive social identity (Tajfel and Turner 1986; Turner 1999), but also in undertaking collective action to subvert hegemonic societal mechanisms and structures (van Zomeren et al. 2008).

However, one of the gaps in collective action theories, as noted by Psaltis, Carretero and Cejahic-Clancy, is how various forms of representation about self and others are entangled with ideologies such as nationalism in divided societies. For example, what gets defined as 'official' memory reflects the power of certain groups and ideologies in society to define the past according to their interests, often by silencing alternative and competing memory discourses (Conway 2003; Epstein 2001;

Middleton and Edwards 1990). Efforts to change these representations—e.g. by promoting 'prejudice reduction' interventions through intergroup contact—may not always be successful or may actually work to strengthen dualisms of good/bad and perpetrator/victim (Dixon et al. 2012). Yet, if such dualisms are so rigid and the cycle of nationalism is simply renewed every time through different means, then one wonders about the prospects of collective action for reconciliation.

This tension is particularly evident in historical narratives taught in schools in many conflict and post-conflict societies, whereas such narratives provide a framework through which children make sense of and lay claim to a national collective memory (Davies 2004; Siegel 2002). History curricula implore students to remember the nation's glories, leaders and warriors through practices which aim at establishing a historical consciousness that 'aligns forgetting with evil forces' (Eppert 2003, p. 186) that threaten to destroy the nation's identity and its very existence. In fact, one of the functions of collective memory is to highlight the victimhood of the in-group and silence the traumatic experiences of the out-group members, what has become known as one-sided victimization narrative (Bekerman and Zembylas 2012).

However, students and teachers are not dopes answering the mandates of 'politics of memory' (Todorov 2003; Simon 2005). Instead, a sense of rupture with official historical narratives and essentialized identities may be grounded in the notion of *dangerous memories*, for this idea challenges assumptions that 'transmitted memories' are endlessly powerful and thus can facilitate conflict transformation processes. Dangerous memories are not a particular kind or function of memory that can be isolated and defined, points out Ostovich (2002, 2005); rather, they are 'a *disruptive* practice of and from memory' (2002, p. 239, added emphasis). Any memory can become dangerous when it resists the prevailing historical narratives. What makes though a memory to be disruptive and therefore valuable to facilitate conflict transformation?

Dangerous memories are disruptive, for example, when they call for solidarity with the 'enemy' on the basis of common human suffering. These kinds of disruptions come as dangerous memories when we remember events of the past that question our consciences and assumed horizons; 'dangerous', then, takes the meaning of challenging, critical and hopeful while propelling individual and collective consciousness into a new process of narrativization. Re-claiming forgotten connections with others involves acts of compassion, self-criticality and resistance to the status quo.

As we are trapped in egotistic and ethnocentric mentalities, dangerous memories interrupt our endless cycle of selfishness and open up our eyes to the suffering of others (Metz 1972, 1980). As Metz notes in the context of violence and hatred in former Yugoslavia,

> [T]he memory of suffering became a shroud for the whole nation and a stranglehold on any attempt at interethnic rapprochement. Here a particular people have remembered only their own suffering, and so this purely self-regarding *memoria passionis* became not an organ of understanding and peace, but a source of hostility, hatred and violence. (Metz 1999, p. 230)

Following the spirit of the political theology of Metz means that the patterns of past violence and hatred may be subverted and solidarity with 'enemies' can be inspired through the memory of common suffering with others. In other words, dangerous memories could facilitate conflict transformation by highlighting practices grounded in solidarity with others. For example, this solidarity requires a constant openness and criticality to one's self and transformation and a willingness to recognize our connections to another's suffering—through attention to their memories of suffering such as listening to their stories and working with them to alleviate suffering.

The relevance of dangerous memories to critical education has been discussed by Giroux (1997) who suggests that,

> transformative intellectuals need to begin with a recognition of those manifestations of suffering that constitute historical memory, as well as the immediate conditions of oppression. The pedagogical rationality at work here is one that defines radical educators as bearers of 'dangerous memory,' intellectuals who keep alive the memory of human suffering along with the forms of knowledge and struggles in which such suffering was shaped and contested. (p. 105)

But how easy is to question hegemonic forms of collective memory and identity in education and highlight dangerous memories grounded in solidarity with the Other's suffering? In the following sections of the chapter, we provide two examples that show both openings and closures in terms of for how dangerous memories could facilitate conflict transformation.

The first example comes from formal efforts to reform history education in the Greek Cypriot and Turkish Cypriot educational systems in divided Cyprus; the second example, which is presented in the section that follows, comes from the non-formal work of civil society organizations.

History Teaching in Cyprus: Educational Reforms at the Formal Level

In general, one could claim that the story of reforming history education in both communities of Cyprus is no different from similar reform efforts in other countries, especially divided ones, in which school history understood and taught as heritage clashes with a new paradigm of history teaching grounded in historical methodologies, constructivist epistemology and critical thinking (for more details, see Makriyianni et al. 2011; Papadakis 2008; Psaltis et al. 2011). Yet, what is unique in this case, as is, of course, in each particular setting in which this clash is manifest, is how *inclusions* and *exclusions* are generated and enacted, strategically or less strategically, and with which consequences (see Klerides 2014).

Greek Cypriot Educational System

The latest reform effort in the Greek Cypriot educational system started in 2004 with the appointment by the government of an Educational Reform Committee to prepare a report on the reforms that needed to be undertaken in the Greek Cypriot educational system. The 'manifesto' that was produced, as the report was called, dealt with all school subjects and the need to initiate reforms at many levels. The main idea of the manifesto was the need for ideological re-orientation and restructuring of the educational system to adopt humanistic ideas rather than reproducing largely 'Greek values' and knowledge. With regard to history, the manifesto highlighted the values of promoting multiperspectivity and reconciliation and suggested the revision of history textbooks in accordance with new approaches of history teaching. Not surprisingly, the manifesto caused a variety of reactions that ranged from the support of its proposal, the avoidance of discussing ideological issues, up to its heavy criticism and rejection—mainly from conservative circles and the Greek Orthodox Church (see Makriyianni et al. 2011). The main issue whether history education should continue to promote the Greek national identity over a common Cypriot identity was lingering in public for several years and received a great coverage from media and politicians.

In 2008, the newly elected government (led by a leftist president) appointed a Scientific Committee to reform the curricula for the Greek Cypriot educational system. The Committee produced a framework promoting a democratic and humane school. In addition to this central Scientific Committee, special subject matter committees were appointed to produce their specific proposals for each school subject. The special committee for history education was consisted of five historian academics; no academic experts in history education were appointed in the committee. The decision was to include academics suggested by different political parties, while no history educators were included. Also, working groups of teachers were appointed to collaborate with academics in producing the new curriculum for each school subject. The approach of the history education academic committee focused on substantive knowledge and a single narrative approach, while pedagogically their approach was rather outdated. The final proposal ended promoting national identity and substantive understanding of history, while also including general references to historical thinking, multiperspectivity, and the importance of distinguishing between primary and secondary sources (Perikleous 2010). The proposal did not include aims regarding the development of historical thinking or the inclusion of sensitive and controversial issues for that matter.

While the working groups of teachers started producing new curricular and pedagogical materials in history education, the newly elected government in 2013 (led by a centre-to-right president) froze the process and appointed a new Scientific Committee to prepare a formative evaluation of the new curricula developed. With regard to history education, the evaluation report of this committee confirmed that there was a clash between two views: on the one hand, history teaching as heritage that leads to ethnocentrism; and on the other hand, history teaching that emphasizes multiperspectivity and critical thinking. The suggestion of the Committee was that the curriculum for history education should be revised, especially with regard to pedagogical issues, didactic approach, and the development of historical thinking. It was also suggested that there should be clear objectives and indicators regarding knowledge, skills and the development of critical thinking and evaluation of historical sources.

Various studies at the time of these reform efforts show a stark reality: how the ethnic division of Cyprus is rescaled down not only to official curricula and textbooks but also to classroom and school life through the creation of spaces that often dismiss the possibility of introducing approaches such as the teaching of sensitive and controversial issues (Zembylas and Kambani 2012) or they prevent openings for dangerous memories that challenge one-sided victimization narratives (e.g. Makriyianni et al. 2011; Perikleous 2010; Zembylas 2015; Zembylas et al. 2016). For example, even though teachers may acknowledge the benefits of approaches such as teaching controversial issues in history instruction, they may still feel strongly about the inappropriateness and non-feasibility of such approaches in the light of particular emotional, social and political circumstances. Thus, we need to remember that new paradigms or approaches such as 'new history' or the teaching of controversial issues that may encourage dangerous memories and facilitate conflict transformation take a different meaning in some settings over others and their application to these settings may not be as unproblematic as it may be argued by their supporters (Klerides 2014). Next, we show some of the developments in history teaching in the Turkish Cypriot educational system.

Turkish Cypriot Educational System

Similar to the Greek Cypriot educational system, the Turkish Cypriot educational system too sees history education 'as a tool to create national subjects' (Karahasan and Latif 2010, p. 23). Although this notion is still the dominant paradigm, the Turkish Cypriot experience shows that grass roots initiatives have played an important role in the 'dynamics of change' (Beyidoğlu Önen et al. 2010, pp. 117–122).

Although there has never been an attempt to revise history textbooks in the Turkish Cypriot community, towards the end of the 1990s and in the beginning of 2000s, the efforts for change came mostly from a grass roots movement. Especially after the banking crisis (Beyidoğlu Önen et al. 2010), towards the end of the 1990s, many Turkish Cypriots faced big economic challenges that led them to question the political status quo (Beyidoğlu Önen et al. 2010; Karahasan and Beyidoğlu, forthcoming). Electing Mehmet Ali Talat as the new leader in 2004 after the long-time presence of leader Rauf Denktash was a big change, because Denktash was the leader of Turkish Cypriots since the late 1970s; the change of administration was interpreted as dissatisfaction with the old regime that ruled for decades.

One of the first things that the new CTP (Republican Turkish Party) government, centre-left, did was to appoint a committee for revising Turkish Cypriot history textbooks, which were in use from 1974 till 2004. As a result of this initiative, the committee came up with new Cyprus history textbooks in a very short period of time. These textbooks were considered as more 'progressive', and they were positively included towards a 'federal united Cyprus'. Interestingly, the whole process of reform did not take place through a public consultation, but it was initiated from the government itself (Beyidoğlu Önen et al. 2010; Latif 2010; Papadakis 2008; Vural and Özuyanık 2008). The textbooks that were in use from 2004 till 2009 were grounded in the idea that 'Cyprus is the homeland of Cypriots', which was a departure from past textbooks. The textbooks in use from 1974 till 2004 depicted Turkish Cypriots as the ones who were rightful and victims, whereas Greek Cypriots were presented as bad and perpetrators (Beyidoğlu Önen et al. 2010).

The reform of history textbooks in 2004, however, created something unprecedented: it gave the opportunity or 'legitimate claim' to new administrations that every time a government changes, textbooks are subject to change too (Beyidoğlu Önen et al. 2010; Karahasan and Beyidoğlu, forthcoming). In other words, this initiative for change opened 'Pandora's Box' for subsequent governments to change history textbooks whenever they come to power. That was the reason why one of the first things that UBP (National Unity Party), centre-right, did when it came to power in 2009 was to change the textbooks that were in use from 2004 till 2009. Only in three months time, the authorities produced new Cyprus history textbooks, which brought back the previous ethnocentric lens (Karahasan and Latif 2010, p. 28).

Pedagogically speaking, there was an important shift in the way textbooks were structured after 2004. Instead of following the predominant 'banking model' (Freire 2000), according to which the teacher knows everything and students know nothing, the textbooks of 2004 encouraged student participation, multiperspectivity and active learning. Similarly, the textbooks of 2009 were grounded in a student-centred approach; however, time limitations seemed to prevent teachers from using the books in the way the writers envisioned.

In general, the experience of the formal reform efforts in the Turkish Cypriot community shows once again that while some 'progressive' narratives were included, they were once again excluded as a result of political change. Thus, although in 2004 there was a wave towards a 'federal united Cyprus' (Beyidoğlu Önen et al. 2010; Latif 2010; Papadakis 2008; Vural and Özuyanık 2008), this approach was replaced with the previous ethnocentric dominant discourse in 2009 after UBP came to power. Similar to the Greek Cypriot experience, the Turkish Cypriot experience shows how history education has been used by political parties as a way to promote particular history narratives to its people. This experience also shows the tensions that (re)surface between 'new history' and heritage and consequences of these tensions in terms of providing openings or closures for dangerous memories in formal education.

Efforts at the Non-formal Level: The Role of Civil Society Organizations in History Teaching

As stated by Bilali (this volume), the role of civil society organizations is significant in order to create awareness in history education, especially in relation to the prospects of dangerous memories, because as non-formal education providers, NGOs can often touch on issues that formal education may not dare to do. Specifically, two main NGOs in Cyprus have had important contribution over the last decade or so in the creation of education spaces to talk about history and peace education in non-mainstream ways; these organizations are the *Association for Historical Dialogue and Research* (AHDR) and *POST Research Institute* (POST RI). Both NGOs have been working on peace and reconciliation in Cyprus, especially since 2003: (a) to make people aware that the traumatic past is not something Cypriots should get trapped into, but the past can be dealt with productively; (b) to help people realize that 'dangerous memories' can constitute a positive way that people can move forward; and (c) to contribute to the creation of a new united Cyprus in which all Cypriots (Turkish Cypriots, Greek Cypriots, Maronites, Latins, Armenians and whoever lives in Cyprus) have educational opportunities that are based on human rights, democratic ethos and respect of differences.

AHDR, a bi-communal NGO, established in 2003, has been working on a wide range of projects and activities, including projects and activities, such as teacher training workshops and the creation of supplementary educational materials. In the past few years, AHDR published many supplementary materials for history teaching in Cyprus with an emphasis on multiperspectivity and empathy in history teaching. Some examples are the following: *Thinking Historically about Missing Persons: A Guide For Teachers* (Chapman et al. 2011); *Learning to investigate the history of Cyprus through artefacts*—*Teacher's Guide and Museum Activity booklet for Students* (Argyrou et al. 2011); *Introducing Oral History: When People's Stories Become History* (Fischer et al. 2011); *Our Children, Our Games* (Uludağ and Makriyianni 2011); *The Ottoman Period in Cyprus: Learning to Explore Change, Continuity and Diversity* (Samani et al. 2011); and *A Look at Our Past* (2011).

It should also be noted that AHDR's publications, except *Our Children, Our Games* (Uludağ and Makriyianni 2011), which was written in Greek and in Turkish only, are always trilingual, considering the importance of reaching out all the different groups in Cypriot society and abroad. Besides publishing supplementary educational materials for teachers, AHDR also organizes conferences and cultural activities for peace and reconciliation in Cyprus at its premises, located in the Buffer Zone in Nicosia. This space is also known as the 'Home for Cooperation' (H4C), which has become a cultural centre, where one can get language, dancing classes as well as space for conferences and meetings. H4C is now becoming an intersection point for both communities in the buffer zone. Alongside the supplementary materials, AHDR also produced a 'policy paper' in education by arguing that '…the current system of education in Cyprus fails to promote the notion of living in a multi-cultural, multi-lingual, and multi-faith society' (2013, p. i), and providing recommendations addressed to different stakeholders for transforming the current education systems on both sides of the divide.

POST RI, a Turkish Cypriot NGO based on the north side of the island, is another civil society organization with the aim of bringing positive change to education in Cyprus. Since its establishment in 2002, POST RI took part in different projects for unification of the island by using peace education as an approach. POST RI organizes film festivals, lectures and discussions, and undertakes research on history education. In 2004, POST RI implemented the first bi-communal project with AKTI (a Greek Cypriot environmental NGO) to explore the presence of nationalistic elements in school textbooks of the last year of primary school in both sides of the divide; the publication was titled *Education for Peace*. The success of this project led POST RI to a continuation of the project, titled *Education for Peace II*; however, this time the focus was only on the Turkish Cypriot side. *Education for Peace II* provided a comparative analysis of the history textbooks in secondary school that were in use from 1974 till 2004, including the revised textbooks developed when the Republican Turkish Party (CTP), centre-left party, came to power. The success of the *Education for Peace II* led POST RI to work extensively continuing the third and last leg of the project titled *Education for Peace III*, which analysed the textbooks in use at the high school level from 2004 to 2009, including some that are being used nowadays. Although the findings of the last project were discouraging in terms of the openings created for dangerous memories, the work of POST RI in general could be seen as providing significant understanding of the current situation and suggesting possibilities for encouraging the emergence of dangerous memories in peace education. POST RI's works are not limited to peace education but also in other areas like geography education and gender issues in the field of education (e.g. Birey and Beyidoğlu Önen 2013).

Overall, the findings of POST RI regarding history education in the north show that Turkish Cypriot history education went through an ethnocentric version of history according to which Turkish Cypriots were the ones who suffered from Greek Cypriots (Beyidoglu Önen et al. 2010). However, according to POST RI's (2010) study, this representation changed drastically with the revised textbooks in 2004 and promoted common social history, instead of a segregated version of 'good-us' versus 'bad-them'. As noted in the previous section, this representation changed once again when the Nationalist Unity Party (UBP), centre-right, took power and revised the textbooks in 2009 (Karahasan and Latif 2010).

In general, one of the most important contributions of POST RI is that it shows precisely how textbook revision in Cyprus is a deeply politicized process. However, an equally important contribution is the sort of pedagogies that are identified to promote reconciliation and highlight dangerous memories. For example, POST RI's publication *Past Traumas: The Representation of History and Peace Education* (Karahasan 2013) underlines the importance of dealing with traumatic past in productive ways and offers pedagogical ideas to deal with various educational challenges. This publication emphasizes that textbook revision is not the only or even the most important means of promoting peace and reconciliation, especially when political circumstances do not allow for such reforms. The way that history is taught might be argued to take priority over textbook reform, especially when such reform is felt to be too sensitive and thus best left until later (Davies 2016).

In summary, both AHDR and POST RI's contributions are valuable in the creation of learning spaces in which past traumatic issues in Cyprus can be talked about constructively in ways that formal curricula, textbooks and pedagogical practices do not dare to do yet. The work that is being done by both of these civil society organizations shows how the intervention of NGOs provides important openings, both academically and personally for those who look for alternative ways of engaging with history teaching. Civil society organizations, then, can open up ways or prepare the ground for formal educational efforts in both educational systems to make more bold moves. To the extent that there is some 'transference' of productive learning spaces from non-formal to formal settings, it is expected that these openings could greatly enhance the processes of conflict transformation in Cyprus.

Conclusions and Implications

The examples provided in this chapter highlight two important aspects in relation to history teaching and the prospects of promoting dangerous memories to facilitate conflict transformation. First, the politics of memory and past trauma are unavoidably entangled with pedagogies, history textbooks and reform efforts. Students and teachers *learn* how to remember the past trauma and sustain negative emotions about the Other through everyday social and educational practices in formal education settings. Consequently, when the politics of memory and trauma are not somehow accounted for in educational reform efforts, they risk perpetuating the hegemonic psycho-social ethos. Taking into consideration the politics of memory and trauma is valuable in making strategic decisions about how history teaching could realistically enhance the ability to actively promote conflict transformation.

The second important aspect in history teaching is that reconciliation pedagogies might often be suppressed in formal educational settings, while there may be more openings in non-formal ones. These differences of approaches reflect the political circumstances and the larger ideologies and hegemonies that lie behind them. Again, these differences as well as the political circumstances under which efforts are undertaken have to be strategically accounted for, if stakeholders want to create relevant openings that highlight dangerous memories and promote reconciliation pedagogies.

We would like to end the chapter by paying particular attention to the link between dangerous memories and reconciliation pedagogies and its importance for conflict transformation. Generally speaking, reconciliatory pedagogical practices are the pedagogies which foreground the need to elaborate how we might learn to live together with ever-increasing emotional and political complexities 'by focusing attention on aspects of pedagogy such as dialogue, the 'discourse of possibility', remembering and witnessing, and the affective dimensions of difficult, contested knowledge' (Hattam et al. 2012, p. 6). A reconciliatory ethos in history curriculum and teaching would help students from conflict-affected communities become aware, both at an emotional level and at an intellectual level, of the shared meanings, visions and ethical interdependence that can constrain as well as promote mutual understanding and communal interaction.

The examples shared in this chapter show the challenges that exist at different levels for highlighting dangerous memories that can be pedagogically approached to promote reconciliation, especially at the formal education level. Yet, the development of reconciliation pedagogies, even at the non-formal level through the work of NGOs is equally important to other reform initiatives, all of which must be designed contextually and strategically. In this regard, reconciliation pedagogies developed by civil society organizations can actively facilitate conflict transformation by helping to gradually dismantle the system of entrenched myths and antagonistic or one-sided trauma narratives that perpetuate division between Greek Cypriots and Turkish Cypriots.

In general, reconciliation pedagogies may offer two important things. First, they provide a space where educators and students can question common sense assumptions and the politics of hegemonic trauma narratives, thus creating spaces for dangerous memories to arise. Second, these pedagogies also provide opportunities for traumatized students to work through feelings of trauma and rehumanize the Other (McKnight 2004). Through dealing with the emotional challenges of trauma, teachers and students from each community may begin to empathize with the Other (McCully 2010); thus, by becoming sensitive to the emotions of trauma and mourning, teachers and students can begin to confront the ideological and political aspects of *chosen traumas* (Volkan 1979, 1988, 1997) within each community.

Social psychological pillars such as rehumanization, empathy and criticality through education are invaluable tools and mechanisms to promote conflict transformation. While these suggestions do offer some important approaches to facilitate sustainable peace and reconciliation, history teaching and education alone cannot do much for conflict transformation;

both Greek Cypriots and Turkish Cypriots must be actively engaged through collective action and solidarity to address the structural limitations mentioned earlier at the widest social and political level.

REFERENCES

Argyrou, E., Blondeau, B., Izzet, V., Ertaç, G., Ktori, M., & Makriyianni, C., et al. (2011). *Learning to investigate the history of Cyprus through artefacts: Teacher's guide and museum activity booklet for students.* Nicosia: AHDR.

Association for Historical Dialogue & Research. (2013). *Policy paper: Rethinking education in Cyprus/Politika öneri belgesi: Kıbrıs'ta eğitimi yeniden düşünmek/Κείμενο πολιτικής: Διαφοροποιώντας την αντίληψή μας για την παιδεία στην Κύπρο.* Nicosia: AHDR.

Bekerman, Z., & Zembylas, M. (2012). *Teaching contested narratives: Identity, memory and reconciliation in peace education and beyond.* Cambridge: Cambridge University Press.

Beyidoğlu Önen, M., Jetha-Dağseven, S., Karahasan, H., & Latif, D. (2010). *Re-writing history textbooks—History education: A tool for polarisation or reconciliation?* Nicosia: POST Research Institute.

Birey, T., & Beyidoğlu Önen, M. (2013). *Toplumsal cinsiyet ve öğretmenlik: Öğretmenlerin bakış açısı* [Gender and teaching: Teachers' perspective]. Retrieved 7 July 2017 from https://postresearchinstitute.files.wordpress.com/2011/02/toplumsal-cinsiyet-ve-c3b6c49fretmenlik.pdf. Nicosia: POST Research Institute.

Booth, W. J. (1999). Communities of memory: On identity, memory and debt. *American Political Science Review, 93,* 249–263.

Bourguignon, E. (2005). Memory in an amnesic world: Holocaust, exile, and the return of the suppressed. *Anthropological Quarterly, 78,* 63–88.

Chapman, A., Perikleous, L., Yakinthou, C., & Celal Zincir, R. (2011). *Thinking historically about missing persons: A guide for teachers.* Nicosia: AHDR.

Conway, B. (2003). Active remembering, selective forgetting, and collective identity: The case of bloody sunday. *Identity: An International Journal of Theory and Research, 3,* 305–323.

Davies, L. (2004). *Education and conflict: Complexity and chaos.* New York: Routledge.

Davies, L. (2016). The politics of peace education in post-conflict countries. In A. Langer & G. K. Brown (Eds.), *Building sustainable peace: Timing and sequencing of post-conflict reconstruction and peacebuilding.* Oxford, UK: Oxford University Press.

Dixon, J., Levine, M., Reicher, S., & Durrheim, K. (2012). Beyond prejudice: Are negative evaluations the problem and is getting us to like one another more the solution? *Behavioral and Brain Sciences, 35*(6), 411–425.

Eppert, C. (2003). Histories re-imagined, forgotten and forgiven: Student responses to Toni Morrison's *Beloved*. *Changing English*, 10, 185–194.
Epstein, J. (2001). Remember to forget: The problem of traumatic cultural memory. In J. Epstein & L. H. Lefkovitz (Eds.), *Shaping losses: Cultural memory and the Holocaust* (pp. 186–204). Chicago: University of Illinois Press.
Fischer, C., Costache, S., & Makriyianni, C. (2011). *Introducing oral history: When people's stories become history*. Nicosia: AHDR.
Freire, P. (2000). *Pedagogy of the oppressed*. 30th anniversary edition. (M. B. Ramos, Trans.). New York & London: Continuum.
Giroux, H. (1997). *Pedagogy and the politics of hope: Theory, culture and schooling*. Oxford: Westview Press.
Hattam, R., Atkinson, P., & Bishop, P. (2012). Rethinking reconciliation and pedagogy in unsettling times. In P. Ahluwalia, S. Atkinson, P. Bishop, P. Christie, R. Hattam, & J. Matthews (Eds.), *Reconciliation and pedagogy* (pp. 1–9). New York: Routledge.
Hill, J. (2000). *Becoming a cosmopolitan: What it means to be a human in the new millennium*. Lanham, MD: Rowman & Littlefield.
Karahasan, H. (Ed.). (2013). *Past traumas: The representation of history and peace education*. Nicosia: POST Research Institute.
Karahasan, H., & Beyidoğlu Önen, M. (forthcoming, 2016). Northern Cyprus. In S. Lässig, M. Repoussi & L. Cajani (Eds.), *History education under fire: Textbooks and curricula in international perspective*. Basingstoke: Palgrave.
Karahasan, H., & Latif, D. (2010). Education for peace III: Textual and visual analysis of the upper secondary school Cyprus history textbooks: Comparative analysis of the old and New Cyprus history textbooks. In M. Beyidoğlu Önen, S. Jetha-Dağseven, H. Karahasan, & D. Latif (Eds.), *Re-writing history textbooks—History education: A tool for polarisation or reconciliation?* (pp. 13–96), Nicosia: POST Research Institute.
Kansteiner, W. (2002). Finding meaning in memory: A methodological critique of collective memory studies. *History and Theory*, 41, 179–197.
Klerides, E. (2014). Educational transfer as a strategy for remaking subjectivities: Transnational and national articulations of 'new history' in Europe. *European Education*, 46(1), 12–33.
Latif, D. (2010). Dilemmas of moving from the divided past to envisaged united future: Rewriting the history books in the North Cyprus. In Ingo Richter (Ed.), *Special issue: Legitimation and stability of political systems: The contribution of national narratives—The International Journal for Education Law and Policy* (pp. 35–46).
Makriyianni, C., Psaltis, C., & Latif, D. (2011). History teaching in Cyprus. In E. Erdmann & W. Hasberg (Eds.), *Facing mapping, bridging diversity: Foundations of a European Discourse on history education, Part 1* (pp. 91–138). Germany: Wochen Schau Wissenschaft.

McCully, A. (2010). The contribution of history to peace building. In G. Salomon & E. Cairns (Eds.), *Handbook on peace education* (pp. 213–222). New York, NY: Psychology Press.

McKnight, A. (2004). Historical trauma, the persistent of memory and the pedagogical problems of forgiveness, justice and peace. *Educational Studies: A Journal of the American Educational Studies Association, 36,* 140–158.

Metz, J. B. (1972). The future in the memory of suffering. In J. B. Metz (Ed.), *New questions on God* (pp. 9–25). New York: Herder and Herder.

Metz, J. B. (1980). *Faith in history and society: Towards a fundamental practical theology.* New York: Seabury.

Metz, J. B. (1999). In the pluralism of religious and cultural worlds: Notes toward a theological and political program. *Cross Currents, 49,* 227–236.

Middleton, D., & Edwards, D. (Eds.). (1990). *Collective remembering.* London: Sage.

Olick, J. K. (1999). Collective memory: The two cultures. *Sociological Theory, 17,* 333–348.

Ostovich, S. T. (2002). Epilogue: Dangerous memories. In A. Confino & P. Fritzsche (Eds.), *The work of memory: New directions in the study of German society and culture* (pp. 239–256). Urbana and Chicago: University of Illinois Press.

Ostovich, S. T. (2005). Dangerous memories and reason in history. *KronoScope, 5*(1), 41–57.

Papadakis, Y. (2008). Narrative, memory and history education in divided Cyprus: A comparison of schoolbooks on the "History of Cyprus". *History and Memory 20*(2), 128–148.

Perikleous, L. (2010). At a crossroad between memory and thinking: The case of primary history education in the Greek-Cypriot educational system. *Education 3–13, 38*(3), 315–328.

Psaltis, C., Lytras, E., & Costache, S. (2011). *History educators in the Greek Cypriot and Turkish Cypriot community of Cyprus: Perceptions, beliefs and practices.* UNDP-ACT. ISBN: 978-9963-703-05-0.

Samani, H., Mavrada, M., Onurkan Samani, M., & Georgiou, M. (2011). *The Ottoman period in Cyprus: Learning to explore change, continuity and diversity.* Nicosia: AHDR.

Siegel, M. (2002). "History is the opposite of forgetting": The limits of memory and the lessons of history in interwar France. *The Journal of Modern History, 74,* 770–800.

Simon, R. (2005). *The touch of the past: Remembrance, learning, and ethics.* New York: Palgrave MacMillan.

Streich, G. (2002). Is there a right to forget? Historical injustices, race, memory, and identity. *New Political Science, 24,* 525–542.

Tajfel, H., & Turner, J. C. (1986). The social identity theory of intergroup behaviour. In S. Worchel & W. G. Austin (Eds.), *Psychology of intergroup relations* (pp. 7–24). Chicago, IL: Nelson-Hall.

Todorov, T. (2003). *Hope and memory: Reflections on the twentieth century.* London: Atlantic Books.

Turner, J. C. (1999). Current issues in research on social identity and self-categorization theories. In N. Ellemers, R. Spears, & B. Doosje (Eds.), *Social identity: Context, commitment, content* (pp. 6–34) Oxford, UK: Blackwell.

Uludağ, G., & Makriyianni, C. (2011). Çocuklarımız oyunlarımız/ Τα παιδιά μας, τα παιχνίδια μας *[Our children, our games].* Nicosia: AHDR.

van Zomeren, M., Postmes, T., & Spears, R. (2008). Toward an integrative social identity model of collective action: A quantitative research synthesis of three socio-psychological perspectives. *Psychological Bullettin, 134*(4), 504–535.

Volkan, V. (1979). *Cyprus-war and adaptation: A psychoanalytic history of two ethnic groups in conflict.* Charlottesville: University Press of Virginia.

Volkan, V. (1988). *The need to have enemies and allies: From clinical practice to international relationships.* Jason Aronson: Northvale, NJ.

Volkan, V. (1997). *Bloodlines: From ethnic pride to ethnic terrorism.* Boulder, CO: Westview.

Vural, Y., & Özuyanık, E. (2008). Redefining identity in the Turkish-Cypriot school history textbooks: A step towards a united federal Cyprus. *South European Society and Politics, 13*(2), 133–154.

Zembylas, M. (2015). *Emotion and traumatic conflict: Re-claiming healing in education.* Oxford: Oxford University Press.

Zembylas, M., Charalambous, C., & Charalambous, P. (2016). *Peace education in a conflict-troubled society.* Cambridge: Cambridge University Press.

Zembylas, M., & Kambani, F. (2012). The teaching of controversial issues during elementary-level history instruction: Greek-Cypriot teachers' perceptions and emotions. *Theory and Research in Social Education, 40,* 107–133.

Zerubavel, E. (1996). Social memories: Steps to a sociology of the past. *Qualitative Sociology, 19,* 283–299.

Authors' Biography

Michalinos Zembylas is Professor of Educational Theory and Curriculum Studies at the Open University of Cyprus. He is also Visiting Professor and Research Fellow at the Institute for Reconciliation and Social Justice, University of the Free State, South Africa. He has written extensively on emotion and affect in relation to social justice pedagogies, intercultural and peace education, human rights education and citizenship education. His recent books include *Emotion and Traumatic Conflict: Re-claiming Healing in Education* (Oxford, 2015), *Methodological advances in research on emotion and education* (with P. Schutz; Springer, 2016) *and Peace Education in a Conflict-Troubled Society* (with C. Charalambous and P. Charalambous; Cambridge, 2016).

Hakan Karahasan graduated from Radio-TV and Film in 2000 at Eastern Mediterranean University (EMU). Then, he took his MA in English Studies at the Department of English Literature and Humanities at EMU. Currently, he is a Ph.D. candidate in Communication and Media Studies and also works as a senior instructor at Near East University, Department of Film Making. In 2009–2010, he was a guest researcher at the Department of Communication Disciplines—Semiotics (now, the Department of Philosophy and Communication) at the University of Bologna, under the supervision of Anna Maria Lorusso. Since 2004, he got involved in *Education for Peace* projects with POST Research Institute and took part in analysing history education on the northern part of Cyprus. His studies were mostly published in various journals in Cyprus and in Turkey, including the book that he edited entitled, *Past Traumas: The Representation of History and Peace Education*, published by POST Research Institute in 2012.

Open Access This chapter is licensed under the terms of the Creative Commons Attribution 4.0 International License (http://creativecommons.org/licenses/by/4.0/), which permits use, sharing, adaptation, distribution and reproduction in any medium or format, as long as you give appropriate credit to the original author(s) and the source, provide a link to the Creative Commons license and indicate if changes were made.

The images or other third party material in this chapter are included in the chapter's Creative Commons license, unless indicated otherwise in a credit line to the material. If material is not included in the chapter's Creative Commons license and your intended use is not permitted by statutory regulation or exceeds the permitted use, you will need to obtain permission directly from the copyright holder.

The Teaching of Recent and Violent Conflicts as Challenges for History Education

Mario Carretero

THE NEED OF AN INTERDISCIPLINARY APPROACH TO STUDY HISTORICAL REPRESENTATIONS

This is a book about history and therefore about the past. This is also a book about dramatic events that have happened in various societies at different and recent times. In this vein, let us start this chapter with an example of 1838 but being discussed nowadays.[1] "The human cargo was loaded on ships at a bustling wharf in the nation's capital, destined for the plantations of the Deep South. Some slaves pleaded for rosaries

---

This paper has been written with the support of Projects EDU2015-65088P from the DGICYT (Ministry of Education, Spain) and also the Project PICT2012-1594 from the ANPCYT (Argentina) coordinated by the author. Also this paper has been written during a stay as Visiting Fellow from La Sapienza University (Rome). My gratitude to this institution and to Professor Giovanna Leone for her very valuable comments on this topic.

M. Carretero (✉)
Autonoma University of Madrid, Madrid, Spain
e-mail: mario.carretero@mac.com

as they were rounded up, praying for deliverance. But on this day... no one was spared: not the 2-month-old baby and her mother, not the field hands, not the shoemaker... Their panic and desperation would be mostly forgotten for more than a century. But this was no ordinary slave sale. The enslaved African-Americans had belonged to the nation's most prominent Jesuit priests. And they were sold, along with scores of others, to help secure the future of the premier Catholic institution of higher learning at the time, known today as Georgetown University".[2]

About 180 years later of this incident, the University of Georgetown has decided to offer compensations to the descendants of this episode of 1838. And these compensations are being offered in a context of investigating historically what happened with these 234 slaves and open to public discussion slavery as a general problem of the USA and as a specific problem of the role of US universities in relation to this issue.[3] Interestingly enough, the National Museum of African American History and Culture has been recently inaugurated being the first important and national museum of this kind.[4]

Definitely this is a very fascinating example of how historical events and representations are not only present as theoretical knowledge in books and archives but on the contrary they are also very alive and can also influence our daily lives as both individuals and societies. The decision of this North American University can only be understood in the context of how slavery has been an important matter on the past of the USA but only recently is being a significant issue in its history (Baptist 2014). As it is well known, the recent past of this country was heavily influenced by slavery as an economic institution, which had an enormous influence on its economic, political, and social and cultural development. Very famous historical events as the Civil War, after the decision of the President Abraham Lincoln of abolishing slavery, and the assassination of Martin Luther King Jr. (1968) because of his activity defending civil rights, cannot be fully understood if we do not take into account that by 1800 about one-third of the population of the South States of USA were slaves from African origin. After the defeat of the South states by the North ones and the abolition of slavery in the whole country, civil rights were not really equal for whites and African-Americans. On the contrary, numerous cases of oppression still existed and this is precisely the main reason for the protests on civil rights leaded by Martin Luther King Jr. by the 1960s.

All this is rather well known and is part of Western popular knowledge due to a number of cultural productions, Hollywood films and TV series being very influential ones. But the question, which makes this example meaningful to the matters considered in this book, has to do with how the representation of the past called "history" has being considering this important issue and what kind of implications has this for present individuals and societies.

At this point, we have to establish a classical distinction framed by an also classical question. This is to say, what kind of "history" are we referring to? Elsewhere we have distinguished among at least three kinds of meanings for this label. I mean academic history, also called historiography, school history and popular history. Elsewhere I have considered the main theoretical and empirical differences among these three meanings (Carretero and van Alphen 2017), and it could be considered that the interaction of the three of them make what finally is considered "historical culture" (Carretero et al. 2017), which is not necessarily just only one of them. On the contrary, it could be said that historical culture is the final product of a rich, complex and continuous interaction among the three of them, as it can be seen, for example, in the chapters of this book. In this vein, all of them present specific cases of how representation of the past is both produced and consumed (Wertsch and Rozin 2000) by different societies and groups being all of them examples of what academic and professional historians are considering uses of history. In this vein, the chapters in this book of Bentrovato and Bellali in part 1 and Pingel and Zadora in part 2 are very good and specific examples of how that interaction is taking place in different national and regional present contexts.

In this occasion, our reference to this issue will be briefer and we will introduce these differences by the comparison among the way these three "histories" have considered the slavery in the USA, as an example of how historical knowledge can be much more surprising than we probably think about it. Let us start by historiographical knowledge. In this case, it is fascinating to see how the topic is receiving an increasing interest by North American historians, which means that it was not considered for a number of years. Of course one wonders how this could happen taking into account its importance and enormous influence. In general terms, it could be said that probably slavery was not important because slaves were not the main actors of the US historiographical narrative which like many others is a national one, and it is devoted to the master narrative of the nation (vanSledright 2008). Definitely this has been changing in the last years.

Let us move to school history. In this case, research by Epstein (2009) has clearly indicated how high school North American students having an African-American origin overtly reject numerous school contents about the past of their nation. This is due mainly because they consider these contents as not representative of their past. Consequently, there is a process of cultural and educational resistance in relation to hegemonic historical school contents, which include textbooks and teachers lessons. As a matter of fact, US history textbooks have received numerous criticisms because of their contents, which traditionally were not inclined to include minorities in their contents. It is important to notice that in this case the so-called minority is bigger than the population of many European Union states. Interestingly enough, these processes of resistance studied by Epstein (2009) and other authors are also showing that not only African-American but also the rest of students are not being taught essential parts of the construction processes of their nation.

And finally if we consider popular history in general terms, it can be said that films and TV series are, for example, *Kunta Kinte*, based on the novel *Roots: The Saga of an American Family* (Haley 1976), *Forrest Gump* (1994) and a number of similar and related cultural productions have very much influenced the view we all have about slavery and other recent events in the USA and, as a consequence, in other parts of the planet. Thus, many of these films have been able to show not only the cruel details of slavery but also its importance as a social and economic institution and the way it determined the life of millions of people for generations. In sum, the access to the representation of the past of those important topics comes from an interaction of the three types of historical knowledge and not only from one of them, as stated above. Also any of these types of historical knowledge is definitely influenced by the other two. Therefore, academic history is not the only one, which establishes reliable and valid representations of the past. Historiography is also a social practice and as such could be influenced by specific views about what will be studied and how. For example, it could "forget" to study slavery for a number of years, as it is being considered in this case. Thus, in the last decade research has been able to show that most of historiographical productions since nineteenth century has been basically influenced by the idea of nation (Berger 2014). In other words, the main subject of academic historical narratives has been the nations as such, and this has implied both an exclusion of heterogeneity and the construction of imagined homogenous national people (Anderson 1983/1991). Obviously slaves, natives and women were not included in that idealized and essentialist canon. And this is probably one of the reasons the present decision of Georgetown University is surprising us even nowadays.

Meanwhile, school history was created as a compulsory subject matter by all nineteenth-century school systems precisely to indoctrinate students with their national histories. There is more than anecdotal evidence that school history and historiography as an academic profession were born mostly at the same times everywhere (Berger 2014). Thus, it can be said that to a great extent school history was born as the little sister of national historiographies. But it is important to take into account that unfortunately the school history has not experienced the same transformation as national historiographies did particularly since the second half of twentieth century when the Annales School (Burke 1990), the History of Mentalities (Braudel 1990), the History of Private Life (Aries and Duby 1992), The History of Gender (Rose 2010), the Global History (Conrad 2016) and other trends introduced enormous changes in this field. On the contrary, school history has suffered a number of changes, which will be presented below but still in many societies historical contents play a role, which is closer to the local nationalistic goals and their associated tensions than to present renovated historiographical approaches (Foster 2012).

It is important to consider that popular history (Groot 2016)—from historical novels, museum exhibitions, heritage sites, to films, television shows and documentaries, Web sites and apps—has experienced an enormous expansion since the fifties due to the enormous development of media and particularly the digital revolution. In this respect, the words of a very prestigious historian as Le Goff should be considered: "Memory (as popular history) is a conquest, it must seek and preserve that what allows it to construct itself from a perspective of truth. It must dispel false legends, black or golden, about such episodes of the past, collect the maximum amount of documents and confront contradictory memories, open up the archives and impede their destruction, know to look for the memory expelled to the taboos of history during certain periods in certain systems in literature or in art, and recognize the plurality of legitimate memories" (Le Goff 1990, p. 15). It is important to take into account that Le Goff wrote this paragraph in a presentation of a book about how the collapse of communist countries after the fall of

Berlin's wall triggered an intense process of recovery of collective memories about essential portions of the past silenced by soviet historiography, which severely censored historiographical research. As Hein and Selden (2000) showed, these attempts to censor history were also successful at least in relation to a number of events in democratic countries as Japan, West Germany and the USA.

In this vein, it is important to mention that for centuries human beings consumed historical representations basically through heritage related to monuments, traditions and museums. In general terms, most of this knowledge was considered in a fixed and dogmatic manner (Lowenthal 2015). But nowadays popular history is playing an important role having an influential interaction with both academic history and school history. As Kansteiner (2017) has noted, historians did not pay attention to historical films until rather recently because these were not considered reliable views on the past. But as mentioned before films and other products of popular history have been very influential in our views on various topics as slavery and its influence on the development of societies.

In conclusion, the study of how different representations of the past are both produced and consumed by individuals and societies needs to be studied from an interdisciplinary point of view (Carretero et al. 2017). It is striking that the research agendas of the historical discipline, the philosophy of history, history education and popular historical culture are still so separate. So far the boundaries have been blurred only in rare instances (Berger et al. 2012; see also Retz 2015 for an analysis of the interface of academic history, school history and the philosophy of history), although these fields can learn a lot from each other. Without this kind of approach, it is almost impossible to understand how a social and cultural phenomenon as the so-called history wars (Grever and Stuurman 2007; Taylor and Guyver 2012) is taking place since the beginning of the 1990s when globalization started its increasing trend. Most of the chapters of this book have to do with different cases of these wars and should be understood in that context where just one discipline is not enough to make sense of its profound meaning.

In this vein, this chapter deals with these objectives. Firstly, a view on the contributions and advances of history education in the last decades will be presented. This will allow us to examine the context of possible educational changes to be implemented in the cases presented in the chapters of this book. The specificity of teaching violent and recent events, related to political conflicts which are still running in many cases, will be taken into account. As it can be easily imagined, it is not the same to teach, for example, the history of Roman Empire than to discuss in the classrooms about a national civil war that happened one or two decades ago. In this respect, most of the present advances on history learning and teaching research have to do with **how** to teach and learn historical contents (Seixas 2017). On its part, most of the research on history textbooks has to do with **what** is included in the textbook. In other words, the first kind of research has to with the **consumption** by citizens of historical contents and the second one with the cultural **production** of them. As it is well known, these two cultural processes do not follow always parallel tracks. This is to say, what is in the minds of the students is not necessarily in the textbooks and vice versa. In this chapter, I will argue that in the area of research of history education, and particularly in the field of the role of history education for conflict resolution and reconciliation, we need to establish a more meaningful relation between these two areas of research if we pretend to implement possible, effective and meaningful improvements in the future. Also, the issue of **for what purposes** should history be told will be considered because it affects also the objectives of this book.

History Education as an Evolving Field

Regarding the production of representations about the past, different researchers have considered the existence of competing objectives of history education (Barton and Levstik 2004; Wineburg 2001). Carretero (2011) has redefined these objectives as "romantic" and "enlightened," because their features and functions stem from their intellectual roots in romanticism and the enlightenment, respectively. In that sense, history has been taught in all national school systems so as to make students "love their country" (Nussbaum and Cohen 2002) and to make them "understand their past" (Seixas 2004). In a romantic vein, history education is a fundamental strategy used to achieve: (a) a positive assessment of the past, present and future of one's own social group, both local and national, and (b) an identification with the country's political history. In an enlightened vein, history education aims at fostering critical citizens' capability of informed and effective participation in the historical changes happening nationally and globally. This can involve a critical attitude toward their own local or national community, or even larger political units. Recently, this has been translated in several countries into the following disciplinary and cognitive objectives: (a) to understand the past in a complex manner, which usually implies mastering the discipline's conceptual categories (Carretero and Lee 2014); (b) to distinguish different historical periods, through the appropriate adequate comprehension of historical time (Barton 2008); (c) to understand historical multicausality and to relate the past with the present and the future (Barton 2017); and (d) to approach the methodology used by historians, such as comparing sources (Wineburg et al. 2010).

The main and almost exclusive objective of history education in many countries has been since the end of nineteenth century the national indoctrination of students via the transmission of an invented national past. History education received much critique during the decades between WWI and WWII, because it became clear that its contents and approaches were saturated with blind nationalism and a very stereotypical view of other nations, nationals and their pasts, particularly of neighboring countries. For example, Boyd (1997) has analyzed the pioneer contribution to this respect of Altamira (1891), a Spanish intellectual who contributed meaningfully to the League of Nations and who was the author of one of the first books on history education. As a matter of fact, it was even suggested to eliminate it from the school system. The enormous human and political catastrophe of WWII demonstrated that blind nationalism was a real and unfortunate fact. Since the 1970s and 1980s, history education's interest in providing students with a critical view of social and political issues of different societies in the past has increased. One of the important factors contributing to this improvement has been the gradual inclusion of social sciences contents in history curricula, as some important educational thinkers were able to foresee (Dewey 1915; Piaget 1933). This feature has implied that school historical contents have tried to incorporate questions and explanations related to how societies change across times and not to include just single and closed narratives about the past of the nations.

In this vein, the field of history education suffered an important change in the early 1980s when Dickinson et al. (1984), (Shemilt 1980) published a number of books and papers that introduced innovative ideas on this theoretical and applied area of research. Up to this point, the teaching of history faced two main problems. On the one hand, a number of researchers indicated a very low performance on school historical knowledge (Ravitch 1987), probably due to a lack of interest in learning about it, which was not significant enough for the students. On the other hand, history as a school subject was characterized by rote memory and copy and paste practices. Enormous list of dates, battles and main characters were the typical contents of school history in most of educational systems. For example, most high school history textbooks in the USA never had less than 500 pages, but at the same time research in text understanding was clearly showing that students had a very poor comprehension of basic history contents constituted by canonical historical narratives such as the one on the Boston Tea Party (Beck and McKeown 1994; Barton and Levstick 1996).[5]

Unfortunately, even nowadays this continues to be the usual picture. Reacting to this situation and with a much more active and constructive view on learning in mind, a number of educational proposals started to be developed in the 1980s. For example, in the UK the *13–16 History Curriculum* was developed and applied in a great number of schools (Shemilt 1980). These developments were based on the importance of academic discipline for educational practice. This is to say, the goal of education rather than transmitting a considerable amount of consolidated academic knowledge was to initiate students in the practice of historiographical procedures through an emphasis on their own cognitive activity. In this respect, Collingwood (1946) was an influential author, as in *Idea of History* he developed his metaphor of the historian as a detective. Thus, the *13–16 History Curriculum* proposed that students had to find out, for example, how and why a specific and decisive historical event had happened instead of just memorizing an enormous list of names, places and specific dates, including also specific predetermined glorious narratives. Also, from this new educational perspective, students had to contemplate the role played by some main characters. For this purpose, students had to examine and critically discuss a number of data and historical texts about that event in order to test their hypothesis. In this vein, the general idea was to base history education on thinking abilities and active knowledge and not only on just an accumulative process of storing information.

At that time, the work by two celebrated psychologists, Piaget (1966) and Bruner (1966), also resonated in the field. Both authors defend a constructivist view on learning and share the idea of knowledge developing in the student's own cognitive activity. They were considerably successful defending the idea of the students' discoveries as a sign of autonomous and active cognition. Furthermore, Bruner's idea of establishing meaningful relations between school contents and academic disciplinary developments was quite influential.[6] In this vein, one of the main advances developed by Dickinson et al. (1984) was the difference between first- and second-order concepts in history. First-order concepts were related to specific historical concepts such as "monarchy" and "feudalism." Second-order concepts were related to students' ideas about how historical knowledge is constructed. These involve time, historical causality, significance and evidence. In other words, the idea of history education as a pedagogical endeavor centered not only on specific data but above all on developing disciplinary thinking and reasoning. Accordingly, history classes should be considered an opportunity for thinking historically and not just for accumulating historical information by rote memory (Carretero and Voss 1994). About 20 years later, these initiatives were a basic support for fully developed educational programs, such as the one designed by Seixas (2004; Seixas and Morton 2013) in Canada around the idea of **historical consciousness**, also influenced by German authors such as Rüsen (see Retz 2015, and Seixas 2015, 2016, for reviews on these specific developments). This program has been developing six essential historical "second-order concepts" (causality, etc.) as the center of its educational efforts. According to this initiative, students should accomplish a full understanding of these concepts to achieve a disciplinary view of historical contents.

Some years after the first mentioned British publications, Wineburg (1991) published a seminal empirical paper about historical problem-solving. His work in the USA was influenced by cognitive theories (Chi et al. 1988) relying on the comparison between experts (historians in this case) and novices as an essential research strategy (Limón and Carretero 1998). Wineburg was also convinced of the importance of teaching historiographical methods instead of emphasizing rote memory of historical contents. His support of the importance of developing student's inquiry activity was also clear. More specifically, his study (1991) analyzed the differences between one group of historians—history experts—and a group of high school students in their senior year when faced to solve a historical problem. This task was basically related to the most important events of the Lexington Battle (1776) in the context of the American Revolution. Participants were provided with pictures and documents of that period and had to interpret them as possible historical sources. The fundamental differences found between the two groups were related to the experts using heuristics to base their inquiry. Thus, one conclusion of this work was that the use of three heuristics would significantly improve evidence evaluation on the part of the high school students. The first heuristic was defined as *corroboration* or the act of comparing documents with one another. The second one, *sourcing*, was defined as the act of looking first to the source of the document before reading the body of the text. The last heuristic is *contextualization* considered as the act of situating a document in a concrete temporal and spatial context. These and related ideas produced the development of educational programs like *Reading like a historian* (Wineburg et al. 2011), which has had an enormous impact on schools in the USA and other countries.[7] The approach developed by Wineburg and colleagues (Nokes 2017; Wineburg et al. 2010) emphasized both reading and writing as essential cognitive abilities related to the specificity of history as a discipline and tend to use the term **historical thinking** as the initiatives leaded by Seixas also do (see http://historicalthinking.ca/ and also https://sheg.stanford.edu/). In both cases, the emphasis has been on the cognitive activity of student as a learner of historical knowledge. This underlying idea can be also found on related efforts as the work of vanSledright (2010). But there are also interesting efforts which emphasized the idea of the student as a social learner from an interactionist point of view.

In a European context, van Boxtel and van Drie (2017) have developed a fruitful instructional initiative through a dialogical framework. They consider learning as entering into a community of practice (Lave and Wenger 1991) and achieving specific concepts and procedures. From this point of view, the historians' practice is also based on a dialogical activity. The work by van Boxtel and van Drie stems from the above-mentioned contributions about fostering historical thinking and also emphasizes the use of documents and evidence. However, based on Bakhtin's ideas (1981) about the nature and importance of dialogue, they think that historical expertise is not only based on individual cognitive operations, such as the sourcing, corroboration and documentation related to historical text inquiry. For them, it is also essential to consider dialogical activity, mostly in relation to multiple views on both historical narratives and concepts. Therefore, they confront students in the classrooms with a number of dialogical activities in which they have to compare and evaluate different views on the same historical issue. More specifically, these activities have to do with asking historical questions, connecting events, developments and actions through a historical contextualization, using substantive historical concepts (facts, concepts and chronology) and also historical meta-concepts and supporting claims with arguments and evidence based on evaluated sources. All this always in a context of the importance of dialogue in classrooms activities. The authors maintain that these components are powerful enough both to trigger historical interest in the students and to improve epistemological beliefs Maggioni et al. (2009) about history as a subject matter. They thus help students to understand that disciplinary historical problems have no closed answers already established in a definitive narrative but, on the contrary, that these problems can be investigated and interrogated as ways of inquiring about past societies and looking for different interpretations. Therefore, these efforts try to develop critical thinking and intellectual autonomy among the students using not only reading and writing activities about historical sources in the classrooms, but also an intensive dialogue about them and the conceptual problems they are associated with. These ideas are in line with some recent research (Freedman 2015) that insists on providing more opportunities for students to develop critical thinking through the introduction of a broader variety of sources and to insert their historical evidence in the context of general interpretations or "frames."

How to Improve the Teaching of Recent, Conflicting and Violent Past?

Once we have described the main developments of history education, we will elaborate how these and related contributions could improve it in the contexts related to the papers of this book. As it was mentioned above most of the educational developments in this field have to do with **how** to teach historical contents in order to achieve a meaningful and disciplinary understanding. But most of the chapters of this book have to do with **what** is present or absent in the narratives included in the textbooks, what has been eliminated and what kind of version is being offered to the students and teachers as present and future citizens about recent conflicts. As it was announced above in this part of this chapter, I will argue that a meaningful relation between these two important aspects of history education should be elaborated in order to improve history education in conflicting contexts.

If we examine the historical topics and issues considered by most of the chapters, two features clearly appear. On the one hand, most of the historical events have a **national character** and not a regional or worldwide one. This is to say, these events only make sense in the context of specific national histories. There are only two exceptions in the whole book. In one case (Psaltis, Franc, Smeekes, Ioannou, Žeželj, Chap. 4), similar processes are compared in three different countries. The other case is the study about the teaching of the Holocaust (Bilewicz, Witkowska, Stubig, Beneta and Imhoff, Chap. 6), which is obviously a historical issue affecting several countries. But in this case it is considered mainly in relation to a specific national case, the Polish one. On the other hand, all the papers deal with recent events. This is to say, they are devoted to analyze **recent** issues, which have happened less between 50 and 100 years ago, or even less. In other words, what most of these papers do not consider is a big historical event, for example WWI or WWII, the colonization of America or the industrial revolution, which are classical and common topics in most Western history curricula.

Thus, these two features of being **recent and national** are the main origins of the difficulties for teaching **conflicting historical issues.** The reasons are almost obvious, but it is important to mention them. Precisely because those events happened so recently, there is a direct continuity between past and present historical subjects, as it was easy to see in the example of the slavery of the USA mentioned at the beginning of this chapter. These type of cases are very numerous. They can be found everywhere, and they show how historical knowledge not only is very alive but even it can be said that "history can bite" (Bentrovato et al. 2016). Interestingly enough, these cases appear even in contexts where apparently there is no conflict. For example, in the case of Spain (Valls 2007) most of the direct descendants of the victims assassinated by the Franquist (*circa* 160,000) during the Spanish Civil War (1936–9) are still asking for government support to recuperate the corpses.[8] Neither those victims nor their families have ever received any kind of recognition by the Spanish government. In other words, recent historical conflicts very often trigger emotional judgments and representations, which could last several generations. Therefore, these views tend to be very durable, and they also are very difficult to change as numerous social psychology works have been able to show.

Also, recent conflicting historical events are a very important source of national identities. These identities are also based on remote historical events, which have considered as nations myths of origin by classic historical research (Hobsbawm 1990). But definitely events that have happened less than 50–100 years have a tremendous influence on citizens view on the past because it is considered by citizens also part of the present (Shemilt 2011). As a matter of fact, they are not part of the present, but to some extent it is understandable that people could think of it in that way because definitely these events have consequences in the present. In other words, it is really complicated to establish and to maintain a historical distance which could favor an objective analysis because there are still many present influences like the ones from media and family which in general do not favor the process of beliefs change, revision and possible reconciliation. On the contrary, in general terms these influences tend to maintain consolidated views on recent conflicts because they are part of their belief systems.

In my opinion, there is a key central idea on present developments of history education. This idea was labeled by David Lowenthal (1985/2015) about 30 years ago by the title of his very influential book *The past is a foreign country*, and it was even continued by another very important contribution in our field. I mean the book by Sam Wineburg (1991) Historical thinking *and other unnatural acts*. These two contributions have developed the very essential idea that a clear separation is needed between the past, as part of our cognitive, emotional and social phenomenological experience, and the historical attempts to analyze that past through systematic and analytical ways and disciplinary methods. In my opinion, we need to develop more profoundly these ideas because they have a central importance for both remote and recent historical events.

In other words, history seems to be about everyday, common-sense things. So many people believe that history can be understood simply by applying common-sense understandings. Thus, when historical concepts appear like "king," "bourgeois" or "colonist," people think they refer to their present experience of those concepts but in fact they refer to very different representations. Of course the same could happen with concepts related to relations and institutions and not only to individuals, like "feudalism" and "republican state." This misunderstanding is in the base of most erroneous representations of the past, and it is central to history education. Therefore, in this chapter, I argue that this simplistic view of history learning is a mistake. Four decades of research suggest that thinking historically is counterintuitive (Carretero et al. 2013; Carretero and Lee 2014; Lee 2005), as it is also the learning of scientific concepts. Three decades of research on different subject matters (Vosniadou 2013) have shown us that meaningful learning implies important processes of radical **conceptual change** going from the intuitive notions to more complex ones. In this vein, history requires understanding concepts that differ from everyday conceptions and explanations. Some everyday ideas are completely incompatible with history; many students, for example, believe that we can only really know anything by directly experiencing it (Cercadillo et al. 2017) and vice versa. This is to say, some students think that whatever is experienced directly through viewing a film or a historical image, for example, corresponds necessarily to true knowledge without taking into account that the film and the image are also cultural products which should be analyzed according to theoretical concepts and theories.

Thus, in order to improve students understanding of history as a representation of the past which is unnatural and counterintuitive, it would be important also to contribute to their decentration through the presentation of alternative views. No doubt multiperspectivity could play an essential role in this process. As a matter of fact in the field of social and civic education, the presence of controversial topics in the classrooms has been proved as a very effective and productive way of changing students minds and improving their reflexivity on these issues (Hess 2004). But multiperspectivity has to do basically with **what** students should learn and not necessarily with **how** to learn it.

In this respect, present developments in history education, as the ones described above, related to **historical thinking** and **historical consciousness** could contribute very much to a better learning and teaching methods of recent and conflicting historical events. This is to say, alternative views could be presented emphasizing underlying issues of historical significance, change, causality and time (Seixas and Morton 2013). Let us briefly unpack these important questions.

- **Significance**. The past is full of events. If most of the history curricula in Western countries are related to some set of common topics is because there is a selection of these events based on particular views on our culture. In other words, these views attribute significance to some events compared to others because Western nations share some common views on the past. For example, these views could be related to the colonial experiences (since fifteenth century to nowadays), and they could also generate different and even opposite views on certain phenomena. It is really important for the

students to elaborate and to discuss why and how historical events are selected to form specific narratives about certain periods of the past and also make explicit the underlying cultural belief systems that support those attributed significances.
- **Change**. History implies necessarily to study how human societies have changed through time and space. This is related to the need of establishing connections and similarities among different human groups and societies in diverse moments and milieus of the planet. It also implies to distinguish between short- and long-term changes. Therefore, it is also related to differentiate change and continuity, as it is applied in different historical periods. Very often these processes of change are violent and traumatic, but their importance usually goes beyond the recognition of those dimensions because historical changes also have durable consequences affecting distinct aspects of human societies related to economy, culture, politics and economy.
- **Causality**. That is, the need to see the causality of historical events in a complex way, determined by multiple causes. On the one hand, students very often tend to maintain just a historical perspective based on just one single cause. But social and historical problems are complex because they imply an interaction of different types of causes. Most of dramatic and important historical events are very dependent on contingencies, and the nature of it implies a sophisticated causal representation. On the other hand, it is very important for students to distinguish between immediate and remote causes because they are inclined to see the more recent causes as the only ones or at least as the most influential. The interaction of these two types of causes is also an essential component of historical consciousness that students should achieve.
- **Time**. As it is well known, there is not history without time. This issue will be discussed below, in relation to the understanding of historical narratives. In this vein, historical time is an essential component of the distinction between myths and historical explanations. To understand historical time (in terms of centuries, Christian, Jewish and Islamic chronologies, for example) it is necessary to first comprehend physical time (in terms of hours, days and seasons, etc.). But the comprehension of physical time is not sufficient to understand historical time because this is also associated with cultural and philosophical views on the relation between time and events (Lorenz 2017). All these issues imply important

conceptual issues that should be developed by an innovative and active view of history education.

National Master Narratives and Concepts as an Obstacle for History Education

One of the objectives of this book is related to the problem of how to improve history education in order to overcome political conflicts and to promote reconciliation applying the contributions of social psychology. One important source of information for this purpose comes precisely from social psychological studies that inform us about the features of citizens' intuitive representations of the past. These features are important because they would indicate what should be changed if a complex and historical disciplinary conception of the past is pretended. Thus summarizing a number of studies comparing quantitative studies carried out in numerous countries (Paez et al. 2017), it can be concluded that,

- Lay historical representations tend to be rather concrete and are based on specific, anecdotal and personalistic episodes. Abstract principles and processes are difficult to understand.
- In this vein, wars and national heroes as well as social and political leaders are seen as having had an enormous influence as initiators of historical change.
- Causality tends to be seen in a simple rather than complex way. In other words, historical issues are considered to depend on just one single cause instead of considering them in a multicausal way.
- Recent historical events (i.e., occurring in the last 100–150 years) tend to be seen as much more important than remote ones.
- Historical events and problems are predominantly viewed as situated in the West. That is, historical developments are seen from a colonial perspective. Post-colonial views are not that common even in countries with recent post-colonial experiences. This implies that an international perspective on a historical matter is harder to grasp than a local or national perspective.

These results from social psychology studies have clear educational implications for the teaching and learning process of recent and violent historical conflicts.

But it is also important to realize that historical recent and conflicting events, as the ones mentioned in the chapters of this book, are basically **national** as mentioned before. For this reason, I will discuss present research about how national narratives are understood by students and how this has a clear implication for the understanding of the concept of nation. It is important to notice that historical narratives and concepts are theoretical-related constructs, and both have serious implication for possible educational developments in this area. In this vein, I argue that the complex relation of concepts and narratives is essential to fully understand how history is represented (Carretero et al. 2013). For example in any specific narrative not only is important who is the main actor of the narrative but what kind actor is. This is to say, the actor could be a personalistic and concrete one as a particular political leader or the subject could be an abstract and more complex one as a historical concept like the bourgeoisie. The difference is really important because in the first case the causal structure of the historical event explained by the narrative could be reduced to the particular attempt of a specific person. In the second case, the student needs to apply a more abstract and complex scheme. A clear example of this difference can be seen in the distinction between understanding the Holocaust as a terrible set of events caused by a specific group of people, Hitler and the Nazis, and a more sophisticated representation which situates this terrible issue in the context of various and complex historical agents.

In my work about how the representation of national narratives and concepts (Carretero 2017; Carretero and van Alphen 2014 ; Lopez et al. 2015a, b), six dimensions have been considered. This is to say, (a) who is the narrative's historical actor, (b) an identification process with that actor, (c) a very simple and concrete causal story based on the fight for freedom or territory, (d) the historical narrative itself as a moral vector, (e) the presence of heroes as non-historical figures and (f) an essentialist view of concept of nation.

I will present them summarizing the main empirical findings and developing those implications. But firstly it is important to remember that from a sociocultural point of view (Wertsch 2002) there is a fascinating coincidence between school historical master narratives and the myths of origin which provide ideological support of any nation (Anderson 1983; Hobwsbawm 1990). As Wertsch and Rozin (2000, p. 41–2) recognized, three basic functions of an official history [...] first [...] a kind of cognitive function having to do with cultural and psychological tools required to create what Anderson (1983) has termed "imagined communities", especially nation- states [...] without instruments such as print media, maps, and texts about history, it may be impossible to imagine communities or to "think" the nation [...] a second function of official histories is to provide citizens of nation-states with some sense of group identity [...] the third related function of official histories is to create loyalty on the part of citizens to the nation state.

In this case, both authors, Anderson and Wertsch, are referring mostly to rather remote master narratives and not to recent ones. The so-called official history, which has coined that way by the pioneer of this field the French historian M. Ferro (1984/2004), is opposed to the "un-official" one which is expressed by the representations of minorities groups which do not have the support of the nation-state. But in my opinion these concepts could perfectly be applied to narratives related to more recent events as the ones mentioned in the chapters of this book. It is important to realize that all the official master narratives started at some point of history as cultural artifacts designed to contribute to the invention of the nations and the national communities. Of course the remote ones, for example the narratives of the independence of American countries as a saga of "the people" fighting against the oppression and looking for freedom (van Alphen and Carretero 2015), have a longer tradition than the more recent ones but the latter are closer in time, and this provides stronger ties for the reasons mentioned above.

The first dimension of master narratives analyzed in our studies is the establishment of the historical subject. That is, the establishment of the nation and its nationals as preexisting and everlasting historical subjects. This dimension is crucial because it determines the main protagonist or voice of the narrative. As it is well known, any narrative strongly depends on who its subject is. This historical subject is established in terms of inclusion and exclusion, radically opposing it to other as a coherent and homogenous group. Our results indicate that after years of history instruction both Spanish and Argentinean high school and university students tend to consider the national "people" as a clear a definite historical subject, which already existed even before the political birth of their nations by the beginning of nineteenth century. For example in the case of Spain (Lopez et al. 2015a), our participants think that the

Spanish people were fighting against the moors for several centuries, but it is not the case at all because at that time in the territory of the Iberian Peninsula there were several kingdoms as Castille, Aragon and others. Spain did not exist until several centuries later. In the case our work in Argentina (Carretero and van Alphen 2014), high school students considered that the Argentinean people fought against the Spanish to achieve their independence and they thought of that people as a homogenous entity very similar to what is today the citizenship. But it was not the case. The so-called people who developed the independence of most of American colonies were just a small proportion of the population, which did not include natives, slaves and women. Obviously the concept of citizen at the beginning of nineteenth century has not the same meaning as it has today. As a consequence of this, it can be concluded that there is a trend in human beings to establish a historical continuity in relation to present and past political subjects even though it does not exist at all.

This idea of continuity has been found also by numerous social psychology works (Smeekes 2014). For example in this book, the work of Psaltis et al. (Chap. 4) is a clear example of this. Therefore, there is a clear coincidence between the research from history education and social psychology studies, which constitutes a firm base to suggest a number of educational implications. Probably the most important one is to help the student to deconstruct the mentioned historical subject. In other words, to contribute to a clear representation of the difference between past and present political subjects. Of course this is also related to the improvement in the comprehension of past and present historical subjects as heterogeneous entities instead of homogenous, essentialist and idealized ones. It is also important to take into account that in the case of recent events the notion of continuity is very controversial and difficult to challenge. As a matter of fact around this notion, we find a real conundrum in both epistemological and educational terms. This is to say, if the historical event is a remote one the continuity between the past national subject and the present one is arbitrary and also invented (Anderson 1983). In other words, the Spanish, the Italian or the Jews citizens of fourteenth century, for example, have no real continuity with the present ones because of many reasons (Sand 2010). The most important reason is the process of demographic interaction between different populations due to migrations, wars and other social and political events over the centuries. Also, this is because the very concept of a national group did not exist until the nineteenth century. But when the historical event is a recent one, the continuity does exist. For example, in terms of the example presented in the beginning of this chapter, the slaves sold by Georgetown University by 1834 have descendants and they are of course the continuation of their antecedents. Also they could ask for compensations in terms of real or symbolic actions. Therefore, there is no doubt that in the case of recent events, as stated above, to promote a historical distance implying the deconstruction of the historical subject of the narrative is a very complex matter. In my opinion, this conundrum only has a possible way of solution. I mean to look to the future. This is to say to look for a better future based on reconciliation, and at this point social psychological theories have a significant contribution to offer as it has been stated in Introduction.

The second dimension studied is the presence of an identification process with the mentioned historical subject and its political unit. This dimension is related to the previous one but is focused on a distinctive aspect. For example in one of our studies (Lopez et al. 2015a), students were asked about the presence of the Arabs in the Iberian Peninsula for about 800 years. In many cases, these students used the pronoun "us" in their narrative even though they were referring to events, which happen several centuries ago. Clearly they did as a sign of this identification process, which obviously has also emotional components.

In this case, the educational implications are also very straightforward. It has to do with the development of a teaching strategy devoted to be conscious of this identification process. Probably if this consciousness takes place, it could contribute to a more flexible view on the cultural and national identity of the students and this could help to acquire a more disciplinary view on historical matters.

The third dimension is related to the existence of a "natural" territory belonging "since ever" to the nation, instead of conceiving the correspondence of nations and their territories to be the result of different political, social and historical complex processes along several decades or even centuries. This dimension probably varies among different groups of students coming from different nations because not all the nations have historically developed the same relation with the issue of territories. In our studies, it looks like that both students of Spain and Argentina consider their present territories in an essentialist way instead of in a historicist way, as mentioned above. In one case, students thought that the Spanish territory existed since at least the Roman Empire times. In the case of Argentina, our students defended the idea of an Argentinean territory, which was basically the same than the present one and which existed since the Spanish colonization. Therefore, in both cases the essentialist view on the territory is basically very similar.

In this vein, this is precisely the conceptual and representational change that education should be able to produce. In other words, to move the students from a more intuitive and superficial notion of the territory to a more sophisticated notion. This involves a consideration of how territories have changed at different historical moments and that borders do not last forever. On the contrary, they express different political processes and conventions: in some cases peaceful and democratic ones but in other cases violent and dictatorial ones. In relation to the territorial dimension of the concept of nation, we would like to emphasize the need and the convenience of introducing historical maps to the school teaching activities. Historical maps are an essential part of historiographical literacy and research, because they provide a clear and precise representation of how territories and nations have changed along centuries. But unfortunately, many students tend to consider the present maps as either immutable or they are cognitive anchors for representing historical events and political changes. In relation to this, recent historiographical research has showed that the so-called historical rights are based on rather invented knowledge about historical limits (Herzog 2017). This is to say, many of the ancient historical limits never existed as very precise borders. Therefore, it would be unjustified to use them to maintain territorial rights based on supposed past evidences.

The fourth dimension I have studied in my research has been the presence of mythical and heroic characters in student historical narratives (Carretero and Bermudez 2012). I think this is particularly important for the type of issues related to the chapters of this book. Most of historically recent and violent events include a number of heroic characters. This is to say specific persons who have played an extraordinary role on the main events of those master narratives, as it is the case of national heroes. In this vein, there are a number of fascinating and intriguing issues to be discussed having most of them clear educational implications. Firstly, specific research about students lay views on historical causality shows that they tend to attribute more influence to specific individual characters than to social and political structures (Carretero et al. 1997; Halden 2000). But this importance is much broader in the case of heroes. To some extent, it could be said that students and citizens in general recover the classical Greek meaning of heroes and myths to apply it to master narratives and their protagonists. Let us remember that one of the main differences between historical and mythical explanations is precisely the absence of specific time and space constraints in the latter. It is totally irrelevant, for example, to know Oedipus' date of birth or any other specific temporal and spatial markers. Myths and mythical figures are basically universal and not local narratives. In contrast, one can say that history is making its appearance when time and its specific cultural and spatial constraints are introduced into a narrative. The appeal of mythical national narratives probably builds on how important are myths for present human societies as historical and philosophical research has noted (Gadamer 1999; Lorenz 2014). Also, the classical Greek meaning of hero consists of being something intermediate between the Gods and the human beings and accordingly to be able to perform extraordinary things. These actions are usually in favor of a specific group, national or cultural, of human beings, and they imply a total loyalty and devotion to the hero, which of course become a model for that group. Interestingly enough, it is very common in the field of history education to see how the heroes of specific national groups are either silenced or strongly criticized by the opposite national groups. In other words from a social psychology point of view, the heroes of the in-group is at the same time the antihero of the out-group. For example in our comparative study of Mexican and Spanish history textbooks, Columbus appears in Mexican books either silenced or having no historical merits at all but in Spanish ones is a hero having very important merits from a scientific, cultural and historical point of view (Carretero et al. 2002).

The educational implications of these issues are basically related to the need to favor a historiographical understanding of these main specific characters. This is to say to develop among the students a complex comprehension of the so-called heroes. Probably the first thing to take into account is to develop a reflection on the process of historical invention and selection of national heroes because an important number of them are part of cultural artifacts developed by political elites in order to build national communities. Secondly, it would be important to transmit to the students that most of the extraordinary actions performed by historical characters only can be fully understood in the context of a number of specific historical conditions. In other words, I think it is educationally worthwhile to make the students progress from the universal "programmatic mythology" of nations (Hobsbawm 1990) to the local specificity of historical explanations including their social, political and economic complexity. Also well-established theories of narrative development (Egan 1997) claim that human beings develop a narrative ability which goes through a number of stages: somatic (0–2 years of age), mythical (3–6), heroic (7–10), philosophical (11–15) and ironic (15 and onwards). Thus, if national historical narratives often maintain their mythical and heroic components even during adolescence and adulthood, time at which individuals should be able to generate philosophical and ironic historical narratives, it is work investigating what kind of social psychological mechanisms yield a contrary result.

The fifth dimension of the narratives I have explored in my research is the application of moral features, which legitimize the actions of the nation and the nationals. This is to say students tend to view national master narratives as moral vectors maintained by the values of nation. For example, Carretero et al. (2012) have found that Spanish young adolescents considered that Christians have the right to "recuperate" the territory of the Iberian peninsula, inhabited by the Arabs for 800 years, because it was considered "Spanish territory," as it is nowadays. On the contrary, according to the same students, the Christians have no right to conquer the American territories because they belonged to the natives. Therefore, the master narrative establishes the distinction between "good" and "bad" options, people, and decisions. Typically, the first one is associated with the national "we," and the second one is related to "they." Thus, the logical and moral truth is always on the "we" side. Secondly, master narratives offer living examples of civic virtue, particularly of loyalty. As it can be easily inferred, this loyalty function was essential in the construction of the nation, and it can still be found in many symbolic forms. For example, if we consider the way World Soccer Championship is followed by any citizen in the world, it would be unconceivable that a citizen could support any team belonging to a different nation, even though that team may play better. Of course these students representations receive also the impact of biased textbooks contents, which very often silence a number of violent events, which could be conflicting for the own national representation of the past.

The educational implications of all these conclusions are quite straightforward even though they could be also rather complicated. The first of them is related to help the students to be aware of this relation of moral judgments and historical representations. This is to say to teach the students to work with them. For example, it is clear in the example presented at the beginning of this chapter that the moral implications have to do with the real and symbolic actions developed by Georgetown University to not continue silencing this event, as it can be seen in a specific Web site and also to compensate the descendants. But at the same time it is important to contribute to develop a historical representation, which cannot be reduced to a moral understanding. This is related to the possibility of teaching to the students that if there are two sides in a historical conflict there will be also two moral views, and these two moral views could be preventing the possibility of achieving a complex and rigorous historical representation. In the case of slavery, only one side was historically damaged but in other historical events two or more than two sides have been historically damaged. This book is full of cases.

Finally, the six dimensions of national historical narratives, as they are understood by high school and university students deal with the concept of nation itself. This implies the selection of a general scheme, which provides coherence to the way the concept of nation is used in the whole narrative. This feature implies the conceptual view of the nation and its nationals as naturalized political entities, having a kind of "eternal" and "ontological" nature. The concept of nation appears as a key element to develop critical historical thinking in our students. Some of these skills include the development of critical thinking, the understanding of historical time and change and historical causality and source evaluation (Lee 2005; Wineburg et al. 2011). It has been argued in this chapter that learning to think historically entails navigating counterintuitive ideas (Carretero and Lee 2014). For this purpose, I think a serious educational effort is necessary to prepare students for understanding the past and present complexity of the societies in which they live. This would imply a process of conceptual change from misconceptions and lay views on historical concepts in general but on the concept of nation in particular (Carretero et al. 2013). This conceptual change implies to understand that nations are artificial historical concepts invented by nineteenth century, and not natural ones having an ontological and essentialist meaning. In this vein, they are receiving nowadays an intense process of revision. For example, what is the European Union? A nation? A nation of nations? An empire? Definitely it is a political entity trying to define itself in the context of an intense political turmoil whose roots cannot be understood without a complex representation of their historical origins. In this vein, I would like to emphasize that, as present citizens of a world experiencing an intense globalization process, clearly our learning needs to be closer to a flexible and nuanced concept of nation. Migration processes will be even more intense in the future, and as this is having an enormous cultural impact, the learning of history in and out of school, particularly when it concerns the nation, has to keep up.

CONCLUDING THOUGHTS. THE ROLE OF BOTH HISTORY EDUCATION AND SOCIAL PSYCHOLOGY IN CONFLICT TRANSFORMATION

This chapter has tried to present basically the main contributions of several present approaches to the very difficult problem of how to deal with recent and violent past events in both formal and informal educational contexts. With this purpose in mind contributions from social and cultural psychology, history education and cognitive and developmental psychology have been taken into account along with some classical contributions from political science and present historiographical debates. As a concluding part of this chapter, a summary of applied implications will be presented below. Hopefully, they could contribute to serve as cues to apply most of the findings of the majority of the chapters of this book. Thus, these chapters have shown how historical representations in textbooks and other educational devices are full of biased contents, which do not contribute to transform social conflicts. Therefore, the basic question is this: how these representations could be changed? How present social sciences research could provide insights for this purpose? Four main conclusions will be presented.

1. *The need of an* interdisciplinary *approach.* To deal both socially and educationally with recent and violent events is a very complex issue. On the one hand, these events are an important part of citizens representations and narratives about the past and very often they do not agree with historiographical research. On the other hand, historiographical research itself is neither an impartial nor completely objective discipline because it could also depend in some cases on social and politically biased influence. In sum, any approach intending to transform social and political conflicts based on the so-called troubled pasts should be very aware that an interdisciplinary account is strongly needed because historical culture and representations are the result of a complex interaction of collective memory, historiography, history education and popular

culture. From this point of view, it is very hard to predict which one of these influences will be more decisive on transforming citizens historical representations and therefore which one will be also important in order to possibly contribute to reduce conflicts. But anyway taking into account the frequent interaction of several of these influences from an interdisciplinary point of view will always be a positive decision.

2. *Is progressive history education enough to transform historical conflicts?* Definitely history education research has made enormous progress in the last decades. Initiatives based on historical thinking and historical consciousness approaches have been developing both a theoretical and an applied basis for teaching and learning historical contents in a meaningful way. This is to say with the objective of achieving a constructive and disciplinary understanding and not just a repetitive copy of inert knowledge. But these advances have mainly covered *how* to teach but not necessarily *what* to teach. In other words, historical thinking and historical consciousness approaches have focused on the importance of student's cognitive and constructive activities such as how to carry out inquiries and discussions to deal with historical knowledge. But most of the social and political conflicts having historical roots are focused on the content among different versions implying, for example, the answer to very stereotypical and conflictive questions as "who arrived first to this land?" "who started this war?" or "who is the victim in this episode"? Of course in order to generate a process of change of citizens representations on these issues is important to consider the type of cognitive and social activities promoted in and out of the school—this is to say **how to teach and learn**—but it is also important to consider **what is going to be taught and learned**. In other words, history education should take into account the importance of silencing and censoring processes. For example, the case of slavery in present societies is a very good example of silencing as described at the beginning of this chapter. Unfortunately, censoring is still present in a number of contemporary societies. Thus, both processes are very common in many educational systems and societies, and definitely they do not contribute to reduce the conflict. Present research and applied attempts to improve history education should take this into account if they intend to contribute to transform conflicts. As it is well known,

silencing and censoring could reduce them in the short term but their further implications are always negative in the long term.
3. *Deconstructing the own nation through reflecting on the conflict.*
As mentioned above, political conflicts based on historical representations are very often based on two dimensions. This is to say they have at the same time a national and a recent character. The first feature is not a surprise at all because history education has been traditionally considered an essential piece of most of educational systems since nineteenth century, and even before, to build and maintain national identities. Therefore, it is precisely its national character in interaction with its recency the center of the conundrum to be solved. This is to say any attempt to discuss new information contradicting prior representations, based, for example, on new data obtained by historians, will be facing an intense defensive reaction because citizens national identities will be challenged. But if history education does not go in this direction trying to change stereotypical historical representations there is no way to contribute to conflict reduction and reconciliation. What to do then? This is precisely what previous pages about the teaching of historical narratives have tried to answer. This is to say I have analyzed a six dimensions view of historical narratives emphasizing how each one of them could be approached in such a way that they could help the citizens to contextualize their representations about the past and particularly their view about a monological and essentialist view of past events. As these dimensions have been analyzed before in detail, it is not necessary to consider again their possible contribution to reduce social and political conflicts but I think it is convenient to insist on the dramatic importance of establishment of the historical subject. Usually citizens establish this subject basically through a historical view based on an endurable and almost eternal continuity between themselves and diverse subjects of the past. This is to say when citizens along the world use a "we" as subject of something that happened in the past they represent themselves as the only and genuine descendants of an idealized historical subject which does not exist anymore. In other words, this "we" consists of an incredible mixture of present and past but probably most of the citizens are not really conscious of such a mystification. As stated before, the establishment of this imaginary historical subject is probably the nucleus of the rest of the narratives dimensions

related to cognitive, emotional and moral issues. Therefore, if history education is able to help citizens to deconstruct this idealized historical subject, it is highly probable that the rest of the narratives dimensions will be also affected and social and political conflicts could be reduced, at least from the point of view of their historical representations which usually provide justifications for not trying to look for more peaceful futures. But how to promote a historical critical thinking which could contribute to that deconstruction? Definitely the development of disciplinary historical view among the citizens would be of great help. This is to say the dissemination of the idea that historical representations are not closed views but dynamic and open interpretations of the past, which could and should be changed according to historical research. In this sense, dialogical activities and open-minded discussions would be of great help because they would contribute to the appearance of a reflective attitude among citizens.

4. *Transforming narratives about the Other*

Above we have outlined and elaborated the importance and impact of historical narratives and representations of the past on conflict resolution processes. More specifically, we have focused on national narratives and how these ought and can be deconstructed in order to facilitate more positive social outcomes. In addition to this, we will briefly outline the importance of narratives people usually have about out-groups and/or former enemy.

Because of both our limited capacity to process information and physical/social complexity and social and political influences, we categorize not only objects but also people into groups. The process of differentiating "us" and "them" is a universal element of intergroup relations. Social psychological research shows that we view "us" (the in-group) as better, superior, more diversified and more moral, while we view "them" (the out-group) as inferior, bad, more homogeneous and less moral. Most the chapters of this book have been based on this classical theoretical distinction. These and similar perceptions are even more pronounced in (post) conflict settings marked by grave human rights violations and constitute a major *barrier* to successful conflict resolution and sustainable intergroup reconciliation.

Recent research points to the importance of representing out-group members in a more heterogeneous and positive moral manner. More specifically, research by Bilewicz and Jaworska (2013; also in this volume) indicates that bringing people together while exposing them to stories of heroic rescuers increased positive affect and perceived similarity between Poles and Jews. The narratives of historical rescuers of Jews during WWII overcame the negative impact of the past on intergroup contact. The authors argued that presenting people with stories of heroic helpers is very important for reconciliation after mass violence as it may prevent entitative categorizations of groups as exclusively victims or perpetrators.

In addition, research that examined the effects of a contact intervention containing narratives of moral exemplars on reconciliation processes in the post-genocide setting of Bosnia and Herzegovina (Čehajić-Clancy and Bilewicz, in press) has found that focusing on moral exemplars increased reconciliatory beliefs due to enhanced forgiveness among both former victims and perpetrators.

Consequently, we suggest that the key to reconciliation is the acknowledgment of historical moral variability by realizing that among out-group members some people were perpetrators, but some of them could be also victims, passive or active bystanders and even heroic helpers (Čehajić-Clancy et al. 2016). Exposing people to such individualized and personalized stories of moral out-group members could influence current relations between historically conflicted groups by inducing trust and fostering contact, resulting in reconciliation.

Notes

1. http://www.nytimes.com/2016/04/17/us/georgetown-university-search-for-slave-descendants.html? (Retrieved May 14, 2017).
2. It should be noted that Pope Gregory 16th condemned the slavery by 1839.
3. http://slavery.georgetown.edu/
4. It is also fascinating to see how much time it took to acknowledge the need to remember the history of North American natives in the USA. The National Museum of the American Indians did not open until 2004!
5. It is very interesting to compare the lack of interest on history as a subject matter that many students show in the schools with the enormous interest historical films, novel and documentary citizens have in many societies. This contrast could be indicating a lack of adequate teaching methods in numerous schools all over Western countries.

6. The field of history education witnessed a number of intense debates about the developmental capacities of students. These were related to Piaget versus Vygotsky controversies, so frequent in discussing the influences of development and learning processes on students' educational achievements.
7. For recent developments in history education, it is important to consider a number of related programs and European developments (Thünemann et al. 2014).
8. As it is well known at the time of the Civil War (1936–1939) Spain was divided into two sides, the republican and the national. The first was leaded by the legitimate republican government and the second one was leaded by the General Franco who initiated the conflict by an attempt of coup d'état. Recent studies (Preston 2012) showed that in the national side about 160,000 were killed and that in the republican side there was about 30,000. After the war, the Franquist government provided recognition to these people and economic help to their families.

REFERENCES

Altamira, R. (1891). *La enseñanza de la historia*. Madrid: Fortanet.
Anderson, B. (1983). *Imagined communities: Reflections on the origin and spread of nationalism*. (Rev. ed., 1991). London: Verso.
Aries, P., & Duby, G. (1992). *A history of private life, Vol I: From Pagan Rome to Byzantium*. Cambridge, MA: Harvard University Press.
Baptist, E. E. (2014). *The half has never been told: Slavery and the making of American Capitalism*. NY: Basic Books.
Barton, K. C. (2008). Research on students ideas about history. In L. Levstik & C. A. Thyson (Eds.), *Handbook of research on social studies education* (pp. 239–258). New York: Routledge.
Barton, K. (2017). Shared principles in history and social science education. In M. Carretero, S. Berger, & M. Grever (Eds.), *Palgrave handbook of research in historical culture and education*. Basingstoke: Palgrave.
Barton, K. C., & Levstik, L. S. (1996). "Back when God was around and everything": Elmentary children's understanding of historical time. *American Educational Research Journal, 33*(2), 419–454.
Barton, K. C., & Levstik, L. S. (2004). *Teaching history for the common good*. Mahwah, NJ: Lawrence Erlbaum Associates.
Beck, I. L. & MacKeown, M. G. (1994). Outcomes of history instruction: Paste-up accounts. In M. Carretero & J. F. Voss (Eds.), *Cognitive and instructional on history and social sciences* (pp. 237–255). Hillsdale, NJ: Erlbaum.

Bentrovato, D., Korostelina, K. V., & Schulze, M. (Eds.). (2016). *History can bite: History education in divided and postwar societies.* Göttingen: V & R Unipres

Berger, S. (2012). De-nationalizing history teaching and nationalizing it differently! Some reflections on how to defuse the negative potential of national(ist) history teaching. In M. Carretero, M. Asensio, & M. Rodríguez-Moneo (Eds.). (2012). *History education and the construction of national identities.* Charlotte, NC: Information Age Publishing.

Berger, S. (2014). *The past as history: National identity and historical consciousness in modern Europe.* Basingstoke: Palgrave.

Berger, S., Lorenz, C., & Melman, B. (Eds.). (2012). *Popularizing national pasts. 1800 to the present.* New York: Routledge.

Bilewicz, M., & Jaworska, M. (2013). Reconciliation through the righteous: The narratives of heroic helpers as a fulfillment of emotional needs in Polish-Jewish intergroup contact. *Journal of Social Issues, 69*(1), 162–179.

Boyd, C. P. (1997). *Historia Patria: Politics, history and national identity in Spain 1875–1975.* Princeton: Princeton University Press.

Braudel, F. (1990). *Écrits sur l'histoire II.* Paris: Flammarion

Bruner, J. (1966). *Toward a theory of instruction.* Cambridge, MA: Harvard University Press.

Burke, P. (1990). *The French historical revolution: The Annales School, 1929–1989.* Cambridge: Polity Press.

Carretero, M. (2011). *Constructing patriotism. Teaching history and memories in global worlds.* Charlotte, CT: Information Age Publishing.

Carretero, M. (2017). Teaching history master narratives: Fostering imaginations. In M. Carretero, S. Berger, & M. Grever (Eds.), *Palgrave handbook of research in historical culture and education.* Basingstoke: Palgrave

Carretero, M., & Bermudez, A. (2012). Constructing histories. In J. Valsiner (Ed.), *Oxford handbook of culture and psychology* (pp. 625–646). Oxford: Oxford University Press.

Carretero, M., & Lee, P. (2014). Learning historical concepts. In K. Sawyer (Ed.), *Handbook of learning sciences.* (pp. 587–604). (2nd edn.). Cambridge: Cambridge University.

Carretero, M., & van Alphen, F. (2014). Do master narratives change among high school students? A characterization of how national history Is represented, cognition & instruction. *Cognition and Instruction, 32*(2), 290–312.

Carretero, M., & van Alphen, F. (2017). History, collective memories or national memories? How the representation of the past is framed by master narratives. In B. Wagoner (Ed.), *Oxford handbook of culture and memory.* Oxford, UK: Oxford University Press.

Carretero, M., & Voss, J. F. (Eds.). (1994). *Cognitive and instructional processes in history and social sciences.* Hillsdale: Erlbaum.

Carretero, M., Berger, S., & Grever, M. (Eds.). (2017). *Palgrave handbook of research in historical culture and education*. Basingstoke: Palgrave.

Carretero, M., Castorina, J. A., & Levinas, M. L. (2013). Conceptual change and historical narratives about the nation. A theoretical and empirical approach. In S. Vosniadou (Ed.), *International handbook of research on conceptual change* (pp. 269–287). (2nd edn.). NY: Routledge.

Carretero, M., Jacott, L., & López-Manjón, A. (2002). Learning history through textbooks: Are Mexican and Spanish students taught the same story? *Learning and Instruction, 12,* 651–665.

Carretero, M., López-Manjón, A., & Jacott, L. (1997). Explaining historical events. *International Journal of Educational Research, 27*(3), 245–253.

Carretero, M., Lopez, C., Gonzalez, M.F., & Rodríguez-Moneo. (2012). Students historical narratives and concepts about the nation. In M. Carretero, M. Asensio, & Rodríguez-Moneo (Eds.), *History education and the construction of national identities* (pp.153–170). Charlotte, NC: IAP.

Čehajić-Clancy, S., Goldenberg, A., Halperin E., & Gross, J. (2016). Social-psychological interventions for intergroup reconciliation: An emotion regulation perspective. *Psychological Inquiry, 27*(2), 73–88.

Cercadillo, L., Chapman, A., & Lee, P. (2017). Organizing the past: Historical accounts, significance and unknown ontologies. In M. Carretero, S. Berger & M. Grever (Eds.), *Palgrave handbook of research in historical culture and education*. Basingstoke: Palgrave.

Chi, M. T. H., Glaser, R., & Farr, M. (Eds.). (1988). *The nature of expertise*. Hillsdale, NJ: Lawrence Erlbaum Associates.

Collingwood, R. G. (1946). *The idea of history*. Oxford, UK: Oxford University Press.

Conrad, S. (2016). *What is global history?* Princeton, NJ: Princeton University Press.

Dewey, J. (1915). The aim of history in elementary education. In J. Dewey (Ed.), *The school and society*. Chicago: The University of Chicago Press.

Dickinson, A. K., Lee, P. J., & Rogers, P. J. (Eds.). (1984). *Learning history*. London: Heinemann.

Egan, K. (1997). *The educated mind*. Chicago, IL: The University of Chicago Press.

Epstein, T. (2009). *Interpreting national history. Race, identity, and pedagogy in classrooms and communities*. New York: Routledge.

Foster, S. (2012). Re-thinking historical textbooks in a globalized world. In M. Carretero, M. Asensio, & M. Rodríguez-Moneo (Eds.), *History education and the construction of national identities* (pp. 49–62). Charlotte, CT: Information Age Publishing.

Freedman, E. B. (2015). "What happened needs to be told": Fostering critical historical reasoning in the classroom. *Cognition and Instruction, 33*(4), 357–398.

Gadamer, H. G. (1999). Myth in the age of science. In H. G. Gadamer, *Hermeneutics, religion, and ethics* (pp. 91–102). New Haven, CT: Yale University Press.

Grever, M., & Stuurman, S. (2007). *Beyond the canon: History for the twenty-first century.* Basingstoke: Palgrave Macmillan.

Haley, A. (1976). *Roots: The saga of an American family.* NY: Basic Books.

Halldén, O. (2000). On reasoning in history. In J. F. Voss & M. Carretero (Eds.), *Learning and reasoning in history* (pp. 272–278). NY: Routledge.

Hein, L. E., & Selden, M. (2000). *Censoring history: Citizenship and memory in Japan, Germany, and the United States.* Armonk, NY: M.E. Sharpe.

Herzog, T. (2017). Historical rights to land: How Latin American states made the past normative and what happened to history and historical education as a result. In M. Carretero, S. Berger, & M. Grever (Eds.), *Palgrave handbook of research in historical culture and education* (pp. 91–107). Basingstoke: Palgrave.

Hess, D. E. (2004). Controversies about controversial issues in democratic education. *Political Science and Politics, 37*(2), 257–261.

Hobsbawm, E. (1990). *Nations and nationalism since 1780: Programme, myth, reality.* Cambridge: Cambridge University Press.

Kansteiner, W. (2017). Film, the past, and a didactic dead end: From teaching history to teaching memory. In M. Carretero, S. Berger, & M. Grever (Eds.), *Palgrave handbook of research in historical culture and education* (pp. 169–190). Basingstoke: Palgrave.

Lave, J., & Wenger, E. (1991). *Situated learning: Legitimate peripheral participation.* Cambridge University Press.

Lee, P. (2005). Putting principles into practice: Understanding history. In P. Lee, *How students learn: History in the classroom* (pp. 31–77). Washington, DC: The National Academies Press.

Le Goff, J. (1990). Preface. In A. Brossat, S. Combe, J. Potel, & J. Szurek (Eds.), *Àl'Est, la mémoire retrouvée* [Found memory in the East]. Paris: Éditions La Découverte.

Limón, M., & Carretero, M. (1998). Evidence evaluation and reasoning abilities in the domain of history: An empirical study. In J. Voss & M. Carretero (Eds.), *Learning and reasoning in history* (pp. 252–271). London: Woburn.

Lopez, C., Carretero, M., & Rodríguez-Moneo, M. (2015a). Conquest or reconquest? Students' conceptions of nation embedded in a historical narrative. *Journal of the Learning Sciences, 24*(2), 252–285.

Lopez, C., Carretero, M., & Rodríguez-Moneo, M. (2015b). Telling a national narrative that is not your own. Does it enable disciplinary historical consumption? *Culture and Psychology, 4*, 547–571.

Lorenz, C. (2014). Blurred lines. History, memory and the experience of time. *International Journal for History, Culture and Modernity, 1*(2), 43–62.

Lorenz, C. (2017). "The Times They Are a-Changin". On time, space and periodization in history. In M. Carretero, S. Berger, & M. Grever (Eds.), *Palgrave handbook of research in historical culture and education* (pp. 109–131). Basingstoke: Palgrave.

Lowenthal, D. (1985). *The past is a foreign country*. (Rev. Edn., 2015). Cambridge: CUP.

Maggioni, L., vanSledright, B., & Alexander, P. A. (2009). Walking on the borders: A measure of epistemic cognition in history. *The Journal of Experimental Education, 77*, 187–214.

Nokes, J. (2017). Historical reading and writing in secondary school classrooms. In M. Carretero, S. Berger, & M. Grever (Eds.), *Palgrave handbook of research in historical culture and education* (pp. 553–571). Basingstoke: Palgrave.

Nussbaum, M. & Cohen, J. (2002). *For love of country? A new democracy forum on the limits of patriotism*. Boston, MA: Beacon Press.

Páez, D., Bobowik, M., & Liu, J. (2017). Social representations concepts of the past and competences in history education. In M. Carretero, S. Berger & M. Grever (Eds.), *Palgrave handbook of research in historical culture and education* (pp. 491–510). Basingstoke: Palgrave.

Piaget, J. (1933). Psychologie de l'enfant et enseignement de l'histoire. In *Bulletin trimestriel de la Conférence internationale pour l'enseignement de l'histoire, 2*, 8–13.

Piaget, J. (1966). *The psychology of the child*. New York, NY: Basic Books.

Ravitch, D., & Finn, C. (1987). *What do our 17-year-olds know*. New York: Basic Books.

Retz, T. (2015). At the interface: academic history, school history and the philosophy of history. *Journal of Curriculum Studies, 48*(4), 503–517.

Rose, S. O. (2010). *What is gender history?* London: Polity.

Sand, S. (2010). *The invention of the Jewish people*. London: Verso.

Seixas, P. (Ed.). (2004). *Theorizing historical consciousness*. Toronto, Canada: University of Toronto Press.

Seixas, P. (2015). Translation and its discontents: Key concepts in English and German history education. *Journal of Curriculum Studies, 47*(6), 427–439.

Seixas, P. (2017). Historical consciousness and historical thinking. In M. Carretero, S. Berger, & M. Grever (Eds.). *Palgrave handbook of research in historical culture and education* (pp. 59–72). Basingstoke: Palgrave.

Seixas, P., & Morton, T. (2013). *The big six. Historical thinking concepts*. Toronto: Nelson Education LTD.

Shemilt, D. (1980). *History 13-16 evaluation study.* Edinburgh: Holmes McDougall.

Smeekes, A. N. (2014). *The presence of the past. Historical rooting of national identity and current group dynamics.* (Doctoral dissertation, Utrecht University).

Taylor, T., & Guyver, R. (Eds.). (2012). *History wars and the classroom: Global perspectives.* Charlotte, NC: Information Age Publishing.

Valls, R. (2007). The Spanish Civil War and the Franco dictatorship: The challenges of representing a conflictive past in secondary schools. In E. Cole (Ed.), *Teaching the violent past: History education and reconciliation* (pp. 155–174). New York: Rowman & Littlefield.

Van Alphen, F., & Carretero, M. (2015). The construction of the relation between national past and present in the appropriation of historical master narratives. *Integrative Psychological and Behavioral Science, 49*(3), 512–530.

Van Boxtel, C., & van Drie, J. (2017). Engaging students in historical reasoning: The need for dialogic history education. In M. Carretero, S. Berger, & M. Grever, (Eds.), *Palgrave handbook of research in historical culture and education* (pp. 573–589). Basingstoke: Palgrave.

VanSledright, B. (2008). Narratives of nation-state, historical knowledge, and school history. *Review of Research in Education, 32,* 109–146.

VanSledright, B. (2010). *The challenge of rethinking history education: On practices, theories, and policy.* NY: Routledge.

Vosniadou, S. (Ed.). (2013). *International handbook of research on conceptual change* (pp. 269–287). NY: Routledge.

Wertsch, J. V. (2002). *Voices of collective remembering.* Cambridge: Cambridge University Press.

Wertsch, J. V., & Rozin, M. (2000). The Russian Revolution: Official and unofficial accounts. In J. F. Voss & M. Carretero, *Learning and reasoning in history: International review of history education* (pp. 39–60) London: Routledge.

Wertsch, J., & Rozin, M. (2000). The Russian Revolution: Official and unofficial accounts. In J. F. Voss & M. Carretero (Eds.), *Learning and reasoning in history* (pp. 39–60). New York, NY: Routledge.

Wineburg, S. S. (1991). Historical problem solving: A study of the cognitive processes used in the evaluation of documentary and pictorial evidence. *Journal of Educational Psychology, 83*(1), 73–87.

Wineburg, S. (2001). *Historical thinking and other unnatural acts.* Philadelphia: Temple University Press.

Wineburg, S., Martin, D., & Montesano, C. (2011). *Reading like a historian.* NY: Teachers College.

AUTHOR BIOGRAPHY

Mario Carretero is a Professor of Cognitive Psychology at Autonoma University of Madrid, Spain, where he was Dean of the Faculty of Psychology, and Researcher at FLACSO, Argentina. He has carried out an extensive research on history education from both cognitive and sociocultural approaches. He has published in *Journal of the Learning Sciences* and *Cognition and Instruction*. His recent books are *History Education and the Construction of National Identities* (2012) (co-ed.) and *Constructing Patriotism* (funded by the Guggenheim Foundation) (2011). He has been Santander Visiting Scholar at the David Rockefeller Center for Latin American Studies of Harvard University (2009) and Bliss Carnochan Visiting Professor at the Humanities Center of Stanford University (2011). His present research interests have to do with an interdisciplinary attempt to study history education issues as it can be seen in *Palgrave Handbook of Research in Historical Culture and Education* (2017) (co-edited along with S. Berger and M. Grever).

Open Access This chapter is licensed under the terms of the Creative Commons Attribution 4.0 International License (http://creativecommons.org/licenses/by/4.0/), which permits use, sharing, adaptation, distribution and reproduction in any medium or format, as long as you give appropriate credit to the original author(s) and the source, provide a link to the Creative Commons license and indicate if changes were made.

The images or other third party material in this chapter are included in the chapter's Creative Commons license, unless indicated otherwise in a credit line to the material. If material is not included in the chapter's Creative Commons license and your intended use is not permitted by statutory regulation or exceeds the permitted use, you will need to obtain permission directly from the copyright holder.

Index

A

Abkhaz, 81
Adherence to ingroup narratives, 110
Afghanistan, 43
Association for Historical Dialogue and Research (AHDR), 9, 11, 25, 330
Albania, 105
Allport, 10
Antisemitism, 80, 170, 174, 176, 180–182, 188
Anxiety, 308
Apartheid Archives Project, 87
Apps, 345
Apologies, 6
Arab, 284
Arab Israeli, 23
Arab spring revolutions, 14
ARIA, 236
Armenian–Turkish dialogue, 89
Association for Historical Dialogue and Research, 85, 330
Attitudes, 170
Attribution theory, 12, 307
Authoritarian state, 257

B

BaH, 232
Belarus/Belarusians, 258–270
Belfast (Good Friday) Agreement, 301
Bosnia and Herzegovina, 22, 43, 80, 232
Burundi, 83
Bystanders, 169, 312

C

Cambodia, 1, 43
Categorization, 4
Causality, 350, 355–357, 362, 365
Cause and consequence, 1, 7
CDRSEE, 52
Change, 355
Civil society organization, 10, 11, 18–20, 88, 90, 331
Civil war, 50
Cold War, 233
Collaborative deliberation, 287
Collective action, 14
Collective amnesia, 44
Collective continuity, 8

Collective victimhood, 40
Colonialism, 157, 159–161
Common schools, 302
Common sense knowledge, 126, 127
Communication styles, 22, 207, 223
Conceptual change, 355, 365
Conflict/Conflicting, 77, 278–281, 283, 284, 286, 287, 292–294
Conflict narratives, 54, 55
Conflict resolution, 2, 236
Conflict transformation, 2, 13, 14, 18–20, 23, 24, 39, 40, 54, 55
Confronting History Projects, 80, 91
Consociational devolved government, 302
Constructivist epistemology, 326
Contact, 302
Continuity and change, 7
Controversial issues, 203
Cooperative attitudes, 247
Cooperative interaction, 55
Council of Europe, 9, 245
Counter-narratives, 13, 125, 127, 129, 139, 140
Crimes, 147
Critical inquiry, 278, 293
Critical thinking, 326
Croatia, 8, 20, 43, 80, 104
Cross-border cooperation, 80
Cross-cultural contact, 303
Curriculum, 315
Cyprus, 8, 9, 11, 15, 16, 20, 23, 25, 85, 98, 104, 105, 107–109, 111–113, 115, 322, 326, 327, 329–333

D
Dangerous memories, 322–325, 328, 330, 332–334
Dehumanisation, 57
Democratic Republic of the Congo, 83

Demonisation, 57
Dialogical narrative transformation, 38
Dialogical space, 55
Dialogue, 5, 80, 235, 240, 243
Diffusion, 202, 205
Digital media, 80
Dilemmata of history teaching, 221
Disciplinary integrity, 316
Disciplinary thinking, 350
Discrimination, 312
Dissemination, 22, 205, 207
Distrust, 2
Divided societies, 306
Divisive past, 37
Documenta, 82
Documentaries, 345
Double-edged sword, 91
Dual-narrative approach, 52, 53

E
Educational materials, 80
Emotion-regulation, 3
Empathetic dual-narrative approach, 280
Empathy, 5, 170
Escalation of conflict, 4
Estonia, 208
Ethnic/Ethnicism, 235, 238, 240–245, 247, 250
Ethnocentric, 85
EUROCLIO, 48
Evidence, 350
Exclusion, 312

F
Facing History and Ourselves, 51, 91
Facing Our History, Shaping the Future (FOHSTF), 303
Films, 345
Forgiveness, 1
Formal and non-formal education, 24

Formal education, 330, 333, 334
Former Yugoslavia, 82
Foucault, 147, 148, 152, 153, 162
Foundational myth, 221
Freedom House, 270

G
Gacaca tribunals, 90
Genocides, 81
Georgians, 81
Greek Cypriot, 16, 104, 105, 108
Germany, 170
Guatemala, 43, 61
Guilt, 3, 6, 19, 160, 161

H
Healing the Wounds of History, 90
Hegemonic, 125, 139, 140
Hegemonic narratives, 127, 134
Heritage sites, 345
Higher-order thinking approach, 280
Hindu–Muslim, 53
Historical consciousness, 350, 355, 356, 367
Historical interpretations, 7
Historical knowledge, 348
Historical methodologies, 326
Historical narratives, 77, 81–83, 103, 104–106, 113
Historical significance, 7
Historical thinking, 7, 9, 12, 13, 19, 351, 354, 355, 365, 367
Historical traumas, 321
History, 346
  education, 346
  popular, 346
History curricula, 201
History education moratoria, 43, 45
History teaching, 261, 265, 268, 306, 322, 323, 326–328, 330, 333, 334

History textbooks, 39
History that Connects, 80
Holocaust, 81, 169–172, 174–188, 312
Holocaust education, 170
Home for Co-operation, 25
Humanization, 5
Hutu, 50

I
Identity, 125, 138, 140, 236, 240, 242, 250, 258–261, 264, 267, 270, 271
Iceland, 170
IHJR, 88
Index of Economic Freedom, 270
India, 52
Innovative pedagogies, 80
Interdisciplinary, 8, 9, 18, 23, 346, 366
Interdisciplinary field, 58
Intergroup, 148
Intergroup anxiety, 5
Intergroup contact, 5, 19, 103
Intergroup contact theory, 4, 5, 10, 14, 15
Intergroup dialogue, 81
Intergroup Emotions, 5
Intergroup Emotions Theory, 3
Intergroup encounter, 278, 286, 287, 293
Intergroup reconciliation, 42, 43, 45, 54, 55, 65
Intergroup relations, 100, 103, 110, 113, 125, 134, 150, 151, 155, 163
Intergroup Threat Theory, 5
Iraq, 46
Israel, 9, 23
Israeli–Palestinian, 53, 279, 280

J
Japan, 346
Jewish, 284
Jewish-Arab conflict, 23
Jewish–Israeli, 279
Jews, 176–187
JNA, 106
Joint History Project, 52
Joint history textbook, 86
Joint textbooks, 53, 56, 60

K
Khmer Rouge, 61
Kosovar Albanians, 105
Kosovo, 105

L
Latvia, 208
Learning Each Other's Historical Narrative, 52
Lebanon, 1, 43
Life stories, 235
Living Memorial Museum, 87
Local authorities, 239
Local experts, 239
Local identities, 170, 186, 188

M
Master narratives, 98, 100, 104, 113, 358, 359, 362–364
Memories, 203
Moldova, 170
Moral-exemplars, 170, 184–186, 188
Multiculturalism, 59, 244, 245
Multinarrative, 51
Multiperspective, 51, 59, 249, 330
Museum exhibitions, 345
Museums, 81

N
Naqba, 280
Narrative transformation, 54, 55, 57, 65
National identity, 361
Nationalist Unity Party, 332
National Socialism, 171, 172, 175
Nation building, 259
Nazi/Nazism, 174, 177, 181–183, 185
Needs-based model of reconciliation, 23, 292
Negative stereotyping, 4
Negotiation, 286
NGO, 24, 233, 330
Non-formal education, 322, 323, 330
Northern Ireland, 15, 23, 301
Norway, 170
Novels, 345

O
Official approach, 98, 280
Official truth (or grand narratives/master-narratives), 50, 63
Oral histories, 80
OSCE, 240

P
Pakistan, 52
Palestine/Palestinian, 15, 279
Parrhesia/Parrhesiastes, 148, 149, 151–153, 156–158, 160, 161
Peace Processes and Dialogue, 81
Personal and group transformation, 304
Perspective taking, 85
Piaget, 17, 18, 25, 234
Poland, 83
Polarisation, 302
Positioning, 203

Post-conflict settings, 9, 302
Post-conflict societies, 42
Postconflict textbook revision, 44, 51, 54, 63, 66
POST Research Institute (POST RI), 330
Post-Saddam Iraq, 51
Power asymmetry, 13
Prejudice, 2, 4, 5, 10, 14, 15, 80, 115
PRIME, 86
Process and outcome, 4
Professional identity, 240
Propaganda, 22, 203, 205–208, 210, 223
Propagation, 22, 203, 205, 207, 223

R
Racism, 80
Radicalized, 14
Radio La Benevolencija, 83
Realistic and symbolic threats, 2
Realistic threats, 111
Recognition, 234–236, 240, 247, 250
Reconciliation, 1, 3, 6, 7, 9, 10, 13–15, 19, 20, 23, 24, 77–79, 81, 83, 86, 88, 90, 302
Reconciliation pedagogies, 322, 323, 333, 334
Redefinition of relationships, 39
Reflexivity, 355
Regret, 170
Religious conflict, 301
Remembering Quilt, 90
Reporters Without Borders, 270
Republican Turkish Party, 331
Reunification, 301
Rwanda, 43, 50, 83

S
School of Dialogue, 83
Segregated education system, 302

Self-categorization, 3
Serbia, 8, 20, 80, 104
Significance, 350, 355, 356
Situational Attribution Training, 309
Slovenia, 170
Social cognition, 306
Social comparison, 308
Social identity theory, 3, 4, 8, 307
Socialist Federal Republic of Yugoslavia, 105
Social psychology, 306
Social Representation Theory, 203, 204
Social utility, 316
Societal change, 302
South Africa, 43, 87
Spoiler-groups, 59
SSRB, 259
Stereotype threat, 307, 308
Structural and societal transformation, 4
Structural inequality, 13–15
Supplementary alternative materials, 48
Supplementary materials, 330
Supplementary teaching material, 52
Symbolic threats, 110–113
Symmetry, 234

T
Taken-for-granted assumptions, 322
Teacher's action space, 203, 204
Teaching Divided Histories (TDH), 303
Television shows, 345
Testimonies, 81
Textbook revision, 232, 233, 238, 241, 243, 245, 257–260, 262–268, 270, 271
Theories of practice, 81
Threat, 110
  group-esteem, 110

realistic, 110
  symbolic, 110
Time, 341, 342, 345, 348–350, 355, 356, 359, 360, 361, 363–365, 368, 370, 371
Transformative history teaching, 19
Transformative potential, 250
Transforming conflict narratives, 78
Transition, 221
Transitional justice, 37
TRT, 236
Trust, 3–5, 10, 103, 110–112
Turkey, 16
Turkish Cypriots, 16, 104, 105, 108, 331
Tutsi, 50

U
Ukraine, 170
Ultimate attribution error, 12

UNESCO, 232, 238
United Nations Development Programme, 245
UN protectorate, 105
Upstanders, 312
USA, 346
USAID, 47
USSR, 260, 269

V
Violence, 312

W
Web sites, 345
West Germany, 346

Open Access This book is licensed under the terms of the Creative Commons Attribution 4.0 International License (http://creativecommons.org/licenses/by/4.0/), which permits use, sharing, adaptation, distribution and reproduction in any medium or format, as long as you give appropriate credit to the original author(s) and the source, provide a link to the Creative Commons license and indicate if changes were made.

The images or other third party material in this book are included in the book's Creative Commons license, unless indicated otherwise in a credit line to the material. If material is not included in the book's Creative Commons license and your intended use is not permitted by statutory regulation or exceeds the permitted use, you will need to obtain permission directly from the copyright holder.

Milton Keynes UK
Ingram Content Group UK Ltd.
UKHW032143071224
452069UK00004B/189